The Bicentennial Census

NEW DIRECTIONS FOR METHODOLOGY IN 1990

Constance F. Citro and
Michael L. Cohen, Editors

Panel on Decennial Census Methodology

Committee on National Statistics

Commission on Behavioral and
Social Sciences and Education

National Research Council

NATIONAL ACADEMY PRESS
Washington, D.C. 1985

National Academy Press • 2101 Constitution Avenue, N.W. • Washington, DC 20418

NOTICE: The project that is the subject of this report was approved by the Governing Board of the National Research Council, whose members are drawn from the councils of the National Academy of Sciences, the National Academy of Engineering, and the Institute of Medicine. The members of the commmittee responsible for the report were chosen for their special competences and with regard for appropriate balance.

This report has been approved by a group other than the authors according to procedures approved by a Report Review Committee consisting of members of the National Academy of Sciences, the National Academy of Engineering, and the Institute of Medicine.

This project was supported by funds from the Bureau of the Census, U.S. Department of Commerce.

Library of Congress Catalog Card Number 85-51816

International Standard Book Number 0-309-03626-7

Printed in the United States of America

Panel on Decennial Census Methodology

JOHN W. PRATT (Chair), Graduate School of Business, Harvard University
PASTORA SAN JUAN CAFFERTY, School of Social Service Administration, University of Chicago
ANSLEY J. COALE, Office of Population Research, Princeton University
DONALD DESKINS, Department of Sociology, University of Michigan
IVAN P. FELLEGI, Deputy Chief Statistician, Statistics Canada, Ottawa
WAYNE A. FULLER, Department of Statistics, Iowa State University
JOSEPH B. KADANE, Department of Statistics, Carnegie-Mellon University
BENJAMIN KING, Research Statistics Group, Educational Testing Service, Princeton, N.J.
ALBERT MADANSKY, Graduate School of Business, University of Chicago
ALBERTO PALLONI, Center for Demography and Ecology, University of Wisconsin
JOHN ROLPH, Rand Corporation, Santa Monica, Calif.
COURTENAY M. SLATER, CEC Associates, Washington, D.C.
JOSEPH WAKSBERG, Westat, Inc., Rockville, Md.

CONSTANCE F. CITRO, Study Director
MICHAEL L. COHEN, Research Associate

Committee on National Statistics

Contents

Tables

Figures

Preface

In 1982 the American Statistical Association Technical Panel on the Census Undercount recommended "that the Bureau of the Census sponsor an outside technical advisory group on undercount estimation and related problems" (American Statistical Association, 1984:256). Partly on the basis of that recommendation, the Census Bureau requested the Committee on National Statistics to establish a panel: (1) to suggest research and experiments, (2) to recommend improved methods, and (3) to guide the Census Bureau on technical problems in appraising contending methods with regard to the conduct of the decennial census.

In response to that request, the Panel on Decennial Census Methodology was established and charged with investigating three major issues from a technical viewpoint, setting aside legal considerations:

(1) Adjustment of census counts and characteristics, including exploration of formal criteria to evaluate measures of undercount and alternative adjustment procedures.

(2) Uses of sampling in the decennial census, specifically investigation of whether sampling for coverage improvement and of nonrespondents for follow-up can improve accuracy at a given cost.

(3) Uses of administrative records, including investigation of the possible utility of various types of records for improving the accuracy of census counts and the efficiency of census operations.

At our first meeting, in January 1984, we took a broad view of the charge and identified additional topic areas beyond those listed for possible investigation. We decided that in order to reach sensible conclusions regarding a choice of methodology for the decennial census it was critical to examine uses of census data and the degree of accuracy needed to satisfy each use. We also decided that it was essential to conduct a thorough review of procedures for improving census coverage and of methods of evaluating the completeness of coverage achieved in the census. Well-designed and well-executed coverage improvement programs can importantly reduce errors in the census. Well-designed and well-executed coverage evaluation programs inform users about the quality of the census results and are the source of input data necessary for any type of adjustment of the census counts to reduce errors further.

The panel produced an interim report that focused on recommendations for improvements in census methodology that warranted early investigation and testing. That report, *Planning the 1990 Census: Priorities for Research and Testing* (National Research Council, 1984), addressed three topic areas that were central to the original charge: (1) uses of sampling for the census count, (2) methodologies for evaluating completeness of coverage of the census, and (3) issues related to the adjustment or modification of census counts and characteristics. In addition, the report reviewed the Census Bureau's plans for the 1985 pretest of a two-stage methodology for conducting the census.

This report updates and expands our ideas and conclusions about decennial census methodology. In it we endeavor to assess the merits of investigating proposed changes in the decennial census that represent important departures from past practice and, specifically, to recommend concepts and procedures that we believe the Census Bureau should place high on its list of priority objectives for research and testing directed toward the nation's bicentennial census in 1990.

Our report, following an introduction and overview that presents in collected form the recommendations of the panel, includes three background chapters, on purposes and uses of the decennial census, on methodology of prior censuses and current 1990 census testing plans, and on past experience with coverage evaluation. The report offers general and specific planning recommendations in five areas: (1) overall strategy for planning the 1990 census, (2) procedures for coverage improvement as part of the census, (3) uses of sampling and administrative records in taking the census, (4) adjustment of census counts and characteristics, and (5) measuring the completeness of the 1990 census.

With regard to the key issue of adjustment of census counts, we argue for balance between efforts to achieve a complete enumeration and efforts to improve the accuracy of census figures through adjustment procedures. We believe that adjustment cannot be viewed as an alternative to obtaining as complete a count as possible through cost-effective means. However, the evidence is overwhelming that no counting process will in fact enumerate everyone. Given our belief that the ultimate goal of the census should be the accuracy of the figures, we recommend that the Census Bureau pursue a vigorous program of research on coverage evaluation and adjustment methods that, if successful, would permit adjustment of the 1990 census counts.

With regard to issues related to adjustment and other topics considered by the panel, the emphasis of our report is on the extensive research and testing needed during the next few years to support sound decisions regarding the choice of a particular methodology for the 1990 and subsequent censuses. Given the limited number of testing opportunities available compared with the range of ideas that appear attractive to try out, we believe it is imperative for the Census Bureau to choose among research objectives. We have therefore endeavored to provide timely advice regarding what we believe are the most promising avenues to pursue.

John W. Pratt, Chair
Panel on Decennial
Census Methodology

Acknowledgments

The Panel on Decennial Census Methodology wishes to thank the many people who contributed to the preparation of this report.

The staff of the Bureau of the Census has been extremely helpful, and we would like to thank particularly certain individuals for their assistance. Peter Bounpane, assistant director for demographic censuses, and Barbara Bailar, associate director for statistical standards and methodology, have been very generous of their time in providing assistance to the panel. Other Census Bureau staff who contributed valuable information include: Frederick Bohme, Charles Cowan, Gregg Diffendal, Richard Engels, Robert Fay, III, Penelope Harvison, Roger Herriot, Catherine Hines, Howard Hogan, Matt Jaro, Bruce Johnson, Charles Jones, Eli Marks, Nampeo McKenney, Susan Miskura, Jeffrey Passel, Paula Schneider, John Thompson, David Whitford, Kirk Wolter, and Arthur Young.

A number of members of the broader statistical community gave very helpful presentations at meetings of the panel: Eugene Ericksen of Temple University and Mathematica Policy Research, Monroe Sirken of the National Center for Health Statistics, John Tukey of Princeton University and AT&T Bell Laboratories, and Kenneth Hill and Robert Warren of the Committee on National Statistics. We would also like to thank Harold Nisselson of Westat, Inc., who prepared background material on coverage evaluation programs, Margaret Boone, anthropologist, who made a helpful presentation on ethnographic research, and Judith Rowe of the Princeton-Rutgers Census Data Project for very useful comments on Chapter 2 of the report.

The members and staff of the Committee on National Statistics were valuable resources to the panel in the course of our work. Stephen Fienberg, as chair of the committee, gave us the benefit of his enthusiastic support, direction, and encouragement in the early stages of the project. Committee member David Wallace read the draft report with great care and made detailed, incisive comments that improved the report in important ways. Staff members Edwin Goldfield, Thomas Jabine, Daniel Levine, Margaret Martin, and Miron Straf provided useful guidance and assistance. Kenneth Hill made very helpful comments on Chapters 4 and 8 of the report.

Deserving of special thanks is Julie Kramen, who assisted in the production of many of the tables included in this report.

The panel is grateful to Christine McShane, editor for the Commission on Behavioral and Social Sciences and Education, for her fine technical editorial work, which contributed greatly to the organization and readability of this report. We would also like to thank members of the Commission on Behavioral and Social Sciences and Education and the Committee on National Statistics who reviewed the report and offered cogent comments.

I would like to express special thanks to the panel's own staff. Constance Citro, as study director, stayed on top of everything, attended to myriad administrative matters, chased down elusive details and people, and arranged and ran efficient, productive meetings. Her ability at the same time to write rapidly, accurately, and clearly about anything and everything was continually amazing. Without sacrificing quality, she met schedules no one else thought possible. The buck could safely be passed to her any time, and often was—yet her effort was unstinting, her temper never ruffled. She was aided nobly throughout by Michael Cohen, research associate. He bravely did battle with topics none of the panel would touch, bearing with remarkable stoicism the slings and arrows inevitably ensuing. Together they were responsible for drafting most sections of the report and rewriting patiently to accommodate comments from all directions.

Finally, I wish to thank the panel members themselves for their generous contributions of time and expert knowledge. Several of them prepared background materials for discussion and drafted sections of chapters. Most provided detailed comments on drafts of the report. Of course, no individual member of the panel should or would want to be held responsible for every word or idea expressed, but the report does represent their collective thinking on the issues addressed. They were an unusual pleasure to work with and learn from; the chief reward of a panel chair was amply paid.

John W. Pratt

1
Introduction

Periodic censuses of population are a long-established tradition in the United States of America, with roots going back to the earliest years of the colonial period. The royal colony of Virginia conducted the first census in North America in the early seventeenth century, and censuses of individual colonies were frequently attempted during the colonial era (Bureau of the Census, 1970b:3).

Political necessity led to the requirement for a periodic complete enumeration of the population in the new nation formed after the American Revolution. In the compromise between large and small states made at the 1787 Constitutional Convention, the delegates voted to provide equal representation for each state in the Senate and representation proportional to population in the House of Representatives; the population of each state was to be determined through a decennial census. Article 1, section 2, of the Constitution stipulates:

> Representatives and direct Taxes shall be apportioned among the several States which may be included within this Union, according to their respective Numbers. . . . The actual Enumeration shall be made within three Years after the first Meeting of the Congress of the United States, and within every subsequent Term of ten Years, in such Manner as they shall by Law direct.

Although fundamental issues of the structure of government provided the motivation for the U.S. decennial census, the country's leaders recognized from the beginning that the census could be a valuable source of information for many other purposes. James Madison noted in 1789 (Bureau of the Census, 1970b:4) that Congress:

> had now an opportunity of obtaining the most useful information for those who should hereafter be called upon to legislate for their country, if this bill was extended to embrace some other objects besides the bare enumeration of the inhabitants; it would enable them to adapt the public measures to the particular circumstances of the community.

The first census in 1790 asked the age, sex, and race of each resident. During the next 100 years, the census became firmly established as an important information resource. The centennial census in 1890 asked questions on more subjects than any census before or since, including 30 items on the basic population questionnaire, several housing inquiries, and special inquiries about decedents, inmates of almshouses and prisons, Indians on and off reservations, Civil War veterans and widows of veterans, and several categories of mentally and physically disabled people (Bureau of the Census, 1973b:74-91).

Work is now under way to plan for the nation's bicentennial census of population and housing, scheduled to take place on April 1, 1990. Reflecting a long-standing tradition of improvement and modification to meet changing information needs and to take advantage of technological advances, census-taking in the twentieth century has come to differ in many important respects from census-taking in the nineteenth century. The 1990 census will undoubtedly incorporate the following features that have been introduced into modern U.S. censuses:

- As has been true since 1910, the 1990 census will be directed by a permanent organization, the U.S. Bureau of the Census, with an experienced, professional staff in charge of planning and supervising the operation.
- As in every census since 1940, statistical sampling methods will be used to obtain responses to many census items, so that a large volume of useful information can be gathered without placing the burden on every household of responding to all questions (the 1980 census asked 7 population and 12 housing items of all households, while about 20 percent of households were asked an additional 26 population and 20 housing questions).
- As in the 1970 and 1980 censuses, the U.S. Postal Service will deliver most of the census questionnaires, and households will be asked to mail their completed questionnaires to census offices. Enumerators will

telephone or visit only those households that do not completely respond (95 percent of households were sent questionnaires by mail in 1980 and 83 percent of them returned their questionnaires by mail).

- As has been true since 1960, large computers will be used to process the census returns in a relatively short span of time; in contrast, the 1890 census required almost a full decade to process, even with the introduction of punchcard machines to help the clerical work force.
- As in every census since 1950, intensive effort will be devoted to evaluating the completeness of coverage of the total population and of important subgroups and geographic areas.

The 1990 census will undoubtedly differ as well from the most recent censuses in the United States. Most of the differences are likely to represent incremental improvements and modifications to tried and tested procedures: for example, mailout-mailback techniques may be extended to the remaining 5 percent of the population residing in sparsely settled rural areas that enumerators personally canvassed in 1980. But pressures are growing in this country, as in other Western nations, to address the problems of rising costs of traditional census practices on one hand and to satisfy expressed needs for greater accuracy in the numbers on the other. Consequently, exploration of changes in methods and techniques that mark a greater break with tradition is under way: for example, one proposal that has received much attention is the use of statistical techniques to adjust the field counts for deficiencies in the enumeration.

In the past, major changes in census methodology, such as the use of sampling for content and mailout-mailback enumeration, were often made on a small scale in one census and then more fully implemented in the next. The 1990 census will be part of a continuing evolution that may lead to a methodology in the twenty-first century that differs as significantly from current methodology as current methodology differs from that of the nineteenth century. This report is an attempt to assess the merits of proposed changes in the next decennial census that represent important departures from past practice and, specifically, to recommend concepts and procedures that should be assigned high priority in the Census Bureau's research and testing program for the nation's bicentennial census.

THE PLANNING CYCLE FOR 1990

Planning for the 1990 census officially began in fall 1983 with an appropriation for fiscal 1984. Well before that date, however, substantial work of direct relevance for 1990 was conducted. The 1980 decennial program included several experiments and post-enumeration studies designed to help plan improvements in methodology for subsequent censuses. Pretests carried out in the late 1970s of concepts and procedures considered for 1980 also had results that are useful for 1990 census planning.

To the general public and many casual users of census data, it may appear that the Census Bureau has ample time to plan wisely for the 1990 census, given the start of the planning process more than six years prior to Census Day, April 1, 1990, and the foundation of research already completed in connection with prior censuses. In fact, as a review of the Census Bureau's field test schedule for 1990 indicates, there are relatively few opportunities to test thoroughly changes or modifications to census procedures, particularly if the changes represent major departures from the past. Moreover, evaluation of the likely impact of important changes is hampered by the fact that pretests cannot adequately assess the effects of alternative procedures on public cooperation with the census--only tests conducted under census conditions, that is, experiments incorporated into an actual census as distinct from pretests, can fully address this important question.

The Census Bureau's 1990 census testing program began in spring 1984 with tests of mailing list compilation methods in several localities around the country (Bureau of the Census, 1984b). Two large-scale pretests were fielded in spring 1985. Pretests will also be conducted in 1986 and 1987. Finally, the research and testing program will culminate in 1988 in "dress rehearsals" of the procedures planned for 1990. (See Chapter 3 for an overview of the Census Bureau's 1990 census research program and for a description of the methodology used in 1980.)

This testing schedule means that the Census Bureau's only opportunities for full field testing of new procedures and concepts for 1990 are the pretests in 1985, 1986, and 1987. The dress rehearsals, as the name implies, are not used to test new ideas but to run through the procedures the Census Bureau expects to follow in the decennial census itself. The only changes the Census Bureau anticipates from the dress rehearsals are corrections of problems encountered in the field, not innovations in census procedures at that late date. This schedule not only compresses into a few years the opportunities to test new methodology but also compresses the time available to evaluate the test results. The fact that tests are scheduled no more than a year apart makes it very difficult to complete the analysis of one set of tests in time to affect the design of the next set.

In addition to the compressed time schedule for testing and research, two other critical factors affect the ability of the Census Bureau to modify census methodology: staff and budget resources. The Census Bureau has long been known for the high quality and dedication of its technical staff. The current budget for research on decennial census methodology, particularly for research on the undercount, is large by the standards of earlier censuses. Nevertheless, no agency of government, particularly in the constrained world of the 1980s, can expect to have sufficient staff or resources to try out more than a few promising ideas and concepts. Pressures in the next few years to reduce the federal government's large deficit may make it more than usually difficult to obtain adequate staff and funding to carry out a thorough research and testing program for 1990. Hence, it is critical to designing the best census for 1990 and to being in the best position to plan further design changes for 2000 that the Census Bureau make the most of the testing opportunities afforded over the next few years and establish priorities for testing and research wisely.

THE IMPORTANCE OF CHOICE OF METHODOLOGY FOR 1990

Controversy surrounding population censuses has as long a history in the United States as census-taking itself. According to one review (Bureau of the Census, 1982a: App.IIIb:73), censuses conducted during the colonial period, generally at the direction of the Privy Council or the British Board of Trade, "were seldom regarded as complete or successful, as people perceived them being for the purposes of taxation or conscription and were evasive and uncooperative." The decennial censuses conducted in the new nation had a constitutional mandate according them legitimacy and support. Moreover, one historian (Conk, 1984:7) has noted that: "After the first few censuses, Americans became increasingly interested in the census results . . . [which] showed that the population was growing steadily and extremely rapidly." It quickly became evident in the early nineteenth century, however, that not all areas were sharing equally in population growth and that reapportionment based on census results meant substantial shifts in political power. Hence, as the same historian comments (Conk, 1984:8):

> It is not surprising therefore that nineteenth century Americans who were pleased with the overall thrust of population change claimed that the census proved the virtue of the American way of life or the American system of government. Conversely, those who felt shortchanged by reapportionment or were concerned about the tendencies of population change challenged both the census and the apportionment system.

The first extensive criticism of the census by statisticians occurred in 1843 when the American Statistical Association (ASA) issued a lengthy report that documented glaring errors in the data on education, occupation, and especially the classification by race of persons identified as insane, idiotic, and deaf and dumb. The ASA recommended that these results should be corrected or, at the least, disavowed. Problems with both undercount and fraudulent additions to the count were documented in many early censuses (Bureau of the Census, 1982a:App.IIIb: 81-83).

Congress did not as a general rule respond directly to these criticisms, although occasionally it acted to alter the apportionment of the House when there was strong evidence of gross deficiencies in the population count. Congress gave a third representative to Alabama in 1823 when the claim was made that the 1820 census omitted two counties and in 1860 awarded an additional seat to California because of problems with the census in that state (Bureau of the Census, 1982a:App.IIIb:82). These actions were politically much more palatable than similar actions would be today, because reapportionment legislation up through 1910 added representatives to accommodate population growth rather than allocating a fixed number of seats among the states.

Despite the questions raised about the population enumeration in the past, a review of decennial census history suggests that social and political forces have converged in recent years to make the census in this country--and in other countries as well--a matter of demonstrably greater controversy than before. Several factors are involved.

On one hand lie increased concern with the need to protect the privacy of individual citizens and a sense that the public is oversurveyed and less willing to respond to government inquiries. Indeed, in the last few years, the level of public suspicion and hostility to plans for the census caused the governments of several Western European countries to delay their census programs or cancel them entirely (see Butz, 1984; Redfern, 1983).

On the other hand, legislators have increasingly turned to statistics in handling tough policy decisions. In fiscal 1984, federal grant-in-aid programs allocated at least $80 billion to states and local areas via formulas that depended in important ways on census figures (or statistics based on census figures, such as current population estimates) to determine who received how many dollars (Office of Management and Budget, 1985). As noted above, census data are used by constitutional mandate to determine the number of seats in the U.S. House of Representatives that are allotted to each state. They are used as well in drawing up congressional and state and local legislative districts to meet rigid criteria for equitable representation of the population. Data requirements for redistricting purposes in 1980 included census tabulations of the population by race (white; black; American Indian, Eskimo, and Aleut; Asian and Pacific Islander; other races) and Hispanic origin for each of several million city blocks in urban parts of the country and enumeration districts in unblocked areas (Bureau of the Census, 1982b:79).

In addition to these critical governmental needs, census data support many other major uses. Data from the latest census serve to document the social and economic condition of the country as a whole and are the single most important source of information for small areas and groups in the population. Comparative information from successive censuses illuminates trends over time. Researchers, planners, and decision makers in business, government, and academic institutions make use of census data for a wide range of important planning and analysis purposes. Just a few of the many uses to which census data are put (see Chapter 2 for a detailed review) include:

- Site selection for public service facilities and commercial establishments based on evaluating the socioeconomic characteristics of alternative locations;
- Transportation planning using detailed data on commuting flows; and
- Research into changing rates of population growth for metropolitan versus nonmetropolitan areas and different regions of the country.

Many analyses based on census data have implications for the distribution of political power and wealth among various population groups in the country. For example, census data on the racial, ethnic, age, and sex makeup of occupational groups in labor market areas are used to assess the extent to which work forces reflect the characteristics of the local labor force. These data frequently form the basis of antidiscrimination lawsuits brought against employers. Census data on the makeup of the local population are used to assess--and challenge--the representativeness of grand and petit juries. Census data on earnings cross-tabulated by various characteristics are used to analyze wage disparities within and among occupations and important population subgroups. Findings from such studies can affect outcomes of public policy deliberations, such as the current debate over the issue of comparable pay for jobs of comparable worth. All of these uses have underscored more than ever before the importance of obtaining a complete and accurate count of the population as well as accurate data about characteristics.

Yet to obtain highly accurate data costs money. The 1980 census cost close to $1.1 billion dollars--about $4.75 for each inhabitant of the United States (Bureau of the Census, 1983b:88). The per capita amount is small compared with the per case cost of most government and private-sector sample surveys. Moreover, this total cost includes planning, collection, and processing activities that spanned most of a decade and provided data that are of value for the decade and beyond. Nonetheless, census costs exceeding $1 billion excite comment and invite close scrutiny to determine how they might be reduced. Recently in Canada, the quinquennial census scheduled for 1986 was cancelled because of budget constraints facing the government; it was subsequently reinstated, however, in response to widespread public expressions of concern and its demonstrated cost-effectiveness compared with alternatives. The U.S. decennial census is constitutionally mandated; nevertheless, pressures are likely to be severe in the coming years to attempt drastic cost reductions both in census planning activities and in the enumeration, despite the fact that, compared with other ways of obtaining comparable information, the census is still cost-effective.

The Census Bureau's own research has shown that there were inaccuracies in the 1980 census, both of underenumeration (that is, persons who were missed) and overenumeration (that is, persons who were inadvertently counted twice or otherwise included when they should not have been). Evaluation studies generally point to the conclusion that, overall, the 1980 census produced a small net undercount of the population--that is, the census count, including erroneous enumerations, fell somewhat short compared with an independent estimate. Most significantly, important race, sex, and age subgroups of the population experienced differential rates of net undercount. There is strong evidence that the black population experienced a net undercount of about 5 percent nationwide. Black men ages 25-54 appear to have had the highest net undercount rates--close to 15 percent on average (Passel and Robinson, 1984:Table 3). Coverage estimates for whites and other races are difficult to derive because of the lack of reliable estimates of net legal and illegal immigration. Making a range of reasonable assumptions about the size of the undocumented alien population, it appears very likely that whites and other races experienced net undercount in the 1980 census, but that the rate of undercount was smaller, perhaps significantly smaller than the 1.5 percent rate experienced in 1970 (see Passel et al., 1982:6-8; see also the review in Chapter 5 of coverage estimates for censuses from 1950 through 1980).

Differential net undercount means possible inequities in redistricting, fund allocation, and provision of social services based on census data as well as possibly erroneous conclusions drawn from studies used as the basis for antidiscrimination policies and lawsuits and other socially important purposes. The belief that errors in the census affected representation and fund allocation gave rise to an unprecedented number of lawsuits following the 1980 census. By October 1981, over 50 suits had been filed challenging the census results (Bureau of the Census, 1983b:85). Currently, the judge assigned to a major case in which the State and the City of New York are suing to have the Census Bureau adjust the 1980 census counts is reviewing testimony and preparing to hand down a decision; 23 other cases are awaiting settlement of the New York suit. Analyses by Kadane (1984) and Gilford (1983) indicate that the apportionment of congressional seats may have been affected by the differential undercount. For example, Kadane found that if one of the sets of estimates produced from the 1980 Post-Enumeration Program evaluation were used to adjust the census results, California would have received an additional seat at the expense of Pennsylvania.

PROPOSED CHANGES IN METHODOLOGY

Not surprisingly, many ideas have been proposed by the Census Bureau and others to improve the decennial census. Some are directed principally at improving coverage and reducing differential coverage errors. One idea in this class is to match administrative records, such as driver's license lists and other sources, against the census on a scale even larger than that used in 1980 to identify people who should be followed up to determine if they were improperly omitted from the census count. (See Chapter 3 for a description of the efforts along these lines in the 1980 census.) Other ideas are directed principally at reducing costs. One such approach is to make use of sampling, not only to obtain information on characteristics, as is currently standard decennial census practice, but also as part of the procedure to obtain the count. For example, one could attempt contact with a sample of households that do not mail back their questionnaires, rather than all nonrespondents, in the follow-up stage of census operations. Special coverage improvement procedures could also be carried out on a sample basis.

Two important themes stand out in current discussions of methodology for the decennial census. One relates to the degree of emphasis that should be given to counting versus estimation. A census, no matter how diligently administered, can never be complete or without error. Moreover, it is true of current census methodology that not every record corresponds to a person actually named on a questionnaire; for example, a small percentage of records (about 1 percent in recent censuses--see Chapter 3) represents imputations in situations in which there is good evidence that a housing unit is occupied but repeated efforts have failed to find the residents. Hence, a census, strictly speaking, provides an estimate of the population.

From this recognition has come a view of the decennial process that emphasizes the role of estimation and argues that some of the resources for conducting the census should be shifted from efforts directed toward traditional coverage improvement procedures to efforts directed toward developing the best possible estimates of the total population and subgroups. Input to the decennial year population estimates, in one version of this view (Ericksen and Kadane, 1985), would include not only a well-conducted census, but also information obtained from various programs conducted on a sample basis that would provide a basis for adjusting the census field counts. (Such programs might include matching of samples of administrative lists to census records and follow-up of a sample of households that did not respond to an initial follow-up effort.) Whatever the merits of particular suggestions put forward to incorporate estimation into the census process, the known errors and the incompleteness of the census count mean that the issue of adjusting census figures needs to be addressed.

The other theme relates to the critical importance of evaluation programs in the methodology of the decennial census. Politicians, policy analysts, statisticians, economists, demographers, other social scientists, and users of census data in all sectors have expressed divergent views regarding the most appropriate methodology for conducting the census. But whether they view the census in traditional terms as strictly a counting operation or believe that the census should be the starting point for an estimating process, there is substantial agreement on the importance of evaluating the completeness and accuracy of census statistics.

The Census Bureau has conducted formal evaluation programs for every census since 1950 (Bureau of the Census, no date-a). All of the techniques used to date in this country and abroad, including demographic analysis, reverse record checks, administrative record matches, and post-enumeration surveys (whether recanvassing selected areas or matching independent surveys to census records), have important flaws (see the review of coverage evaluation methods in Chapter 4). In the United States today, the absence of adequate data for estimating net immigration, whether of legal or illegal residents (Marks, 1980), poses particularly severe problems for evaluating the census count even at the national level using the demographic method. Furthermore, if evaluation results were to be used for census adjustment purposes, then reasonably accurate information on the errors of evaluation estimates would also be needed. Nevertheless, with concern over possible inequities in political representation and the distribution of large amounts of federal dollars as well as concern over the adequacy of the data for analysis of the socioeconomic status of important population groups, there has never been a greater need for thorough evaluation of the decennial census. This evaluation is necessary whether the object is to inform users of known errors in the census or actually to modify census results.

While there is widespread agreement that evaluation is important and that the issue of adjustment must be faced, many decisions on methodology for 1990 remain to be made. It is clear that there is no lack of ideas and suggestions that appear useful to investigate. It is also clear that the process of determining a reasonable methodology for 1990 will involve difficult choices.

Ideally, one would like the 1990 and future censuses to improve the accuracy of the data over that in 1980, maintain the amount of useful information collected, and release the results on a more timely basis, while at the same time reducing the burden on the public and lowering costs. The Census Bureau has stated (Bailar, 1984:259) that its minimum goals for 1990 are to:

> (a) Conduct the 1990 Census without increasing the per-housing-unit cost in 1980 dollars. (b) Expedite the availability of the data to users. (c) Maintain a high rate of overall coverage and improve the accuracy of small area data while reducing the overall differential for population groups and geographic areas.

It may be possible to design a methodology that makes gains in the desired direction on each of these dimensions. The more likely situation is that it will be possible to make progress on one or two dimensions but at the price of giving up improvements on the others. Explicit trade-offs reflecting costs and benefits will need to be made in the choice of methodology for 1990 and beyond (see Keyfitz, 1979). Because of the high costs of censuses and the compressed time frame within which they are carried out, making mid-course corrections impossible, it is essential that the methodology to be used be thoroughly tested.

INDEPENDENT REVIEWS OF DECENNIAL CENSUS PLANS

The Census Bureau is actively working on methodology for the 1990 census and has assembled staffs to plan the census and specifically to work on issues of undercount and the possible adjustment of census counts. For many decades, the Census Bureau has also actively sought outside independent review of its plans and proposed procedures. In addition to ongoing advisory committees involving various professional disciplines and advisory committees representing the interests of population groups for whom census results are particularly important, the Census Bureau has asked the National Research Council (NRC) and the American Statistical Association (ASA) to conduct special studies of the decennial census. This report represents the fourth outside review conducted in recent years of key aspects of modern census methodology. A brief discussion of the scope and thrust of the predecessor NRC and ASA studies can help place the current study in context.

The 1969-1972 NRC Advisory Committee on Problems of Census Enumeration

The Bureau of the Census sponsored a study in 1969 by a committee of the National Research Council to provide advice on ways to improve completeness of coverage in the decennial census and intercensal household surveys. (The Office of Economic Opportunity and the Manpower Administration of the U.S. Department of Labor also contributed support for the study.) The Advisory Committee on Problems of Census Enumeration issued its final report, America's Uncounted People, in 1972. The report focused on the need to understand the social and psychological context in which undercount occurs. For example, the committee noted that people may be missed in central city areas because, although members of extended families, they are not attached to a family or household residence, which is the basic unit of enumeration in the census and household surveys. The committee strongly recommended that the Census Bureau broaden its research strategy and knowledge base to include methods and concepts not typically embraced in survey research. The report included specific recommendations to conduct experimental studies of questionnaire wordings and formats and their effects on respondents; explore the utility of communication research for better understanding the reasons for census and survey undercoverage; and carry out localized participant-observer studies to learn more about the impediments to census data collection in different kinds of areas.

The 1978 NRC Panel on Decennial Census Plans

The Census Bureau asked the National Research Council again in 1978 to review decennial census methodology, specifically the plans for the upcoming 1980 census. The NRC's Committee on National Statistics set up the Panel on Decennial Census Plans, which worked within a very short time span, to: (1) examine field procedures, questionnaire design, and special procedures designed to improve the 1980 census coverage, (2) review proposed procedures for handling contested counts, (3) investigate the feasibility of adjusting census counts, and (4) consider evaluation plans for the 1980 census. The panel's report, _Counting the People in 1980: An Appraisal of Census Plans_, made recommendations in many areas. This panel repeated the call of the earlier committee for imaginative work on the cultural and social problems associated with census-taking. In the area of adjustment, the 1978 panel concluded (National Research Council, 1978:132-133) that: "methods of adjustment with tolerable accuracy are feasible" and "on balance an improvement in equity would be achieved." The panel supported implementation of procedures to adjust population counts for underenumeration for purposes of fund distribution and expressed confidence in the Census Bureau to determine the best technical procedures for adjustment. The panel recommended that adjustment "not be applied to the counts used for legislative apportionment nor to the body of census data on the characteristics of the population."

The 1981-1982 ASA Technical Panel on the Census Undercount

The Census Bureau asked the American Statistical Association in 1981 to convene an expert group to review the methods and results of the programs used to evaluate completeness of coverage in the 1980 census and to make recommendations regarding research in the areas of coverage evaluation and adjustment of census counts. This panel made a number of specific research suggestions and also recommended (ASA, 1984:256): "that the Bureau of the Census sponsor an outside technical advisory group on undercount estimation and related problems."

The 1984 Panel on Decennial Census Methodology

In response to the recommendation of the 1981 ASA panel, the Census Bureau asked the Committee on National Statistics at the National Research Council to establish the Panel on Decennial Census Methodology. The charge to the panel was for an investigation of three major issues from a technical viewpoint, setting aside legal considerations:

(1) Adjustment of census counts and characteristics, including exploration of formal criteria to evaluate measures of undercount and alternative adjustment procedures;
(2) Uses of sampling in the decennial census, including investigation of whether, for a given cost, the sampling of lists and areas to improve coverage and sampling of nonrespondents for follow-up can improve accuracy for the total population and for important subgroups;
(3) Uses of administrative records, including investigation of various types of records to determine their possible utility in improving the accuracy of census counts and the efficiency of census operations.

We interpreted this charge to include investigation of closely related topics, notably methods of coverage evaluation and improvement. Coverage evaluation programs provide the necessary input data for any adjustment and serve the important function of apprising users of the quality of the census counts. Procedures for coverage improvement are viewed by the panel as important and desirable even if an adjustment procedure is incorporated into census methodology. The panel also investigated uses of census data and their dependence on the accuracy of the census figures. Proper evaluation of the consequences of changes in collection methodology requires an understanding of important uses of the data being collected.

The charge to the panel related to analysis of decennial census methodology and not to other population programs of the Census Bureau. However, in the course of the panel's work, it became clear that the census could not be considered completely in isolation. Demographic and related social and economic statistics are used continually over the decade following each census, and current information is needed for these uses. The Census Bureau has a number of formal programs for updating some of the census information. Hence, the census is the central part of a broader statistical system designed to produce data needed to implement legislation, assist in decision making both by industry and government, and help understand changes taking place in our society. Although the panel did not undertake a study of population statistics programs other than the census, we did consider the quality of census data compared with the quality of postcensal population estimates. The panel makes a recommendation to assess the need for a mid-decade census in 1995 in light of the impacts of errors in postcensal population estimates on major data uses, such as fund allocation (see the discussion in Chapter 2).

The work of the panel differs in several important ways from the efforts of its predecessors. This is the first panel to be asked explicitly to consider important changes in decennial census methodology from the perspective of cost as well as effectiveness. A theme running through the charge to the panel is to design a methodology that improves accuracy compared with previous censuses but costs no more, and ideally less, in constant dollars.

Other important differences have to do with the timing of the panel's work in relation to the cycle of decennial census planning. The panel was convened at a point in the cycle when it could benefit from the availability of extensive material regarding the experience in the most recent census. At the same time, the panel carried out its work in an early stage of the planning cycle for the next decennial census before decisions on methodology were fixed. Hence, the panel has been in an unusually good position to provide suggestions and guidance regarding the research and testing program for 1990. In fact, the panel's role has been one of assessing and reacting to Census Bureau research and pretest plans for 1990 rather than attempting to recommend, at this stage in the process, the adoption of specified procedures and concepts as the methodology for the 1990 census. The panel does not presume to have the answers regarding the "best" methodology for the decennial census. We have endeavored to state our position and to recommend directions for needed research on critical issues of what constitutes cost-effective methodology, particularly the relative emphasis to be given to counting versus estimation.

MAJOR THEMES OF THE REPORT

Several themes run through this report. The first major theme can be expressed as the need for balance between traditional and new procedures in the choice of census methodology for 1990. Indeed, balance has characterized the historical evolution of decennial census methodology. The panel does not propose that the Census Bureau make radical innovations in decennial census methodology in the near term. The census is a massive and complex operation and major changes should be made only with care and after thorough evaluation--including tests carried out under actual census conditions. Nonetheless, the panel believes that it is important to implement changes on some dimensions for 1990 and to undertake planning that may lead to further changes in the future.

Most important, the panel argues for balance between efforts to achieve a complete enumeration and efforts to improve the accuracy of census figures through adjustment procedures. The panel believes that adjustment cannot be viewed as an alternative to obtaining as complete a count as possible through cost-effective means. The United States has a long tradition of a census as a complete enumeration in which it is a civic responsibility to participate in the census process. The panel believes it is important to continue this tradition and important that census methodology should strive for a complete enumeration via counting procedures, including the use of cost-effective special coverage improvement programs. However, the panel also believes that the ultimate goal of the census should be the accuracy of the census figures. The evidence is overwhelming that no counting process, however diligent, will in fact enumerate everyone. Hence, the panel recommends that the Census Bureau carry out a vigorous program of research on coverage evaluation and adjustment methods that, if successful, would permit adjustment of census figures as part of the methodology for the 1990 census (see the discussion in Chapters 7 and 8).

A second and related theme concerns cost-effectiveness. The panel has not attempted to apply formal cost-benefit analysis to decennial census methodology, but has endeavored to identify those proposed changes that show the most promise of improving accuracy without increasing costs or of reducing costs without importantly impairing accuracy. In this regard, the panel's recommendation for research designed to develop appropriate and feasible methods of adjustment of the census counts, together with the Census Bureau's stated goal to contain costs for the 1990 census, implies that some budget resources must be shifted from coverage improvement to coverage evaluation and adjustment. Specifically, the panel argues that coverage improvement programs used in previous censuses should be carefully reviewed to determine their efficacy. Costly programs that neither correctly added significant numbers of people to the count nor importantly reduced differential undercount should be dropped from the Census Bureau's plans for 1990 (see the discussion in Chapter 5). Effective programs, however, should be further refined through testing and research, and the budget should make room for testing some new ideas in this area.

While not favoring extensive use of sampling to obtain the count, the panel supports research on using sampling in the later follow-up stages of census operations and in some coverage improvement programs, such as the program to recheck the vacancy status of housing units. Limited use of sampling may effect measurable cost savings with minimal sacrifice of accuracy (see the discussion in Chapter 6). Careful use of sampling for certain coverage improvement programs may, in fact, improve accuracy by reducing duplications and other erroneous enumerations, in addition to identifying missed households and people.

In considering cost and accuracy, the panel believes it is important to look at the characteristics data collected in the census as well as the population count. There is strong evidence that important subject items have severe reporting problems. The panel recommends a strategy of looking closely at each item proposed for inclusion on the questionnaire to determine: (1) the need for that item, (2) the level of geographic detail required by users, and hence whether the item must be asked of all households on the short form, or whether it can be asked of a sample on either the long form or on a much smaller follow-on survey, and (3) whether some other source could provide higher-quality data. The panel suggests exploring the use of administrative records together with sampling to obtain data on some housing structure characteristics (see Chapter 6). Such data could be more accurate than individual responses on the census form. Costs initially may be high, but should decline over time. This particular use of administrative records has the advantage that it should present no actual or perceived threat to individual privacy.

A third major theme of the report concerns the strategy for designing the 1990 census, whatever the particulars of the methodology may turn out to be. The research plans drafted by the Census Bureau staff are extremely comprehensive and ambitious. The staff has clearly tried to include all reasonable ideas for consideration in the research and testing program. The panel commends the Census Bureau's efforts to design and carry out a thorough research and testing program that will support sound decisions regarding methodology for the 1990 and later censuses.

The panel believes, however, that in most areas the Census Bureau must choose among all the ideas and procedures proposed for testing, given constraints on available staff and budget resources and the limited time available to analyze test results and use them to guide decisions on methodology. The exception concerns research related to adjustment, including research on coverage evaluation methods. In this area, the panel believes that research must proceed on a broad front if effective methodologies are to be developed for 1990. In other areas, the panel has endeavored to recommend strategies for choosing priority projects for inclusion in the 1990 census research and testing program and has also recommended the use of less costly research methods, where appropriate, including more detailed analysis of 1980 census results, in place of full-scale field tests. Finally, the panel recommends specific concepts and procedures for research and testing that we believe show special promise for improving the methodology of the decennial census in 1990 and beyond.

OVERVIEW OF THE REPORT AND RECOMMENDATIONS

This section provides an overview of the report and a summary of the panel's recommendations. The report is organized as follows: Chapters 2, 3, and 4 provide background on the decennial census that is helpful for understanding the subsequent exposition of the panel's recommendations. Chapters 5 through 8 provide general and specific recommendations in several areas. Each chapter includes one or more appendixes that provide additional details for the interested reader on topics discussed in the text. Below we briefly summarize the contents of each chapter and list the panel's recommendations.

Chapter 2--Purposes and Uses of the Decennial Census

In choosing an appropriate and cost-effective methodology for a data collection program, it is important to understand the kinds of uses that are made of the statistics. The chapter gives a brief overview of the uses of census data historically and then describes the range of uses of the modern census; most importantly, the census is virtually the only source of comparable data on basic counts and detailed characteristics for small areas and small groups in the population. Two appendixes provide additional information on uses and users of census data: Appendix 2.1 reviews state and local government uses, and Appendix 2.2 provides a case study of government, business, and academic uses in the State of New Jersey.

The chapter includes a review of the limited body of research that has attempted to measure the effects of census data errors on key uses, such as reapportionment, redistricting, and allocation of federal funds to states and localities. Finally, the chapter reviews data on errors in postcensal population estimates for small areas, which appear to greatly exceed errors in the census itself. The panel recommends serious consideration of the need for a mid-decade census program in 1995 to improve the quality of postcensal estimates:

> 2.1. We recommend that the Census Bureau assess the need for a mid-decade census, particularly by studying the effect of errors in postcensal population estimates compared with errors in the decennial census on major data uses. Unless these studies do not support the value of a mid-decade census, the Census Bureau should proceed with preparations and make every effort to secure funding to conduct a census in 1995.

Chapter 3--Census Methodology: Prior Practice and Current Test Plans

This chapter briefly reviews the procedures used to conduct the 1980 census and compares and contrasts the 1980 census methodology with procedures used in previous modern censuses in the United States and in other Western countries. The discussion covers the following stages in the census process: development and checking of address lists, enumeration, follow-up, coverage improvement, data processing, and post-census evaluation. The chapter also summarizes the Census Bureau's current research and testing plans for the upcoming 1990 census, with particular emphasis on the plans for pretests in spring 1986, and presents the panel's overall assessment of these plans.

The panel has several major concerns with the research and testing program proposed for 1986. The program outlined appears too ambitious for the time remaining before the census and for the staff and budget resources likely to be available, particularly if key data are to be analyzed in time to support major decisions. In the panel's view the program also places too much emphasis on field testing over other kinds of research, including further analysis of existing data. The panel suggests in this chapter some ways to scale back the 1986 testing program and in subsequent chapters provides detailed recommendations for research priorities in specific areas of census methodology.

3.1. We recommend, to ensure cost-effective field testing and preservation of adequate resources for analysis, that the Census Bureau attempt to identify research and testing proposals for 1986 that:

(a) Can be pursued with other research methods and omitted from the 1986 field test program;
(b) Can be safely deferred for research or testing until 1987 or until the dress rehearsals;
(c) Are unlikely to be viable for 1990 but should be incorporated on an experimental basis into the 1990 census as a test for future censuses; and
(d) Should be omitted entirely from consideration for the 1990 census, based on previous census experience or other survey research results.

3.2. We recommend that the Census Bureau make full use of data from the 1980 census and from experiments carried out in 1980 to help guide planning for 1990. To this end, we recommend that the Census Bureau assign a high priority to completion of 1980 census methodological studies, and we encourage further analysis of these data where appropriate.

Appendixes to Chapter 3 provide more detailed expositions of two aspects of current census methodology--sequential hot-deck imputation, used to assign values to census records for missing responses (Appendix 3.1), and iterative proportional fitting, used to calibrate responses obtained from samples of households to responses obtained from the entire population (Appendix 3.2). These techniques have potential use, as discussed in Chapter 7, in carrying out an adjustment of the census counts.

Chapter 4--Evaluating the Decennial Census: Past Experience

This chapter reviews the history of coverage evaluation of population censuses in the United States from 1950 through 1980. Broadly speaking, there are two major classes of coverage evaluation techniques--micro-level methods based on case-by-case analysis of samples of units such as persons or households and macro-level methods involving analysis of aggregate census data, including comparison of census totals with external data and analysis of internal consistency. The chapter identifies strengths and weaknesses of each of the major micro-level methodologies used in the United States and Canada, including post-enumeration surveys, reverse record checks, and administrative records matches, and of the major macro-level method, demographic analysis. Although the chapter does not contain recommendations, it does provide important background material for the panel's conclusions presented in Chapter 8 regarding research on coverage evaluation estimation methods for the 1990 census. Chapter 4 includes two appendixes providing technical details on coverage evaluation based on multiple lists (Appendix 4.1) and on operational aspects and modeling of computer matching (Appendix 4.2). Matching of records from the census to records obtained from one or more surveys or administrative lists is a critically important component of most methods of evaluating the completeness of coverage of the population obtained in the census.

Chapter 5--Taking the Census I: Improving the Count

This chapter focuses on the problem that not all population groups are counted equally well in the census and discusses procedures for improving the count, including procedures used in past censuses together with some new ideas. Most programs directed toward coverage improvement are expensive. They may also introduce error by duplicating or otherwise erroneously adding persons. In general, however, the panel believes that the costs of well-designed and well-executed coverage improvement programs represent money well spent for improving the census figures. The chapter first reviews what is known about hard-to-count groups in the population and about groups that have exhibited problems of erroneous enumerations. (The text provides a summary of the literature, and Appendix 5.1 provides a more in-depth review.) The chapter then reviews the performance of special programs directed toward coverage improvement in the 1970 and 1980 censuses, including estimates of cost and numbers of persons and housing units added to the count. The panel makes recommendations for coverage improvement related to items on the questionnaire and to enumeration procedures.

The panel first notes the importance of gaining understanding of the problems of undercount and overcount in the census.

5.1. We recommend that the Census Bureau assign a high priority to the completion of studies of undercount and overcount in the 1980 census.

5.2. We recommend that the Census Bureau set up a timetable and assign staff to permit completion of the analysis of 1990 coverage evaluation results in time to be used in planning the first pretest of the 2000 census.

The panel next discusses priorities for research and testing directed toward improvement of items on the questionnaire that relate to coverage, including the questions on race and Hispanic origin. It is important to understand what responses to the race and ethnicity questions mean if appropriate estimates of coverage rates for race and Hispanic groups are to be developed. This section reviews the history of race and ethnicity questions in the census, considers techniques for developing race and ethnicity questions, and discusses issues of data comparability, including comparability of race and ethnicity data from census to census and comparability with information collected in vital statistics records.

5.3. We recommend that the Census Bureau test a variety of question designs for the race and ethnicity information to be collected in the 1990 census, including some that combine the collection of information on Hispanic origin with the other race and ethnicity information.

5.4. We recommend that the Census Bureau, in addition to other methods that it has traditionally employed, use the technique of focus group discussions as one means to develop questions on particularly sensitive items such as race and ethnicity.

5.5. We recommend that, in 1990 as it did in 1980, the Census Bureau collect, tabulate, and release data on race and ethnicity in such a way that the data can be reaggregated as necessary to obtain maximum feasible comparability with 1980 and 1970.

5.6. We recommend that the Census Bureau, the National Center for Health Statistics, and other relevant federal agencies work closely together to design questions and response editing rules on race and ethnicity that minimize conceptual differences between census and vital statistics records to the extent feasible. The Office of Management and Budget should act as necessary to facilitate such coordination.

The next section of the chapter reviews experience in the 1970 and 1980 censuses with questions on the short form designed to aid in achieving a complete and accurate count, such as questions probing for a complete roster of household members. The discussion notes problems posed for an accurate count by the mobility of the population and recent trends in living arrangements that have resulted in growing populations with two or more usual residences (for example, retired people with summer and winter homes). The panel suggests a question for testing directed toward improving coverage of young adults and children in hard-to-count areas.

5.7. We recommend that the Census Bureau give high priority in its planning for 1990 to research and testing of questions and enumeration procedures that address problems of accurately counting persons in the process of moving, households with second (vacation) homes, and persons with more than one usual place of residence.

5.8. We recommend, as one procedure to consider for improving coverage of hard-to-count groups, that the Census Bureau pretest a question asking parents for names and addresses of children who are not part of the household. This question should be included in the 1986 pretests.

The last section of the chapter provides the panel's overall assessment of special enumeration procedures designed to improve the count. While believing that programs such as the recheck of vacant units can make important contributions to improving coverage, the panel does not subscribe to the view that every coverage improvement idea that is suggested or has been used in the past should be included in the plans for the next census. The panel recommends paring down the list of programs to be considered for 1990 and the list requiring early field testing.

5.9. We recommend that the Census Bureau review coverage improvement programs used in past censuses and proceed with research and testing directed toward use in 1990 of those programs that: (1) exhibited a high yield in terms of numbers of missed persons correctly added to the count and/or contributed significantly to reducing differential undercoverage, (2) exhibited low-to-moderate costs per person correctly added, and (3) did not add many persons incorrectly. Programs that do not satisfy these criteria should be dropped from consideration unless: (1) the program exhibited low total dollar costs and had demonstrable public relations or goodwill value in previous censuses or (2) there is some particular reason to believe a revised program will yield greatly improved results.

5.10. We recommend that the Census Bureau conduct full-scale pretests in 1986 only of those coverage improvement programs that require such testing. Furthermore, we recommend that the Census Bureau use focus groups that include members of hard-to-count populations as one means to explore coverage improvement techniques and to narrow the range of options to be field-tested.

Chapter 6--Taking the Census II: Uses of Sampling and Administrative Records

This chapter addresses two major methods that have been proposed to improve the cost-effectiveness of the decennial census-the uses of sampling in obtaining the count and the use of administrative records. The chapter considers the merits of replacing the census with a large sample survey, using sampling in the follow-up stage of census operations, and using sampling for various coverage improvement operations. It also discusses the traditional use of sampling to obtain characteristics detail. Finally, the chapter considers the use of administrative records along with sampling for improving the quality of certain census items.

With regard to sampling for the count, the discussion notes problems of replacing the census with a large sample survey. The panel believes that a survey would result in less complete coverage compared with a census and that there would be only minor cost savings in sampling on the scale necessary for satisfaction of present demands for small-area data from the census. The use of sampling for follow-up of households that do not return their census questionnaires has some of the same drawbacks, but sampling could prove cost-effective in the final stages of follow-up in which it is very expensive to count an additional person. Although the Census Bureau has dropped plans to study the use of sampling for follow-up and for coverage improvement programs such as the recheck of vacant units in 1986, the panel supports research in these areas. The panel also supports further testing of telephone follow-up of nonresponding households, which was tried experimentally in 1980. Finally, the panel discusses the need to maintain machine-readable records of the follow-up history of individual households that will permit detailed analysis and simulation of different sample designs.

6.1. We recommend that the Census Bureau not pursue research or testing of a sample survey as a replacement for a complete enumeration in 1990.

6.2. We recommend that the Census Bureau include the testing of sampling in follow-up as part of the 1987 pretest program. We recommend that in its research the Census Bureau emphasize tests of sampling for the later stages of follow-up.

6.3. We recommend that the Census Bureau keep machine-readable records on the follow-up history of individual households in the upcoming pretests and for a sample of areas in the 1990 census, so that information for detailed analysis of the cost and error structures of conducting census follow-up operations on a sample basis will be available.

6.4. We support the Census Bureau's plans for further testing of telephone follow-up procedures in 1986. We recommend that the Census Bureau review the implications for sample-based follow-up operations of the operational difficulties that were encountered in the 1980 telephone experiment.

6.5. We recommend that the Census Bureau consider the use of sampling for those coverage improvement programs that are implemented in the final stages of census operations and where there is potential for significant cost savings. We recommend that the Census Bureau simulate sampling in the Vacant/Delete Check program in an upcoming pretest.

The chapter then reviews the use of sampling for content items in the census. Historically, in every census since 1940, some items have been asked of only a sample of the population in order to reduce response burden and processing costs while obtaining the benefits of additional data. Sample designs and sampling fractions have differed in recent censuses. The Census Bureau is currently considering a design for 1990 that would include a short form containing items asked on a 100 percent basis, a long form containing additional items asked of a large sample, and a follow-on survey of a small percentage of short-form households administered within a few months of Census Day that would obtain yet other information. The panel did not offer specific recommendations in this area, but noted that the criteria for including items in the follow-on survey have not been explicitly articulated but should be to permit thorough assessment of the need for the survey and for the inclusion of particular items.

6.6. We recommend that the Census Bureau refine and make more explicit its criteria for inclusion of items in the proposed follow-on survey that is being considered for the 1990 census.

The last section of the chapter discusses the use of administrative records and sampling for improving the accuracy of content items. The concern over completeness of population coverage in the census can obscure equally valid concerns over the accuracy of the content. There are well-documented problems with the reporting of content items such as income, utility costs, and age of structure. The panel recommends research and testing directed toward improving the data quality of key items. The research program should include design of operations to verify, and possibly adjust, responses as part of the census operation and investigate the possibility of obtaining some items from administrative records sources. The panel makes a specific recommendation with regard to housing structure items.

6.7. We recommend that the Census Bureau conduct research and testing in the area of improved accuracy of responses to content items in the census. We recommend further that the content improvement procedures examined not be limited to reinterviews of samples of respondents, but include the use of administrative records.

6.8. We recommend that the Census Bureau investigate the cost and feasibility of alternative ways of obtaining data on housing structure items. Possibilities include: (1) obtaining housing structure information on a sample basis from administrative records and using this information to verify and possibly to adjust responses in the census; (2) obtaining structure information solely from administrative records and dropping these items from the census; and (3) asking structure questions of a knowledgeable respondent such as the owner or resident manager. We recommend that any trial use of a "knowledgeable" respondent procedure include a check of the data obtained from such respondents against data from administrative records.

Two appendixes to Chapter 6 provide additional information related to use of sampling to obtain the census count. Appendix 6.1 gives very rough cost estimates for conducting the census on the basis of different-sized samples; Appendix 6.2 develops illustrative costs for conducting follow-up operations of a sample of nonrespondents. Appendix 6.3 develops in further detail the panel's suggestion for obtaining improved data on housing structure items by means of local administrative records.

Chapter 7--Adjustment of Population Counts

In this chapter, the panel presents its basic position on the issue of adjustment of the census counts. The chapter considers criteria or yardsticks for measuring the increase in accuracy of census information that adjustment might produce and addresses problems of consistency and timing posed by adjustment. The chapter discusses what is known and recommends further research on procedures that could be useful for adjustment. Three appendixes provide additional technical discussion. Appendix 7.1 supplies the mathematical expressions for various yardsticks discussed in the text; Appendix 7.2 discusses in greater detail hierarchical Bayesian techniques that have been proposed for use in adjustment; and Appendix 7.3 discusses a problem raised by the aggregation of synthetic estimates.

The chapter begins with consideration of the need for adjustment to improve the accuracy of the census numbers, particularly to reduce differential coverage errors across geographic locations and demographic groups. The panel is led to recommend development of adjustment procedures, but as a complement to--not a substitute for--continued efforts to improve census coverage. If public perception of the importance of being counted should deteriorate, this would have serious consequences for the accuracy of the figures, adjusted or not.

<u>7.1</u>. Completeness of the count is an important goal, both for ensuring the accuracy of the census and for establishing the credibility of the census figures among all users. Adjustment should not be viewed as an alternative to obtaining as complete a count as possible through cost-effective means. Nevertheless, the ultimate goal is that of the accuracy of the published figures. Given the likelihood that the census will continue to produce different rates of undercoverage for various population groups, and given

the equity problems caused thereby, we recommend that work proceed on the development of adjustment procedures and that adjustment be implemented if there is reasonable confidence that it will reduce differential coverage errors.

The chapter next considers criteria for evaluating the numbers produced by the census (based on either unadjusted or adjusted counts), considering both the errors in the numbers themselves and the resulting loss to society due to erroneous treatment of political jurisdictions in terms of representation, fund allocation, and other uses of the data. The panel discusses yardsticks or loss functions, that is, numeric measures of the impact of census errors, from the viewpoint of the data user and as they relate to adjustment. The discussion notes that no adjustment procedure can be expected to simultaneously reduce the error of every piece of census information for every geographic area; rather, there is an important net social gain if differential coverage error is generally reduced. The panel believes it is substantially more important to reduce the overall error per person than the overall error per place and recommends that loss functions for measuring total error take into account the population size of each jurisdiction. In discussing technical considerations concerning choice of loss functions, the panel concludes that good adjustment procedures should be expected to perform well for a range of loss functions. Where the choice of adjustment procedure depends importantly on the choice of loss function, this suggests that the particular adjustment procedure has weaknesses that need to be addressed.

7.2. In measuring the total loss associated with an adjustment procedure, we recommend that the contribution to this loss attributable to a geographic region should reflect its population size. Thus, we recommend against loss functions based solely on the number of political entities losing or gaining through adjustment.

7.3. We believe that, in general, the results of an adjustment are likely to be affected more by the quality of coverage evaluation data and the models and methodology used than by the choice of loss functions. Given a family of loss functions with relatively similar objectives, it should be possible, and desirable, to determine an adjustment procedure that has good performance for most or all of them. We recommend that the Census Bureau investigate the construction of adjustment procedures that are robust to a reasonable range of loss functions.

The next section of the chapter discusses the problem of estimating the likely range of error introduced by the particular procedure adopted for an adjustment. Although error can be measured only imperfectly, information about the distribution of error is important in the same way that sampling variances for sample surveys provide useful information.

7.4. We recommend that the Census Bureau explore methods for providing estimates of errors associated with estimates of census over- and undercoverage, with a view to publishing such error estimates along with coverage evaluation results and any adjusted census data that may be issued.

Adjustment of census data could create problems of internal consistency of microdata from the census with aggregate statistics. The panel believes that internal consistency is an important quality for general purpose statistics, such as those produced by the decennial census, which have a wide range of output and many uses. The section discusses reasons to prefer carrying down any adjustment of population estimates for larger geographic areas to the level of the individual micro-records and reviews methods, such as weighting and imputation, for accomplishing this.

7.5. The panel believes that it is important to strive for internal consistency of published census figures. Should adjustment appear feasible and effective, methods exist for distributing adjusted totals for aggregated groups down to subgroup values. We recommend that one of these methods be used to achieve internal consistency of census figures.

Adjustment also presents problems of timing. Current law requires submission of state population counts for purposes of reapportionment within 9 months after Census Day and of small-area counts within 12 months after Census Day for purposes of redistricting. The panel discussed the pros and cons of various scenarios with regard to release of adjusted data if it does not prove possible to implement a full-scale adjustment in time to satisfy the above constraints. Congress clearly will need to stipulate which scenario is preferable for apportionment purposes.

<u>7.6</u>. Census data used for reapportionment and redistricting are required by law to be produced no later than specific dates. It is possible that adjustment of the 1990 census will prove feasible and effective in all respects, except for the ability to meet the required deadlines. This should not necessarily preclude subsequent issuance of adjusted data for other uses. In this situation, we recommend that the Census Bureau seek determination by Congress of whether it desires that adjusted data be used and will therefore extend the deadlines, or wishes to adhere to current deadlines and will therefore stipulate the use of unadjusted (or partially adjusted) data for reapportionment and redistricting.

The remaining sections of Chapter 7 review possible technical approaches to the use of data from coverage evaluation programs for adjusting the raw census figures (detailed discussion of these programs is in Chapter 8). The review covers procedures for starting out, that is, for developing estimates for a limited number of large geographic areas, and procedures for carrying down, that is, for using the large-area estimates to develop adjustments for small areas and ultimately for the microdata records. The discussion considers the Census Bureau's plans for research and testing of adjustment procedures in upcoming pretests and makes recommendations for priority research areas.

<u>7.7</u>. The panel recognizes that considerable work is still necessary and likely to lead to improved procedures for adjusting census data. We therefore support the Census Bureau's stated plans to pursue, internally, research and development of adjustment procedures, and we also recommend that the Census Bureau vigorously promote and support related statistical research in the academic community.

<u>7.8</u>. The panel supports the Census Bureau in its plans for a 1986 pretest of adjustment operations, including the production of mock tabulations of

adjusted census data. We recommend analysis of the resulting adjusted and unadjusted data sets, to help identify the strengths and weaknesses of the particular methods tried.

7.9. We recommend that research on adjustment include: (1) investigations of the assumptions underlying the procedures, (2) an attempt to evaluate empirically the more important of the assumptions as well as the sensitivity of methods to violation of assumptions, (3) study of methods used for carrying down estimates to lower levels of aggregation, and (4) a study of the impact of adjustment on uses of census data.

Chapter 8--Measuring the Completeness of the 1990 Census

This chapter presents the panel's recommendations for research and testing to design effective coverage evaluation programs for the 1990 census. For adjustment to be feasible, evaluation programs must be good enough to provide estimates of net undercoverage that are reliable for at least large geographic areas and have error properties that are broadly understood. Coverage evaluation programs also provide valuable information for users of the data and for the Census Bureau in planning subsequent censuses. Although in general the panel recommends that the Census Bureau narrow its 1990 census research and testing objectives, in the area of coverage evaluation the panel believes it is too soon to focus on one method to the exclusion of others. The panel makes several recommendations related to the Census Bureau's currently preferred method of pre- or post-enumeration surveys and also recommends vigorous research related to alternative methods, including reverse record checks and systematic observation. Appendix 8.1 discusses estimation methods and estimates for the illegal alien population, and Appendix 8.2 provides estimates of variance and cost for a large systematic observer study.

The chapter begins with a review of the problems associated with each of the major methods of coverage evaluation and considers the Census Bureau's current plans for research and testing directed toward coverage evaluation of the 1990 census. The panel argues against the Census Bureau's decision to concentrate on post-enumeration (or possibly pre-enumeration) survey methodology as the principal means of coverage evaluation in

1990, notes that the Census Bureau should not put itself in the position of lacking a means of adjustment if there are problems with the operation for matching survey with census records, and urges completion of 1980-based studies related to coverage evaluation.

8.1. We recommend that the Census Bureau conduct research and tests of alternative coverage evaluation methodologies in addition to the post-enumeration survey, specifically reverse record checks and systematic observation.

8.2. We agree that matching algorithms are very important to the success of several adjustment methods. We recommend that the Census Bureau investigate the development of a fallback position in case adequate matching is not available in 1990.

8.3. We recommend that the Census Bureau complete and report analyses of 1980-based tests related to coverage evaluation, especially the Census/CPS/IRS Match Study.

The chapter next considers possible improvements and recommends priority research areas for each major coverage evaluation method in turn. The demographic analysis method, which uses data from independent sources including birth and death records to estimate the number of persons at the time of the census in a given age-race-sex category, currently suffers from the absence of data on undocumented aliens. The panel recommends research into using demographic analysis for estimates of the native-born population. The reverse record check method, which traces the current location of a representative sample of newborns, immigrants, and persons counted in the previous census or coverage evaluation program, has a greater problem in tracing in the United States because of the 10-year interval between censuses (as opposed to 5 years in Canada, where the method has been used extensively). The panel recommends completion of a current experiment to test alternative methods of tracing. The chapter discusses at length the method of post-enumeration (or pre-enumeration) surveys, in which a sample of households is interviewed and matched with records in the census, and identifies several problem areas for particular attention in the Census Bureau's research.

Finally, the chapter discusses the idea of using systematic observers to provide independent estimates of the population in a sample of areas, including but not limited to areas that have proved particularly hard to count in previous censuses. This method is suggested because it may have the potential to surmount the problem observed repeatedly in the history of coverage evaluation, namely that persons who are missed by the census are also likely to be missed by an independent survey or other data source.

8.4. We recommend that the Census Bureau conduct research into using demographic analysis to develop estimates of coverage for the native-born population. The research should consider whether these estimates could usefully be combined with other estimates of coverage.

8.5. We recommend that the Census Bureau move quickly to complete the Forward Trace Study to determine the feasibility of using forward trace methods in a reverse record check program for 1990. If the methodology is effective, a national sample for this purpose needs to be initiated by 1986.

8.6. We support the Census Bureau's research directed toward developing the 1990 Post-Enumeration Program and recommend that such research emphasize the following areas:

(a) Reduction of post-enumeration survey nonresponse;
(b) Reduction of unresolved matches between records for individuals listed in the post-enumeration survey and the decennial census;
(e) Validation of the assumptions and/or development of alternative methodologies with respect to netting-out of overcounts and undercounts with reference to the place of enumeration; and
(d) Investigation of alternatives to the assumption that the inclusion of individuals in the post-enumeration survey is unrelated to their inclusion in the decennial census and the estimation of the strength of this relation.

8.7. We recommend that the Census Bureau initiate a research program on systematic observation with a view toward the use of this method for a sample of areas at the time of the 1990 census.

In the area of adjustment-related research, including coverage evaluation methods, the panel acknowledges that many technical and operational issues need to be resolved if adjustment procedures are to be developed in time for their use in the nation's bicentennial census in 1990. Overall, while much effort will be required, the panel is optimistic that substantial progress can be made.

2
Purposes and Uses of the Decennial Census

The panel reviewed uses and users of decennial census data with several objects in mind. The first purpose of the review was to document major uses of the census and identify their data requirements to permit the panel to evaluate the likely impact of changes in methodology. The second purpose was to assess--or at least to inquire into--whether some uses could not be satisfied as well or almost as well by other data collection programs. The third purpose was to examine the sensitivity of each major type of use to the accuracy of the data.

An inescapable conclusion from our review is that, given the multiplicity of important purposes served by the census, major changes in census methodology should not be made without careful consideration of their ramifications for a broad spectrum of uses. At the same time, we believe that investigation of alternative approaches to data collection might reveal opportunities to remove some questions from the census (particularly from the long form) or to make other changes that would free funds for efforts to improve the data that are collected. Examination of the sensitivity of uses to the accuracy of the census is needed to understand the consequences of census errors and to determine the benefit of devoting additional resources to improving the data. How much difference would it make in the distribution of revenue sharing dollars, for example, if the differential net undercount among ethnic groups in the population could be reduced from about 4 percentage points (the apparent difference between blacks and all others in 1980) to 2 percentage points? Would this improvement make more or less difference than improved measurement of per capita income, which also enters into the revenue sharing formula?

The panel's review of uses of the census stems from the belief that decisions on methodology for a data collection program should consider the various purposes the program is intended to serve. If a statistical program were being designed de novo, the responsible agency might go through the following steps:

- Identify the fundamental purposes the program must serve and the minimal requirements for subject matter and geographic area detail, needed accuracy of the data, and frequency of data collection required to satisfy these purposes;
- Identify secondary purposes that it would be desirable to accommodate and their data requirements;
- Identify methodologies that, at a minimum, can serve the basic purposes;
- Further evaluate those methodologies on other criteria, such as ability to satisfy secondary purposes and public acceptability;
- Determine costs for each methodology of serving the basic purposes and the incremental costs of serving additional purposes; and
- Select the optimal methodology.

In the case of the decennial census, with its long history of serving many uses and users, its unique role in determining political representation, and its operational complexity, methodological choices cannot be nearly as cut-and-dried as the above scheme would suggest. It is not easy to rank uses in order of importance--what may be of marginal direct value to federal officials may be of great value for local planners or business people, and it is not clear how to weight these different assessments. Having made a decision to assign a lower or higher priority to a given use leads to further problems of implementation. On one hand, it is hard to reconcile users to a decision to scale back the level of detail or accuracy provided or to stop serving a need altogether. On the other hand, it is hard to make changes to tried-and-tested procedures to accommodate new uses or to improve the level of detail or accuracy provided, even if cost were no particular object.

The panel did not attempt to resolve these difficult questions, but undertook a more limited review of census uses and users with the objectives set forth at the outset. The chapter begins with a brief overview of the uses of census data in the American past. Subsequent sections review the distinguishing features of the modern census that shape the uses made of the data, give examples of major types of applications, and endeavor to draw implications for census methodology from the data requirements for important uses. The chapter then reviews the limited body of research that has attempted to measure the effects of census data errors on key purposes, such as reapportionment and fund allocation. The concluding section reviews research on the magnitude of errors introduced in postcensal population estimates compared with errors in the census itself and discusses the implications of the research results for the utility of a mid-decade census.

HISTORICAL USES OF CENSUS DATA

Originally, the main purpose of the decennial census in the United States was to determine the population count in every state for apportioning seats in the House of Representatives. Very soon, however, the census was expanded to collect additional information beyond basic demographics, and policy makers and analysts began to use the data for many purposes.

In the nineteenth and early twentieth centuries, census data are known to have served at least the following types of uses:

• Scholarly analysis. For example, Frederick Jackson Turner's landmark work on "The Significance of the Frontier in American History" (1894) rested on analysis of census data.

• Input to public policy decisions. Census results strongly influenced the debate at the turn of the century that culminated in the National Origins Act of 1924, which severely restricted immigration (Conk, 1984:10-13). A noted Civil War historian has suggested that the 1860 census results were a factor leading the South to secede rather than accept growing Northern population--and therefore political--dominance (Nichols, 1948:460-461).

• Use for allocation of federal funds to the states. Between 1887 and 1921, the Congress passed laws providing for allocation of funds to the states for programs of vocational education, agricultural extension, conservation, highways, and public health using formulas that included census population counts. These laws laid the foundation for the grant-in-aid system. By 1930, the total funds distributed by formula amounted to about $100 million, 3 percent of the federal budget (Conk, 1984:18-19).

- Public information and population analysis. From the beginning, Americans have been keenly interested in what the census results show about their own place of residence and how it stacks up against others. Census results have found their way into countless speeches, student themes, and newspaper and magazine articles describing and extolling local areas and reporting changes over time.

All the historical uses of census data described above have their counterparts today. Users of early censuses would be astounded by the extent and depth of analysis made possible by modern computer technology, but they would readily recognize many types of applications.

DISTINGUISHING FEATURES OF THE MODERN CENSUS AND ITS USES

The modern census in the United States has evolved in response to demands for data to serve a wide range of purposes, many of which are not served by any other data collection program. The need to satisfy particular kinds of important purposes has shaped census methodology, and, conversely, the distinguishing characteristics of the census program have created a set of expectations among users regarding data they look for in the census.

This section organizes a discussion of uses of the present-day census according to three main features that together differentiate the census from other data collection programs: population counts for small areas, small-area and subgroup characteristics, and historical time series. Questions posed are: What is the census currently expected to provide that other data collection vehicles do not? What kinds of benefits do users anticipate from census data as opposed to data from other sources? What are the implications of user expectations for proposed changes in methodology? Appendix 2.1 describes applications that state and local governments--two important user groups--make of census data. Appendix 2.2 depicts the range of uses within a single geographic area--New Jersey--among private, public, and academic users. It also describes the various distribution channels through which census data are made available to users.[1]

Basic Counts for Small Areas

The census is the source of complete head counts, including basic information about age, race, and sex, and of residential housing counts obtained in a consistent manner throughout the country for small as well as large geographic areas. The census provides counts not only for the nation as a whole and for large areas such as regions, states, and metropolitan areas, but also for counties, congressional districts, cities and towns, and minor civil divisions of counties. In addition, in what represents a vitally important and relatively recent development, the census provides counts for local areas including census tracts, block groups, and city blocks.

Local areas identified in the census are typically quite small in population (as are some political jurisdictions, such as towns and villages--see Bureau of the Census, 1982b:Ch.4). Census tracts--first delineated in several large cities for the 1910 census--generally have between 2,500 and 8,000 residents and are currently identified in every metropolitan area and some nonmetropolitan counties. Block groups along with enumeration districts covered the entire nation in 1980 (the former were tabulated where there were city blocks and the latter elsewhere) and averaged about 800 population. There were over 2.5 million city blocks in 1980 identified in urbanized areas, cities of 10,000 or more population outside urbanized areas, and in other areas that contracted with the Census Bureau to tabulate block statistics. By 1990, blocks will be identified in all areas of the nation. All of these types of small areas are often used as "building blocks" in putting together information for nonstandard census areas, such as school districts, neighborhoods, police precincts, urban renewal areas, etc.

In contrast, the largest federal sample survey ever conducted, the 1976 Survey of Income and Education,

---

[1]See U.S. House of Representatives (1982) for additional documentation provided by many users from government, private business, and academic institutions of their needs for census data.

covered enough households (200,000) to provide reliable data for states and metropolitan areas but not for any smaller areas. Regularly recurring federal surveys, such as the American Housing Survey and the Health Interview Survey, contain just enough households (currently about 40,000) to produce reliable information for large states and metropolitan areas. The Current Population Survey (CPS), which includes about 60,000 households, is now designed to produce estimates for all states and also large metropolitan areas but cannot support estimates for smaller areas. Some localities conduct their own censuses (usually contracting with the Census Bureau) or surveys, but these efforts do not generate comparative data for other areas.

Sample surveys, even the most thoroughly conducted ones, also do not obtain as complete a coverage of the population as the decennial census. The Census Bureau estimates that the Current Population Survey (after imputation for refusals and other cases of nonresponse, but before ratio estimation using census-based current population estimates) covers only 93 percent of the census total (Hansen, 1984:138).

Various administrative records systems can potentially provide complete counts for small as well as large areas, but no currently existing system covers the entire population in a consistent manner. Among large federal systems, Internal Revenue Service (IRS) records, while covering most persons, exclude those who do not file tax returns or who are not listed as dependents and, in addition, overcount persons who both file a return and are reported as a dependent on someone else's return. Social Security administration records likewise both undercount, excluding children who have not yet applied for a card and adults who have never worked or applied for a card and are not yet eligible for Medicare, and overcount, including some decedents and persons with more than one social security number. Moreover, the address information needed to determine individuals' specific place of residence is not fully available from these sources--many IRS addresses represent place of business or legal domicile rather than place of residence and social security addresses typically are current only for those receiving benefits (see Alvey and Scheuren, 1982). Other limitations of administrative records include the difficulty of generating data on families and households and the paucity of characteristics information.

Among the major uses of basic counts from the census are the following:

• Reapportionment of the U.S. House of Representatives according to the distribution of population among the states. Title 13 of the U.S. Code includes a provision requiring the Secretary of Commerce to report state population totals to the President within nine months after Census Day, i.e., by December 31 of the census year.

• Redistricting within states and localities to meet stringent court-mandated criteria for equal size and compactness of election districts and for appropriate representation of race and ethnic groups. Under current law, the Census Bureau is to provide to the states within one year after Census Day a computer tape containing small-area population counts. The tapes provided April 1, 1981, contained total population plus race and Hispanic origin for blocks, enumeration districts, and, where specified by the state, precincts.

• Benchmarking of postcensal population estimates. Census counts by age, race, and sex are the starting point for current population estimates produced between census years for geographic areas ranging from the nation as a whole to states, counties, and all 39,000 political jurisdictions recognized for federal revenue sharing.

• Calibration of data from other collection programs. Census-based current population estimates by age, sex, race, and Hispanic origin are the basis for weighting the output from federal surveys such as the Current Population Survey and the Health Interview Survey.

• Calculation of vital rates. Census counts and census-based population estimates by age, race, sex, and geographic area serve as denominators for rates of births, deaths, marriages, and divorces produced for the nation and the states from the vital statistics program.

• Allocation of federal and state dollars to states and localities. A large number of grant-in-aid programs include the total population as one element in the allocation formula. The best known of these programs is general revenue sharing.

• Determination of eligibility for funding from government programs and of local rights and responsibilities. A number of grant programs have thresholds for eligibility; for example, the Job Training Partnership Act generally designates service delivery areas as counties or cities with 200,000 or more population. Most states classify counties and municipalities by size and accord various rights and responsibilities to each size class.

• Public planning and decision making. For example, cities examine census counts by police precinct, school district, fire precinct, and many other kinds of administrative areas built up from census geography such as city blocks to allocate personnel and budget in proportion to population and housing, to redraw administrative areas to equalize demands for basic services, and to serve as a starting point for projecting future public needs.

• Business planning and decision making. Retailers locating sales outlets, for example, compare population density and demographic characteristics in areas surrounding possible sites.

• Comparison and ranking of areas, such as cities and metropolitan centers, by population, for many purposes such as advertising, marketing, and public information. Even the most casual review of the nation's media quickly reveals the extent of reliance on census and census-based statistics for articles, maps, and graphs on national, regional, and local social and economic characteristics (see Rowe in U.S. House of Representatives, 1982:424-428, for data on use of federal statistics in *The New York Times*).

As noted at the outset of this chapter, the panel believes that the uses of census data should be examined periodically, by the Census Bureau and others, to reassess their importance and the possibilities for meeting them from alternative sources. Some uses of basic small-area counts may appear unimportant or even frivolous and not worth expenditure of public funds. However, other uses are fundamental to our federal governance (including reapportionment and redistricting) or to the efficient delivery of goods and services in the public and private sectors, and demonstrate why basic small-area counts constitute the heart of the census program.

Most of the important uses of basic census population (and housing) counts cited impose the requirements that data be collected in a complete and comparable way for all manner and size of geographic areas, with consequent implications for proposed changes in methodology. The requirement for comparable data across areas strongly implies the need to obtain estimates of the population more or less at a point in time. The requirement for comparable data argues as well for the need to standardize processes of data treatment and estimation to the extent practicable. The fact that users expect to be able to obtain counts for very small areas, such as blocks and tracts, and to use these counts to reaggregate the data into other kinds of areas such as school districts or police precincts, implies the need to incorporate any estimation or imputations used into the microdata records so that consistent totals can be produced for whatever tabulations are requested.

It is of course possible to challenge these arguments or to state that other considerations must take precedence. However, the panel in subsequent chapters evaluating proposed changes in methodology justifies the premise that comparability and consistency of census figures are requirements that methodological innovations should satisfy unless there are compelling reasons not to do so.

With regard to the requirement for completeness or accuracy of basic census counts, the picture is somewhat less clear. Ideally, every user would like a completely accurate set of numbers, but it is recognized that it is impossible to obtain a perfectly complete count. The question becomes the tolerable level of accuracy for a particular application. For many uses of the basic counts, such as allocating police personnel in proportion to neighborhood population, the level of accuracy currently embedded in the numbers is probably quite acceptable. With regard to reapportionment, there is evidence, discussed below, that the differential errors in the 1980 census counts may have affected the allocation of one or two seats, a matter of some concern to the states involved.

Evaluation of the need for increased accuracy of census counts for uses in fund allocation formulas is difficult. Most formulas include other factors besides the population counts. The available limited evidence on the effect of errors in the basic counts on equity in fund allocation is reviewed in a separate section below. For many programs that allocate predetermined amounts of public monies, and for other key uses such as determination of political representation, it is the differential errors among population subgroups and geographic areas that cause the most serious concern. Differential errors in coverage of basic age, race, and sex groups also have implications, discussed below, for postcensal population estimates and for important series, such as vital statistics that use census figures in the denominator. With regard to uses of the counts as thresholds, inaccuracy assumes importance in cases in which coverage error places an area on the wrong side of a threshold. Legislation and administrative practices often provide avenues of appeal for areas that believe they have grown enough to cross a threshold or not declined enough to drop below a threshold even though the census numbers say otherwise (see appendixes). In sum, although the picture is mixed, there is ample evidence that errors in the counts matter for important purposes and that methodologies showing promise to reduce errors (see discussion in Chapter 7) should be given serious consideration.

Small-Area and Subgroup Characteristics

In addition to head counts and basic characteristics such as age, race, and sex, the census obtains detailed data for many other characteristics on a comparable basis for small as well as large areas and for subgroups of the population. The 1980 census included in total over 30 population and 30 housing items covering a broad range of topics; most items--26 of the population and 20 of the housing questions--were asked of samples of households rather than of everyone. Census products, which include computer files as well as printed documents, cross-tabulate these items in a variety of ways. In order to protect the confidentiality of individual responses, more detailed tabulations are provided for larger than for smaller geographic areas. Summary tape file 1 from the 1980 census contains over 300 items of data (such as the count of married women age 15 and over) for individual blocks and enumeration districts and summary tape file 5 has over 1 million data items (such as the number of Hispanic women in a certain age and income category) for all metropolitan areas and large cities and counties.

These data make it possible to carry out a wide variety of comparative studies of geographic areas and population components. To list just some examples, census characteristics data are used on a cross-section basis for:

- Government planning, analysis, and decision making at all levels, including:
  - -- Assigning local agency personnel to currently defined police or fire precincts and redefining precincts using census geographic building

blocks and census socioeconomic data on the population and housing of each area;

- -- Identifying the most "disadvantaged" areas in a city for locating service facilities;
- -- Conducting traffic planning studies related to peak loadings and based on cross-tabulated information on place of work and place of residence;
- -- Identifying concentrations of groups that are targets or potential targets of government programs (poor elderly persons living alone, youth without previous work experience, work-disabled persons);
- -- Allocating funds to states and localities by means of formulas (for example, age of housing is a factor in one formula used for community development block grants and children in poverty is a factor in the formula for some educational assistance programs); and
- -- Redesigning major statistical programs, such as the Current Population Survey.

• Business planning and decision making, including:

- -- Locating retail outlets in terms of market potential based on area socioeconomic characteristics, such as income, occupation, education, home ownership, and housing value;
- -- Comparing the market potential of different cities, ZIP codes, or census tracts within cities; and
- -- Assessing the availability of needed occupational skills in different labor market areas.

• Basic and applied socioeconomic research, including:

- -- Analyzing groups that represent reaggregations, for example, persons in high-tech industries aggregated from detailed industry breakdowns;
- -- Issue-oriented analyses, for example, study of the assimilation of different immigrant groups or projections of shortages in selected occupations;
- -- Analysis and legal testimony related to affirmative action and equal employment opportunity programs and challenges to the representativeness of juries; and

-- Analysis of relationships, for example, characteristics of persons who moved during the past 5 years, characteristics of families with adult children living at home.

Although questions have been raised about the necessity of having the census collect all the characteristics data, the census does not by any means collect every kind of item that business leaders, government officials, and researchers might want. This is true even though the marginal cost of additional questions is low relative to the large fixed cost of obtaining the count and basic demographic information. Moreover, the items that are collected are not all obtained from every household or tabulated for every area. Over the decades, budget and operational constraints, demands for privacy, and considerations of the burden on the public have led the Census Bureau to a methodology that imposes the following kinds of restrictions on the data collected and tabulated:

(1) The Census Bureau carefully reviews proposed items to be sure that the need for them justifies expenditure of public tax dollars. While the data are useful for many marketing and business planning purposes, the Census Bureau will not include questions solely for such purposes. For example, questions on number of pets are proposed and turned down virtually every decade. Similarly, questions that were asked in censuses through 1970 on appliances, such as clothes dryer and TV, were eliminated from the 1980 census. In prior decades, these items were justified for analysis of changes in standard of living in different areas of the country, but they no longer are.

(2) The Census Bureau also carefully reviews items to determine whether they are needed at the block level and hence must be included on the short form administered to every household; whether tabulations for somewhat larger areas are sufficient so that the item should be included on one or more versions of the long form sent to only a sample of households; or whether some other vehicle (such as the CPS) could provide adequate geographic detail.

(3) Question detail is limited to what it is judged self-respondents can handle in a reasonable amount of time and with a minimum of confusion. For example, the income question in the census specifies fewer categories than the corresponding questions in the Current Population Survey and many fewer categories than the corresponding

questions in the Survey of Income and Program Participation. (The SIPP is administered in person by interviewers and the CPS in person or over the telephone.)

(4) What is asked of every household is limited to what will fit on two facing pages; the number of items asked of a sample of households is limited to what will fit on two additional pages per person plus a page and a half of housing items. Forms are designed and most questions formulated for machine tabulation.

(5) Cross-tabulations are limited for smaller areas in order to protect the confidentiality of replies and prevent identification of individuals.

The decennial census does not cover as many subjects or cover specific subjects in as great depth as many surveys, but it provides many more analytically relevant explanatory variables than most administrative records systems. The detail it provides can be cross-tabulated in a multiplicity of ways without adversely affecting reliability or raising confidentiality considerations. The census is virtually the only source of detailed comparable characteristics as well as totals for small areas and small groups in the population.

There are several important implications for methodology stemming from these distinguishing features of the census. Many of these are the same as for the basic counts: for comparative analysis the need to obtain a reading more or less at a point in time, the need to standardize all processes of data treatment and estimation, and the need for consistency across various tabulations and retrievals--whether planned or ad hoc. Finally, there is limited evidence that the relatively small errors in the census population count, though possibly significant for analysis of certain very specific subgroups, are rarely significant for most cross-sectional uses of characteristics data. For these uses, the improvement or adjustment of counts is less significant than the reduction of errors and biases in content (e.g., misreporting of marital status by single mothers, miscoding of occupation and industry, errors in income reporting, etc.). As an example, evidence, discussed below, indicates that errors in the income component of the revenue sharing formula have more impact on fund distribution than errors in the population component.

Historical Time Series

The census in the United States provides updates at 10-year intervals of head counts and characteristics for population groups and areas, permitting analysis of changes over time. (Since the Census Bureau does not follow individuals from census to census, longitudinal micro-level data do not exist.) Many of the kinds of uses referenced above, ranging from local planning to market research to scholarly analysis, gain added significance when they are carried out from census to census on a comparable basis. For example, there is keen interest not only in the level of wages of women relative to men and of blacks relative to whites, but also in changes in the relative levels over time by occupation and geographic location.

The time-series character of the census has additional implications for methodology above and beyond the cross-sectional considerations already discussed. Changes in methodology need to be assessed not only in terms of the cross-sectional dimension but also from the point of view of their likely impact on consistency over time. Put differently, if a change is likely to disrupt comparability with the previous census, the gains in the cross-sectional dimension need to be substantial.

Considerations of comparability over time are important for characteristics; they are important as well for the basic counts. There are some important uses of population data for which variability in accuracy of census population counts, from census to census or among population subgroups, is disturbing. A possible change in coverage of a few percentage points for the black or Hispanic population can introduce considerable uncertainty into comparisons of growth rates for various segments of the population. Moreover, because censuses are used to calibrate postcensal population estimates, which are used as population controls for national surveys such as the CPS, changes in coverage create discontinuities in time series that are difficult to interpret. Possibly more important are the uses of population figures as denominators of rates for which the numerators are independently obtained, for example, mortality and birth rates. Changes in coverage over time interfere with analyses of trends in these rates, and differential coverage of blacks and whites, for example, affects comparisons of death rates for specific diseases.

One consideration regarding periodicity of the census is whether 10 years is the optimal interval. A decennial census is mandated in the Constitution for reapportionment. The Congress passed legislation requiring a mid-decade census in 1985 and every year ending in 5 thereafter; however, funds were never appropriated to carry out the 1985 mid-decade census. It appears to be the case that errors in postcensal estimates dwarf errors in the census itself (see further discussion below) and, therefore, depending on the cost, it might be cost-effective to conduct a mid-decade census to improve the data for purposes such as fund allocation.

EFFECTS OF CENSUS ERROR ON KEY USES: REVIEW OF RESEARCH

This section reviews extant research that attempts to measure the impact of errors in the census on important uses of the data. Typically, this is done by implementing one or more types of "adjustment" of the census figures and comparing results of using the pre- and postadjusted data set. Considering the political and economic power that flows from the census through reapportionment, redistricting, and fund allocation, as well as the concern over possible inequities in the distribution of power resulting from coverage and other errors, there has been relatively little research on what difference census errors make for the allocation of votes and funds. Moreover, the research studies reported in the literature and reviewed below are subject to limitations in scope and method, so that their findings must be viewed with caution.

The focus on research directed to reapportionment, redistricting, and fund allocation is not meant to suggest that these are the only important uses of census data or that errors may not be a problem for other uses. As should be evident from the previous discussion, census data are used for a wide range of research, planning, and public policy purposes. However, virtually no research has been carried out on the effects of census errors for purposes other than allocation. Keyfitz (1980) has expressed the opinion that a considerable margin of error is tolerable for most research and planning purposes. Others have argued that, as an example, the use of census data for establishing and monitoring equal employment opportunity programs places requirements for accurate coding of occupation for age, race, and sex groups in small geographic areas that the census currently does not meet (see Conk, 1981).

Before proceeding to review the published studies on effects of census errors for reapportionment, redistricting, and fund allocation, we should be clear about what is encompassed in the term "census errors" and what is not. There are many kinds of error in collected data. In the census context, errors include:

- Coverage error (households/persons omitted; households/persons erroneously included);
- Unit nonresponse (households/persons known or believed to exist but lacking forms);
- Item nonresponse (households/persons with one or more items blank); and
- Misresponse (for example, underreporting or overreporting of income).

In addition, the data become less useful the longer the time interval between collection and release.

Current census methodology includes procedures to attempt to correct for some of the sources of error noted above, specifically, unit nonresponse and item nonresponse. However, these procedures are never completely accurate and may introduce added error. Most research studies have focused on coverage errors in the census; a few have also looked at the interaction of coverage error and misresponse for selected items. Users, such as government and business planners, when asked, have often noted that delays in release of census tabulations much more adversely affect their use of the data than do coverage or content errors.[2]

What none of the research covers and what the discussion in this chapter does not attempt to address are considerations of "error" in the larger sense. That is, even if a data set were completely accurate, it could well be the case that the application of the data in a formula resulted in an inequitable allocation because the

---

[2]Based on notes of Constance F. Citro from the session on census undercount, annual meeting of the Association of Public Data Users, October 25-26, 1984, Washington, D.C.

variables did not in fact relate to the intended purpose (see Keyfitz, 1980).

Finally, the panel recognizes the very difficult problems in attempting to assess the implications for census methodology, particularly with regard to adjustment, of research findings about effects of census errors. Such an assessment rests first on one's judgment about the quality of the research, specifically as to: (1) the accuracy and completeness of the estimates of errors in the census applied in each study and (2) the completeness and appropriateness of the methodology used for evaluating the effects of applying a certain set of correction factors. (For example, need a study of general revenue sharing replicate all aspects of the complicated formulas to assess adequately the implications of estimated census errors?)

Assuming that the research results appear creditable, one must further make a judgment as to whether the measured effects of census errors are sufficiently important to warrant adjustment, particularly given that any adjustment procedure may itself add error and given the cost associated with developing adjustment procedures and gathering the input data for those procedures. In other words, granting that a data set can never be completely accurate, one must decide what constitutes sufficient accuracy for particular uses and whether adjustments that can be made represent sufficiently significant improvements. Is it tolerable, for example, to have two congressional seats misapportioned because of coverage errors in the census? Four seats? Six seats? Is it tolerable if research suggests that coverage errors do not affect apportionment, but coverage and content errors result in the states receiving, on average, about 1 percent more or less revenue sharing funds than they should? Two percent more or less? Four percent more or less? Is it tolerable if areas with high proportions of blacks who are more poorly counted than whites receive less in federal funds from all the population-based formula programs than they should?

Ultimately, these are political judgments. The panel has concluded from the research discussed below and so stated earlier in this chapter its belief that errors in the census do make a difference for important purposes. Throughout the remainder of the report, the panel supports research and testing of methods that show potential to reduce errors within reasonable cost limits. The panel's recommendations are directed both to methods for coverage improvement (see Chapter 5) and methods for adjustment of the enumerated counts (see Chapter 7).

Effects of Errors on Reapportionment

Siegel (1975) carried out a study of the implications of coverage errors in the 1970 census for the allocation of congressional seats among the states. The study first developed several sets of estimates of net undercoverage for states, using the technique of synthetic estimation (see Chapter 7) to carry down national estimates of undercount for major population groups. The different estimates included:

(1) A set that applied what the authors believed to be the best estimates of the national rates of net undercount for age, sex, and race groups (black, white, other) to the counts for each group within each state;
(2) A set that applied the national rates of net undercount for race groups only; and
(3) A set that in addition applied the national rate of net undercount for the black population to the population of Spanish heritage within each state.

Each of these sets of estimates produced similar geographic distributions of net undercount rates, with nine states having net undercount rates of 3 percent or higher, compared with the national average of 2.5 percent. Three additional sets were produced as modifications of the second scenario as follows:

(4) A set that assumed that persons below the poverty line in each race group had twice the net undercount rate of persons not in poverty;
(5) A set that assumed that the net undercount rate for each race group varied inversely with the level of median family income for the state; and
(6) Finally, a set that assumed that the net undercount rate for each race group varied inversely with the median years of school completed for that group within each state.

Scenarios (5) and (6) resulted in 11 and 10 states, respectively, with net undercount rates of 3 percent or greater, while only 8 states had net undercount rates of 3 percent or greater under scenario (4).

Correcting the state populations using the net undercount estimates developed under each scenario and running the corrected figures through the currently used apportionment formula--a method called "equal proportions"--gave the following results. Only the fifth and sixth scenarios changed the apportionment from that using the unadjusted census figures. Under scenario (5), Alabama gained one seat and California lost one seat, while, under scenario (6), Alabama gained one seat at the expense of Oklahoma.

Carlucci (1980) noted that a subsequent Census Bureau study (Siegel et al., 1977) that developed alternative estimates of net undercoverage in the 1970 census for states showed a greater impact of coverage errors on apportionment. Adjusting the census figures with one set of estimates developed in this later study produced a change of one seat between Tennessee and Oklahoma, while the use of another set produced changes of two seats involving California, Texas, Ohio, and Oklahoma.

Kadane (1984), in a study of the consequences of coverage errors in the 1980 census for reapportionment, developed estimates of the population by state based on the results of the 1980 Post-Enumeration Program, specifically the PEP series 2-9 estimates (see Chapter 4 for a description of PEP). Application of Kadane's estimates for reapportionment gave California an additional seat at the expense of Pennsylvania.

Finally, a simulation study performed by Gilford (1983) of congressional apportionment based on different sets of state population estimates from the PEP showed that the results are sensitive to the estimates used. Gilford contends that the PEP results should not be used for adjustment because (p.2): "adjustment of state population counts can cause counter-intuitive changes in apportionment" and "the extreme volatility of apportionment results based upon adjusted census counts--attributable solely to the random characteristics of the particular PEP sample selected--renders the PEP unsuitable as a basis for adjusting the census for apportionment purposes." It should be noted that the counterintuitive changes reported by Gilford are largely the result of the fact that states are not allocated fractional representation. As Siegel (1975:13-14) commented, "Under the method . . . used to determine the number of Congressmen from each State, the shift in the population of a State required to produce a change in the State's representation, may be merely a few hundred persons or a few hundred thousand persons, depending on the precise populations of all the States." Moreover, Gilford used all 12 sets of PEP estimates, some of which are regarded as less plausible than others. There remain the conclusions that: (1) coverage errors in the 1970 and 1980 censuses affected at least one or two congressional seats and (2) considerable uncertainty remains as to the particular states (both winners and losers) that might have been affected. However, with respect to point (2), in Gilford's analysis for 1980, California gained at least one congressional seat under every scenario explored.

Effects of Errors on Redistricting

Determining the boundaries of congressional election districts, as well as districts for state legislative offices, is a state function. Prior to the "one man, one vote" Supreme Court decisions in the early 1960s (*Reynolds* v. *Simms* and *Baker* v. *Carr*), the states redistricted when absolutely necessary because reapportionment changed the number of seats and on occasion when the party in power believed it would be advantageous politically. States were notorious in allowing districts to vary greatly in population size. The Supreme Court decisions mandated strict requirements for population equality (no greater than a 1 percent difference in population between the largest and smallest congressional district and no greater than a 10 percent difference among state legislative districts--see Carlucci, 1980) as well as compactness and contiguity of districts. In addition, the Voting Rights Act and growing awareness by minority groups of the effect of the composition of election districts on their political strength led to demands backed up by court actions for equal representation of important population groups. Hence, today, in addition to redistricting due to reapportionment (Bureau of the Census, no date-b:1):

> States and localities are forced to redistrict because of challenges brought in court or because the Justice Department clearance mandated by the Voting Rights Act fails to occur. Between 1967 and 1978, some two dozen cases concerned with state or congressional redistricting went to the Supreme Court.

Census small-area data are critical for the modern redistricting process to meet the standards set by the courts. Currently, P.L. 94-171 requires that the Census Bureau transmit small-area population data to each state within one year after Census Day. To permit achieving equal population size among districts, the 1980 census P.L. 94-171 computer tapes provided to the states by April 1981 tabulated the population for each city block or enumeration district in unblocked areas. Although not required by law, the Census Bureau added race and Hispanic origin data to the tapes, as it was clear that states would need these data to justify their plans to the Justice Department and to survive court challenges. The states are currently requesting that the Census Bureau provide P.L. 94-171 data in 1991 with the addition of separate counts of the voting-age population.

It is possible that differential coverage errors among population groups and areas could affect the degree of population equality actually achieved by a redistricting plan based on the decennial census data. The study by Siegel (1975), mentioned above, assessed the likely effects of coverage errors in the 1970 census on the composition of districts within a state or city. Given a predetermined number of seats, Siegel noted that a new legislative district must be carved out of existing districts, one of which must be eliminated. The possibility that adjustment of the census counts would result in an additional seat going to an area within a state or city at the expense of another area depends on the average size of the districts, the differential coverage rates of major population groups, the proportionate distribution among areas of the major groups, and the number of contiguous districts with high undercoverage rates. Siegel's analysis, assuming different rates of coverage of the white and black populations and different proportions of whites and blacks within areas, indicates that the possibility of a shift in the number of congressional districts for the regions of a state was very small. Siegel estimated that the chances of a shift in state legislative districts or city council districts were somewhat greater, but still small.

Carlucci (1980) applied Siegel's calculations to New York City, as an example, and judged that an adjustment for undercount in 1970 would not produce additional representation for that city. However, Carlucci pointed out that, if one made the additional assumption that all groups other than whites were undercounted at the same rate as blacks, given that New York City's population in 1970 was one-third nonwhite, it appeared very likely that the city would have been entitled to another congressional seat plus additional seats in the state legislature.

If the Census Bureau were to adjust the counts for use in redistricting, there is the problem that P.L. 94-171 imposes very tight time constraints for delivery of tabulations to the states. In 1980, even when adjustment had been ruled out, the tight timetable limited the checking that the Census Bureau could accomplish, and the redistricting counts consequently contained processing and geocoding errors (Bureau of the Census, no date-b:2)

> The rush to get them out necessitated less than complete checking of all of the thousands of small area counts in each state, and there were errors. The Bureau discovered many of these errors in routine reviews, and the redistrictors discovered many as they began to atttept to draw new districts. In general, these errors were geographic misallocations, that is, people were counted but in the wrong block. Occasionally, processing errors were discovered and it was necessary to add persons to the count, rather than shift numbers from one block to another.
>
> The Bureau issued a series of count corrections in the months and years following the distribution of the redistricting figures. In some cases, these corrections were enough to make it appear that the distribution achieved in the original plan drawn on the basis of the April 1, 1981 numbers was not as good as it should be. Redistrictors began to question how final the P.L. 94-171 numbers were and whether or not the states should draw new plans. The Bureau's reply was that it had furnished the best numbers it had on April 1, 1981 and the counts were final <u>as of that date</u>, but subsequent reviews had surfaced errors that would be corrected as soon as they became known. Such a process had taken place following previous censuses. The correction process caused concern in many states, but . . . no state was forced to draw a new plan on the basis of corrections alone.

Not only can processing errors discovered after the fact and differential coverage errors affect the population equality achieved by a redistricting plan, but also the passage of time between censuses obviously affects the relative representation among districts that differ in their rate of population growth. However, it appears that states do not want to draw new plans more often than once after each decennial census because of the difficulty of getting any plan approved by the legislature and through Justice Department clearance and/or court challenges. In fact, members of the Conference of State Legislatures stated that, if the mid-decade census authorized by P.L. 94-521 (but never funded) were to provide small-area statistics, they would go to Congress and seek to have the law changed to preclude the use of such data for redrawing state legislative districts. (The law already includes a prohibition against the use of mid-decade data to reapportion the House of Representatives or to draw new congressional districts--see Bureau of the Census, no date-b.) Nevertheless, it is worth noting that apportionment and districting plans are used for about 10 years, during the course of which substantial population shifts occur whose effect on the "one man, one vote" principle probably dwarfs any effects introduced by errors in the census counts. These effects tend to disadvantage areas of disproportionate population growth.

Effects of Errors on Fund Allocation

From a small beginning around the turn of the century, federal grant-in-aid programs have grown enormously in scope and amount. Prior to 1930, federal grant programs for state and local assistance were limited in purpose, used simple allocation formulas involving factors such as total population or population density, and consumed less than 3 percent of the federal budget. As of the 1980 census, there were over 100 programs that distributed money to states and localities for a wide range of purposes by means of complex formulas including census or census-based data elements. A conservative estimate of the funds distributed via formula in fiscal 1981 was $80 billion, close to 15 percent of the federal budget (Emery et al., 1980). As of fiscal 1984, funds distributed by formula amounted to about $80 billion, or about 10 percent of the budget (Office of Management and Budget, 1985). In addition, many states have formula-based programs of aid to their local governments. Table 2.1 lists selected federal grant programs and indicates the

TABLE 2.1 Uses of Census Data in Selected Federal Grant-in-Aid Programs

Program	Data Items Used for Allocation and/or Eligibility	Fiscal 1984 Expenditures (billions)
Education		
Adult Education Act (P.L. 89-750)	Title III: allocates same base amount to all states and then remainder based on state share of persons age 16 and older with less than 4 years of high school completed (excluding persons ages 16-19 currently enrolled).[a]	$0.8 (includes career and vocational education)
Career Education Incentive Act (P.L. 95-207)	Allocates funds to states based on state share of population ages 5-18.[b]	See adult education
Education Consolidation and Improvement Act (P.L. 97-35)	Chapter 1, Educationally Deprived Children: allocates funds to school districts based on district share of children ages 5-17 in poverty.[a]	$3.4
	Chapter 2, Consolidation of Federal Programs for Elementary and Secondary Education: allocates funds to states based on share of children ages 5-17.[b]	$0.4
Head Start	Allocates 87% of available funds to states based on state share of children under 18 in AFDC families and children under 6 in families in poverty.[a]	$1.0
Higher Education Act (P.L. 89-329)	Title IV-C, Work Study Program: allocates 90% of funds to states as follows: ⅓ based on state share of persons enrolled full time in postsecondary schools; ⅓ based on state share of high school graduates; ⅓ based on state share of related children under 18 in families with income under $3,000.[a]	$0.5
Public Libraries (P.L. 84-597)	Allocates funds to states based on share of population.[b]	N.A.
Vocational Education Act of 1963 (P.L. 94-482)	Title I, Part A, State Vocational Education Programs: allocates 50% of funds to states based on share of population ages 15-19; 20% based on share of population ages 20-24; and 15% based on share of population ages 25-65.[b]	See adult education
Employment and Training		
Job Training Partnership Act (P.L. 97-300)	Eligible Service Delivery Areas (SDAs) must be one or more counties or cities of 200,000 or more current population (or a rural CETA prime sponsor or an exception approved by the governor).[b]	$3.0 (all programs)
	Title II, Part A, Adult and Youth Programs: allocates ⅓ of funds to states based on state share of unemployed in areas of substantial unemployment; ⅓	

TABLE 2.1 (Continued)

Program	Data Items Used for Allocation and/or Eligibility	Fiscal 1984 Expenditures (billions)
	based on state share of excess unemployed; ⅓ based on state share of economically disadvantaged population. Uses same formula to allocate 78% of each state's funds to SDAs.[c]	
	Title II, Part B, Summer Youth Employment and Training: uses Part A formulas.	
	Title III, Dislocated Workers: allocates ⅓ of funds to states based on state share of unemployed; ⅓ based on state share of excess unemployed; and ⅓ based on state share of persons unemployed 15 or more weeks. State-required matching percentage is reduced 10% for each 1% higher than average unemployment in previous year.[c]	
General Revenue Sharing		
(State and Local Fiscal Assistance Act of 1972 as amended, Title I)	Allocates funds to states according to 1 of 2 formulas: (1) Allocates funds based on state share of total population times tax effort (state and local taxes divided by personal income) times ratio of state to national per capita income.[b,d] (2) Allocates ²⁄₉ of funds based on state share of total population; ²⁄₉ based on state share of population divided by per capita income; ²⁄₉ based on state share of urbanized population; ⅙ based on state share of tax effort; and ⅙ based on state share of state income taxes.[b,d]	$4.6
	Allocates 100% of state funds to general units of government in each state based on local-government-unit share of total population for units in the state times tax effort times the ratio of government unit to state per capita income.[b,d]	
Housing		
Community Development Block Grants (Housing and Community Development Act of 1974 as amended, Title I)	Eligible areas are cities with 50,000 or more population, metropolitan counties with 200,000 or more population, and some nonmetropolitan areas.[b]	$4.4 (includes Urban Development Action Grants)
	Allocates 80% of funds to cities and counties according to 1 of 2 formulas:	

TABLE 2.1 (Continued)

Program	Data Items Used for Allocation and/or Eligibility	Fiscal 1984 Expenditures (billions)
	(1) Allocates ¼ of funds based on area share of total population for all eligible areas; ½ based on area share of persons in poverty; ¼ based on area share of overcrowded dwelling units with more than 1.01 persons per room.[a,b] (2) Allocates ⅕ of funds based on area share of the growth lag for all areas; ³⁄₁₀ based on area share of persons in poverty; and ½ based on area share of older housing built before 1940.[a,b]	
Federal Housing Act of 1949 as amended	Title 502, Housing Assistance Programs: Eligible areas to receive insured and/or guaranteed loans include nonmetropolitan areas with under 10,000 population and areas between 10,000 and 20,000 that face credit-shortages.[b] Allocates ³⁄₁₀ of funds for insured loans to states based on state share of rural population living in inadequate housing; ³⁄₁₀ based on state share of total population; ³⁄₁₀ based on state share of rural population in poverty; ¹⁄₁₀ based on state share of per capita housing cost.[a,b] States distribute funds for insured loans to districts (groups of counties) and from districts to counties using same formula. Funds for guaranteed loans are distributed using similar formulas, except that the share of rural households with incomes between $15,000 and $20,000 replaces the rural poverty factor.	$3.3
Public Assistance		
Aid to Families with Dependent Children (AFDC—Social Security Act, Title IV)	Determines federal matching percentage of state expenditures based on state share of 3-year average per capita income.[d]	$6.6
Low Income Home Energy Assistance (P.L. 97-35)	Allocates funds to states based on households below the lower living standard income level and below 125% of poverty.[a]	$1.9
Medicaid (Social Security Act, Title XIX)	Determines federal matching percentage of state expenditures based on state share of 3-year average per capita income.[d]	$19.2

TABLE 2.1 (Continued)

Program	Data Items Used for Allocation and/or Eligibility	Fiscal 1984 Expenditures (billions)
Public Works		
Construction Grants for Wastewater Treatment Works	Allocates ½ of funds to states based on formula A and ½ based on formula B: (A) Allocates ¼ of funds based on state share of total population and remainder based on state share of need (based on construction costs and population projections).[b] (B) Allocates funds based on maximum of state share of total population and state share of needs.[b]	$2.5
Recreation		
Urban Park and Recreation Recovery Program (P.L. 95-625)	Title X: Eligible areas for funds are central cities of metropolitan areas, places of 40,000 or more population, and counties of 250,000 or more population that score above the median on a composite variable including population density, net change in per capita income, percentage of unemployed, percentage of households with cars, population under 18 and 60 and older, and percentage of population in poverty.[a,b]	$0.03 (est.)
Social Services		
Community Services Block Grants (P.L. 97-35)	Allocates funds to states based on state share of population in poverty.[a]	$0.4
Older Americans Act of 1965 as amended (P.L. 89-73)	States must submit a plan for services and designate Planning and Service Areas (PSAs), generally as counties or groups of counties based on total persons 60 and older and low-income persons 60 and older.[a] Outreach required of PSAs with large numbers of persons 60 and older with limited English ability.[a] Title III, Parts B and C, Supportive Services and Senior Centers and Nutrition Service: allocates funds based on population 60 and older.[b] Some states allocate funds to PSAs based on each PSA's share of persons 60 and older below poverty.[a]	$0.7
Runaway Youth Act (P.L. 96-509)	Allocates funds to states based on number of children under 19.[b]	N.A.

TABLE 2.1 (Continued)

Program	Data Items Used for Allocation and/or Eligibility	Fiscal 1984 Expenditures (billions)
Social Services Block Grants (Title XX of Social Security Act)	Allocates funds to states based on state share of total population.[b]	$2.8
Transportation		
Highway Research, Planning and Construction (Title 23, U.S. Code)	Primary Systems Program: allocates 2/9 of funds to states based on state share of total land area; 2/9 based on state share of rural population (including places under 5,000 outside urbanized areas); 2/9 based on state share of mail delivery route mileage; and 1/3 based on urban population.[a] High-Hazard Locations Program: allocates 3/4 of funds to states based on state share of total population and 1/4 based on state share of public road mileage.[b]	$11.2 (all programs)
Urban Mass Transportation Act (modified by 1982 Surface Transportation Assistance Act)	Section 5: provides funds for approved projects of metropolitan transportation agencies. Surface transportation entitlement is determined for an urbanized area based on average of its share of total urbanized area population and its share of population density.[a]	$3.9

NOTE: Except for AFDC and Medicaid, the programs distribute shares of a fixed amount of funds. This is either because the allocation formula is explicitly share-based or because the amounts allocated are proportionately reduced to fit within an appropriations ceiling for the fiscal year. The allocation formula descriptions in the table omit many features affecting fund distribution such as hold-harmless and minimum and maximum amount provisions.

N.A. = Not available.

[a]Decennial census data are the only reliable source for some or all formula elements.

[b]Can use census-based current population estimates and/or Current Population Survey (CPS) data for some or all formula elements. CPS data are controlled to census-based current population estimates.

[c]Data source is Bureau of Labor Statistics (BLS) local area unemployment estimates. These are calibrated to the CPS, which is calibrated to census-based current population estimates.

[d]Data source is Bureau of Economic Analysis (BEA) per capita income estimates, based on BEA personal income estimates divided by census-based current population estimates.

SOURCES: Bryce (1980); Emery et al. (1980); Gonzalez (1980); Herriot (1984: various unpublished attached documents such as copies of laws provided by federal agencies); Maurice and Nathan (1982); Office of Management and Budget (1985).

data elements used in fund distribution. (See Appendix 2.1 for a description of some state grant programs.)

There is no requirement for federal funds to be allocated according to formula comparable to the constitutional mandate for reapportionment or court requirements for redistricting. Indeed, the present administration has worked to reduce the scope and extent of both formula-based and categorical federal grant-in-aid programs. However, it is clear that Congress has become accustomed to use formulas that eliminate the need for case-by-case decisions regarding fund applications from states and localities. It is likely that some formula-based programs will continue and that new programs of state and local assistance will in many cases be formula-based. Hence, research on the effects of errors in the census on the distribution of federal funds should contribute importantly to the making of sound choices for decennial census methodology.

Unfortunately, the available research to date in this area is severely limited both in method and in scope. No research has been completed that looks at the total set of grant programs; most research has concentrated on one program--general revenue sharing. Several factors have prevented a comprehensive analysis, including the lack of documentation of the formulas used and the complexity of many formulas. Emery et al. (1980:74,77) in a study attempting to document all of the formulas in use, noted:

> Among the formula grant programs . . . one-fourth failed to report the existence of a formula to OMB while others reported the existence of a formula but did not specify the factors involved. The lack of central documentation and the variability in agency documentation cause a large part of the uncertainty concerning how statistics affect assistance payments. . . . Notwithstanding the considerable vested interest and controversy surrounding the topic, the total number of programs having statistical allocations, the amount of money involved and the quality of data employed in calculating payments are unknown quantities.

With regard to complexity of the formulas, the same authors note (p.77) that "the simplest allocation formulas involve a calculation of a State's share of dollars based on the State's share of the total U.S. population. However, most allocation formulas are far more complex, involving more than one statistical factor and constraints such as minimum and maximum awards."

Two key aspects of fund allocation formulas affect the extent to which errors in the census result in inequitable distribution of grant program monies. First, whether a program distributes funds on a per capita basis or as shares of a fixed total sum is a major determining factor in whether adjustment for census errors will cause a large change in the amount of funds an area receives. Obviously, errors in coverage relate directly to maldistribution of funds under programs that operate on a per capita basis. In contrast, maldistribution of funds under programs that allocate shares of a fixed total will generally occur only if the eligible areas experienced significantly different rates of net undercoverage. The exception is a program with a share-based formula that also includes an eligibility threshold; in this case, coverage errors will directly affect the number of jurisdictions that are eligible to share in the fund allocation and hence will affect the distribution of the fixed total amount. At present, almost all grant programs that use formulas operate to distribute shares of a fixed total, either because their formulas are explicitly share-based or because of ceilings on the total amounts that per-capita-based programs can disburse during a fiscal year. Only a few of these programs include eligibility thresholds (see Table 2.1).

The second important aspect of a program's formula is whether it includes only population counts or whether there are additional factors. To the extent that other factors dominate the formula, errors in coverage per se have less effect on fund distribution under the program.

Siegel (1975) analyzed the implications of adjusting the census counts in each state for a program that was assumed to allocate $1 billion purely according to each state's share of total population. He found that, depending on which set of population estimates was used (see description of his scenarios in the discussion of reapportionment above), only 5 to 11 states experienced a 1 percent or greater shift in their fund allotment even though 50 states (including the District of Columbia) had estimated net undercounts of 1 percent or greater under each scenario. The scenario that had the greatest effect modified the national undercount rates by race to take account of median family income; under this scenario 6 states experienced a shift in funds of 1 to 1.9 percent, 4 states a shift from 2 to 2.9 percent, and the District of Columbia a shift in funds of over 4 percent.

Most research in this area has focused on the general revenue sharing program, first authorized in 1972. The program distributed over $5 billion to 39,000 governmental units including states and localities in fiscal 1981 and over $4.5 billion to localities in fiscal 1984 under formulas based on population, per capita income, and tax effort factors. (States no longer receive revenue sharing funds, but the program still determines first the amount to be allocated in total to the localities in each state and then applies a separate formula to determine the share of each state's total for specific localities--see Table 2.1.)

Siegel (1975), in an extension of the analysis just described, simulated the distribution of revenue sharing funds among the states. He compared the distributions using unadjusted 1970 census population and income data with distributions using: (1) adjusted population data but assuming that per capita income remained as before (that is, assuming that uncounted persons had the same income as counted persons); (2) unadjusted population data but per capita income data adjusted to Bureau of Economic Analysis control totals; and (3) adjusted population and per capita income data.

The results showed that simply adjusting population never made any large numbers of changes in funds apportioned to the states under general revenue sharing. Using the basic synthetic adjustment of population by age, race, and sex, the distribution of funds shifted by more than 1 percent for only 5 states and by more than 2 percent for only the District of Columbia. Using a modified population adjustment based on median family income, 8 states experienced a shift of 1 percent or more and 5 states a shift of 2 percent or more. Adjusting per capita income alone resulted in more significant changes--25 states experienced a shift of 1 percent or more and 14 states a 2 percent or greater shift, with 4 of those states experiencing a shift of 6 percent or more in their share of funds. Adjusting population and per capita income together also resulted in a larger number of changes, especially using the modified population adjustment based on median family income together with the income adjustment--under this scenario fully 32 states experienced a shift of 1 percent or more in their fund allocation, 17 states a shift of 2 percent or more, and 5 states a shift of 6 percent or more.

Several studies have examined the effect of census errors on distribution of revenue sharing funds to localities. Siegel (1975:22) noted that "the role of the income component is even more dominant when the General Revenue Sharing formula is applied to counties and cities," because the income component in the tax effort factor as well as the per capita income factor requires adjustment. In addition, the formula for allocation to localities includes constraints so that no local area may receive less than 20 percent or greater than 145 percent of the state's average per capita payment or more than 50 percent of the sum of its taxes and intergovernmental transfers. Siegel (1975:23) concluded that prior studies (Hill and Steffes, 1973; Savage and Windham, 1973; Strauss and Harkins, 1974; Grindley et al., 1974) "all fail to make adequate allowance in the application of the formula for the understatement of the income component or to take account of the apportionment features of the Act."

Robinson and Siegel (1979) carried out an illustrative study of the effects of 1970 census coverage and income reporting errors on distribution of general revenue sharing funds to localities within the states of Maryland and New Jersey. The results were similar to the findings in the earlier Siegel study for states in that adjustment of income had a greater effect than adjustment of population on shifts in the distribution of funds; however, the effects of adjustment were greater for local areas than for the states. States and local areas experienced similar average percentage shifts in fund distribution with just the population factor adjusted--0.6 percent for the 50 states and D.C., 1.0 percent for the 155 local jurisdictions in Maryland, and 0.7 percent for the 567 local areas in New Jersey. With income alone adjusted, the average percentage shift in funds was 1.8 percent for the states, 4.1 percent for the Maryland local areas, and 4.4 percent for the New Jersey local areas; while, with both income and population adjusted, these figures became, respectively, 1.9 percent, 8.5 percent, and 9.1 percent. The local areas most affected by adjustment were those not constrained by the minimum and maximum allotments specified in the formula.

Another way of looking at the impact of census errors is on a per capita basis, that is, how much lost revenue from various fund allocation programs each additional uncounted person represents for a state or local area. Maurice and Nathan (1982) undertook to answer this question for three different programs: (1) general revenue sharing, (2) the Community Development Block Grant program, and (3) mass transit subsidies provided under section 5 of the Urban Mass Transportation Act. They investigated the simultaneous impact of a synthetic population adjustment using 1970 census national net undercount rates by race for 573 areas (central cities of standard metropolitan statistical areas or cities with more than 50,000 residents). Over half the cities had estimated net undercount rates of greater than 2 percent and almost one-fifth had estimated net undercount rates exceeding 3 percent with the application of the synthetic adjustment.

Maurice and Nathan (1982:253) note that assertions are often made that each uncounted person represents a significant sum of money lost to a jurisdiction, e.g., the New York City planning department estimated that the city would lose $200 per year in federal aid for each resident missed in the census. In contrast, they find (1982:266): "For the majority of cities, the total change in allocation [for the three programs] resulting from an undercount adjustment of population is in the range of plus or minus $5 per uncounted person." For 18 large cities, the total change ranged from a loss of $11.80 (for Minneapolis) to a gain of $15.40 (for Philadelphia). They explain this result as a consequence of three phenomena: (1) the synthetic method of population adjustment produces small changes in cities' shares of the national population, (2) population is not the only factor in most fund allocation formulas, and (3) one of the most important programs--community development block grants--includes a population growth lag variable in one formula used by older distressed cities that gives larger allotments to cities with larger net undercounts.

Maurice and Nathan found greater effects of adjustment for coverage errors in the public service employment portion of the Comprehensive Employment and Training Act (CETA) program. For selected large cities, the change in fund allotment under this program ranged from a loss of $2 per uncounted person for Los Angeles to a gain of $35 for New Orleans. However, they note that this finding could be sensitive to the assumptions used regarding the labor force status of uncounted persons. They also note that this component of CETA was not included in its successor program, the Job Training Partnership Act.

Finally, most of the studies of the effects of census errors on fund allocation have found that, typically, more jurisdictions "lose" by an adjustment than "gain" compared with the distribution of funds using unadjusted census data. For example, Robinson and Siegel found that

31 states, 114 (of 155) local areas in Maryland, and 315 (of 567) local areas in New Jersey would have been worse off with both population and income adjusted than when unadjusted census data were used for the allocation of general revenue sharing funds. However, this type of analysis suffers from two problems. First, as discussed more fully in Chapter 7, the appropriate standard of comparison in determining winners and losers resulting from an adjustment procedure is not the unadjusted census count but the true population (see also the discussion in Bryce, 1980:119-120). Second, the panel argues in Chapter 7 that an adjustment should be evaluated not by counting the number of areas gaining or losing but by taking into account the population size of each area. (In this regard, the "winners" in Maryland in the Robinson and Siegel study included the city of Baltimore, with 23 percent of the state's total population.)

Summing up, there appears to be evidence that coverage errors affect fund allocation, but to a relatively small degree. Errors that do have an appreciable effect are those related to income reporting. We should caution, however, that the studies reported in the literature are of limited scope and are not simply generalizable to all federal fund allocation programs. Furthermore, the adjustment techniques used were by and large unsophisticated; adjustment procedures that introduced greater complexity, such as the Siegel procedure that modified national net undercount rates by race to take account of state median family income, generally produced larger effects.

EFFECT OF ERRORS IN POSTCENSAL ESTIMATES

As mentioned previously in this report, the census can be viewed as part of a more comprehensive statistical system providing both census and postcensal data for the uses described above, including the distribution of funds and other mandated purposes. It is instructive to compare the effect of errors in the census with those arising in the updating process as well as from using outdated census information because more current statistics are not available.

The Census Bureau recently completed an evaluation of the quality of county and subcounty postcensal population estimates and made the results available to the panel. The evaluation was carried out by preparing population

TABLE 2.2 Percentage of Error in County Population Estimates for 1980 by Metropolitan-Nonmetropolitan Residence

Percentage of Error	Metropolitan Counties (%)	Nonmetropolitan Counties (%)
Less than 1.0 percent	19.8	15.5
1.0 to 2.9 percent	33.8	29.2
3.0 to 4.9 percent	20.5	23.2
5.0 to 9.9 percent	20.2	24.5
10.0 percent or more	5.6	7.5
Average absolute percentage of error	3.7	4.3

NOTE: Several different population estimation methods are used by the Census Bureau. These data and the data in Tables 2.3, 2.4, and 2.5 are for the method with the smallest absolute errors in 1980.

SOURCE: Unpublished Bureau of the Census tabulations.

estimates for 1980 in the same ways they were made during the postcensal years of the 1970-1979 decade and comparing the estimates with the 1980 census counts (see Starsinic, 1983, for a description of the method and a report comparing 1980 estimates with the census counts for states). The comparisons show that the size of the errors in the postcensal estimates for areas below the state level dwarf those in the census. This is not a reflection on the Census Bureau. A considerable amount of research has been conducted on the methodology for population estimation and the estimates have been improving over the years. However, there are at present inherent limitations in the data bases used to prepare the estimates and statistical manipulation can only partially correct for them.

Tables 2.2 through 2.5 (extracted from forthcoming Census Bureau publications) illustrate the nature of the problem. The 1980 estimates for 7.1 percent of the 3,142 counties in the United States had errors of 10 percent or more. The errors tended to be concentrated in the smaller counties: 18.8 percent of counties with population under 5,000 and 9.4 percent of those between 5,000 and 10,000 had errors of 10 percent or greater. However, errors of this size were not solely a small county phenomenon. Of the 412 counties with 100,000 or more persons, 2.2 percent were off by 10 percent or more. Of course, the evaluation covered 1980 and the errors accumulate over time, so that these results probably reflect the situation only in the

TABLE 2.3 Selected Measures of Accuracy of County Population Estimates for 1980, by Size of County

Population of County	Average Absolute Percentage of Error	Percentage of Counties With Errors of 10.0 Percent or More
Less than 5,000	6.1	18.8
5,000 to 9,999	4.8	9.4
10,000 to 24,999	4.1	7.1
25,000 to 49,999	4.0	5.5
50,000 to 99,999	3.8	3.2
100,000 or more	3.0	2.2
Total	4.2	7.1

SOURCE: Unpublished Bureau of the Census tabulations.

last few years of the decade. Even so, the potentially large impact on uses of the data is disturbing.

The situation is even more serious at the subcounty level. The average absolute percentage error among the 35,644 subcounty areas analyzed was 15.2 percent. As in the case of counties, the smaller areas were subject to greater errors, with the average percentage error ranging from 35 percent for areas with less than 100 persons to 4 percent for those with over 100,000 population. Forty-eight percent of all areas had errors of 10 percent or greater. Of the 160 areas with 100,000 or more persons, 4.4 percent had errors between 10 and 19 percent. Both positive and negative errors existed. For example, of the 6,012 places with errors of 25 percent or more, the errors were in the negative direction for 2,320 places and in the positive direction for 3,692. The difference in population estimates between some pairs of places could thus be off by more than 50 percent of their populations.

These errors contrast with those in the census, where even the black-white differentials in coverage are not large enough to make it likely for places to be undercounted by more than a few percentage points. A comparison of the two sets of errors suggests that the emphasis on census errors in the past few years has been somewhat misplaced, and that users of the data would have been better served if some of the funds used to reduce undercoverage in the 1980 census could have been used to improve postcensal data.

A detailed analysis of the postcensal estimates is not within the scope of the charge to the panel. However, we

TABLE 2.4 Percentage of Error in Subcounty Population Estimates for 1980

Percentage of Error	Percentage of Places
−25.0 or more	6.5
−24.9 to −15.0	8.6
−14.9 to −10.0	8.2
− 9.9 to − 5.0	12.7
− 4.9 to − 0.1	15.4
0.0 to 4.9	14.1
5.0 to 9.9	9.7
10.0 to 14.9	6.7
15.0 to 24.9	7.6
25.0 to 49.9	7.0
50.0 or more	3.4

NOTE: There were 35,644 places for which estimates were made and evaluated.

SOURCE: Unpublished Bureau of the Census tabulations.

strongly urge the Census Bureau to examine the cost-effectiveness of a mid-decade census compared with the cost-effectiveness of the extra effort required to achieve the last one-half to one percent coverage improvement in accuracy of the decennial census. If, as we suspect, a mid-decade census would significantly improve the usefulness of the data for key purposes, such as allocation of federal and state funds, compared with marginal coverage improvement efforts in the census, this fact should be transmitted to the administration with a strong recommendation that funds be budgeted for a mid-decade program for 1995. We realize that diverting some coverage improvement funds from the decennial census to the mid-decade census will only partly support the latter program. The additional support needed would be more than justified, in our view, if further study demonstrates the value of a mid-decade census for importantly improving overall data quality. A mid-decade census program may also afford operational advantages for census-taking, such as facilitating retention of experienced staff, that would further improve data quality and/or reduce the per person costs.

We recognize that the temper of the times is not conducive to the initiation of new programs, but we believe that statisticians have the responsibility to describe the facts and recommend the actions they believe are sensible. We think it highly likely that reallocation of funds from marginal efforts to achieve small reductions in the decennial census undercount to a mid-decade pro-

TABLE 2.5 Selected Measures of Accuracy of Subcounty Population Estimates for 1980, by Size of Area

Population of Area	Number of Areas	Average Absolute Percentage of Error	Percentage of Areas With Errors of: Less Than 10%	10% to 19.9%	20% or More
Total	35,644	15.2	51.9	24.5	23.6
Under 100	2,425	35.1	21.4	20.0	58.6
100-499	11,085	19.8	37.5	26.9	35.6
500-999	6,613	13.2	52.2	27.7	20.2
1,000-2,499	7,141	11.6	58.6	26.3	15.1
2,500-4,999	3,348	9.6	66.7	22.6	10.6
5,000-9,999	2,212	8.3	72.3	20.6	7.1
10,000-24,999	1,740	6.5	80.6	14.4	4.9
25,000-49,999	636	5.5	84.9	11.9	3.1
50,000-99,999	284	4.5	93.3	6.0	0.7
100,000 or more	160	3.9	95.6	4.4	-0-

SOURCE: Unpublished Bureau of the Census tabulations.

gram would improve overall data accuracy and thus contribute to equitable political representation, fund allocation, and public administration. The panel urges that these issues be thoroughly explored before the 1990 census plans are finalized.

Recommendation 2.1. We recommend that the Census Bureau assess the need for a mid-decade census, particularly by studying the effect of errors in postcensal population estimates compared with errors in the decennial census on major data uses. Unless these studies do not support the value of a mid-decade census, the Census Bureau should proceed with preparations and make every effort to secure funding to conduct a census in 1995.

APPENDIX 2.1

STATE AND LOCAL GOVERNMENT USES OF CENSUS DATA

Government agencies at all levels--federal, state, and local--are heavy users of census data. This appendix reviews typical applications of census data made by state and local agencies.[1] At these levels of government, the decennial census is an invaluable and unmatched resource in providing comparable small-area and subgroup data.

STATE USES OF CENSUS DATA

State governments use census tabulations in ways that are similar to federal and local uses and in ways that are unique to the states' role in the federal system. Based on a review of uses specified by a reasonably representative group of states (Alaska, Connecticut, Florida, Georgia, Illinois, Indiana, Iowa, Missouri, Montana, New Jersey, New York, Oregon, Tennessee, Virginia, Wisconsin), the kinds of applications described below are typical for this level of government.

Use for Redistricting

The states determine the boundaries of congressional election districts, as well as districts for state legislative offices. Under the "one man, one vote" requirements imposed by the courts for equal population size and compactness of districts, small-area census data are essential for the task of redistricting. The chapter text indicated the data requirements for this use of the decennial census figures and reviewed potential

[1]Much of the material in this section comes from a survey of federal, state, and local government agencies initiated by the Census Bureau in fall 1982 requesting information on specific needs for subject matter and geographic detail from the census for uses mandated in legislation. The responses are summarized in Herriot (1984). Many agencies indicated other kinds of uses in addition to mandated ones.

problems posed by differential undercoverage and by discovery of other kinds of errors, such as processing mistakes, subsequent to release of the redistricting tabulations one year after Census Day.

Use to Classify Local Governments

All the states denominate various categories of local governments, such as municipalities or townships, by population size and accord varying rights and responsibilities to each size class. For example, compensation of county clerks in Missouri is established as a function of population size and assessed valuation. This application uses census figures as thresholds, and hence coverage errors can be important if a locality is put in the wrong size class. However, many state statutes include language that permits localities to submit alternative population counts, for example, from special censuses.

Use to Allocate State Funds

Many states have programs to allocate state monies to localities on the basis of formulas similar to federal programs like general revenue sharing. For example, the State of Alaska has a state revenue sharing program that distributes money to municipalities and unincorporated places. The State of Florida allocates its 2 cents per gallon gasoline tax to counties via a formula that includes three terms for each county:

> One-fourth the ratio of the county land area to the state, plus one-fourth the ratio of the county population to the state, plus one-half the ratio of the county gasoline tax dollars to the state.

Most states with a motor vehicle fuel sales tax distribute the receipts using a formula including local population counts. Many states likewise distribute the proceeds of consumption or nuisance taxes, such as parimutuel, cigarette, and alcoholic beverage taxes, on the basis of population (Bryce, 1980:112-113). The State of New York allocates funds for building code enforcement to counties and cities using a formula that includes each area's share of the total noninstitutionalized population and of total real property valuation, while Iowa allocates day care center funds on the basis of numbers of children under 7 and low-income families. The equity of the distribution of monies under these various state programs is presumably affected by differential undercoverage. The chapter text discusses what is known about the effects of errors in the census count on fund allocation formulas for various federal grant programs.

Use for Equal Employment Opportunity Purposes

Every state in the nation has requirements, in legislation or executive order, for state agencies to implement one or more kinds of equal employment opportunity (EEO) or affirmative action programs with regard to hiring and personnel practices. State agencies make use of census data to establish affirmative action goals and to monitor how well equal employment opportunity programs are meeting their goals. The most common data requirements are for occupation by race and sex for counties and cities. Many states also need data on occupation and industry by age, veteran status, disability, and language spoken. After 1980, the Census Bureau provided a special EEO file that contained detailed occupation cross-tabulated by sex, race, and Hispanic origin, plus years of school completed tabulated by age, sex, race, and Hispanic origin for counties, cities of 50,000 or more population, and metropolitan areas. The Census Bureau's Data User Services Division sold over 330 copies of this file directly to users, in addition to providing copies to all State Data Centers (from information furnished by Michael Garland, Chief, Data User Services Division).

There are many related applications of census data by the states in the area of antidiscrimination efforts. The State of Missouri anti-redlining statute requires the Department of Commerce to monitor bank compliance using data on the characteristics of the housing stock (number of units, tenure, etc.) and of the population (race and income) by census tract in several cities.

EEO applications of census data require tabulations of groups such as blacks and Hispanics that are known to be covered less well than other groups. Moreover, these applications require additional data such as occupation and income, and it may well be that errors or problems with these items have greater impact on the validity of conclusions drawn or actions taken on the basis of the cross-tabulations than simply differential undercoverage by race.

Use for Implementation of Federal Programs

Many federal programs that distribute funds to states and localities require applications for specific programs or projects rather than simply allocating dollars according to formula. States use census data to support grant applications of all kinds. For example, the State of Florida Department of Health and Rehabilitative Services needs data on the elderly population (persons 60 and over) by race in each county to justify funds for social and nutrition services programs under the Older Americans Act; the Florida Department of State, Division of Library Services, needs census data on income by age, race, and Hispanic origin for counties and cities for funding under the Library Services and Construction Act.

Use for Statewide Planning

The states use census data for many kinds of planning purposes. Just to name a few examples, the Alaska Department of Natural Resources requires small-area data on population, income, employment by industry, household size, and permanent versus seasonal residence for planning various park and recreation programs. The Florida Department of Transportation has statute-based requirements for census data on population, density, income, auto ownership, and employment by occupation and industry for small areas for statewide transportation planning. The Florida Department of Education needs census data on age, sex, education, income and poverty by county, and current county population estimates by single years of age for community college, state university, and adult education program planning. The Missouri Department of Agriculture uses county population categorized by age to plan publicity for the Missouri State Fair, and the Department of Mental Health develops measures of prevalence of mental disorders, alcoholism, and drug abuse, and plans service programs using census tract data. The State of Indiana uses county and census tract population and counts of housing units with basements in planning nuclear civil protection.

A related use is to determine workload needs for various state services. For example, under its Omnibus Crime Control and Safe Streets Act, the State of Montana uses census data for counties and cities on sex, race, age, and income to estimate personnel needs and workloads for public safety programs.

LOCAL AGENCY USES OF CENSUS DATA

Local governments exhibit many of the same kinds of uses of census data as do the states, including use of the data for redistricting.[2] If anything, localities have a greater need for census data for very small areas, such as blocks and tracts.

Typical census data uses cited by specific local governments include the following:

- Use for transportation planning, including planning of highways and other commuter transportation modes and forecasting airport demand (Orange County, Fla.; Pueblo Regional Planning Commission, Colo.; Corpus Christi, Tex.; Tri-County Regional Planning Commission, Harrisburg, Pa.; Lincoln City-Lancaster County Planning Department, Neb.; City of Detroit, Mich.).
- Use for planning local building and development projects (Houston, Tex.; Tri-County Regional Planning Commission) and for obtaining mortgage revenue bonds (Amarillo, Tex.).
- Use for services assessment and planning, such as needs assessments for human resources services in local community target areas using data on the elderly living alone, female-headed families, and children by census tract (Houston); development of state-mandated community services area plan (Orange County).
- Use to support grant applications for state and federal funds, for example, determination of transit subsidies from the regional transit authority using population and automobile availability by small area (Detroit); applications to the state small communities program using data by block and tract on population, housing, employment, income and poverty (Tri-County Regional Planning Commission); support of applications for family planning services project grants using data on

[2] Much of the material in this section comes from the Census Bureau survey previously cited (see Herriot, 1984). This survey obtained responses from a small number of cities--less than 20--and most of these cities noted that they had relatively few mandated uses of census data. However, the examples of census data use discussed in this section appear to represent typical local applications.

ethnicity, age, income and poverty for women ages 15-44 (County of San Diego Department of Planning and Land Use, Calif.).

Some formula grant programs, in addition to the categorical programs, place data requirements on localities above and beyond the need for the items that go into the formula. For example, the HUD Community Development Block Grant (CDBG) program has one set of data needs to determine fund allocation, another set to use in a Housing Assistance Plan (HAP) that each locality must develop before the CDBG funds to which the locality is entitled can be released, and yet a third set to monitor the impact of the program on housing for low- and moderate-income, minority, and female-headed households.

APPENDIX 2.2

CENSUS DATA USE IN NEW JERSEY--A CASE STUDY

This appendix endeavors to sketch a picture of census data uses and users in one geographic location. New Jersey was chosen because of ready availability to the panel of relevant information. Examples of uses from all sectors--public, private, academic--are included.

DISTRIBUTION CHANNELS

Before describing users and uses, it will help orient the exposition to identify the various channels for distributing census data within New Jersey. The federal government offers documents, including census publications, for sale through the U.S. Government Printing Office and, by law, makes free reference copies available to the nation's 1,350 depository libraries. Rowe has estimated (U.S. House of Representatives, 1982:424) that perhaps as much as 50 percent of census data use is by the millions of people who visit libraries every day to obtain needed information on a variety of subjects.

Census data in nonprinted form, including tabulations on computer tape (summary tape files), tabulations on microfilm and microfiche, and samples of individual microdata records (public use microdata sample files), are sold directly by the Census Bureau's Data User Services Division (DUSD). Census tape files serve a growing need for more elaborate and extensive analysis than printed reports can readily serve. The tapes contain many more data items than can be printed in a manageable set of volumes and offer the advantage that the user can readily reprocess the data using computers. The availability of samples of microdata records (with identifying information removed) has greatly expanded the capabilities for original analysis and retabulation of the census responses to suit the user's needs.

The Census Bureau has also set up a network of state data centers that receive publications and computer tapes containing the census tabulations for their state for redistribution to users. The typical structure includes a lead agency in the state government that works with the state library and one or more universities to provide a full range of user services, plus a number of affiliates that provide basic reference services throughout the state. Currently, there are data centers in 49 states, Puerto Rico, and the Virgin Islands (Riche:1984b).

New Jersey is one of the states with an active state data center. The New Jersey State Data Center is housed in the Department of Labor and Industry and works with the New Jersey State Library and with Princeton University and Rutgers University to provide a full range of processing and reference services to users. The center has as local affiliates the planning boards for each of the state's 21 counties plus the Delaware Valley Regional Planning Commission. In addition, all county libraries receive State Data Center materials.

Finally, a growing number of private firms are in the business of supplying users with census (and other public) data. A recent survey by American Demographics (Riche, 1984a) identified 68 firms that repackage and resell government statistical data, one of which is located in New Jersey. While these firms handle some general information requests, most of their work is for clients who need specific tabulations or analyses that often require extensive processing of computerized census data. Many of these firms provide a range of services based on census data, such as profiles and projections of local area characteristics for site selection and market analysis; relating client information such as number of accounts to census characteristics for ZIP codes or other areas; and development of sampling frames and designs for local surveys. Other firms specialize in such services as using census data for election campaigning and voter registration drives, affirmative action planning and legal actions, and fulfillment of regulatory requirements. In fact, it is probably the case that these firms serve more users of census tapes than does the Data User Services Division. The DUSD supplies tape copies to users and will prepare special summaries of the confidential microdata tapes, but does not make extracts or special tabulations of publicly available data tapes. The DUSD filled over 5,100 orders for 1980 census computer tapes from 1981 to 1983 (from information furnished by Michael Garland), representing a small fraction of total user orders for tapes and analyses and tabulations produced from the data tapes.

TABLE 2.6 Data Requests Received by the New Jersey State Data Center's Lead Agency by Type of User and Data Source, 1983

	Data Source					
Type of User	Census of Population and Housing	Economic Censuses	Other Censuses	Other Federal Data	Lead Agency Data	Total
Academic	7.0%	3.7%	4.2%	9.5%	6.6%	6.8%
Business	22.9	54.3	43.5	22.9	28.3	27.7
Government	58.6	33.3	19.3	22.7	19.5	39.9
Private individuals	11.5	8.6	32.9	44.9	45.6	25.6
Total number	2,024	243	331	568	965	4,131
Percentage of overall total	49.0%	5.9%	8.0%	13.7%	23.4%	100.0%

SOURCE: Connie O. Hughes, director, New Jersey State Data Center, personal communication to Constance F. Citro, March 1984.

PROFILE OF STATE DATA CENTER USERS AND USES

The New Jersey State Data Center lead agency-the Office of Planning and Research (OPR) within the State Department of Labor and Industry--serves a large number of census data users each year. The agency has tracked data requests received by phone and reported that in 1982 phone requests totalled 3,600, rising to over 4,100 in 1983 (from information provided by Connie O. Hughes, director of the State Data Center). The increase resulted despite the policy effective July 1, 1982, of reduced direct service to the general public due to budget cuts incurred by OPR. Fully half the requests in 1983--over 2,000--were for data from the 1980 decennial census. Almost three-fifths of the census requests were received from other government agencies, about one-quarter from businesses, 10 percent from private individuals, and 7 percent from academia. Table 2.6 shows the distribution of requests by type of data (1980 decennial census, economic censuses, other censuses, other federal data, OPR data) and type of user.

The Princeton University Computer Center, which works closely with the lead agency, reported on a week's sample of census use in spring 1984 (from information provided by Judith S. Rowe, associate director). Projects that took some amount of staff time included:

• A study of migration patterns and the demographic characteristics of the 1975 residents of the service area of a utility company in Texas, using the public use microdata sample files (PUMS);

• A study of migration from Long Island compared with migration from similar metropolitan areas, including age, occupation, income, and other characteristics of out-migrants, for a Long Island newspaper, using the PUMS;

• Development of profiles from the PUMS of recruitment pools (age, income, race) by district for the four military services;

• Construction of a data set merging selected summary tape file 1 and summary tape file 3 data for minor civil divisions and unincorporated places on housing and homeowners for a private company that is supplying data to realtors;

• An analysis of voting behavior in Chicago using summary tape file 1 to define neighborhoods along race and ethnic lines for an undergraduate student in political science;

• An analysis of need and ability to pay for home health care using summary tape file 4 tables on age and income for a graduate student at Wharton, employed at a New Jersey hospital; and

• An analysis as part of a continuing study of commuting patterns in New Jersey using the Urban Transportation Package of special tabulations of place of work and journey to work data for a professor in the transportation program.

The Rutgers Center for Computer and Information Services, the other main component of the New Jersey State Data Center, described its activities for 1983 (from information furnished by Gertrude J. Lewis, project leader). The center keeps current copies of *Rutgers University Guide to Machine Readable Data Files* in all of the university's libraries, and sophisticated users can access the available files, which include census and other data sets, without the center's active help. In 1983, almost 30 different departments specifically requested the center's machine-readable data files. For the decennial census files, the center handles phone calls from many business firms inside and outside the state. Users are encouraged to do their own computing with census data. Three times a year, the center offers seminars on using census files and also offers special seminars on request.

Examples of census data use at Rutgers include:

- Two faculty members in the Department of Sociology compared health needs of the poor with their service utilization using PUMS files and data from the National Center for Health Statistics;
- A faculty member in sociology and urban studies analyzed change in housing prices and characteristics between 1970 and 1980 at the minor civil division level both for research and instruction to undergraduates and graduates;
- A staff member of the affirmative action department used data from the special EEO file to construct figures on availability of minorities and women to determine utilization in the university's work force;
- A faculty member in the Department of Agriculture/ Economics compared state and county population figures among cities and places in the United States for 1970 and 1980;
- A professor in the Graduate School of Management carried out research on travel behavior between 1970 and 1980 with emphasis on transportation and the energy crisis;
- A graduate student in geography for his doctoral thesis used census population and housing characteristics to correlate the rate of subsidies at the census tract level in Manhattan;
- Undergraduate students in geography extracted census data and mapped the data using SAS/GRAPH;
- A graduate student in the School of Criminal Justice correlated census demographic data at the block group level with criminal data for his dissertation;
- A researcher in the Center for Urban Policy Research assists research personnel throughout the year in accessing American Housing Survey and decennial census data. These projects cover a variety of topics, such as assessing population change for planning boards and studying segregation and integration within the state; and
- A research student in the Department of Agriculture/Economics accessed census data to analyze factors affecting employment change between 1970 and 1980 in rural communities in the United States.

GOVERNMENT USES OF CENSUS DATA IN NEW JERSEY

The State of New Jersey regularly uses census data for many purposes, typical of state governments across the country. These uses include:

• Redrawing congressional and state legislative districts.

• Classifying local governments. A review of the state code in 1973 identified over 800 statutes that referenced population data; most of these references classified local governments by size and stipulated the rights and responsibilities of each class. For example, the term of office of street commissioner is three years in cities of the second class, with population of 100,000 to 250,000.

• Apportioning state funds to localities. New Jersey apportions motor vehicle fuel and general sales tax dollars to local jurisdictions based on population.

• Apportioning other kinds of services. New Jersey law states that localities may not grant retail liquor licenses in excess of 1 for every 3,000 population nor wholesale liquor licenses in excess of 1 for every 7,500 population, "as shown by the last then preceding Federal census" (although a municipality with fewer than 1,000 population can have one wholesale and one retail license in any case); members of the board of trustees for a community college that serves more than one county are allotted to each county based on population.

• Meeting equal opportunity requirements. New Jersey requires all agencies to develop equal employment opportunity plans and to monitor their progress in meeting EEO goals using data on the civilian labor force by race and sex for the state, counties, and cities; the Department of Banking uses data on housing stock characteristics such as number of units and tenure and on population by race and income for all incorporated places to enforce the state's anti-redlining statute.

• Approving applications. The Department of Banking approves applications for bank charters and bank branches based on economic feasibility determined from analysis of population, number and size of households and income by census tract for the area to be served; the Division of Mental Health and Hospitals allocates funds to community agencies according to past performance and need-based plans submitted by each agency that analyze data on age, income, marital status, race, and other characteristics for the census tracts and places served.

3
Census Methodology: Prior Practice and Current Test Plans

The panel believes it is important to consider proposed changes in the methodology of the decennial census in the context of past experience. Changes that depart greatly from recent methodology need careful consideration of their costs and benefits. Review of practices in previous U.S. censuses and in the censuses of other Western nations can also suggest ideas that may be worth adopting for future censuses in the United States. The purpose of this chapter is to provide background for the discussion and recommendations in subsequent chapters on proposed changes in methodology. The chapter first describes the methodology followed in taking the 1980 decennial census. The description is not meant as a comprehensive account but as an overview to acquaint readers new to the decennial census process with the basic procedures and their chronology. Next, the discussion briefly references alternative procedures that were followed in previous U.S. censuses and related procedures used in other Western nations.

The remainder of the chapter provides an overview of the Census Bureau's research and testing plans for the 1990 census as currently formulated. The panel offers a general assessment of these plans and makes recommendations directed to strategies for selecting priority projects. Subsequent chapters provide detailed recommendations on pretest and research plans in specific areas.

1980 CENSUS METHODOLOGY

It is convenient for descriptive purposes to divide the process for the 1980 census into eight components. These are (roughly in chronological order):

(1) Development of a master address list of residential housing;
(2) Development of lists of special places, e.g., institutions;
(3) Checking of address list prior to the census;
(4) Enumeration;
(5) Follow-up;
(6) Coverage improvement;
(7) Data processing;
(8) Post-census evaluation.

These eight headings give a quick overview of how the census was taken with the methodology of 1980: (1) a master address list of housing units was constructed from a variety of sources; (2) other kinds of group housing were added in; (3) these addresses were checked for completeness and accuracy; (4) forms were then delivered and collected by mail and by enumerators; (5) complete responses were sought for incomplete questionnaires, including forms that were completely blank, and for questionnaires that were not returned; (6) alternative enumeration methods were used to obtain responses from hard-to-count elements of the population; (7) the questionnaire data were converted into computer-readable form, incomplete or inconsistent information was imputed, and final census products (counts, cross-tabulations, and sample public use microdata files) were created; and as a last step, (8) the accuracy of the final set of records was evaluated to inform users of the quality of the data presented and to help design the next decennial census. The following sections more fully describe each of these eight components. The discussion draws heavily on Bureau of the Census (1982b, 1983b), Bounpane (1983), and National Research Council (1978).

Development of Master Address List of Residential Housing

Building on the experience of previous censuses, the Census Bureau made the fundamental decision for 1980 to enumerate the vast majority of the population--about 95 percent of the total--using mailout-mailback procedures. Use of the mails required construction of a comprehensive address list. For purposes of this step in 1980, the Census Bureau divided the United States into three types of areas: (1) mail areas for which the Census Bureau purchased commercial mailing lists, (2) mail areas for which Census Bureau staff developed the mailing list, and (3) conventional (non-mailout) areas.

Areas for Which Commercial Mailing Lists Were Used

For urban areas that met certain requirements: (1) the Census Bureau had a computerized geographic coding file for the area, (2) the area was located within the Postal Service city delivery boundaries, and (3) computerized commercial mailing lists were available for the area, the Census Bureau purchased several of the more complete and accurate commercial lists and used them to develop a master tape address register (TAR). In New York City, Philadelphia, and Chicago, the Census Bureau merged the 1970 census master address list with the commercial mailing lists obtained and in New York City also merged the 1978 census dress rehearsal list into the master TAR list. Elsewhere the 1970 lists were not used. This procedure represented an extension of the 1970 process wherein the Census Bureau purchased only one mailing list. The 1980 TAR areas accounted for over 50 percent of all residences.

Mail Areas for Which Commercial Mailing Lists Were Not Used

For the remaining mail areas, which accounted for over 40 percent of all residences, Census Bureau personnel "prelisted" each area, that is, compiled a list of addresses in the field. In 1980, field staff were instructed to "knock on every door with no callbacks, that is, conduct a physical canvass of all potential residences, including an attempted contact, to help determine whether the address was indeed a residence and was occupied. Where the canvassers could not make personal contact with occupants during this stage, they obtained information on occupancy status from neighbors, landlords, etc.

Conventional (Non-Mailout) Areas

There were some areas of the United States for which the Census Bureau felt it was more cost-effective to enumerate by conventional means, i.e., by sending out an enumerator to obtain a completed questionnaire instead of asking residents to mail back a form. The enumerators compiled the address list at the time of enumeration in these areas, which contained about 5 percent of the total residences of the United States and were mostly thinly populated.

Development of Lists of Special Places

For the 1980 census, the Census Bureau compiled from a variety of sources lists of so-called special places in which people live in nonresidential settings, including college dormitories, military bases, naval vessels, hotels, motels, and shelters, and institutions such as hospitals, nursing homes, and penitentiaries. The population residing in special places is not insignificant--about 3 percent of the total in 1980 (Bureau of the Census, 1982c:53)--and such places can pose special problems for obtaining a complete and accurate enumeration.

Checking of the Master Address List Prior to the Census

After compilation of the master address list, the next step was to implement several checks for accuracy and completeness. In the TAR areas (urban areas for which the Census Bureau purchased computerized commercial mailing lists), U.S. Postal Service staff conducted three checking operations and Census Bureau enumerators conducted yet a fourth.

The Postal Service carried out an advance post office check (APOC) in summer 1979--mail carriers checked address cards for completion and accuracy while following their regular routes. Census enumerators made a second check of the master address list in early 1980, the precanvass, to verify that every address still existed and was assigned to the correct geographic area. The enumerators also added missed or newly built residential units to the list. The Postal Service carried out the third and fourth checks in the TAR areas just prior to Census Day, April 1.

In the casing check, three weeks prior to enumeration, mail carriers received addressed census questionnaires with instructions to note any addresses to which they deliver mail for which they did not receive a questionnaire. Finally, during the actual delivery of the census questionnaires, mail carriers again noted addresses for which they did not have questionnaires--the time of delivery (TOD) check. In the prelist mail areas where census enumerators had developed the address list, only the casing and time of delivery checks were performed. The various address check programs represented an expansion of similar programs that were conducted in 1970.

Enumeration

Enumeration--what is generally thought of when one hears the word census--was the next step. In the mailout areas of the country, mail carriers delivered the census questionnaires two or three days prior to Census Day, April 1, 1980. Each questionnaire included instructions for the respondents to fill out and mail back the completed form to the local district office. For most questions, respondents were to blacken circles that could be read by the Census Bureau's computerized data input system (FOSDIC), while other questions required handwritten entries. In the 1970 mail census areas, questionnaires went out in the mail to 60 percent of residential addresses and were received back in the mail from 86 percent of the occupied residences. In 1980, 95 percent of addresses got questionnaires in the mail and 83 percent of occupied households mailed them back. In most areas in 1980, five of every six households received short-form questionnaires containing a limited set of population and housing items; every sixth household received the long-form questionnaire containing the items asked of every household plus additional items asked just of the one-sixth sample. In places of under 2,500 population, one in two households received the long form. Overall, about 20 percent of households received the long form.

As one of several experiments conducted as part of the 1980 census in selected district offices, the Census Bureau tested the use of a somewhat different procedure for delivering the questionnaires, called update list/leave. In this procedure, enumerators instead of mail carriers delivered the questionnaires, and at the same time updated the address list (see Chapter 5 for some results of this experiment).

In the conventional areas, the Postal Service delivered unaddressed short-form questionnaires to all households several days before April 1. Householders were instructed to fill out their form and wait for an enumerator. Beginning on Census Day, enumerators visited each household and picked up a completed form or helped the residents complete the form, at the same time compiling a list of addresses. At designated households, enumerators helped the residents complete the long-form questionnaire.

In both mailout-mailback and conventional areas, specialized procedures were used to obtain questionnaires (individual census reports) containing just the population items from persons living in various types of group quarters, such as military bases, naval vessels, college dormitories, prisons, and hospital chronic wards. At places offering transient residence, such as hotels, motels, and missions, Census Bureau staff enumerated travelers who had no one at their usual home to count them and other persons with no usual place of residence.

Follow-Up

In the 1980 census mail areas, the first stage of follow-up began two weeks after Census Day. This stage concentrated on obtaining questionnaires that had not been sent back to one of the 375 district offices (unit nonresponse). Enumerators were instructed to return, a total of four times if needed, to residences that did not mail back a questionnaire. At the end of this process, enumerators as a last resort asked neighbors and landlords for any information that they might have about the residents and completed basic demographic and housing items on the questionnaire. Census office staff also followed-up over the telephone households that mailed back an incomplete questionnaire to obtain the missing information (item nonresponse). In several district offices, on an experimental basis, Census Bureau office staff followed up nonresponding households over the telephone using directories ordered by address (see discussion of this experiment in Chapter 6).

A second stage of personal follow-up in the mail census areas began two to three months after Census Day. In this stage, census enumerators implemented several specific coverage improvement procedures, described in the next section, followed up the very small percentage of nonresponding households (estimated at about 2 percent) for which not even "last resort" information was obtained in the first stage, and also followed up for missing items on otherwise complete questionnaires for which the earlier telephone follow-up was not successful. Follow-up operations conducted by the 37 district offices in conventional areas were similar to the second stage of follow-up in mail areas. Chapter 6 describes the 1980 census follow-up experience in more detail.

District offices, on average, completed all follow-up operations about five to six months after Census Day in mail census areas and four to five months in conventional areas. For a small percentage of housing units (less than 0.5 percent of the total) from which questionnaires were not obtained by the end of follow-up, the district office "closed out" the case. For some of these units, the office knew the household size, but for others there was no knowledge of whether the unit was occupied.

Coverage Improvement

Coverage improvement is a term encompassing several different approaches to the collection of information from households that were missed by the master address list, or from individuals within otherwise-enumerated households who were missed or elected not to respond. The various address checks carried out prior to Census Day were part of the coverage improvement effort for the 1980 census. In addition, Census Bureau staff implemented several post-Census Day coverage improvement programs--primarily in mail areas during the second stage of follow-up:

(a) _Checks Based on Responses to Coverage Questions; Whole Household Usual Home Elsewhere Check._ Enumerators visited addresses at which a respondent in a small apartment building (less than 10 units) reported more housing units than listed for the structure on the master address list, households that reported more residents on the front of the questionnaire than on the inside pages (the dependent roster check), households whose respondents indicated some uncertainty about who was considered a household member, and households with persons listed as having their usual place of residence elsewhere to make sure all households and persons were properly counted.

Whole households reporting usual residence elsewhere were checked to be sure that the occupants were counted only once at their usual residence.

(b) Vacant/Delete Check. In 1980 a second independent enumerator revisited every unit classified as vacant in the first stage of follow-up (or at the time of enumeration in conventional areas) to determine if the unit had actually been occupied on Census Day and also to try to identify and enumerate persons who moved into the unit after Census Day who had not been enumerated at their former residence. The Census Bureau implemented this check in response to findings from the 1970 census indicating that a nontrivial proportion of housing units enumerated in the census as vacant was actually occupied. In 1970, however, in contrast to the complete recheck of vacancy status carried out in 1980, Census Bureau staff rechecked only a sample of units initially declared vacant and used the results to carry out a computer imputation for other units.

(c) Nonhousehold Sources Program. For areas with large minority populations, the Census Bureau district office staff clerically performed a cross-match between census records and lists of names and addresses from outside sources, including driver's license lists, records of the Immigration and Naturalization Service, and, in New York City, welfare records. Enumerators visited addresses at which persons were identified from the match who might have been omitted from the count.

(d) Prelist Recanvass. In mailout-mailback areas for which Census Bureau staff developed the address list and only two of the pre-Census Day address checks were performed, the field staff rechecked the list for completeness during the second stage of follow-up.

(e) Post-Enumeration Post Office Check (PEPOC). In all conventional areas, mail carriers noted addresses that did not appear to be on the address list; these addresses were followed up by Census Bureau personnel. This program was previously implemented in the 1970 census on a sample basis in rural areas of the South.

(f) Casual Count. In major urban areas, Census Bureau field personnel visited places where persons who had no fixed address or who were missed at their residence might be found, such as skid row districts, pool halls, employment offices, etc.

(g) Were You Counted. The Census Bureau had special forms printed in news media inviting persons who believed that they were missed by the census to complete the forms and send them in. The district office staff checked their records to see if persons sending in these forms were already included.

(h) Local Review. The Census Bureau provided preliminary housing unit and population counts to local officials after completion of the first stage of follow-up. Officials reviewed the counts and indicated possible problem areas that were field checked and corrections made as needed.

The coverage improvement efforts for the 1980 census represented a considerable expansion in number and scope over the 1970 effort. In addition to the procedures described above for identifying missed persons and households, programs aimed at increasing public cooperation, particularly among hard-to-count groups, were greatly expanded. The latter included special publicity efforts, assistance centers that the public could call or visit for help in filling out census forms, and the availability of foreign-language questionnaires. Chapter 5 describes the experience with coverage improvement in 1970 and 1980 and provides program-by-program estimates of both cost and yield, or net additions to the count of population and housing units.

Data Processing

The next step in the decennial census process was to take the raw data collected from the enumeration, follow-up, and coverage improvement stages, create computerized household and person records, and edit these data records prior to producing and distributing the final census counts, cross-tabulations, and sample microdata files. The reader should note that no names or addresses were retained on the computerized files. In 1980 computer editing of the raw data involved four steps: (1) imputation for unit nonresponse, (2) imputation for item nonresponse (see Appendix 3.1 for definition and description of the sequential hot-deck imputation method used), (3) weighting the records containing long-form data collected from about 20 percent of the households by iterative proportional fitting (see Appendix 3.2 for definition and description), and (4) implementing various suppression routines on the cross-tabulations and sample microdata records to protect the confidentiality of individual respondents' answers. In addition, clerks manually coded handwritten responses to long-form questions on occupation, industry, place of work, and other items, a step that preceded computer processing of the long-form information.

As mentioned above, for less than 0.5 percent of all addresses, census enumerators were not able to obtain even last-resort information. For these close-out cases, the Census Bureau, where necessary, first imputed the occupancy status of the unit and then, for units designated as occupied, "substituted," that is, imputed using sequential hot-deck imputation (see Appendix 3.1) a filled-out questionnaire from a randomly selected neighbor. Of the total population count in 1980, 0.3 percent represents persons who were imputed in this manner (Bounpane, 1983:31). In addition, the Census Bureau made substitutions for persons and housing units for which the last-resort information obtained in the second stage of follow-up was inadequate and, in a very few instances (0.1 percent of the total), for which a questionnaire was inadvertently damaged during processing. The total of substituted persons including close-out and last-resort cases was 1.5 percent of the final 1980 population count (Bureau of the Census, 1983d:Table B-4).

For questionnaires with missing or inconsistent information, computer programs allocated or assigned, again using sequential hot-deck imputation, the responses of a geographically nearby respondent with similar characteristics as determined from the completed portion of the census questionnaire. Some consistency edits did not require hot-deck imputation but were made on the basis of other information within the same data record. About 10 percent of the total households in 1980 had one or more short-form items imputed, and almost 45 percent of people receiving the long-form questionnaire had one or more items imputed (Bureau of the Census, 1983d:Table B-4; 1983f:Table C-1; see also Citro, 1984).

As mentioned before, about 80 percent of households received the short form, while a sample of about 20 percent received the long form. (The sample was selected systematically rather than randomly, that is, every sixth address, or, in places under 2,500 population, every other address, was designated for the sample.) Both types of forms included a common set of basic demographic and housing questions. Publications and data tapes containing just the short-form items were produced from the entire set of census records (complete count), but data products that cross-tabulated these items with the other items asked on the long form were produced in a second pass of only the sample records. Without adjusting sample weights, the marginal tabulations of basic characteristics contained in the complete count and sample data products would agree only within bounds of sampling error. The Census Bureau forced these marginals to agree closely through reweighting the sampled cases using a technique called iterative proportional fitting (see Appendix 3.2). Forcing agreement promoted consistency in the census tabulations, reduced the variance of the estimates, and also probably reduced any biases that may have occurred in the sample selection.

Finally, prior to release of tabulations and data files to the public, the Census Bureau implemented computer programs to suppress information that might permit identification of individual respondents. For example, characteristics of minority populations in areas that had fewer than 15 such persons were not released (Bureau of the Census, 1982b:103-106).

Post-census Evaluation

The Census Bureau implemented a variety of programs to attempt to evaluate the quality of the census in 1980. Programs to evaluate the completeness of census coverage of the population, i.e., the completeness of the count, included the Post-Enumeration Program (PEP) and demographic analysis. Other programs evaluated the quality of responses for particular content items. Chapter 4 describes coverage evaluation programs carried out in 1980 and prior censuses.

The reader should not gain the impression from the above description that every step in the decennial census process flowed smoothly or was conducted exactly as planned. Each stage experienced problems, some of design and some of implementation. A major goal of the research and testing program that has begun for the 1990 census is to identify modifications to census methodology that promise to facilitate the census process and enhance the quality of census data. Before turning to a review of the Census Bureau's current research plans, the two sections that follow briefly review the highlights of methodologies used in previous U.S. censuses and in other Western nations to indicate the range of possibilities.

METHODOLOGY USED IN PREVIOUS CENSUSES

It is natural to begin this discussion with the 1950 census, which was the first population census in the United States to have comprehensive programs for evaluation of completeness of coverage. The 1950 census (see Bureau of the Census, 1955) relied exclusively on personal enumeration to obtain responses to census questions. Enumerators went door-to-door with sheets (line schedules) that had room to list 30 persons on the front--one person to a line--and up to 12 housing units on the back. Enumerators asked every fifth person an additional set of questions and every thirtieth person a few more questions, generating sampling rates of 100 percent, 20 percent, and 3.3 percent. There was no prior compilation of an address list, although the Census Bureau estimated total housing unit counts by block for most cities of 50,000 or more population to use as a check on the completeness of the enumeration. On an experimental basis in 1950, the Census Bureau tested the use of a list/leave self-enumeration procedure whereby enumerators listed addresses and left questionnaires for households to fill in and mail back to census district offices. The Census Bureau also tested the use of household instead of line schedules.

The 1960 census (see Bureau of the Census, 1966) used a combination of mail and personal interview enumeration techniques. In areas covering roughly 82 percent of the population, enumeration involved a two-stage list/leave procedure. In these areas, several days before April 1 the Postal Service dropped off household questionnaires called advance census reports (ACRs) that contained the 100 percent items. Residents were asked to fill in the answers and wait to give the ACR to an enumerator. Enumerators came to all households and transcribed the 100 percent items to computer-readable forms. If the household had not answered the questions, the enumerator obtained answers at that time. The best estimate is that 60 percent of households had the forms filled out and waiting before the enumerator arrived. At every fourth household, the enumerator left a long-form questionnaire, which the household was to fill in and mail back to census district offices. A different set of enumerators followed up for sample questionnaires that were not returned--about 20 percent of the sample--and for vacant units in the sample. In the remaining areas of the country covering about 18 percent of the population, the enumeration involved a single-stage approach. The Postal Service delivered unaddressed questionnaires. Enumerators visited each household and obtained answers to the 100 percent items and also to the sample items for designated households.

The 1970 census (see Bureau of the Census, 1976a) foreshadowed in most respects the methodology adopted for 1980. This census extended the use of the mails in conducting the enumeration. In areas of the country encompassing roughly 60 percent of the population, the Postal Service delivered questionnaires to all households several days prior to Census Day with instructions to the residents to complete and mail back the forms. Four-fifths of the households received the short-form questionnaire, while the other fifth received one of two versions of the long form (one version was sent to 15 percent and the other was sent to 5 percent of households). In the remaining areas of the country covering roughly 40 percent of the population, the Census Bureau used conventional enumeration procedures similar to the single-stage procedure used in rural areas in 1960. In one change from 1960, the unaddressed short forms sent to households in the conventional areas were already in computer-readable format. On an experimental basis in 1970, the Census Bureau tested use of mailout-mailback procedures in selected areas that would otherwise have been enumerated conventionally. The success of this experiment led to the decision to expand the mailout-mailback procedure to over 95 percent of households in 1980.

The 1970 census was the first to implement specific programs designed to improve coverage, including both checks of the master address list prior to Census Day and programs, such as a recheck of units classified as vacant, conducted after the first stage of follow-up. For 1980 the Census Bureau greatly expanded the number and scope of coverage improvement programs. Unlike 1970, for which two of the programs--the National Vacancy Check and the Post-Enumeration Post Office Check--were implemented on a sample basis, an early decision was made to carry out all coverage improvement programs on a 100 percent basis in 1980.

METHODOLOGY USED IN OTHER WESTERN COUNTRIES

There is a wide range of methodologies used to carry out periodic censuses in other Western nations. The following text very briefly highlights major features of census methodology in eight countries--Australia, Canada, and Great Britain; France, the Federal Republic of Germany, and the Netherlands; Sweden and Denmark. (For the last six countries, the discussion draws heavily on Redfern, 1983.) Obviously, procedures that work well in one country may not be applicable to another for many reasons, such as different public perceptions and attitudes or differences in population size and consequent scale of census operations. Nonetheless, it is useful in reviewing census methodology in the United States to be aware of what is being done elsewhere.

Australia currently conducts a census every five years using a list/leave/pickup procedure. Enumerators deliver questionnaires, while at the same time compiling an address register. Several days later, enumerators revisit each household to pick up the completed questionnaires. Field operations generally close out within two weeks of Census Day. Australia uses post-enumeration survey techniques to evaluate the completeness of the count and, based on the results, produces adjusted population totals for states, which are used for reapportionment of the legislature and fund allocation. Characteristics data, however, are not adjusted (see Doyle, 1980).

Canada also conducts a quinquennial census using a list/leave/mailback procedure (see Fellegi, 1980a). Beginning on Census Day, enumerators canvass their assigned areas, compile an address register, and leave questionnaires at each address with instructions for householders to fill them in. As in the United States, 80 percent of the households receive a short form and 20 percent a long form. In all areas of significant population concentration, householders are asked to mail back their census forms, while, in sparsely populated areas, enumerators call back to pick them up. In both types of areas, enumerators follow up for unit and item nonresponse. Enumerators are held entirely responsible for conducting a complete and accurate census in their districts--the same person in each area performs the initial list/leave and follow-up operations. Enumerators' work is subject to quality control. Most field work ends in about three weeks.

Great Britain conducts decennial censuses using list/leave/pickup techniques. Enumerators, who are recruited, trained, and paid by the central government rather than local agencies--in contrast to the practice in most countries of continental Europe--deliver and retrieve questionnaires in their areas. The enumerators for the most recent 1981 census completed field operations within about two months of Census Day. The questionnaire in 1981 included relatively few items--16 questions for each person and five questions on housing and cars. No questions were asked on income, ethnicity, marital history, or childbearing history. Sampling was not used in the field, but responses to questions that required manual coding, such as occupation, were processed on a 10 percent sample basis.

The recent 1982 census in France used conventional enumeration techniques as well. The enumerator staff, who were recruited and supervised by the local administrations, collected data using three main forms: one for each individual, for each housing unit, and for each building. Questions asked of each individual were relatively few in number compared with the United States; for example, questions were not asked on ethnicity, language, income, or journey to work. There was a relatively large number of questions on housing. Most items, although obtained from 100 percent of the population, were processed on a 25 percent sample basis. The French are considering a system of mailout-mailback of a short form to every three in four households and using enumerators to obtain responses to a long form at the remaining one in four addresses.

The Federal Republic of Germany last conducted a census of buildings and houses in 1968 and a census of population in 1970 with conventional enumeration techniques. The 1970 census used two forms: a long form administered in 10 percent of the enumeration districts and a short form administered in the remaining 90 percent of districts. The local communities played a major role in the field work, recruiting and training enumerators, checking the census returns against the local population registers, and correcting one or the other set as necessary. The federal government planned a combined population and housing census for 1983, with a single form containing a shorter list of questions than the 1970 long form. However, public opposition to the census forced the government to postpone it indefinitely. The opposition stemmed from considerations of privacy and confidentiality and specifically objection to the practice in the 1961 and 1970 censuses of using individually identifiable census information to correct the local population registers (see Butz, 1984, for a description of the controversy).

The Netherlands most recently carried out a census of population in 1971 administered by the municipalities, which generated an initial address list from the local population registers, recruited, trained, and paid the enumerators, and used the census returns to update the registers. The census operations were completed and data published, but about 2.3 percent of the population failed to cooperate as a consequence of public debate about computers and privacy. The 1971 census had a separate form for each person, and the questionnaire for heads of households included about 60 items. The plans for the 1981 census specified important design changes, including: (1) abandoning the practice of using census returns to update the local registers (on the basis of results from the 1971 census showing the registers to be very complete); (2) obtaining demographic information from the registers; and (3) administering a short form to four in five addresses asking solely for the number of housing units, households, and residents in each household, and a long form to the remaining 20 percent of addresses similar in length to the 1971 questionnaire. However, public concern about confidentiality of the data and disappointing response to a pretest in 1979 led the Central Commission on Statistics to recommend that the 1981 census be cancelled. In its place, the commission acted to increase the size of the Labor Force Survey from about 2.5 to 5 percent in spring 1981, to carry out a 1 percent housing survey in fall 1981, and to obtain basic demographic information from the population registers.

Sweden currently conducts a quinquennial census using mailout-mailback techniques. For the most recent census in 1980, forms were mailed to each person age 16 or over and to each married couple with names and personal reference numbers preprinted from the local population registers. The form asked only for a list of adults permanently living in the home and for details of the person's labor force activity. The mail return rate in both 1975 and 1980 was about 97 percent. The statistics office linked the returns to the population registers to obtain demographic data including age, sex, marital status, and citizenship and obtained data on housing from returns made by owners of real estate for tax assessment purposes. The Swedish government is actively pursuing the concept of a completely register-based census but is encountering considerable public concern.

Denmark has been the pioneer of a census based completely on administrative registers rather than enumeration. Denmark instituted local population registers beginning in 1924 and in 1968 created an automated central population register with a unique reference number for each person. The 1970 census in Denmark was the last conducted using enumeration techniques. In 1976 Denmark used the central population register to obtain a set of demographic data for all persons for statistical purposes. In 1977, the national government created a central register of buildings and dwellings, based on declarations made by property owners for tax assessment purposes, and made various other improvements in relevant administrative records systems. The government used the following registers to carry out a completely register-based census in 1981:

- Central population register;
- Central register of buildings and dwellings;
- Registers of wages and salaries paid to each employee as reported by employers to the tax office;
- Registers of income as returned by individuals to the tax office;
- Registers of employment insurance and unemployment benefits;
- Central register of enterprises and establishments;
- Register of educational achievements; and
- Geographic address coding files.

Problems posed by this census methodology in Denmark are numerous: (1) the central population register is generally believed to be of high quality but contains records for persons who have emigrated; (2) some data items, such as means of travel to work, are not available; (3) other items, notably occupation, have serious reporting problems; and (4) there have been delays in obtaining data from some registers, notably the tax office records. Chief arguments made in its favor, compared with traditional enumeration techniques, is that costs and burden on the public are greatly reduced and that data are available for items, such as income, that were never included in conventional census questionnaires. There has been very little public objection in Denmark to the large-scale linkage of records involved in a register-based census. No evaluation information exists on the completeness and accuracy of the 1981 Denmark census.

Government and academic statisticians in the United States have suggested modifications in this nation's census methodology that would incorporate concepts and procedures used elsewhere. The Census Bureau, as previously described, tested use of a variant of the list/leave/mailback technique in the 1980 census update list/leave experiment. More extensive use of administrative records has been proposed for purposes ranging from address list construction to improvement of coverage and selected content items (see Brown, 1984). Alvey and Scheuren (1982) have advocated research on the concept of an administrative records census and developed a preliminary assessment of the coverage and subject detail that could be expected from existing administrative records systems, such as Internal Revenue Service and Social Security Administration records. Other proposed modifications to census methodology in this country include the use of sampling for obtaining the count and adjustment of field counts for incompleteness of coverage. The next section describes the Census Bureau's current plans for research and testing directed to the choice of methodology for the 1990 census.

CENSUS BUREAU RESEARCH PLANS FOR 1990

The Census Bureau staff has been actively working since 1983 to design and implement a research and testing program for the 1990 census. The staff prepared detailed research plans in late 1983 and early 1984 on the following topics, each of which relates to an area of interest to the Panel on Decennial Census Methodology (the most recent version is cited in each case):

- "Uses of Sampling for the Census Count" (Miskura et al., 1984) proposes research on several applications of sampling for obtaining the count, including: replacing the census with a large sample survey, following-up only a sample of households that fail to mail back their questionnaires, and implementing coverage improvement and content verification programs on a sample basis.
- "Research Plan on Adjustment" (Hogan, 1984b) describes an ambitious and wide-ranging research program directed toward improvement in methods for evaluating census coverage and development of methods for adjustment of census counts and investigation of their implications for census data uses and users.

• "Record Linkage Research Plan" (Jaro, 1984a) discusses plans to develop automated procedures for matching records for use in coverage evaluation programs and other aspects of census methodology. This research plan is directed toward a critical problem area for most methods of coverage evaluation--determining in an accurate and timely manner which persons captured in an independent survey or set of administrative records were or were not enumerated in the census.

• "Research Plan on the Uses of Administrative Records for the 1990 Census" (Brown, 1984) discusses possible uses of administrative records for coverage and content improvement and evaluation, content collection, special place enumeration, and as a replacement for the census.

• "Residence Rules for the 1990 Decennial Census" (Herriot and Speaker, 1984) reviews the rules of residence that are used in the census to determine who should be counted and to assign persons to geographic areas.

The first field activities directed toward the 1990 census involved tests of alternative methods of compiling address lists in urban and rural areas that were conducted in several localities in spring 1984 (Bureau of the Census, 1984b). Concurrently, the Census Bureau staff developed specific plans for the first full-scale pretests to be carried out in spring 1985 (Bureau of the Census, 1984b). In this round of tests, the Census Bureau experimented with various automated procedures to improve census operations in Tampa, Florida. In addition to testing use of these automated procedures in a second location, Jersey City, New Jersey, the Census Bureau conducted a test of a two-stage census operation in the latter city.

The two-stage procedure involved collecting only short-form information from all housing units in the first stage and later contacting a sample of housing units during an administratively separate second stage for long-form information. Households in the second-stage sample were asked to respond to all the short-form items once again, in contrast to the procedure used in 1960, wherein respondents were asked to repeat only name and relationship for each household member.

In conjunction with the Tampa pretest, the Census Bureau is conducting a post-enumeration survey of a sample of blocks as part of its research and testing program on coverage evaluation methods. The test will include an administrative records match for two typically hard-to-count groups, minority males ages 18-40 and minority children under age 10.

In summer and fall 1984, Census Bureau staff began to develop goals for a much more extensive pretest program to be carried out in spring 1986 (see Matchett, 1984; Johnson, 1984). The 1986 pretest objectives incorporated some of the ideas outlined in the research plans cited earlier and omitted others. Subsequently, some changes were made to the pretest plans (see Bureau of the Census, 1985b), but most of the objectives initially identified were retained. The process for planning the 1990 census pretests is actively ongoing; the description that follows summarizes the main features of the pretest objectives for 1986 as they were defined in spring 1985.

Effort is to be directed in 1986 toward tests of specific methods and procedures in the following areas:

- Feasibility of Adjustment-Related Operations. This area includes tests of coverage evaluation based on pre-enumeration and post-enumeration surveys of samples of blocks in an urban test site and a post-enumeration survey in a rural site. The plans include using the results from the urban post-enumeration survey to simulate all operational aspects of carrying out a full-scale adjustment of the census figures for the urban site by the end of 1986. (See Chapters 7 and 8 for additional description.)
- Automation. The Census Bureau proposes to test two major processing alternatives: (1) a system of separate collection and processing offices for use in urban areas and (2) a system of local offices that combine collection and processing for possible use in rural and selected suburban areas. The urban test will include experiments with different data entry techniques. In all instances, the intent is to develop automated processing systems that provide greater management control of the questionnaires and of the address list and that permit entry of responses into computer-readable form on a flow basis. In contrast, the 1980 census local district offices relied exclusively on clerical staff to manually check-in and review questionnaires, update the address list, and perform other operations. Questionnaires were sent in batches to one of three centers for data entry and computer processing.
- Native-American Enumeration Techniques and Procedures. The Census Bureau proposes to test various

methods to improve coverage and accuracy of enumeration on American Indian reservations, including obtaining tribal rolls and designating tribal liaisons, modifying the training procedures for indigenous enumerators, and advancing travel expenses for enumerators.

• Rural Area Techniques and Procedures. This area includes testing alternative methods of improving questionnaire delivery and coverage in rural areas that were conventionally enumerated in 1980 and also in prelist areas for which Census Bureau staff developed the mailing list in 1980 rather than working with commercial lists. (See Chapter 5 for further description.)

• Coverage Improvement. This area includes tests to improve the effectiveness of at least a dozen coverage improvement procedures that were used in 1980, such as address checks, a program to recheck the status of units originally classified as vacant, a program to check administrative records against census returns to identify possibly uncounted persons, local review of preliminary census counts, and others (see Chapter 5).

• Enumeration Methods for Multiunit Structures With Mail Delivery Problems. Procedures proposed for testing include refining the various checks that are conducted of the mailing list to identify likely problem addresses (for example, buildings with a central mail drop) and to use an update list/leave procedure for multiunit structures with delivery problems, for which census enumerators rather than Postal Service staff deliver the questionnaires and update the mailing list at the same time. (See Chapter 5 for further description. The update list/leave test may be deferred until 1987.)

• Follow-up Procedures. Included in this area are proposed tests to use telephone follow-up for households that do not mail back questionnaires and to use computer-assisted telephone interviewing of households whose questionnaires fail one or more edits. (A proposal originally included to test the use of sampling for follow-up of households that do not mail back questionnaires was dropped; see Chapter 6.)

• Geographic Support System. Various tests are proposed of aspects of the geographic support system, including the address control files, maps, and geocoding files that assign addresses to pieces of census geography.

• Outreach. The Census Bureau proposes to test a number of ideas for improved outreach and advertising for the decennial census.

• Questionnaire Design and Content. This area, like coverage improvement, includes a large number of ideas and procedures for testing, such as: a general-purpose follow-on survey of short-form households about two months after Census Day; alternative race and ethnicity questions; questions about noncash income; questions about second residences to help minimize both overcounting and undercounting; the use of a structure questionnaire to ask some housing items of a knowledgeable respondent, such as the building manager instead of each household. (See further description in Chapters 5 and 6.)

• Tabulation and Publication Systems. This area includes tests of procedures to improve processing of the short-form tabulations that are produced for local review and for redistricting use by the states.

• Work Force Issues. This area includes tests of ways to improve the selection, retention, and productivity of enumerators, for example, using teams of enumerators in hard-to-count areas.

The concepts and procedures proposed for testing listed under each of the above headings represent those that remained after a prior selection process. Moreover, although the staff originally assigned the objectives to three priority categories, top Census Bureau planners have indicated that their intent is to request funding for all the 1986 pretest objectives. The rationale is that there are few opportunities to test new or improved census procedures and hence that the Census Bureau must move forward to test as many promising ideas as possible. The planned tests generally include efforts, often substantial, to improve upon 1980 census methodology, but do not include radical changes in methodology, such as replacing the census with a large sample survey or obtaining census information completely from administrative records. A potentially very significant improvement over 1980 census methodology could result from the effort to develop automated procedures that can expedite data processing and lead to more timely availability of the data. Adjustment of the census counts, if it were to be implemented based on the research and testing of coverage evaluation and adjustment methods currently going forward, would also represent an important change for the 1990 census.

Finally, in fall 1984, the Census Bureau prepared a position paper updating its research plan on adjustment and proposing a specific research program for coverage evaluation in 1990 and possible adjustment of the census counts (Wolter, 1984). In brief, this paper described the Census Bureau's plans to develop and test a design for a post-enumeration or possibly pre-enumeration sample survey to use as the major coverage evaluation program providing information that could be used for adjustment. The paper indicates that the currently preferred design is for an independent survey, instead of an existing data collection vehicle such as the Current Population Survey and for a compact area cluster sample as opposed to list sample, that is, a sample including all residences within selected small geographic areas, such as city blocks. The Census Bureau explicitly ruled out using the reverse record check methodology or administrative list matching, except possibly as an adjunct to the independent survey.

The paper also described plans to design and test operational procedures that could be used to adjust the census results. The paper stated that the Census Bureau's goals are to develop procedures that, if successful, would permit adjustment of all census figures, including the population count and characteristics, in time for delivery of adjusted state population counts to the President by December 31, 1990, and in a manner such that the individual micro records could be aggregated in any possible way for tabulations and analysis. The paper acknowledged that development of satisfactory coverage evaluation and adjustment procedures would require many important improvements in methodology, including successful implementation of a fast and accurate computer matching program. (See further discussion in Chapters 7 and 8.)

ASSESSMENT AND GENERAL RECOMMENDATIONS

The panel believes it can contribute to the choice of methodology for the 1990 census by providing a careful critique of the Census Bureau's research and testing plans. How well the Census Bureau designs its research and testing program will crucially affect its success in improving accuracy and timeliness of the 1990 census while containing costs.

Review of 1985 Pretest Plans

The panel's interim report, which was prepared to provide early guidance to the Census Bureau regarding proposed research and pretest plans, commented extensively on several aspects of the 1985 pretest plans, particularly the two-stage census pretest in Jersey City. The panel, on balance, did not support this methodology and recommended that research be carried out based on prior censuses before reaching a decision to commit resources to a field test (see National Research Council, 1984:Ch.3). The Census Bureau field staff suggested that a two-stage procedure would make it possible to speed collection of the count in the first stage and thereby significantly improve the timeliness of the basic information. The Census Bureau believed it was important to obtain an early determination of the likely gains in timeliness from a two-stage procedure and, hence, proceeded with the test as planned.

The panel did not scrutinize plans for the Tampa pretest of automation procedures because the panel is not specifically addressing operational aspects of the decennial census relating to field control of the address list, data entry, and so on. However, the panel supports efforts by the Census Bureau to develop improved automated procedures that have the potential to speed up data collection, improve accuracy, and reduce costs. The panel also supports efforts to automate matching operations that may be used in coverage evaluation and coverage improvement programs.

The panel commented in the interim report on the coverage evaluation tests being conducted in Tampa and on other research in progress related to coverage evaluation and adjustment. Chapters 7 and 8 of this report comment further.

Finally, the panel recommended in the interim report that a question asking parents for names and addresses of children not residing in the household receive early testing as a coverage improvement measure (National Research Council, 1984:24). At present such a question is being considered for testing in 1987 (see further discussion in Chapter 5).

Review of 1986 Pretest Plans

For this report the panel reviewed the Census Bureau's descriptions of proposed 1986 pretests and the proposed coverage evaluation and adjustment research program, along with the research plans listed earlier and other documents. We provide below an overall assessment of the

Census Bureau's 1990 research and testing planning process and recommend strategies for choosing priority projects. Subsequent chapters present recommendations on pretest and research plans in specific areas.

The panel has several major concerns with the research and testing program outlined for 1986. These concerns relate to the time schedule for planning the 1990 census, budget and staff resources, and the emphasis given to field testing over other kinds of research.

The panel has noted elsewhere that there is not much time to get ready for 1990. On the face of it, this reality may appear to argue for the need to test as many ideas as possible as early as possible. On the contrary, however, the panel suggests that it is likely to be self-defeating to try to handle a very large and many-faceted testing program. To be useful for making timely decisions on census methodology, test data must be obtained, analyzed, assessed, and discussed and the findings used to design subsequent tests. This process is itself time-consuming and requires ample staff and other resources (such as computer resources). If too many studies are planned for a testing cycle, there is a danger that there will not be sufficient time to obtain and assimilate results from more than a fraction of the tests for use in planning further studies or in making choices of methodology to use for the census.

Moreover, field tests are very resource-intensive, and budget resources and staff time devoted to designing and implementing a wide range of pretests are likely to take away from budget resources and staff time available to obtain and digest the pretest results. Even though ample funds may have been allowed for the analysis phase, these funds are typically more at risk of diminution than the funds for the actual tests themselves. If the costs of testing exceed estimates, as frequently happens, the most likely outcome is a reduction in budget available for analysis.

The panel believes that the Census Bureau should give greater recognition to the problems involved in a large-scale testing program posed by the constraints of calendar and staff time needed to evaluate and assimilate the results. We believe that the Census Bureau will need to pare back its 1986 testing program if key data are to be analyzed in time to support major decisions. The program outlined appears too ambitious for the time remaining before the census and for the staff resources likely to be available.

The Census Bureau should exercise greater selectivity in several ways. First, the planning staff should carefully review all the proposed pretests to determine if some ideas should be dropped from the research and testing program entirely. We recommend a strategy of identifying the more promising projects and pursuing only those projects from the top of the list that fit the overall time and resource constraints, even though this entails the risk that useful ideas will be ignored. Some ideas that cannot be accommodated in the 1990 research program should be considered for testing on an experimental basis in the 1990 census itself with a view toward further improvements in methodology for the year 2000.

Second, Census Bureau staff should determine if there are useful ideas that can be pursued without requiring the time and expense of full-scale pretests. There are a number of projects listed in the Census Bureau's pretest package that we believe can be researched with much less expense and effort via other methods, such as thorough review of the Census Bureau's own previous tests and research. The panel suggests elsewhere in the report projects for which the Census Bureau could usefully carry out research in 1986 that does not involve field tests of the kind planned for 1985 and 1986. One example is investigation of the feasibility of using administrative records to obtain improved housing structure data (see the discussion in Chapter 6).

Moreover, research other than field tests carried out in 1986 could be very helpful for designing pretests for 1987. For example, research on new questions or alternative question wording could be carried out initially by means of focus groups and laboratory experiments, in addition to the National Content Test (a large mail survey) planned for 1986. The 1986 field tests should include tests of questions related to coverage improvement (see the discussion in Chapter 5) but could well omit other question tests in order to simplify the logistical problems and costs of fielding the tests. Results from the National Content Test and small group research carried out in 1986 could suggest further question tests for the 1987 field program.

Finally, there may be proposed tests of procedures that do not need to be conducted until the 1988 dress rehearsals. For example, one proposed project is to test automated searching and updating for persons found in the Casual Count operation. This operation was low in cost in both 1970 and 1980 but also low in yield in terms of number of persons added to the count. Assuming it is worthwhile to continue the program, it does not appear that the program merits extensive testing. It could be omitted from 1986 and 1987 tests and incorporated into the dress rehearsals, which will include every procedure planned for 1990; an advantage of this approach is that by 1988 the Census Bureau should have made a decision on the type of automation system that it will use in the field.

Recommendation 3.1. We recommend, to ensure cost-effective field testing and preservation of adequate resources for analysis, that the Census Bureau attempt to identify research and testing proposals for 1986 that:

(a) Can be pursued with other research methods and omitted from the 1986 field test program;
(b) Can be safely deferred for research or testing until 1987 or until the dress rehearsals;
(e) Are unlikely to be viable for 1990 but should be incorporated on an experimental basis into the 1990 census as a test for future censuses; and
(d) Should be omitted entirely from consideration for the 1990 census, based on previous census experience or other survey research results.

In Chapters 5 through 8 we comment on the Census Bureau's proposed research and testing program in specific key areas of census methodology related to the panel's charge, including: coverage improvement methods (Chapter 5), uses of sampling and administrative records (Chapter 6), adjustment methods (Chapter 7), and coverage evaluation methods (Chapter 8). The reader should note that, given the particular nature of its charge and its expertise, the panel did not undertake to review many other important aspects of census methodology, such as enumeration procedures, geographic support systems, and data entry procedures.

Chapters 5 through 8 provide specific recommendations of ideas and procedures that the panel regards as high priority for research and testing as soon as possible, as well as ideas that the panel believes can safely be given a lower priority or show little promise and should be dropped. The panel's recommendations generally indicate a preference for the use of less resource-intensive research methods whenever possible and appropriate.

The panel's recommendations in many instances call for the Census Bureau to complete studies or reanalyze data that are already available from the 1980 census and the experiments and pretests conducted for 1980.

In general, the panel believes that research with existing data is likely to result in important additions to knowledge with low expenditure of costs compared with other methods. Obviously, more expensive methods, including full-scale field tests, are required to develop the methodology for 1990, but the research and testing program should provide resources to exploit existing data as well.

> Recommendation 3.2. We recommend that the Census Bureau make full use of data from the 1980 census and from experiments carried out in 1980 to help guide planning for 1990. To this end, we recommend that the Census Bureau assign a high priority to completion of 1980 census methodological studies, and we encourage further analysis of these data when appropriate.

APPENDIX 3.1

AN OVERVIEW OF SEQUENTIAL HOT-DECK IMPUTATION

The Census Bureau makes use of an extremely sophisticated sequential hot-deck imputation to correct for item nonresponse in the decennial census. We briefly describe some of the features of this system. Due to its complexities, we do not attempt a complete description; see Bureau of the Census (1983e) for further information.

The individual records are processed sequentially.[1] At the start of this process, an imputation table exists that has initial values stored in it for use with various combinations of nonresponse. For example, when, at the early stages of this process, a record is encountered with age and sex missing but race, etc., responded to, this table will have an entry that will give reasonable values for the age and sex of an individual with similar characteristics. However, as more complete (or at least more complete than the nonresponse represented by entries in the imputation table) questionnaires are processed, substitute values are continually used to replace the values in the imputation table. The benefit of this substitution arises from the geographic continuity implied by the processing of the census questionnaires. The closer the donor respondent is to the nonrespondent in the census processing, the closer the two are likely to be geographically. This procedure amounts to the use of detailed geographic stratification for imputation purposes.

Although the above description gives the fundamentals of the sequential hot-deck procedure used by the Census Bureau in imputing for the decennial census data set, there are several further complications, two of which we touch on here. Both of these complications relate to the difficult problem of using an imputation mechanism that will produce a "consistent" data set when the process is finished. These two examples may give some idea of the magnitude of the problems encountered in devising an imputation procedure for the decennial census data set.

---

[1]The short-form records and long-form records of the decennial census are treated separately. However, the differences between the imputations for the two forms are only of degree and not of kind.

First, it is important to understand that the order of imputation of variables is key, since there is a strong dependence between the answers given on the census questionnaire. For example, consider the situation of yes-no questions followed by further responses if the answer to the previous question was yes.

Second, consider the case of imputing age of spouse. A simple-minded suggestion would be to substitute the age of spouse for a similar respondent. Unfortunately, it is quite easy to impute the "existence" of situations that one would consider to be rather unlikely, such as spouses substantially older or younger than their mates. This is something that one might characterize as weak inconsistency. To avoid the above possibilities, the Census Bureau imputes so that the difference between the spouse's and his or her mate's ages is substituted. (One might also consider substituting based on the ratio of their ages.) This lessens the problem of having spouses and mates of vastly different ages. However, it does not necessarily address the difficulty of spouses with siblings older than their mother or father. Single cases such as age of spouse, if identified, can be treated. However, these possibilities must be noticed so that the need for these additional features in the imputation process is appreciated. Fellegi and Holt (1976) provide a solution to the problem of consistency of imputations--whether carried out one variable at a time or in a multiple mode.

One of the major motivations to the use of hot-deck imputation is that imputation of averages and zeros, as well as other types of cold-deck methods, which are relatively effective as far as estimates of means and central tendencies of the data set are concerned, severely distort the remainder of the distribution, especially the variance, of the affected variables. This is because the values imputed are far less variable than the observed responses would have been. This is especially true of imputation of averages, whose use clearly results in a reduction of the estimate of the variance of any estimate based on the data set with imputations. Hot-deck imputation avoids this by imputing typical values from the raw data set, thereby attempting to mimic the variance of the hypothetical complete data set.

A relatively recent advance, termed multiple imputation (Rubin, 1978), which represents an expansion of the simple imputation strategy, may often lead to more accurate inference than single imputation. In his paper, Rubin demonstrates that at least in some simple situations, e.g., estimating a mean from a simple random sample with some random nonresponse, this generalization of imputation gives rise to an unbiased estimate of the variance of the sample mean.

Ideally, it is highly desirable to control the level of imputation (by achieving high levels of good response) so that imputation will be more for user convenience than to affect the estimated mean and variances of the variables concerned.

APPENDIX 3.2

A DESCRIPTION OF ITERATIVE PROPORTIONAL FITTING

One component of the census process briefly described in Chapter 3 is the data processing component, which includes a step to relate the long-form to the short-form information. The long-form information published by the Census Bureau is acquired on a sample basis. However, for the subset of variables that also appear on the short form, information is available for all respondents. In order to promote consistency between the short-form and the long-form tabulations as well as to reduce variance and any sample biases, the Census Bureau adjusts some of the sample information so that the sample estimates agree with the 100 percent information. Iterative proportional fitting has been used by the Census Bureau since 1970 to accomplish this. Iterative proportional fitting uses the 100 percent information at an aggregate level--that is, cross-tabulations for geographic "weighting" areas of broad categories of some of the short-form variables (see Bureau of the Census, 1983f)--to weight the individual long-form records.

In a more general context, the objective of iterative proportional fitting is to allocate population totals for aggregated groups down to individual records by weighting the individual records so that totals for individuals over the subgroups agree with population totals for the aggregates. Therefore iterative proportional fitting has potential for carrying down information from coverage evaluation programs, which is necessarily collected at an aggregate level, to the individual record level of the decennial census data set. This would ensure that the adjusted data set would be consistent, in a manner described in Chapter 7, and would also have smaller variances. Consider the two-way table given in Table 3.1. The n_{j+} and n_{+i} in Table 3.1 are the sample totals (for example, from the long form). The m_{j+} and m_{+i} are the row and column totals from the superior source (for example, the short form). The problem is to use the m_{j+} and m_{+i}, the row and column marginal totals, to adjust the elements of the table.

Iterative proportional fitting was first proposed in Deming and Stephan (1940). The first step of this algorithm reweights the entries in column 1 by the factor m_{+1}/n_{+1}. Then, assuming the values throughout all columns in the table have been altered in this manner, a

TABLE 3.1 Notation for Iterative Proportional Fitting for a Small Two-Way Table

	Demographic Group 1	Demographic Group 2	Demographic Group 3	Sample Total	Population Total
Age group 1	n_{11}	n_{12}	n_{13}	n_{1+}	m_{1+}
Age group 2	n_{21}	n_{22}	n_{23}	n_{2+}	m_{2+}
Age group 3	n_{31}	n_{32}	n_{33}	n_{3+}	m_{3+}
Sample total	n_{+1}	n_{+2}	n_{+3}	n_{++}	
Population total	m_{+1}	m_{+2}	m_{+3}		m_{++}

new table of n_{ij} is created and the same operation is performed by rows, etc. After each iteration, each individual cell has been assigned a weight that applies to each member of the cell. The iteration proceeds until convergence (see Fienberg, 1970). The procedure can also be applied to multiway tables of more than two dimensions. Iterative proportional fitting will, in general, reduce the variance of the resulting single cell estimated totals.

Because the adjustment factor uses row and column totals from the sample data in the denominator, a zero row or column total will clearly require a modification to allow the resulting estimates to be finite. It is common practice to combine adjacent rows or columns if one row or column total is zero or small. If there are many zero cells in the interior of the table, the rate of convergence may be adversely affected.

Iterative proportional fitting provides the user with weights, which can be used to construct estimates of other characteristics. When iterative proportional fitting is used for the purpose of assigning weights, and not merely for adjusting tables of cross-classified counts, it is often called raking ratio estimation. Iterative proportional fitting is a generalization of synthetic estimation (described in Chapter 7), which is used on one-way contingency tables.

4
Evaluating the Decennial Census: Past Experience

Evaluation of the decennial census is an important element of the census process. Not only does it provide users with some understanding of the limitations of the information provided, but also the Census Bureau uses the results to help improve the census methodology for administration of the next census. This chapter describes the various methods that have been used in the United States to evaluate the completeness of coverage in decennial censuses and what is known about the strengths and weaknesses of each method. It also provides information on comparable experience with coverage evaluation in Canada.

Errors in the census can be classified as coverage error or content error. Coverage errors are those that affect the population count and include cases of omission from the census of housing units and persons as well as cases of erroneous enumeration or inclusion. Omissions of persons can occur, among other reasons, because occupied housing units--and hence all of their residents--are inadvertently overlooked or are believed to be non-residential or vacant at the time of the census, because individual members of a household are not reported by the household, because persons with more than one usual place of residence, such as college students away from home or persons with a vacation home, are not counted at either address, and because some persons do not have usual places of residence as the term is commonly used. Erroneous enumerations also can occur for many reasons, for example, because persons who moved between Census Day and field follow-up are enumerated at both locations, because persons with more than one usual residence are enumerated more than once, because "out of scope" persons, such as those who were born or migrated to the United States after Census Day or were temporary visitors to the United States, are counted, because of fictitious questionnaires filled out by interviewers ("curbstoning"), and so on. Typically, questionnaires using information from neighbors, landlords, etc. ("last resort" and "close-out" cases), rather than actual contact with residents, are not treated as coverage errors unless, upon checking in a coverage evaluation program, the information turns out to have been erroneous.

Net coverage error is the difference between total (gross) omissions from the census and total (gross) erroneous inclusions. The main goals of coverage evaluation programs are to measure the net coverage error for the total population of the nation and, when possible, for important demographic subgroups and subnational geographic areas.

Content error includes errors in reported characteristics such as age and income. Estimates of net coverage error for particular population groups in the census often reflect the joint effects of enumeration error and content reporting error. For example, estimates of the net coverage of a particular age group will include the effects both of net coverage of people in the age group and of the net transfer of people to and from the age group as a result of age misreporting.

Census error evaluation studies are carried out for a number of purposes. Historically, evaluation results--both estimates of coverage and content errors--have been used to help improve the methodology for subsequent censuses and to suggest promising avenues for research and testing leading to other methodological changes. They have also been disseminated to users to provide general information on the quality of the data. In recent years, the possibility has been discussed of using evaluation results to adjust census statistics in order to improve the accuracy of the census counts. To date, the most closely related census operations to adjustment both occurred in 1970, when two programs--the National Vacancy Check and the Post-Enumeration Post Office Check--were conducted on a sample basis and the results were used to generate imputations of occupied housing units, occupants, and their characteristics in the census. The two programs accounted for 0.5 and 0.2 percent, respectively, of the total 1970 population count (see Chapter 5).

This chapter describes and assesses programs designed to evaluate completeness of census coverage of the population excluding for the most part consideration of content error evaluation programs (discussed briefly in Chapter 6).

Studies directed solely to evaluation of coverage of housing units and not persons are also excluded. Chapter 5 reviews specific findings from both population and housing coverage evaluation programs regarding gross undercount and overcount among groups in the population.

Finally, the discussion concerns only direct estimates of net national undercount derived from coverage evaluation programs. Methods of making small-area estimates (for example, synthetic estimates that apply national net undercount rates to subnational geographic areas) are not considered, nor are methods for "strengthening" direct estimates (for example, the Fay-Herriot methodology employed in the 1970s to adjust census income statistics used as input for postcensal per capita income estimates for allocation of general revenue sharing funds). Chapter 7 discusses possible uses of coverage evaluation results for adjustment purposes, including methods for carrying adjustments down to smaller geographic areas and methods for strengthening the estimates. Chapter 8 presents the panel's suggestions and recommendations for improved methods of coverage evaluation for the 1990 census.

METHODS OF COVERAGE EVALUATION

Broadly speaking, there are two major classes of coverage evaluation techniques: micro-level methods and macro-level methods. Micro-level or direct methods are based on case-by-case analysis of samples of units such as persons or households. Macro-level or analytic methods involve analysis of aggregate census data, including comparison of census totals with external data (such as vital statistics or other records) and analysis of internal consistency (for example, analysis of sex ratios by age group and of cohort changes between censuses). A variety of micro-level methods have been used in the past for coverage evaluation. An important distinction among micro-level methods is the source of the evaluation data: administrative records or survey data. The main macro-level method is demographic analysis. A variety of methodological procedures exists for both micro and macro approaches, and both approaches have been used for content evaluation.

Micro-level case-by-case coverage evaluation methods usually require two samples to estimate net coverage error. The first is the "P sample," or sample of the population from a source other than the census itself. The P sample provides an estimate of gross underenumeration. The second is the "E sample," or enumeration sample selected from the census itself. By definition, the E sample cannot contain any missed persons but is made up of both correct and erroneous enumerations, and therefore provides a basis for estimating these components. The union of the P and E samples provides estimates of net coverage error.

Fellegi (1984) has classified micro-level coverage evaluation methods by treatment of the P sample:

- "Do it again, but better." This involves a post-enumeration survey (PES) in which a sample of areas is revisited by specially selected and trained enumerators who try to do a better job of counting than the census.
- "Do it again, independently." This involves an independent survey that is matched to the census. Typically, the results are used to develop net coverage estimates with so-called capture-recapture or dual-system techniques. The 1980 Census Post-Enumeration Program (PEP), which matched the April and August Current Population Survey (CPS) records to the census, is an example. Matches of CPS to census records in 1950, 1960, and 1970, which were also carried out for purposes of content evaluation, produced as by-products estimates of gross omissions only.
- Reverse record checks. In this method, samples drawn from four frames--(1) persons counted in the previous census, (2) postcensal births, (3) postcensal immigrants, and (4) persons determined through coverage evaluation to have been missed in the previous census--are located to determine whether they are still residing in the area, and the resulting estimated number of residents is compared with the census total. The 1960 census in the United States tested a reverse record check approach; Canada relies heavily on this method for coverage evaluation.
- Administrative records matches. By these methods, records or samples of records from one or more administrative systems (for example, social security records) are matched to the census. The Census Bureau has conducted coverage studies of specific population groups based on administrative records matches, for example, using Medicare data to study coverage of persons 65 and over. One method, sometimes called the composite list,

has been detailed in Ericksen and Kadane (1983; they refer to it as the "megalist" method).

There are other possible sources for the P sample that have been suggested or experimented with in the past:

• Records of household composition generated by participant observers in local areas. (Experience with a single participant observer study in 1970 is described in Chapter 5.)

• Multiplicity or network surveys, in which census respondents are asked for names of relatives, such as parents or children, not living in their household. This approach was used with limited success in the 1977 Oakland pretest for the 1980 census (see discussion in Chapter 5). It was also used to evaluate coverage in the 1978 Richmond dress rehearsal, but most of the analysis was never completed.

• Lists generated by localities. The 1980 census included a provision for local review of preliminary field counts as a coverage improvement method (see Chapter 5). The Census Bureau also evaluated coverage in New York City with reference to local lists furnished by the city as part of its lawsuit protesting the 1980 census count (see Ericksen, 1983; Ericksen and Kadane, 1983). However, no attempt has been made to base evaluation--or adjustment--of the census on lists or other ad hoc data supplied by localities.

COVERAGE EVALUATION PRIOR TO 1980: MICRO-LEVEL METHODS

The completeness of the census count and the quality of the data have concerned census officials and data users since the first census in 1790. However, formal evaluation of the census originated in the mid-twentieth century. (The discussion in this section of the history of census coverage evaluation programs in the United States draws heavily on Bureau of the Census, 1978b, no date-a.) The social and economic problems of the 1930s and 1940s stimulated increased interest in census data for policy purposes and correspondingly increased interest in the accuracy of the figures. The development of probability sampling methods and improvements in vital statistics records over the two decades prior to 1950 made it possible to develop reasonable measures of accuracy.

There was no formal coverage evaluation effort in conjunction with the 1940 census, although outside researchers carried out limited macro-level analysis of coverage among certain age groups.

The Census Bureau experimented successfully with micro-level coverage evaluation programs using post-enumeration survey techniques for the 1945 Census of Agriculture, the 1947 Census of Manufactures, and the 1948 Census of Business. These efforts led to the decision to evaluate coverage in the 1950 Census of Population and Housing using a large post-enumeration survey.

The 1950 Census Post-Enumeration Survey

The post-enumeration survey coverage evaluation methodology used in the 1950 census (see Bureau of the Census, 1960) was predicated on the notion that errors in the census were largely due to failures to implement correctly census definitions and procedures and to imperfections in materials and procedures that led to respondent misunderstanding and reporting error. Hence, the approach used to evaluate both coverage and content errors was to "do it again, but better."

The 1950 PES used a combination area and list sample. A sample of the land area of the United States was used to identify erroneous omissions of entire households (P sample). A list sample of persons enumerated in the census was also used to: (1) check within-household errors in population coverage, both omissions and erroneous enumerations, (2) identify erroneous inclusions of entire households, and (3) measure the quality of answers to specific census questions (content evaluation). The area sample contained 280 primary sampling units, 3,500 segments (generally containing 6-10 housing units) and about 21,000-25,000 households. To reduce costs in canvassing two independent samples, the list sample was largely drawn to include most of the households in the area sample segments.

To obtain a high level of accuracy in the PES, interviewers were very carefully selected, trained, and supervised; more detailed questions were asked than in the census; and interviewers were instructed to obtain responses from each adult rather than allow proxy responses. The per case cost of the PES was about 20 times the per case cost of the census itself. Interviewing took place in August and September 1950.

The interviewers for the area sample were required to make a complete canvass of their assigned segments, note any dwelling units not included in the list sample for the sample segments as possibly omitted from the census, and obtain housing information for these units and information for each person living in them as of Census Day, April 1. (Hence, the 1950 PES used the household composition rule later termed PES-A, of determining the persons living at the address as of Census Day, as opposed to the rule termed PES-B, of determining where the persons found by the PES were actually living on Census Day.)

Interviewers for the list sample were to visit each household, determine whether there were other people that should have been enumerated at that address as of April 1, determine whether one or more persons or the whole household was erroneously enumerated, and obtain responses to housing and population questions for purposes of content evaluation. All the interviewer records from both the area and list samples were then matched to the census files.

The net undercount estimated by the PES was 2.1 million persons or almost 1.4 percent, the difference between erroneous omissions (2.2 percent) and erroneous inclusions (0.9 percent). The gross errors included persons who were counted in the wrong place and, hence, showed up as omissions for one place and erroneous inclusions for another. At the national level, such omissions and inclusions balance out. The PES also provided estimates of gross and net coverage error for the four regions of the country (Northeast, North Central, South, and West) by urban/rural residence and for population subgroups classified by age, race, sex, and various socioeconomic characteristics such as income and occupation.

Evidence from several other sources, including a quality check conducted as part of the PES, demographic analysis, and independent record checks for selected population groups, indicated that the PES net coverage error was too low--probably by as much as 2 percentage points (see discussion in a later section regarding demographic analysis and independent record checks). The PES quality check, which involved withholding from the list sample interviewers some names of persons actually enumerated in the census, found that the interviewers missed about 12 percent of these people. It appeared that interviewers were less effective in identifying cases in which the census missed one or more members of an enumerated household than in identifying errors involving whole households, in part due to the problem of persons moving between Census Day and the PES. The PES by design did not include transient quarters, such as hotels, and hence missed a population group believed to have a high net undercount in the census. However, the major reason postulated for the understatement of net undercount estimated by the PES is what is often termed "correlation bias," namely, the tendency for the PES to miss, although perhaps to a lesser degree, the same types of people who are missed in the census (see discussion in a later section of this chapter).

Coverage Evaluation in the 1960 Census

The experience with the 1950 Post-Enumeration Survey led the Census Bureau to undertake a more elaborate coverage evaluation program for the 1960 census (see Marks and Waksberg, 1966). The program included another post-enumeration survey and several kinds of record checks, including a reverse record check, in addition to demographic analysis.

The 1960 Post-Enumeration Survey

The 1960 PES again used two samples, an area sample and a list sample. The area sample contained 2,500 segments comprising about 25,000 housing units drawn from the 1959 Survey of Components of Change and Residential Finance. Enumerators were instructed to list all structures and housing units in their segments, to reconcile their listings with Survey of Components and Residential Finance data and census data, and to identify missed housing units and the number of people living in them. The list sample was selected independently of the area sample and comprised a national sample of about 15,000 housing units and group quarters drawn from census enumerators' listing books for about 2,400 enumeration districts in 335 primary sampling units covered in the Current Population Survey. The sample averaged about two clusters of three housing units each per enumeration district. The list sample interviewing began in May, only one month after Census Day, to endeavor to minimize problems stemming from movers and lack of recall on the part of respondents. The interviewers were given the list of housing units, but not the names of the occupants, and were instructed to enumerate independently the units, ascertaining the household composition as of Census Day as well as the composition in May. The interviewer records from the area and list samples were matched to census records, with special efforts made to determine: (a) whether persons in each unit in May who were not resident there on Census Day had been enumerated somewhere else and (b) whether the actual residents of the unit on Census Day had all been included.

The 1960 PES estimated the national net undercount at 3.3 million people, or 1.9 percent of the total population. The area sample provided estimates of persons in missed or erroneously enumerated housing units and the list sample provided estimates of missed or erroneously enumerated persons in otherwise enumerated households. The program produced net undercount estimates for age, race, and sex population groups but not for any other population classifications nor for subnational geographic areas. Again, evidence from demographic analysis and other sources indicated that the PES underestimated the net undercount--probably by about 1 percentage point. The 1960 PES estimated a higher proportion of missed persons in otherwise enumerated households compared with the 1950 effort (about two-fifths of the total of missed persons in 1960 compared with only one-quarter in 1950) but was still considered to have been relatively more successful in identifying missed households than missed persons within households.

1960 Record Check Studies of Specific Population Groups

The 1960 census coverage evaluation program included several record check studies developed in response to the evidence that post-enumeration surveys tend to miss the same kinds of people that the census misses. Two of the studies were directed toward evaluation of coverage of specific population groups, namely college students and elderly persons. Based on samples of students enrolled in college in spring 1960 and elderly recipients of social security benefits in March 1960, the Census Bureau estimated that the census experienced a gross undercount of between 2.5 and 2.7 percent of college students and 5.1 to 5.7 percent of the elderly (Marks and Waksberg, 1966).

The 1960 Census Reverse Record Check

The Census Bureau also carried out a reverse record check study to estimate net national undercount in 1960, similar to the methodology used in Canada. For the reverse record check in 1960 (see Bureau of the Census, 1964b), the Census Bureau constructed an independent sample of the population as of April 1 from four sampling frames:

(1) Persons enumerated in the 1950 census;
(2) Children born after April 1, 1950, and before April 1, 1960, as registered with state bureaus of vital statistics;
(3) Persons missed by the 1950 census but found by the 1950 PES; and
(4) Aliens registered with the Immigration and Naturalization Service as resident in the United States in January 1960.

The sample totaled about 7,200 persons (excluding about 400 persons found to be "out of scope" because they had died or moved out of the country or for some other reason), of a universe believed to consist of about 98 percent of the total U.S. population. Population groups not represented in the four samples included:

(1) Persons missed by both the 1950 census and the 1950 PES;
(2) Persons missed in the 1950 census in Alaska and Hawaii, which the 1950 PES did not cover;
(3) Citizens (mostly Puerto Ricans) outside the continental United States in 1950 but in the United States in 1960;
(4) Unregistered intercensal births;
(5) Aliens arriving after 1950 who became citizens before 1960;
(6) Aliens entering the United States between February 1 and April 1, 1960; and
(7) Aliens resident in January 1960 but not registered with the Immigration and Naturalization Service.

Two population groups were represented twice in the four samples:

(1) Persons missed in 1950 at their usual place of residence and erroneously enumerated at another

address (represented both as missed persons in the PES and enumerated persons in the census) and

(2) Aliens registered in 1960 and enumerated in the United States in 1950.

The Census Bureau attempted to trace each sample person to his or her address as of April 1, 1960; obtain responses to a questionnaire (by mail or in person when necessary), verifying the address and providing characteristics data to assist in determining enumeration status in the census; and match each questionnaire to the census records. For persons not found in the census or when there was doubt as to the person's enumeration status, the Census Bureau made further efforts to determine whether the person was counted.

Despite their best efforts, a definite match status (counted in the census or missed) could not be assigned to almost 1,200 of the sample cases (16.5 percent of the total). Over three-fourths of the failures to match were due to an inability to obtain a current address. Among the four samples, the sample drawn from the 1950 PES had the highest proportion of cases for which a definite match status could not be assigned--over 24 percent.

Using different assumptions about the rate at which the census counted persons for whom a definite enumeration status could not be obtained, the Census Bureau estimated gross omission rates from the reverse record check of between 2.6 and 4.7 percent of the total population. (The range for the sample drawn from the 1950 PES was 5.7 to 10.5 percent and for the sample of registered aliens 7.3 to 15.4 percent.) Subtracting the PES estimate of 1.3 percent erroneous enumerations in the census gave estimates of net undercoverage of between 1.3 and 3.4 percent. Marks and Waksberg (1966) narrowed the range of reasonable net undercount estimates from the reverse record check to a band of 2.5 to 3.1 percent. These estimates compare with the net undercount estimate of 1.9 percent from the PES and an estimate of 2.7 percent from demographic analysis. The small sample size of the reverse record check and uncertainties stemming from the match failures precluded deriving coverage estimates for population subgroups or subnational geographic areas from the 1960 reverse record check.

Reverse Record Checks in Canada

Since 1961, Canada has relied on reverse record check methodology to estimate the completeness of coverage achieved in its quinquennial censuses. Fellegi (1980a:280) notes that demographic analysis, given its vulnerability to migration estimates, is not useful in Canada because emigration is both significant and not well measured. He notes as well (1980a:281) the problems with the assumption that the probability of being missed in a survey is independent of the probability of being missed in the census as reasons not to use the Canadian monthly Labour Force Survey as the basis for constructing net coverage estimates. This problem is largely obviated by a reverse record check, which does not rely on dual-system estimation. Matching problems are also less consequential, since an estimate of the total population can be prepared after tracing, without matching with the census files. (Matching may play a useful role during tracing; it is also needed to identify a set of micro records of persons missed by the census for use during evaluation of the next census.)

The Canadian reverse record check program (see Gosselin and Theroux, 1977, 1978a, 1978b, 1979) combines samples from four mutually exclusive but together almost comprehensive sampling frames: (1) the previous census, (2) the register of intercensal births, (3) the list of intercensal immigrants, and (4) persons missed in the previous census as identified in that census's reverse record check. Conceptually, a sample drawn from these four frames covers all persons to be enumerated in the current census, except illegal immigrants and unregistered births (the latter are rarities in Canada because of its "baby bonus" program). Fellegi (1980a:281-282) summarizes the reverse record check (RRC) procedures as follows:

> The operation consists of meticulously tracing the current address of every selected person, and then of checking the census records to see whether they were included there. The key to the success of the project is the tracing operation--and we were able to trace conclusively in each of the last four censuses about 95 per cent of the selected persons. . . . As part of the tracing operation all selected persons who appear to have been missed by the census are contacted by an interviewer, partly to find out whether there may have

> been another address at which they could have been enumerated, partly to collect some basic census information from them. As a result, the RRC project provides not only estimates of national or provincial under-enumeration rates, but it also results in a microdata base [that] . . . has a rich analytic potential to describe the "profile" of those missed by the census.

The reverse record check of the 1976 Canadian census estimated undercoverage of both persons and occupied housing units at about 2 percent (Fellegi, 1980a:285-286). No E sample has been used to date in Canada (though one is planned for 1986) because the emphasis has been toward deriving information for lessening the gross undercount. Furthermore, Canada does not make use of the same array of coverage improvement programs as the Census Bureau that probably contribute to overenumerations.

Coverage Evaluation in the 1970 Census

Because of the problems with the post-enumeration survey methodology used to estimate net undercoverage in the 1950 and 1960 censuses, the Census Bureau made no plans to carry out a comparable program for the 1970 census but placed chief reliance on the method of demographic analysis (see discussion in a later section). Several other programs, including the CPS-Census Match and record checks for specific population groups, contributed to knowledge of coverage problems.

The CPS-Census Match

The approximately 56,000 households included in the March 1970 Current Population Survey sample were matched to the 1970 census records. Although the match was performed primarily for purposes of content evaluation (using the subsample of about 10,000 CPS households that received the census long forms), it also served to evaluate coverage of housing units. Data on missed persons were tabulated but never published (see Siegel, 1975).

The Census Bureau constructed estimates of gross undercoverage for the total population and subgroups from the CPS-Census Match using dual-system estimation techniques. The CPS-Census Match estimated a gross under-coverage rate of 2.3 percent for all persons, compared with the demographic analysis estimate of 2.2 percent. The CPS-Census Match estimate is higher than the demographic estimate, at least in part because of the absence of an E sample to estimate erroneous overenumerations in the census. The CPS-Census Match estimates were adjusted for additions to the census count resulting from imputations based on the National Vacancy Check, the Post-Enumeration Post Office Check, and some "close-out" procedures, but they were not adjusted for erroneous additions to the census, such as duplicate enumerations.

Record Check Studies of Specific Population Groups

The Census Bureau carried out two record check studies in 1970 directed toward coverage evaluation. For the Medicare Record Check, a sample of approximately 8,000 persons age 65 and over was selected from Medicare health records and matched to the 1970 census records. The overall gross omission rate for this population group as estimated from the study was 4.9 percent, a somewhat lower rate than that estimated for elderly social security recipients in 1960.

For the D.C. Driver's License Study, the Census Bureau matched driver's license records with census records for about 1,000 males, ages 20-29, living in a set of selected tracts in the District of Columbia, and who obtained or renewed their licenses in the District of Columbia between July 1969 and June 1970. About 14 percent of the cases were identified as missed in the census, with an additional 10 percent who were probably missed but for whom a definite match status could not be determined. This project was designed as a feasibility study. Analysts recommended that future studies: (1) narrow the sampling time reference, (2) update the address information after sampling and before matching, and (3) have the Postal Service review the list prior to matching.

COVERAGE EVALUATION PRIOR TO 1980: MACRO-LEVEL METHODS

Researchers inside and outside the Census Bureau have used aggregate methods to assess the completeness of census coverage since the beginning of coverage evaluation efforts in the United States. The principal macro-level method is termed demographic analysis, whereby independent estimates for the population in various categories (typically, age, sex, and race) are constructed and compared with the census counts. In ideal form, the process of constructing an independent estimate for an age-race-sex group, for example, black men ages 25-29 in 1970, is as follows:

(1) Obtain from vital statistics records the count of births of black males occurring between April 1, 1941, and April 1, 1945 (and apply appropriate corrections for underregistration);

(2) Subtract the count (obtained from vital statistics records) of deaths occurring between April 1, 1941, and April 1, 1970, to black males born in the above time period;

(3) Add the count (from Immigration and Naturalization Service statistics) of black male immigrants to the United States born in the above time period who arrived between April 1, 1941, and April 1, 1970;

(4) Subtract the count (estimated as best possible) of black male emigrants from the United States born in the above time period who left the country between April 1, 1941, and April 1, 1970.

The resulting estimate can then be compared with the 1970 census count for black men ages 25-29 to determine the net undercount or overcount of that group in the population.

The above procedure is fairly reliable for population groups for which birth registration data are complete (essentially those born in 1935 or later), for which illegal immigration is negligible, and for which emigration is also negligible. Data sources are not available that permit accurate estimates either of illegal immigration or of emigration. Given the gaps in the data, various methods have been used to construct "demographic" estimates for particular population groups. For example, data from Medicare records are currently used to construct independent estimates of the population age 65 and over, rather than using the demographic method outlined above.

Demographic analysis cannot be performed for population groups defined according to other characteristics, such as income or education, because of the absence of appropriately classified registration information. It has also not been possible to use the method for subnational geographic area coverage estimates, because of lack of data on internal migration flows. The method provides estimates of net national coverage error for age-sex-race groups for which illegal immigration and emigration are small, but it does not distinguish among the components of error--gross omissions, gross overenumerations, and content errors such as age misreporting. Nonetheless, the method has been extensively developed in the United States and is regarded as providing more accurate estimates than other methods of net undercoverage for the 1950, 1960, and 1970 censuses at the national level. The sections below briefly review the history of demographic analysis of census coverage in the United States prior to 1980.

Demographic Analysis Prior to 1950

After the 1940 census there was some macro-level analysis by outside researchers of the completeness of the coverage. With a grant from the Social Science Research Council, Daniel O. Price (1947) compared aggregate census data for men ages 21-35 by race with selective service registration data and estimated a net undercount of 3 percent for all men and 13 percent for black men in this age group. P.K. Whelpton of the Scripps Foundation for Population Research, using vital statistics data, estimated that white and nonwhite children under age 5 had net undercount rates, respectively, of over 6 percent and over 15 percent in the 1940 census (Bureau of the Census, 1944).

Demographic Analysis in 1950

Ansley Coale of Princeton University carried out an extensive analysis (1955) to develop demographic estimates of the population in 1950. For age groups under 15, he used birth registration statistics as the basis for his estimates. For older groups, ages 15-64, he relied on comparisons with the results of preceding censuses (with appropriate allowances for mortality and net immigration). An important assumption underlying his method was that within each age-sex group the relative net undercoverage was identical in the 1930, 1940, and 1950 censuses. For persons age 65 and older, Coale used the 1950 Post-Enumeration Survey results. Coale estimated net undercount for the total population in 1950 at 3.5 percent, 5.4 million people.

Coale's net undercount estimate of 3.5 percent is 2.5 times the estimate from the PES of 1.4 percent. The Census Bureau developed a "minimum reasonable estimate" of 2.4 percent net undercount based on PES results for persons age 40 and older, birth registration data for persons under 15, and examination of sex ratios for persons ages 15-39 (Bureau of the Census, 1960:5-6). Demographic analysis at the Census Bureau subsequently led to refinements in Coale's 1955 estimate. The latest estimate (Siegel, 1974) puts the 1950 census net undercount at 3.3 percent of the total population.

The 1950 census evaluation program included a Test of Birth Registration, designed to evaluate the completeness of vital statistics on births. (A similar study was carried out as part of the 1940 census.) For 1950, census enumerators filled out cards for infants born between January 1 and April 1, 1950. These cards were matched to birth registration records for the corresponding period. The results, used in Coale's work and other demographic analysis studies, indicated that the registration system recorded 98 percent of all births (compared with 93 percent in 1940), including 99 percent of white births and 94 percent of all other births (Siegel and Zelnick, 1966).

An extension of this project, the Infant Enumeration Study (Bureau of the Census, 1953), matched birth records for January through March 1950 to the infant cards filled out by census enumerators to assess completeness of coverage for newborns. The study found that about 96 percent of infants under 3 months old were enumerated. In about 82 percent of cases in which an infant was missed, the parents were also missed.

Demographic Analysis in 1960

Census Bureau staff and university scholars carried out several studies in the early 1960s to evaluate completeness of coverage in the 1960 census. Siegel and Zelnick (1966) summarized these studies and presented a "preferred analytic composite" estimate of 3.1 to 3.2 percent net undercount of the population in 1960.

Undercount percentages for persons under age 25 were derived from population estimates for this group based on birth registrations (adjusted for underregistration using the results of the 1940 and 1950 birth registration test), registered deaths, and estimated net external migration. The estimation method used for whites age 25 and older was quite complex. The method represented an extension to 1960 of coverage estimates for 1950 published in Coale and Zelnik (1963) for the native white and total white population by age and sex.

Coale and Zelnik constructed estimates of annual births and birth rates for the native white population from 1855 to 1934 using single-year age distributions available in every census since 1880. For each cohort, they estimated the proportion that could be expected to survive each intercensal decade based on mortality data, then used those figures (adjusted for immigration) to estimate the number of births that should have occurred a certain number of years before a given census to account for the number of persons enumerated at a certain age in that census. This description is an oversimplification, as various complex adjustments were required to attempt to compensate for deficiencies in the census single-year age distributions and the mortality records. From the estimated annual birth data for native whites, Coale and Zelnick constructed estimates of total population, by age and sex, then of coverage errors for the native and total white population of each age and sex group in each census from 1880 to 1950.

The 1960 coverage estimates for nonwhite women 25 years and older represented extensions of the estimates developed by Coale (1955) for this group in 1950, using an iterative technique assuming that age patterns of undercount were similar in the 1930, 1940, and 1950 censuses. The 1960 coverage estimates for nonwhite men 25 and older were the result of applying expected sex ratios to the estimated nonwhite female population (whose coverage errors are lower) and comparing the results with the census counts.

Siegel (1970) updated the 1960 coverage estimates to incorporate population estimates for the elderly based on Medicare data. Siegel (1974) published the current "preferred" estimate that the 1960 census undercounted the population by 2.7 percent or 5 million people. The preferred demographic analysis estimate is 1.4 times the estimate from the 1960 PES and falls within the range of 2.5 to 3.1 percent estimated in the 1960 reverse record check.

Demographic Analysis in 1970

The Census Bureau relied on demographic analysis as the principal method of evaluating coverage in the 1970 census. The data used for the demographic estimates included birth and death statistics, life tables, immigration data, Medicare enrollments, and data from previous censuses. Siegel (1974) published a range of estimates, with the "preferred" estimate that the 1970 census undercounted the population by 2.5 percent. The range of estimates stemmed from differing assumptions regarding net undercount in the 1960 census and population change in the following decade.

The preferred estimates were developed as follows. Population estimates for persons under 35 were based on adjusted birth statistics, projected forward to 1970 by accounting for deaths and estimated net migration. The birth data were adjusted for underregistration using the results of the 1940 and 1950 birth registration tests and of another study of completeness of birth registration for 1964-1968 (Bureau of the Census, 1973e). For the latter study, a sample of about 15,000 children born between 1964 and 1968 who were included in the Current Population Survey or the Health Interview Survey from June 1969 to March 1970 were matched to birth records. The study found that 99.2 percent of births during this period were registered, including 99.4 percent of white births and 98 percent of all other births.

Population estimates for white women ages 35-64 in 1970 represented extensions to 1970 of the 1950 estimates for white women ages 15-44 developed by Coale and Zelnick (1963) based on estimating annual births. Population estimates for black women ages 35-64 represented extensions to 1970 of 1960 estimates for these cohorts developed by Coale and Norfleet W. Rives, Jr. (1973). The Coale and Rives study constructed estimates of the black population and of black birth rates for the period 1880 to 1970, starting with the assumption that the "true" population in 1880 could be represented by "model" tables of stable population age distributions.

The population estimates for white and black men ages 35-64 were derived by applying expected sex ratios (males per 100 females) to the corresponding female population estimates. Finally, estimates of persons 65 and over were derived from Medicare data, adjusted for persons not enrolled and further adjusted for consistency with expected sex ratios for the elderly population.

Subsequent work with new data permitted refinements in the 1970 coverage estimates. The latest estimate is that the 1970 census had a net undercount rate of 2.2 percent (Passel et al., 1982). The revision was primarily attributable to increased allowances for emigration during 1960 to 1970, for Medicare underregistration at ages 65-69 in 1970, and to small changes in estimated completeness of birth registration for 1935-1970.

As described more fully in Chapter 5, demographic analysis estimates of net undercount in every census since 1950 indicate better coverage for women, on average, than for men, and for whites than for persons of other races. During the 1970s, Census Bureau researchers endeavored to develop coverage estimates for states (Siegel et al., 1977) and for the growing Hispanic population (Siegel and Passel, 1979), but these efforts were frustrated by lack of reliable data. The growing interest in coverage estimates for subnational areas and for other population groups besides blacks and whites, coupled with severe data problems, such as absence of data for estimating illegal immigration and emigration and for reliably estimating internal migration, led the Census Bureau to decide that demographic analysis could not be the principal coverage evaluation method for 1980. The Census Bureau planned, in addition to demographic analysis, to carry out a program to match an independent survey to the census (the P sample) and recheck a sample of census records (the E sample). The results would be used, through dual-system estimation, to construct coverage estimates for the nation, states, and large metropolitan areas. The 1980 Post-Enumeration Program and the demographic analysis efforts carried out for 1980 are discussed in detail below.

THE 1980 POST-ENUMERATION PROGRAM

In 1980, the Census Bureau implemented a coverage evaluation program closely related to the post-enumeration surveys used in conjunction with the 1950 and 1960 decennial censuses. The aim of this program, called the 1980 Post-Enumeration Program (PEP), was to provide estimates of net undercoverage in the 1980 census, with considerable geographic detail, possibly down to the level of states and large cities.

The basic methodology of the 1980 Post-Enumeration Program was "do it again, independently." Thus, the sample recount was not intended to be more complete than the census, only independent of the census. If the independence assumption applies, then the estimate of the number missed can be arrived at via a model similar to the one used in the estimation of wildlife populations, called capture-recapture. When used in the context of the census, the model is referred to as dual-system estimation (see Marks et al., 1977, and Sekar and Deming, 1949, for an early use of the capture-recapture methodology in a census context).

In the case of wildlife populations, a sample of the population is taken and identified or tagged. It is assumed that every member of the population has an equal chance of being tagged. Then another independent sample is taken. Again at this second stage, it is assumed that every member of the population has an equal chance of being tagged, although not necessarily the same chance as at the first stage. The population thus falls into four mutually distinct groups: (1) those caught the first and the second time, (2) those caught the first time but not the second time, (3) those missed the first time and caught the second time, and (4) those missed both times. The total population is the sum of these four groups. The difficulty is that the fourth group's number is unknown.

At this point the assumption of independence is used. The population that was caught the first time is estimated to have the same probability of being captured the second time as the total population. Thus, the percentage of the population caught the first time that is also captured the second time is assumed to be the same as the percentage of the entire population that is captured the second time.

It has long been thought that either the independence assumption or the assumption of equal capture probabilities or both are very likely seriously in error. The failure of the assumption of independence is sometimes referred to as "correlation bias." It is commonly believed (and partially supported by Valentine and Valentine, 1971) that certain persons, such as undocumented aliens, others wishing to avoid detection by authorities for a variety of reasons, and those either with multiple residences or living in quarters that are not clearly residential, are missed by both the census and sample surveys more frequently than the joint assumptions of independence of capturing mechanisms and equal capture probabilities would yield.

In the application of dual-system estimation to the 1980 census, the two assumptions of equal capture probability at each stage and the independence of capture probabilities, which are generally believed not to hold, were modified as follows. The Census Bureau stratified the population into subpopulations and used dual-system estimation separately in each stratum. Thus the two assumptions used were that the individuals within these strata had equal probabilities of capture and that the capturing mechanisms operated independently within strata. The strata were defined using the variables age, race, sex, ethnicity, and area of residence.

Notationally, for each stratum, if n_1 are caught the first time, n_2 are caught the second time, m are caught both times, and we are interested in estimating N, the total population, it follows from the two assumptions given above that:

$$m / n_1 = n_2 / N \quad \text{and hence } \hat{N} = (n_1 \times n_2) / m.$$

Parallel to the wildlife example, in the 1980 census dual-system estimation model, the census served as the first method of capture and the Census Bureau used the Current Population Survey sample of households as the post-enumeration survey, the second capture mechanism.

Unlike the wildlife situation, it is not always easy to ascertain whether an individual was included in the census. The individuals themselves cannot reliably respond to this question, partly because a member of a household may not know whether another member completed a questionnaire that included them. To determine which people counted in the post-enumeration survey were also counted in the census, a match of individuals in the post-enumeration survey and the census was carried out, matching by information on name, address, sex, age, and race. Ideally, one would need to match both the PES to the census and vice versa to be able to identify inaccuracies and errors in both the lists. While it is conceptually straightforward to search the census records for Current Population Survey records, the procedure used in 1980 did not facilitate matching a substantial percentage of census records to the Current Population Survey. The purpose of such reverse matching could be to determine records in the census that were either erroneous enumerations or duplications. Therefore, as mentioned above for previous post-enumeration surveys, a sample of census records was taken, called the E sample.

Below we give details concerning both the P sample and the E sample.

Finally, there are two populations that were not sampled by the Current Population Survey: individuals in military barracks and the institutional population. For these populations, a supplemental sample was drawn. We do not describe the treatment of these samples of group quarters further here.

The P Sample

The P Sample comprised the April and August 1980 samples of the Current Population Survey. Samples for two months were used so that the overall sample size would be large enough to provide fairly reliable estimates of undercoverage for states and major cities. (Due to the current design of the Current Population Survey, samples taken four months apart have no overlap.) Each CPS month included about 70,000 households and about 185,000 individuals.

To obtain the P sample information, the Current Population Survey interview was supplemented with two pieces of information: (1) a sketch map of the major roads so that residences could be located unambiguously on census maps and (2) for the August CPS interview, a list of all places of residence of each person between January 1 and the time of the interview, as well as information that would help to validate the geographic locations. The address for each interview was then geocoded to the census enumeration district. The census questionnaires for that enumeration district--and only that enumeration district--were then clerically searched for a person with closely matching information on name, address, sex, age, and race.

If no matching census record could be found, or if there was not enough information to ascertain match status, a follow-up interview was attempted. An inherent asymmetry should be noted here. The Current Population Survey enumerations were followed-up for verification, but the census enumerations were considered valid without follow-up. The E sample was intended to account for this asymmetry.

The E Sample

The E sample, as mentioned above, was designed to verify the accuracy of the information provided in the census, specifically, to count possible overenumeration from each of the following sources: (1) records placed into the wrong census enumeration district, (2) records resulting from erroneous enumerations, e.g., individuals born after Census Day, and cases fabricated by census enumerators (called curbstoned cases), and (3) multiple records for the same individual. For measurement of net error, these cases would be subtracted from the gross undercoverage estimates.

In the administration of the E sample, 100,000 census questionnaires were selected and follow-up enumerators were sent into the field to detect erroneous enumerations and incorrect geocoding. A 50 percent subsample of the questionnaires in the E sample was also checked for duplicates.

The Combined Estimate

The dual-system estimation was then modified to reflect geocoding errors, erroneous enumerations, and duplications--these add wrongly to the number of nonmatches in the census and therefore should be subtracted from the census count. (Also subtracted from the census count were the number of field imputations[1] that were also not matchable by CPS records.) If d represents the estimated number of duplications in the census, g the estimated number of persons placed into the wrong enumeration district, ee the estimated number of erroneous enumerations, and i the number of field imputations, the estimate of the total population then becomes:

$$\hat{N} = (\{n_1 - d - g - ee - i\} \times n_2) / m.$$

There were inconsistencies between the treatment of census and the CPS cases, which also further complicated matters. For example, the degree of verification of inclusion in the two lists differed, with the census operating under somewhat more flexible rules concerning what individuals might serve as a substitute respondent for a particular individual. This difference might have

[1]Field imputations are those that did not result from damaged questionnaires.

accounted for relatively more enumerations in the census than in the Current Population Survey.

Aside from any assumptions underlying the models used in the 1980 Post-Enumeration Program, the quality of the collected data and the data processing affect the reliability of the resulting estimates. One assumption concerning data quality and processing is that there is always enough information to be able to decide whether two records match. Another implicit assumption is that, given sufficient information to assign match status to two records, there are no errors in the matching algorithm. Slight relaxations of the above two assumptions, e.g., that they hold for a very large majority of the cases, would probably still permit the calculation of reliable estimates. In the remainder of this section we discuss the incompleteness in the P and E samples in the 1980 PEP and how the Census Bureau attempted to compensate for the lack of completeness.

For the P sample there are three major sources of missing data:[2] (1) household noninterviews in the CPS; (2) failure to attempt or complete follow-up interviews for initially unmatchable CPS cases; and (3) failure to obtain acceptable follow-up interviews for initially unmatchable CPS cases, including sufficiently precise April 1 addresses. For the E sample there is one primary source of missing data: failure to obtain acceptable follow-up interviews.

In April 1980, the percentage of Current Population Survey (P sample) interviewees that were refusals, temporarily absent, or did not respond for other reasons was about 4.4 percent. One approach in the PEP was to treat these cases as nonrespondents. A second approach was to search CPS records for interviews for preceding and succeeding months for these cases, thus permitting attempts to match them to the census. (The CPS is a rotating survey and respondents are asked to furnish information for a total of 8 months in a 16-month period.) The majority of these households could be matched to the census. The successful search for interviews in neighboring months was referred to as a "Type A noninterview." Type A noninterviews were used in some calculations of census undercoverage and not used in others.

---

[2]Some material in this section taken from conversations with Robert Fay, III, U.S. Bureau of the Census.

Besides the decision of whether to include Type A noninterviews, two other decisions arose over the inclusion or exclusion of certain data. First, when the E sample search was unable to determine where a person included in the census resided on Census Day, postal carriers were consulted. These data were not considered by the Census Bureau to be of high quality (see Cowan, 1983). Second, the information on date and place of residence from August CPS movers (i.e., CPS interviewees in August who had lived elsewhere on Census Day) was determined also not to be of high quality.

Most CPS interviews that did not match to the census were followed-up in the field in order to: (1) determine or confirm April 1 address and (2) improve the quality of information on the precise geographic location of the Census Day address. Of the cases in which the follow-up interview was complete, the majority (60 percent) had been correctly geocoded and the correct enumeration district's questionnaires had been searched for a match. Therefore these cases were given the status of not matched to the census. However, some follow-up interviews were not attempted or completed. Of those that were completed, some were considered to be unacceptable because the interviewers could not follow the fairly strict protocol on required features such as self-response. Finally, for a large number of cases, the follow-up interview was completed but the resulting address information was incomplete or in some other way not precise enough to determine the proper enumeration district for the residence. Occasionally the respondent reported "I don't know" or refused to answer.

A rough summary of the incompleteness in the April P sample is provided in Table 4.1. The situation for the August P sample is worse, primarily due to the problems with movers, as noted above. As a rough approximation, by adding the 4.4 percent rate of refusals for households to the 4.0 percent rate of unresolved matches (this is an approximation because percentages of households and individuals cannot strictly be added together), we arrive at the fact that, for over 8 percent of the people in the PEP, a match status could not be determined from the data collected. This compares with the percentage net undercount, which is probably less than 2 percent on a national level.

In order to take account of these missing data, the Census Bureau used various forms of imputation, as well as other approaches described below, to arrive at 12

TABLE 4.1 Response and Match Resolution Rates for April 1980 Current Population Survey (P Sample) by Race

Percentage of April P Sample Households by Race and Response Status for Series 3 Estimates[a]			Percentage of April P Sample Individuals in Responding Households by Race and Ethnicity and Match Status for Series 3 Estimates[a]			
Race	Responded	Did Not Respond	Race and Ethnicity	Matched	Nonmatched	Unresolved
Total	95.6	4.4	Total	92.6	3.4	4.0
White	95.7	4.3	Black	85.8	7.4	6.8
Other	94.5	5.5	Nonblack Hispanic	87.7	5.5	6.8
			Other	93.8	2.7	3.5

[a] Series 3 estimates, described more fully in the text, did not use Type A noninterview information but reweighted these cases to behave identically to the interviewed cases.

SOURCE: Wolter (1983:Exhibit B).

different sets of estimates of undercoverage for states, major cities, and remainders of states. The formation of these 12 estimates resulted from various choices concerning which CPS month to use, the treatment of information considered of questionable quality, and the treatment of unresolved matches. The Census Bureau used a combination of weighting and imputation, the weighting representing essentially imputation of the average matching rate for individuals of the same demographic characteristics. Thus, weighting did not make use of as much information as the imputation, e.g., it did not use information about the cause of the incompleteness.

Some of the choices resulting in the 12 estimates were: (1) choosing whether to use Type A noninterviews for matching decisions or using weighting to assign matched status, (2) choosing whether to use Post Office information for the E sample or to treat these cases as noninterviews and use weighting to assign match status, (3) choosing whether to use information from any movers in August or to treat them as noninterviews and use weighting to assign match status, and (4) in general, for both the E sample and the P sample, choosing to use weighting for all incomplete cases or to use imputation. As a result of these choices, plus the choice of which CPS month (April or August) to use as well as other choices not mentioned here, the Census Bureau developed 27 estimates of undercoverage for states and major cities. Later, this number was reduced to 12 estimates

TABLE 4.2 Scheme to Identify Various 1980 PEP Estimates

Code	Month	P Sample Treatment / E Sample Treatment
2-9	Apr	P — With Type A noninterviews E — Post Office results considered noninterviews
3-9	Apr	P — Without Type A noninterviews E — Post Office results considered noninterviews
2-8	Apr	P — With Type A noninterviews E — With Post Office results
3-8	Apr	P — Without Type A noninterviews E — With Post Office results
5-8	Aug	P — Movers used E — With Post Office results
5-9	Aug	P — Movers used E — Post Office results considered noninterviews
10-8	Aug	P — Movers treated as noninterviews E — With Post Office results
3-20	Apr	P — Without Type A noninterviews E — Incomplete cases treated as simple noninterviews
2-20	Apr	P — With Type A noninterviews E — Incomplete cases treated as simple noninterviews
14-20	Apr	P — Incomplete cases treated as simple noninterviews E — Incomplete cases treated as simple noninterviews
14-8	Apr	P — Incomplete cases treated as simple noninterviews E — With Post Office results
14-9	Apr	P — Incomplete cases treated as simple noninterviews E — Post Office results considered noninterviews

NOTE: Every estimate in this table made use of clean-up information, essentially more extensive efforts to collect follow-up interviews, etc.

SOURCES: Cowan and Bettin (1982:14); Cowan (1983:32-33).

that the Census Bureau felt all represented reasonable alternatives. Table 4.2 provides the definitions of these 12 sets of estimates. They are denoted by a two-integer hyphenated code, in which the first number describes a treatment of the P sample, and the second number indicates a treatment of the E sample.

There are a number of reasons, both a priori and a posteriori, supporting the various individual estimates from this list of 12 estimates. For example, estimate 10-8 reduces the problem for movers when using the August P sample. Also the handling of incomplete interviews in the 14 and 20 series of estimates is similar to that used in the Canadian census. These points among others are detailed in Bailar (1983c).

The use of these 12 estimates produced very different estimates of undercoverage for national demographic groups, as shown in Table 4.3. Some analysts have suggested that the number of acceptable estimates should be

TABLE 4.3 1980 PEP Estimates of Percentage Undercoverage for Demographic Groups at the National Level

Estimate Code	National	Black	Nonblack Hispanic	Other
2-9	1.4	6.7	5.6	0.3
3-9	1.3	6.3	5.3	0.2
2-8	1.0	5.6	4.4	0.0
3-8	0.8	5.2	4.1	−0.1
5-8	1.6	4.3	6.4	0.8
5-9	2.0	5.4	7.6	1.1
10-8	0.2	2.7	3.6	−0.4
3-20	1.6	6.9	5.5	0.4
2-20	1.7	7.2	5.8	0.6
14-20	−0.3	2.5	1.2	−0.8
14-8	−1.0	0.7	−0.2	−1.4
14-9	−1.1	2.0	1.0	−0.6

SOURCE: Cowan and Bettin (1982:Tables III-1,12).

narrowed considerably. For example, Ericksen (1983) would discard all but the 2-8, 2-9, 3-8, and 3-9 estimates as either based on August data, which had a higher rate of cases with unresolved match status, or as making use of extreme assumptions in the adjustments for missing data. However, even within this restricted set, the national undercount rate ranges from 0.8 to 1.4 percent.

1980 DEMOGRAPHIC ANALYSIS

In the years prior to 1980, demographic analysis had provided what were considered to be the most trustworthy estimates of undercoverage for certain demographic groups at the national level. However, demographic analysis for 1980 is generally considered to be significantly less accurate than for any of the previous three censuses (even though the reliability of some components of the estimates probably improved). In this section, we briefly describe the data sets and models used to calculate the 1980 demographic analysis estimates of undercoverage. (The main source for this section is Passel, 1983.)

The demographic method developed a preliminary estimate of the April 1980 national population of 226.0 million based on the so-called preferred estimate of the undercount for 1970 (see Bureau of the Census, 1974a). The 1980 decennial census counted 226.5 million. It was generally assumed that some undocumented aliens were counted in the census but that a sizable percentage were not. Since the demographic estimates incorporated undocumented aliens only indirectly by assuming that net illegal immigration was equal to another unknown, namely emigration of legal residents, it was generally assumed that the census had experienced an undercount nationally, but it was difficult to estimate how much.

As more and improved data concerning the components of population change, births, deaths, and legal migration became available, better estimates were made. These estimates (Passel et al., 1982) were an improvement over the April estimates; however, they could not make use of data on recent fertility, mortality, or immigration nor of 1980 Medicare data, which were not yet available.

Work has continued on improving coverage estimates based on demographic analysis. To understand the nature of these improvements, we discuss in turn each of the major data components of demographic analysis separately for persons under and over age 65.

The Population Under Age 65

Birth Records

For 1980, population estimates based on virtually complete birth registration can be obtained only for the population under age 45. However, even for the years of virtually complete birth registration (1935 to the present), correction factors are used that are based on tests of the completeness of birth registration records for the white population. In addition, the demographic estimates had to use preliminary data on the number of births in 1979 and 1980, since final information on 1979 and 1980 birth registration did not become available until late 1983. Birth registration data are incomplete for persons between ages 45 and 64. Coale and Zelnik (1963) and Coale and Rives (1973), using stable population and other analysis methods, constructed estimates of the number of births for the years before 1935.

Death Records

Death statistics are used with very little correction for underregistration. Two minor exceptions are: (1) a small adjustment for the underregistration of infant deaths between 1935 and 1960 and (2) the use of Medicare records for deaths of people over age 70 between the years 1970 and 1980. Some smoothing of the death rates is also used.

Legal External Immigration

Records on immigration from 1935 to 1980 are provided by the Immigration and Naturalization Service (INS). Final data for most age, sex, and racial groups for the years 1979 and 1980 had not been provided to the Census Bureau by INS by late 1983. The overall effect on the preliminary estimates is thought to be small. Emigration is only indirectly measured. Differences in estimates from consecutive censuses of the number of foreign-born persons has provided estimates of the net change in the foreign-born, which, when combined with immigration data, can be used to provide estimates of emigration. This technique is due to Warren and Peck (1980).

The Population Age 65 and Over

For the population age 65 and over, Medicare data are used to provide estimates of coverage; however, Medicare does suffer from a small amount of underregistration (Bureau of the Census, 1974a). The population figures used in the demographic estimates contained adjustments for the underregistration.

Undocumented Immigrants

The most serious deficiency in the population balance equation used for demographic analysis is the lack of information on the net flow of illegal or undocumented immigrants into the United States. A comprehensive discussion of this problem is contained in a recent National Research Council report on immigration statistics (Levine et al., 1985). The estimates of the number of undocumented aliens residing in the United States at the time of the 1980 census ranged from 2 to 12 million. No records of entries or departures are available for undocumented aliens (although some losses to the undocumented population through death may be included in numbers of registered deaths), so this population is impossible to incorporate into the standard demographic analysis. Various attempts have been made to estimate the size of the undocumented population, or particular components of it, using for example the 1960, 1970, and 1980 censuses of Mexico or Immigration and Naturalization Service data (see for example Goldberg, 1974; Bean et al., 1983; see also Appendix 8.1). Unfortunately, the results of these analyses are not precise enough to do more than set broad limits, between 2 and 4 million, on the size of the undocumented population resident in the United States in 1980 (Levine et al., 1985).

Warren and Passel (1983) applied a modified form of demographic analysis to the foreign-born population enumerated by the 1980 census to estimate the number of undocumented aliens included in the census, a necessary preliminary step to estimating undercoverage of the legally resident population. Upon removing the undocumented aliens included in the overall count, this method estimated that the census had a 0.5 percent national undercount of the legally resident population, with a 5.3 percent undercount for blacks and a 0.2 percent overcount for whites and other races (see Chapter 5). These numbers agree fairly well with PEP estimates 3-8 and 2-8, given in Table 4.3.

Many other factors besides the quality of the data sets are involved in the reliability of estimates based on demographic analysis. For example, there is a large amount of uncertainty in the racial and ethnic categorization used in demographic analysis, both between censuses and between any census and other sources, such as vital statistics records. Furthermore, the models of the completeness of birth registration are themselves based on data that made use of matching studies, which are generally error-prone. Finally, subnational estimation procedures using demographic analysis are still undergoing research. The possibility of developing useful estimates in the near future appears to be small, due to the lack of estimates of interstate migration (see Siegel et al., 1977).

RECENT USE OF ADMINISTRATIVE LISTS FOR COVERAGE EVALUATION

The existence of administrative records, for example the Internal Revenue Service personal income tax files, Medicare records, and social security records, raises the possibility of basing a coverage evaluation program on these administrative lists. Roughly speaking, one would match samples of these lists (various possibilities have been suggested for how this might be done) and then make use of dual-system estimation or some generalization to estimate the undercoverage of the census list (see Appendixes 4.1 and 4.2 for discussions of multiple list methods and the matching of administrative records). The major advantage of such an approach is that household-based coverage evaluation programs, such as the Post-Enumeration Program, are better designed to account for missed households rather than missed individuals in enumerated households. Quite possibly, a large number of these missed individuals are included on administrative lists.

The use of administrative records and multiple list methods as a major component of a decennial census coverage evaluation program on a national level has never been attempted in the United States. However, the Census Bureau has performed several tests on a national basis. The Census Bureau has also used administrative records in studies of gross omissions for limited populations. Examples of the former include the IRS/Census Direct Match Study (see Childers and Hogan, 1984a, and Chapter 5 below) and a three-way CPS/Census/IRS match study (see Hogan, 1984a). Examples of the latter include a study that matched Medicare records with census questionnaires (see Bureau of the Census, 1973d) and two studies that matched, respectively, social security beneficiaries and college students with census files (see Marks and Waksberg, 1966, and previous discussion above). None of the studies mentioned--except the as yet unreported CPS/Census/IRS match study--explored the difficulties of using more than one list besides the census list. Considering the differential undercoverage present in any one currently proposed list, such testing is highly desirable.

Assuming that at least two lists are to be used (along with the census list), there are two primary methods proposed that make use of multiple lists to estimate the rate of census omission. The first method, composite list formation, merges all but the census list into a super list or composite list. (Sampling is almost certainly used in the merging process due to the expense of matching two large files.) The composite list is then matched with the census file. The estimation of the rate of omission, arrived at by estimating the number of people not represented by either the composite list or the census, follows from the use of dual-system estimation, described above and in Appendix 4.1. The second technique, which we call the multilist method, proceeds by completely matching samples from every administrative list with each other and with the entire census list. This results in a multidimensional contingency table with the count in every cell determined by an individual's inclusion or omission by the various lists. The cell representing the number of individuals missed by every list must be estimated in order to estimate the omissions rate in the census. (These two methods, composite list and multilist, as well as a third, less often proposed method using covariate information for modeling within the contingency table, are discussed more fully in Appendix 4.1.)

Composite list and multilist methods each make certain assumptions. Failure of these assumptions would cast serious doubt on the reasonableness of the resulting estimates of omission rates. When using the composite list method or when completely matching all lists, it is necessary that:

(1) The lists are available for the entire United States;
(2) There exists an identifier, such as social security number, or a suitable number of common responses that permit matching;
(3) There is very low item nonresponse and misresponse for variables used in matching;
(4) The addresses on the various lists are the address of residence; and
(5) There are few false matches and few false nonmatches, and the treatment of unresolved matches through imputation of matching status is effective.[3]

In using the composite list method, it is also necessary that:

[3]We point out that it would be desirable to provide quantitative bounds instead of the qualitative expressions used. However, it is currently not possible to do so, due to the lack of research.

(1) The merged list have little differential undercount and
(2) Either the first-order independence assumption used in dual-system estimation nearly hold or the degree of dependence be well estimated.

In using the multilist method, it is also necessary that:

(1) The various lists be weighted so that no identifiable subpopulation is differentially underrepresented on any list and
(2) Either the higher-order independence assumption used nearly hold or the degree of dependence be well estimated.[4]

Investigation of the above requirements for a successful national coverage evaluation program based on the use of existing administrative lists would cause one to be less than optimistic for this application of administrative lists. However, current trends in our society toward increasing computerization, automation, editing, quality control, etc., are likely to increase the possibility of meeting many of the requirements. In addition, progress at the Census Bureau in areas such as automated list matching should benefit the use of administrative records for coverage evaluation. Therefore, it is likely that many of the above requirements may be within reach in the foreseeable future.

The New York City Match

Another test of composite list methods occurred in the lawsuit in which the City and State of New York sued the U.S. Department of Commerce for federal funds that they claim they were deprived of as a result of differential undercoverage. Briefly, the plaintiffs created a composite list, referred to as the "Megalist" (details provided below). At the request of the plaintiffs, the

---

[4]Especially when using a large number of lists, it is helpful (but not necessary) that the lists contain few people who are not supposed to be included in the census, such as people who died before Census Day.

court instructed the Census Bureau to determine the number of people on this list who were residents of New York City on Census Day, 1980, and who were not counted in the census. Once the number of people not included in the census was determined, the plaintiffs arrived at an independent estimate of the number of residents of New York City as of Census Day, 1980. Since the test deals only with New York City, it does not address the difficulties faced with a national application of the methods. However, it is currently the most-developed application of the use of composite list methods for coverage evaluation. (The following discussion is taken from Ericksen and Kadane, 1983.)

In this application of composite list methods, the court directed that the Census Bureau use the following 10 lists:

(1) Consolidated Edison electricity billpayers;
(2) Babies born immediately preceding Census Day;
(3) People who died immediately after Census Day;
(4) New York City public school children;
(5) Persons arraigned in city courts;
(6) Students enrolled at the City University of New York;
(7) Persons in "Medicaid Eligibility File";
(8) Licensed drivers;
(9) Registered voters; and
(10) Recipients of unemployment benefits.

Since there are a substantial number of people included more than once on the above lists, and since it is not possible to match more than a fraction of the population of New York City's residents, a sampling plan was necessary in forming the composite list in order to select the cases to be matched to the census, as well as a procedure that prevented duplicates from being represented in the composite list.

The formation of the composite list proceeded as follows. (See Kadane and Lehoczky, 1976, for a full discussion of the underlying methodology.) First, 8 percent of the enumeration districts in New York City were selected. Next, samples of each list were selected with sampling frequency proportional to the square root of the expected omission rate. Finally:

(1) The lists were numbered from 1 to 10;

(2) The sample from the first list was guaranteed inclusion in the final list;
(3) The sample from the second list was checked against the entire first list; and
(4) For the remaining lists, the samples were checked against all preceding lists, with duplicates removed.

The final combination of lists produced a sample of 16,500 persons, representing a total population of 6.2 million, a large proportion of the approximately 7-8 million residents of New York City. The Census Bureau was ordered to match this list with that of the census for New York City and determine the individuals who:

(1) Were included in the 1980 census;
(2) Were not living in New York on Census Day in 1980; and
(3) Composed the remainder of the list.

In performing the match, it was necessary to trace people included on the composite list to their current address was often necessary to determine to which of the above three categories each of the people belonged (details of the matching and tracing processes can be found in Bureau of the Census, 1982d).

Due to several circumstances, among them the difficulty of tracing people to current addresses, it was not always possible to determine whether an individual had been counted in the 1980 census. Of the 6.2 million cases represented, 5.17 million were located in New York City on Census Day. The remaining 1.03 million represented cases that could not be determined. Of those located in New York City, 4.75 million were determined to be counted in the census, and 0.42 million were determined to be missed by the 1980 census. Those persons missed represent 8 percent of the cases for which a match status could be clearly determined. Ericksen and Kadane believe a more reasonable estimate of the rate of omissions to be at least 10 percent due to the treatment of imputations and the likelihood of the undetermined cases to represent residents of New York City.

Many of the difficulties encountered by this test of an administrative records-based coverage evaluation program were specific to this application and are not due to the general methodology. For example, much of the difficulty in tracing people to current addresses was probably due to the 28-30 month separation between the taking of the census and the tracing operation. Ericksen and Kadane point out their uneasiness about estimates derived from data of which 15 percent is missing (not at random), and they call for methods for reducing and accommodating missing data in this context. To this end they mention a procedure to replace hot-deck imputation of match status for the undetermined cases that is closely related to fractional matching, discussed in Chapter 8. Ericksen and Kadane present various sources of evidence for the reasonableness of their estimates. Finally, they recommend that in future applications of this methodology a smaller number of lists be used.

CONSIDERATIONS FOR ASSESSING ALTERNATIVE COVERAGE EVALUATION METHODS

In assessing the merits of alternative methods of evaluating completeness of census coverage, a number of factors are involved: (1) the error profile for the method, that is, the sources of error for each method, the degree of error contributed by each source, and the likelihood that corrective measures can reduce error; (2) timeliness; (3) feasibility; (4) cost; (5) the extent to which a method meets the needs for coverage estimates, e.g., the provision of small-area estimates; and (6) the extent to which the various sources coincide to give a coherent picture.

Clearly, an error profile that projects optimistically toward substantial improvement in the future is a consideration in the choice of coverage evaluation programs. In considering adjustment based on coverage evaluation data, it is also important to consider the development of an error profile for the census as well so that the two can be compared.

Considerations of timing are important as well. A fast program is particularly desirable if coverage evaluation is to be the basis for an adjustment of the census counts. It is also helpful for census users to have evaluation results available when they are making most use of the census, i.e., in the first few years after the census. Beyond some thresholds, timing is partly a function of the staff resources and effort devoted to the coverage evaluation program. For example, although preliminary results from the 1950 Post-Enumeration Survey were not published until 1953 and final results not until 1960, the study results could undoubtedly have been made available sooner if there had been a perceived need, with the commitment of necessary resources. Micro-level coverage evaluation programs, however, have not been completed to date within a shorter time span than about a year and a half after the census. Preliminary demographic estimates for 1980 were released in mid-1981 and are still being revised on the basis of new data such as updated Medicare records.

Cost is also a consideration. Rough estimates of costs for the censuses conducted from 1950 to 1970 (Bureau of the Census, 1978b:App.A, Tables 1-3) suggest that evaluation programs of all kinds accounted for roughly 1.5 to 2 percent of total costs, with coverage evaluation programs making up perhaps about half the total devoted to evaluation. In 1980, the Post-Enumeration Program cost about $14 million, over 1 percent of the total. These percentages certainly do not appear high considering the need to have good information about the accuracy of the data. For 1990, the panel believes that increased resources should be devoted to coverage evaluation and other adjustment-related programs, in accord with our recommendation to pursue vigorously a program of research and development that could lead to the use of coverage evaluation results for adjustment of the counts (see Chapter 7). We have indicated ways in which cost savings could be achieved in other areas (see Chapters 5 and 6), so as not to increase total costs of taking the census.

It is also vital that coverage evaluation programs provide information at subnational levels of aggregation because of the concern about the equitable distribution of political power and monies. Finally, a way in which a coverage evaluation method can gain acceptance is for it to provide estimates that nearly coincide with estimates given by other coverage evaluation programs based on substantially different statistical models.

ERROR PROFILES FOR COVERAGE EVALUATION METHODS

An error profile of a survey is constructed by first creating a systematic and comprehensive list of the operations that lead to the survey results. The error profile is then a description of the potential sources of error for each operation, the information available about each, and their impact on the survey estimates of interest (Bailar, 1983a; Brooks and Bailar, 1978).

It is not a simple matter to make an exhaustive list of the operations of a complex survey. It is even less simple to make a list of the potential sources of error, particularly in the case of a new measurement approach or an adaptation from another field. However, it is often true that one can identify dominant sources of error--ones whose reduction would materially improve the reliability of final estimates (even if one cannot exactly quantify by how much). It is on these dominant error sources that one must concentrate resources available for improvements since, without reducing them, even major error reduction in other components would lead to only negligible improvements in the reliability of the final product. Chapter 8 makes several recommendations in this direction.

The preceding sections of Chapter 4 have provided an overview of the development of coverage evaluation methods during the past 40 years. The questions remain, what is the current state of knowledge as to the efficacy of the various methods, and what are the expectations for improvements in each of the various methods over the next few years? It is not possible to provide a direct answer to these questions, since research is still at an early stage for many of the techniques. However, by way of summary we present the various operations central to coverage evaluation and a sense of the magnitude of the problem faced in accomplishing each of the operations by the various techniques.

The operations central to coverage evaluation are:

Direct Estimates
- Developing the completeness of the coverage evaluation survey
- Obtaining complete response in survey and census
- Tracing
- Geocoding
- Matching
- Dual-system estimation--independence
- Evaluating the evaluation

Demographic Analysis
- Obtaining component data
  - --Undocumented aliens
  - --Completeness of birth registration
  - --Completeness of death registration

--Legal immigration and emigration
--Internal migration
• Evaluating the evaluation

We now address, in turn, each of these operations and discuss qualitatively the resulting impact that each operation would have on an error profile for the various coverage evaluation techniques.

Components of Direct Estimates Programs

Developing the Completeness of the Coverage Evaluation Survey

Incompleteness of coverage results from the fact that no list, whether based on surveys, administrative records, or a combination, includes the proper representation of the target population--in the present case every resident of the United States. Some groups have a history of being significantly missed in post-enumeration surveys, for example, undocumented aliens. People in urban areas with very low socioeconomic status are missed by post-enumeration surveys and censuses (Valentine and Valentine, 1971). Although reverse record checks omit some of the persons missed in the previous census, undercoverage is probably not as severe with this method as with post-enumeration surveys. However, the problems reverse record checks have in counting undocumented aliens are probably as serious as those of post-enumeration surveys. Administrative list methods may have still less of a problem of undercoverage (although other problems exist, including the fact that gaps in coverage cannot be quantified in terms of age-sex-race groups or other census characteristics).

Obtaining Complete Response in Survey and Census

Incompleteness of response results from the inability to obtain survey forms from some individuals or households on the master address register or from the inability to collect answers to specific questions: for example, unreported or incomplete address was a major cause of unresolved matches in the 1980 PEP (see Cowan and Bettin, 1982). Of the 8.5 percent unresolved matches in the April P sample, over 60 percent were due either to CPS nonresponse or to failure to complete a follow-up interview. For reverse record checks, nonresponse is less serious per se. However, the inability to trace a fraction of the selected population has an effect that is completely analogous to nonresponse. Nonresponse will clearly affect any matching involved in methods based on administrative lists.

Tracing

Tracing is the process of searching, used in the reverse record check, for a present residence address, given information about a residence some time in the past. As mentioned earlier, roughly 12 percent of the sample in the 1960 test of a reverse record check in the United States could not be traced successfully. The use of more intensive tracing methods, as tested in the Forward Trace Study (see Chapter 8), may reduce the rate of failure to trace. (In Chapter 8 we mention that intensive tracing may increase the sensitization of the population.) Recent use of the reverse record check in Canada has been accomplished with a fairly consistent tracing failure rate of 5 percent. Canada has the advantage, compared with the United States, that addresses used for tracing are at most five years out of date. The tracing failure in 1960 in the United States was somewhat higher than the PEP unresolved match rate in 1980; the Canadian tracing failure rate is lower than the 1980 PEP unresolved match rate. Post-enumeration surveys and administrative record techniques do not make use of tracing in estimating the undercount.

Geocoding

Geocoding is the determination of census geography, i.e., census enumeration district, for the address of a record included in the evaluation program. Relative to nonresponse, geocoding does not appear to be a major problem for the PEP. In 1980, incomplete or impossible geocodings, when the address was complete, were responsible for only a small part of the unresolved matches. However, geocoding (more generally geographic errors) affected PEP errors in a more subtle manner: by increasing the apparent *gross* overenumeration and underenumeration levels and thus putting a greater strain on the complex estimation method, cancelling out large offsetting errors. In 1990, the Census Bureau is planning not to use geocoding as a preliminary step prior to matching, but rather to use the address as an alphanumeric string that can be matched directly (see Jaro, 1985). The reverse record check does not depend on a refined level of geocoding. Matching administrative lists to the census depends on geocoding to the same extent as a post-enumeration survey.

Matching

Matching is statistical-based inference as to when information for two records on one or two lists does or does not represent information for the same individual. Matching problems, given complete information, were the cause of only a small percentage of the unresolved matches in the 1980 PEP. For reverse record checks, matching is not intrinsically required to estimate net undercoverage. However, matching is used in the preliminary efforts at tracing. Multiple and composite list techniques are, of course, exceedingly dependent on matching. Matching administrative lists, particularly local lists, is especially troublesome as the number of lists increases, due not only to the increased computation but also to the likely incompatibility of many of the reporting and coding practices for these lists.

Dual-System Estimation: Independence and Equal Capture Probabilities

The problems with the assumption of independence for the inclusion of people in the census and the evaluation study list and the assumption of equal capture probabilities are related to undercoverage problems discussed above. The estimation of undercoverage when using dual-system estimation is believed to be quite sensitive to these assumptions. Information on nonindependence for certain demographic groups (see Kadane and Ericksen, 1985) has indicated the possibility that the undercoverage rates may be higher than those estimated assuming independence (see Chapter 8). Administrative lists have the same sensitivity to the failure of these two assumptions. Reverse record checks do not use dual-system estimation to provide estimates of undercoverage, since the underlying assumption is that the frame used for the reverse record check sample is essentially complete.

Balancing of Overcount and Undercount

The difficulty of balancing over- and undercount, faced by post-enumeration programs that do not sample compact area clusters such as city blocks, has as yet an unknown impact on coverage estimates. The difficulty arises because two different survey vehicles (the P and the E samples in the 1980 PEP) must exactly balance with respect to their estimates (confounded with other estimates) of the number of census enumerations assigned to the wrong geographic area. Since net undercount is estimated as a residual by subtracting the E sample estimates from the P sample estimates, and since both are substantially higher than the net undercount, the latter may be significantly affected by the supposedly offsetting errors not balancing one another. The reverse record check is not subject to this source of error.

Components of Demographic Analysis

Obtaining Data for Undocumented Aliens

This component was clearly the most difficult one for demographic analysis in the 1980 census. Since uncertainty in the number of undocumented aliens in the United States is at least a million or so either way, a major improvement in the precision of the measures of this component of the population is necessary before demographic analysis can be comfortably used in the future.

Completeness of Birth Registration

As time passes, an ever-increasing proportion of the population has been born in the period during which birth registration has been essentially complete. For the 1990 census, reliable information on births will be available for most residents 55 or younger, nearly 80 percent of all residents. Since those age 65 and over will be covered by Medicare information, a fairly small group will remain with less reliable sources of registration. Furthermore, the development of models of the completeness of birth registration is proceeding. This is not a component in need of great attention.

Completeness of Death Registration

Death registration is virtually complete and a very minor contribution to the error in demographic analysis.

Legal Immigration and Emigration

Data on immigration are subject to problems. However, the most problematic component is emigration, for which there is as yet no direct estimate. Relative to other components, legal migration is probably subject to greater error than birth and death records, but to less error than undocumented immigration. An interesting by-product of the reverse record check is the possibility of a direct estimate of emigration.

Internal Migration

Censuses have obtained data on interstate mobility, but their quality is generally considered inadequate for use in coverage estimates. This precludes the use of these data for the development of subnational estimates of undercoverage.

Evaluating the Evaluation

To better determine where the difficulties lie in the application of coverage evaluation programs, especially demographic analysis, there is a need to develop estimates of variability of the estimates of undercoverage. Sensitivity analyses should also be carried out to determine the effect of various assumptions, input data quality, etc., with respect to the resulting estimates. This topic is discussed further in Chapter 7.

When one is considering the major sources of error in coverage evaluation programs, it is necessary to compare the results with an investigation of the errors present in the census. Coverage evaluation programs are attempts to measure errors of the census, and their results are used by the Census Bureau to understand the errors so that action can be taken to make improvements. Chapter 5 presents information gathered from the various methods used to evaluate the coverage of the decennial censuses on differential rates of undercount and overcount among groups in the population.

APPENDIX 4.1

AN INTRODUCTION TO ESTIMATION FROM MULTIPLE LISTS

INTRODUCTION

Government administration generates large lists maintained for various purposes. Examples include social security registration lists, Medicare eligibility lists, and the Internal Revenue Service individual income tax return files. Local governmental bodies have other files, e.g., school enrollment lists, lists of driver's licenses, and voter registration lists. These are referred to as administrative records, which have been put forth as having potential for improving the decennial census.

Although other applications have been suggested (see Alvey and Scheuren, 1982), this appendix deals with using administrative records, or multiple lists, as part of an estimation process to help determine the "true" population count. The estimated count can then be used for coverage evaluation and also, of course, for adjustment, as suggested by Ericksen and Kadane (1985). Estimation from multiple lists is performed through the use of list matching, i.e., the determination of when information for two individuals on the same or different lists is in fact information for the same individual. Appendix 4.2 discusses the operational techniques involved in list matching. This appendix is mainly concerned with the statistical estimation models used in conjunction with list matching, their definition, purpose, and advantages and disadvantages.

An important advantage in using an administrative record match for coverage evaluation is that it does not rely on a household survey or a previous census. As indicated earlier, surveys tend to miss many of the same people as censuses. A second advantage is the possibility of focusing more sharply on the kinds of people most likely to be missed, by including such lists as AFDC recipients, or those collecting unemployment insurance.

For the purposes of this discussion, it is convenient to assume that the matching has been carried out perfectly, that is, every list contains only correct information for its members, especially the address, every list in use has been unduplicated correctly, every list has been purged of erroneous enumerations, there are no false matches, and there are no false nonmatches.

TABLE 4.4 Two-Way Table Underlying Simple Dual-System Estimation

	Caught in the Other List	Missed in the Other List	Population Total
Caught in the census	n_{11}	n_{10}	n_{1+}
Missed in the census	n_{01}	n_{00}	n_{0+}
Population total	n_{+1}	n_{+0}	n_{++}

DUAL-SYSTEM ESTIMATION

The basic model used in estimating the total population from two incomplete lists is called dual-system estimation. (As Chapter 4 details, in other contexts it is referred to as capture-recapture estimation.) The process may be stated as follows. Assume that one has two lists of a population, one from the census, and it matters little if the other list is a sample from a (possibly theoretical) parent list. Given that one has observed the total number of individuals on each list, and the number of individuals jointly on the two lists by matching, how can the remaining members of the population be estimated? These quantities lead to four elements of a two-by-two contingency table, given in Table 4.4. The resulting question is how one estimates the size of the n_{00} cell. (For purposes of this discussion, the important assumption of equal probabilities on the two lists (or more) will be used. Its impact on the estimate is discussed above briefly in Chapter 4.)

In order to estimate the size of the n_{00} cell, or equivalently the n_{++} cell, it is necessary to assume a model relating the entries of the cells. An assumption that is commonly made is that the mechanisms for inclusion in the two lists operate independently, that is, that inclusion in the census given inclusion in the other list is equal to the probability of inclusion in the census, and that this probability is the same for everyone. It follows that:

$$n_{11}/n_{+1} = n_{1+}/n_{++} \qquad (4.1)$$

or equivalently:

$$n_{11}/n_{01} = n_{10}/n_{00}.$$

Therefore, an obvious estimate of n_{++} is $(n_{+1})(n_{1+})/n_{11}$.

More generally we can parametrically specify the relationship between the two ratios in equation 4.1:

$$n_{11}/n_{+1} = k'(n_{1+}/n_{++}) \qquad (4.2)$$

or equivalently:

$$n_{11}/n_{01} = k(n_{10}/n_{00}).$$

In this formulation, it is first necessary to estimate k' or k, in order to calculate n_{++} or n_{00}. When k, sometimes referred to as the cross-product ratio, is determined or believed not to equal 1, the mechanism for inclusion in the two lists is said to have "correlation bias." We discuss correlation bias and the parameter k more fully in Chapter 8.

Many modelers have assumed that k equals 1, i.e., independence of the two processes, although the validity of that assumption is usually uncertain. One method of increasing the intuitive strength of the independence assumption is to stratify the population of one of the lists and to use dual-system estimation separately on each subpopulation. This can be a powerful tool for lessening the impact of dependence (see Marks et al., 1977). However, stratification assumes that one understands the mechanism for being missed on each list and knows what modes of stratification are appropriate.

OTHER ESTIMATION APPROACHES

There are a number of alternative methods of estimation. One approach is to obtain and then merge several lists, then match the resulting composite list to the census. One would then use dual-system estimation on the resulting two-by-two table, assuming that k equaled 1 for this two-by-two table. The merged list is likely to be both more complete and more representative of the population than any of the individual lists, and the values of n_{10} and n_{00} will be smaller. (By representative we mean that no identifiable population, e.g., demographic group or persons residing in a specific region of the country, is missed relatively more often by the composite list than any other identifiable population.)

One can effectively merge a sample of the noncensus lists by sequentially matching them and then matching the merged list with the census. Kadane and Lehoczky (1976)

TABLE 4.5 Multiple List Quantities for the Case of Two Lists and a Census: Three-Way Contingency Table

	Included in Census	Missed in Census		
Included in second sample	n_{111}	n_{011}	n_{+11}	Included in first sample
Missed in second sample	n_{110}	n_{010}	n_{+10}	
Total	n_{11+}	n_{01+}	n_{+1+}	
Included in second sample	n_{101}	n_{001}	n_{+01}	Missed in first sample
Missed in second sample	n_{100}	n_{000}	n_{+00}	
Total	n_{10+}	n_{00+}	n_{+0+}	
Included in second sample	n_{1+1}	n_{0+1}	n_{++1}	Total
Missed in second sample	n_{1+0}	n_{0+0}	n_{++0}	
Total	n_{1++}	n_{0++}	n_{+++}	

NOTE: In this table, each subscript indicates inclusion (1) or exclusion (0) in each of three lists, representing two lists and the census.

present an efficient method for ordering the lists to be sequentially matched. Ericksen and Kadane (1983) applied this technique to prepare their estimate of the proportion of New York City's population that was undercounted in 1980.

Another approach, which we call multilist, is to match completely all the pairs of lists, including the census. If there are j noncensus lists, this requires $(j+1)j/2$ total matches. If one is willing and has the resources to perform all these matches, then one has many estimates of the number of people missed by all the lists from which to choose. The resulting mathematical structure is a 2^{j+1} contingency table (see Table 4.5 for the notation for three lists).

Some estimates of n_{000} are (see Marks et al., 1977):

$$
\begin{aligned}
&(n_{100})(n_{010})/n_{110}, \text{ or } (n_{100})(n_{001})/n_{101}, \text{ or} \\
&(n_{010})(n_{001})/n_{011}, \text{ or } (n_{110})(n_{001})/n_{111}, \text{ or} \\
&(n_{101})(n_{010})/n_{111}, \text{ or } (n_{011})(n_{100})/n_{111}, \text{ or} \\
&(n_{01+})(n_{10+})/n_{11+}, \text{ or } (n_{0+1})(n_{1+0})/n_{1+1}, \text{ or} \\
&(n_{+01})(n_{+10})/n_{+11}
\end{aligned} \tag{4.3}
$$

and various combinations of these nine estimates. The use of the first six of these estimates individually implies something about a parameter similar to the k and k' above being set equal to 1, but these new parameters relate to conditional independence assumptions. It is sometimes believed that these assumptions are more realistic or less sensitive to failure than the unconditional assumptions made with only two lists. Furthermore, by examining other complete subtables, that is, subtables not involving the missing cell n_{000}, various independence and dependence assumptions about the incomplete subtables can be checked, in a weak sense. The last three estimates given in equation 4.3 relate to marginal tables that are equivalent to the pre-merging of two of the three lists. At any rate, if n_{000} is smaller than n_{00} would be, this alone would make the estimation of n_{+++} less sensitive to assumptions.

A third approach, offered by Cormack (1981) and Pollock et al. (1984), is to use covariate information in modeling the probability of an individual's capture in each list. In these papers, the usual log-linear parameterization of the 2^{j+1} contingency table resulting from the complete j-way match is replaced by a parameterization relating, for example, the probability of being captured in the ith list given that the individual was captured in the (i-1)st list. This gives one a different interpretation of the missing cell, whose entry is now a function of the parameters estimated from the nonmissing portions of the table.

There is finally a need in any discussion of multiple list estimation methods to point out the hazards of multiple list matching. The grave disadvantage of multiple list matching is that successful matching assumes a level of administrative sophistication that is unlikely to be the case in practice. Although in theory it seems easy to match individuals between lists, in practice it is far from easy to avoid false matches, false nonmatches, and ambiguous matches that may have a substantial impact on results. All administrative lists contain errors resulting from intentional misreporting, unintentional misreporting, or data entry imperfections; furthermore, records in administrative lists have differing reference dates, and revision practices will vary between lists and between individuals within lists. The inability of the 1980 PEP to match more than 92 percent of individuals between the 1980 census and the April 1980 CPS despite almost exactly equivalent reference dates and extensive follow-up investigations is illustrative of the problems involved. These problems are likely to be even more severe with the use of administrative lists maintained for other purposes with different record-keeping priorities. Some of these issues are discussed in Appendix 4.2.

APPENDIX 4.2

OPERATIONAL ASPECTS AND MODELING OF COMPUTER MATCHING

This appendix describes the physical operations and statistical models underlying the process of matching two lists (or unduplicating one file). The statistical models discussed relate to a different issue from the one addressed in Appendix 4.1 when the models are to be used after the matching has been completed. The models discussed here provide one with an objective means of deciding which records to link as well as estimates of the resulting error rates. A good overview of the subject of matching is presented in Federal Committee on Statistical Methodology (1980).

OPERATIONAL DIFFICULTIES OF MATCHING

Before proceeding, in order to appreciate the overall cost structure of matching, it is helpful to understand the social and operational obstacles to the use of administrative records in list matching. A major concern is the public reaction to any possible encroachment on the confidentiality and privacy of their individual records. In the interests of satisfying respondent concerns over the privacy of the census questionnaires, neither names nor addresses of respondents, except for a small sample of households involved in a few components of the coverage evaluation program, were recorded in machine-readable form in the 1980 decennial census. Thus, in 1980, the Census Bureau was able to assert to uneasy respondents that its files could not be used for large-scale government record linkage. In 1990, the current plans of the Census Bureau are to capture in machine-readable form both name and address for input into a computer matching algorithm. However, the potential for actual invasion of privacy is not very great in coverage evaluation programs, since the number of persons involved is such a small percentage of the total population.

Operationally, there are serious problems in list matching administrative records. First, the quality of the information on many lists is not good. There are duplications, erroneous entries, and missing data. For example, the addresses on social security files, except for beneficiaries, are not current. In addition, the more lists that are merged, the higher the chance of significant undetectable duplication on the merged list--which, when matched against the census, will inflate the estimated undercount.

Many lists, for example the census itself, do not have an identification number, such as the social security number, to facilitate matching. Without such an identification number, matching must make use of such items as name, address, age (possibly birth date), sex, and race. Unfortunately, addresses in administrative records are frequently not the residence address required for a census match but a mailing address or an obsolete address. Finally, the combination of the above complications usually results in a large percentage of cases for which match status cannot be resolved. The treatment of these unresolved cases can have a substantial impact on the resulting undercoverage estimates.

GENERAL ALGORITHM OF MATCHING

The general algorithm underlying matching is based on the similarity of the information for two individuals under comparison in two files. Every record from one of the two files is assigned a 0 or a 1, denoting, say, unmatched or matched. (Later on, we will see that there is an important third class that is assigned a "do not know" status.) Thus, two candidates for matching are identified. If their characteristics, for example, name, address, sex, age, race, and birth date, are the same, or close, the algorithm will assign them a "1" for match status. In the absence of a single error-free identification number, the more discriminating the matching characteristics (e.g., birth date as opposed to sex), the fewer the false matches; and the more error-free the characteristics, the fewer the false nonmatches. The key to matching well is weighting the similarity or dissimilarity of the characteristics information so that few individuals are misclassified.

BLOCKING

Matching, when one of the lists is as extensive as the decennial census, and even for considerably smaller lists, cannot possibly be done by searching the entire large file for each record on the other list. Therefore, the search is limited to a likely subset of the census file. To define this subset, one or more characteristics are chosen, then equivalence classes or blocks of responses for these characteristics are identified, which have the property that when two records are located in different blocks, the likelihood of a match is considered to be quite small. When such a variable, or variables, are found, the large file (the decennial census file) is restructured so that only those records that are located in the same block are checked for possible matches. Blocking necessarily involves a trade-off: incurring some number of false nonmatches in order to reduce costs by a significant margin.

The question of how to block effectively has a statistical framework initially articulated by Fellegi and Sunter (1969). Kelley (1984b) has also investigated this issue.

In 1980, in the Post-Enumeration Program, the blocking used was geographic. Possible matches were searched for only in the same enumeration district as that of the address of the Current Population Survey interviewee. This was necessary due to the limitations of a clerical match. However, the Census Bureau is developing and testing sophisticated software to reduce, possibly to under 40 percent, the percentage of the matching that will need to be handled clerically in 1990. This automation of the matching process should also allow less restrictive blocking to be used.

VARIABLE SELECTION

The selection of identifying variables available in both files can be an important aspect of matching algorithms. However, in the particular case of the coverage evaluation programs for the decennial census, variable selection is more or less predetermined. This is because matching requires the use of short-form information only, such as name, address, age, sex, and race. There are not a great many more variables on the short form to choose from that would help determine match status. When one has more latitude, variable selection is driven by two considerations, as mentioned above: (1) the quality of the response for that variable and (2) the discriminating power of the variable.

A MATHEMATICAL MODEL FOR RECORD LINKAGE

Fellegi and Sunter (1969) developed a mathematical model for matching, or record linkage, which the Census Bureau is using in its software system for automated matching. A brief description follows.

First, assume that one wishes to match files A and B. The ordered pairs of these two files, A X B, is the disjoint union of two sets:

$M = [(a,b);\ a=b,\ a\varepsilon A,\ b\varepsilon B]$ (the truly matched set)
and $U = [(a,b);\ a\neq b,\ a\varepsilon A,\ b\varepsilon B]$ (the truly unmatched set).

In order to determine the match status of any two records, it is necessary to compare their set of characteristics. To do this, a comparison vector is created, which is a vector function of the records, x(a) and x(b), more precisely, of the common identification information contained in the records. This comparison vector is written:

$$g[x(a),x(b)] = \{\ g^1[x(a),x(b)],\ldots,g^k[x(a),x(b)]\ \}.$$

Typically, $g^i[x(a),x(b)]$ is the coded result of the nature of agreement or disagreement between the ith identifying variable (e.g., age) of the two records. All matching inferences about the records (a,b) are made on the basis of the vector g, which codifies the pattern and nature of agreement and disagreement between the pair of records a and b. Three possible decisions can be made based on an examination of the vector function g: (1) decide to link a and b, (2) decide not to link a and b, or (3) choose not to make a decision. This decision rule, which we will denote as d(g), is a function of the comparison vector.

Now, given that one is taking a set of random pairs from A X B, one must consider the likelihood of observing the comparison vector g given, respectively, that the pair (a,b) came from M or came from U. These are written:

$$m(g) = P\{\ g[x(a),x(b)] \mid (a,b)\ \varepsilon\ M\}$$

and

$$u(g) = P\{\ g[x(a),x(b)] \mid (a,b)\ \varepsilon\ U\}\ .$$

The two types of errors associated with a linkage rule are: (1) deciding to link unmatched individuals and (2) deciding not to link matched individuals. Setting these two errors respectively to e_1 and e_2, Fellegi and Sunter defined a decision rule d(g) as optimal if, given all rules that have errors of type 1 less than or equal to e_1, and type 2 less than or equal to e_2 as above, the probability of making no decision is smallest.

The above problem was shown by Fellegi and Sunter to yield an optimal decision rule, which, roughly, decides to link all the cases in which the ratio m(g)/u(g) is high and not to link all the cases in which m(g)/u(g) is low. This is equivalent to a likelihood ratio test. The two threshold levels (above which to link and below which not to link) are determined to yield the two types of error, e_1 and e_2, at prespecified levels.

The difficulty that remains is that of estimating m(g) and u(g). Fellegi and Sunter provide two methods for accomplishing this. One might have prior knowledge from other studies of the errors to which variables involved in linkage are subject. The errors might also be estimated on the basis of comparing a small sample of records that are known to match and observing the lack of agreement in the identifying variables (see Arellano et al., 1984). Iterative procedures are also conceivable in which initial match status is determined, which then provides more refined estimates of m(g) and u(g). Finally, we note that records that cannot be matched at the level of predetermined error rates e_1 and e_2 have to be followed-up--either through clerical matching or by obtaining additional identifying information for them.

5
Taking the Census I: Improving the Count

The charge to the Panel on Decennial Census Methodology called for investigation of methods of conducting the decennial census that could prove more cost-effective than the methodology used in 1980. The 1980 methodology, as described in Chapter 3, included numerous programs designed to improve coverage in hard-to-count areas and of hard-to-count populations and stipulated that all follow-up and coverage improvement operations be carried out as completely as possible. The panel was asked to consider possible alternative methodologies, for example, a methodology that would incorporate adjustment for coverage and content errors. Adjustment, if appropriate methods can be developed and implemented, might not only increase accuracy but also lessen costs by leading to a decision to give somewhat less emphasis to coverage improvement programs during the conduct of the census. Similarly, the panel was asked to consider the uses of sampling for the count and of administrative records as means of reducing costs compared with the 1980 methodology.

Most programs directed toward coverage improvement are expensive, both in absolute terms and often in terms of the cost per person or housing unit identified and added to the census. Moreover, some coverage improvement programs as well as other census procedures may have introduced some overcounts in 1980 by duplicating persons or otherwise erroneously adding persons. In general, however, the panel believes that the costs of well-designed and well-executed coverage improvement programs represent money well spent for improving the count. The panel, from the beginning of its work, identified as a key issue that of reviewing coverage improvement methods with the purpose of identifying particularly promising approaches that should be part of the methodology for conducting the enumeration.

This chapter begins by summarizing the literature on what is known about the characteristics of hard-to-count areas and groups in the population to provide the necessary background for evaluating the cost-effectiveness of coverage improvement programs. The section also summarizes what is known about the problem of overcounting. (Appendix 5.1 provides a more detailed review of the literature on undercounting and overcounting.)

The chapter then reviews the history of efforts directed specifically toward coverage improvement in both the 1970 and 1980 censuses and the Census Bureau's plans for testing coverage improvement methods for 1990. Finally, the chapter presents the panel's recommendations for priority areas for research and testing with regard to coverage improvement.

HARD-TO-COUNT GROUPS IN THE CENSUS: WHAT IS KNOWN

Experience in 1980

Evaluation studies of the completeness and accuracy achieved in the 1980 census are still in progress. Estimates published to date, based on the method of demographic analysis, show the rate of net undercount for the total population in the range of 0.5 to 1.4 percent, depending on the estimate of the number of resident undocumented aliens in the country (see Table 5.1). The highest net undercount rate estimated by demographic analysis for 1980 (1.4 percent) is about three-fifths of the rate estimated for 1970 (2.2 percent) and only two-fifths of the 1950 rate (3.3 percent). The differential rate of undercoverage between the black population and all others has narrowed somewhat for the nation as a whole, as the table shows. The differential in 1980 of 5.5 percentage points between net undercount rates for blacks and all other legal residents is about three-fourths of the 1950 differential of 7.2 percentage points. However, the 1980 differential is over 90 percent of the 1960 and 1970 differentials of about 6 percentage points, and most of the gain achieved by 1980 in narrowing the differential resulted from better coverage of black women and not black men.

Rates of gross and net undercount in 1980 varied by population group and by geographic area, with rates

TABLE 5.1 Net Undercount Rates by Race and Sex From Demographic Analysis, 1950 to 1980 Decennial Censuses (estimated population minus census population as a percentage of estimated population)

Population Category	1950	1960	1970	1980
Total population	3.3	2.7	2.2	0.5-1.4[a]
Male	3.8	3.3	3.1	N.A.
Female	2.8	2.2	1.4	N.A.
Legally resident population	N.A.	N.A.	N.A.	0.5
Male	N.A.	N.A.	N.A.	1.5
Female	N.A.	N.A.	N.A.	−0.4
Black population	9.7[b]	8.0	7.6	5.3
Male	11.2	9.7	10.1	8.0
Female	8.2	6.3	5.3	2.7
White and other races population	2.5[c]	2.1	1.5	−0.2
Male	2.8	2.5	2.1	0.6
Female	2.1	1.7	0.9	−0.9

NOTE: A minus sign indicates net overcount.

N.A. = not available; difference between total and legally resident population probably negligible (except for 1980).

[a] Lower percentage assumes presence of 2 million undocumented aliens in the estimated population; upper percentage assumes presence of 4 million undocumented aliens. The census population used in calculating the total population rates is the actual count, including an estimated 2 million undocumented aliens that were counted.

[b] Blacks and other nonwhites.

[c] Whites only.

SOURCES: For 1950: Siegel (1974:Table 3). For 1960: Siegel (1974:Table 2, Set D estimates). For 1970: Passel et al. (1982:Table 1, column labeled "modified census count"). For 1980: For total population rates shown, Passel et al. (1982:Table 2, assumptions 2 and 4); for all other rates, Passel and Robinson (1984:Table 2). All 1980 rates shown, except for total population, include only legal residents in both the estimated and the census populations.

considerably higher for certain groups than for the population as a whole. The 1980 census experienced overcount as well, and rates of erroneous enumerations also differed to some extent among groups in the population. In addition to demographic analysis, studies that shed light on the kinds of persons who were more poorly counted in 1980 include the Post-Enumeration Program and the IRS-Census Match.

Demographic Analysis

Demographic analysis provides independent estimates of the national population by age, race, and sex that, when compared with the census counts for these categories,

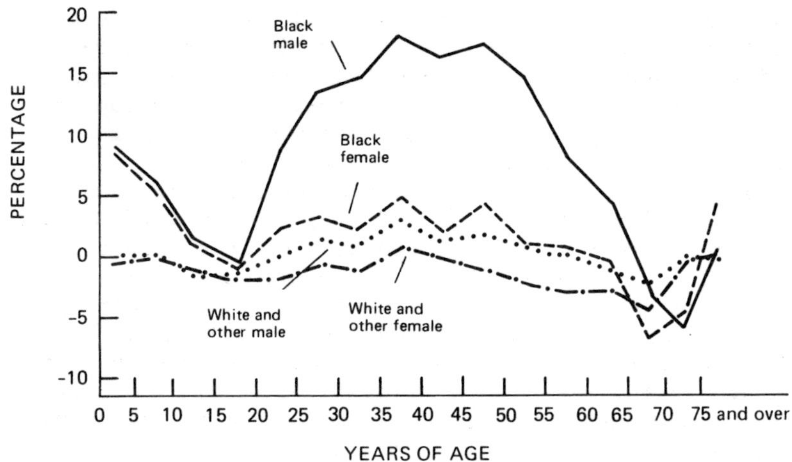

FIGURE 5.1 Percentage net undercount rates by age, race, and sex: 1980 census (legally resident population, determined from demographic analysis).

result in estimates of net undercount. (See Chapter 4 for a description of the methodology, which is based on birth and death records and estimates of net immigration.) For 1980, the presence of a significant but unknown number of undocumented aliens for whom immigration data do not exist complicated the analysis. Preliminary results are available and work is in progress on refining these results. A report on that effort indicates that the preliminary findings will not be altered to any significant degree (Passel and Robinson, 1984).

The net undercount rates for 1980 derived to date by demographic analysis are graphed in Figure 5.1. All points shown are based on estimates of the legally resident population only. Clearly, blacks were more poorly counted than the remainder of the population and men more poorly counted than women. Black men ages 25-54 experienced the highest rates of net undercount, followed by black men ages 20-24 and ages 55-59. Black children of both sexes under age 10 also experienced high rates of net undercount. According to this set of estimates, non-black women experienced small net overcounts in almost every age group. Black men and women ages 65-74 also showed net overcounts.

Data are not shown for undocumented aliens. Warren and Passel (1983) estimated that the 1980 census successfully counted 2.1 million undocumented aliens, and their estimates for age-race-sex groups were subtracted from the census population totals to obtain the net undercount estimates graphed in Figure 5.1. Hill, in a review of recent work on estimating the stock of undocumented aliens (Levine et al., 1985:App.B), concludes that the number of illegal aliens counted in the census can reasonably be estimated in the range from 1 to 2.5 million. He also states that (p. 243), "though no range can be soundly defended, a population of 1.5 to 3.5 million illegal aliens appears reasonably consistent with most of the studies." No firm conclusions are possible about the net undercount among undocumented aliens, given the broad range of estimates both of the total illegal alien population and of those illegal aliens recorded in the census.

Demographic analysis does not provide coverage estimates either for population groups other than the basic age-race-sex categories or for subnational geographic areas. Moreover, demographic analysis does not permit further analysis of net coverage rates in terms of gross undercount and gross overcount. Finally, net undercount rates from demographic analysis for specific age-race-sex subgroups reflect reporting errors, such as age overstatement or understatement, as well as coverage errors per se.

The Post-Enumeration Program

The Post-Enumeration Program (PEP) matched interview records from the April and August Current Population Surveys to 1980 census records to measure underenumeration in the census and rechecked a sample of census records to detect erroneous enumerations. The PEP is a source of information about differential rates of net and gross coverage errors among groups in the population. (See Chapter 4 for a description of the PEP and of the estimates of net undercoverage produced from it.)

To assess the inequity among geographic areas and population subgroups resulting from differential coverage in the census, one must ultimately look at net undercoverage rates. But to identify groups in the population that, for one reason or another, are particularly hard to count and, conversely, groups that are more likely to be overcounted, it is the gross omission and gross overenumeration rates that one needs to examine. Preliminary findings on gross error rates from exploratory analysis of the PEP data at the Census Bureau are summarized below and more fully reviewed in Appendix 5.1. The results presented are largely from the PEP 3-8 series of estimates, which was the first series to be put into a computerized form suitable for this kind of analysis. Examination of gross error rates from several other PEP series of estimates generally confirms the picture shown by the 3-8 series regarding the population groups that were relatively harder to count in 1980 (see Appendix 5.1).

The PEP 3-8 series estimated an overall rate of gross omissions (that is, persons in the Current Population Survey for whom corresponding records were not found in the census) of 5.4 percent, and an overall rate of gross overenumerations of 3.6 percent. (The reader should note that both the gross omission and gross overenumeration rates are overestimates and cannot be subtracted to give an estimate of the net undercount, which was estimated to be 0.8 percent in the 3-8 series--see Appendix 5.1 for explanation.) Given the problems the PEP program encountered in implementation and the resulting uncertainty attached to the estimates, and given the exploratory nature of the analysis that was conducted of gross error rates, we assigned gross omission and gross overenumeration rates for population subgroups to broad categories prior to making comparisons.

With regard to gross omissions, the PEP results indicate the following patterns:

(1) Categorizing the population by ethnicity (race and Hispanic origin), the gross omission rates for blacks, Puerto Ricans, and "other" Hispanics (those not classified as Cuban, Mexican, or Puerto Rican) were over twice the average rate.

(2) Categorizing the population by household relationship, gross omission rates for persons not related to the head of household and for relatives other than parent, child, or spouse were over twice the average rate. In contrast, spouses had a below-average rate of gross omissions.

(3) In contrast to the findings by race and household relationship, the PEP did not estimate large differences in rates of gross omissions between men and women or among age groups. Similarly, large differences were not evident by region of the country or type of area, although central

cities of large standard metropolitan statistical areas (SMSAs with 3 million or more population) had a moderately high gross omission rate compared with the average. Areas enumerated using conventional techniques rather than a mailout-mailback approach had a below-average rate.

(4) Cross-classifying ethnicity and type of place by the mail nonreturn rate for the district office (that is, 100 percent minus the percentage rate at which questionnaires were mailed back from households) produced striking differences in gross omission rates. Blacks and Hispanics in district offices with mail nonreturn rates of 30 percent or higher exhibited gross omission rates more than three times the average, while the gross omission rate for blacks in district offices with mail nonreturn rates of under 15 percent was only moderately above the average rate and the gross omission rate for the corresponding group of Hispanics was close to the average. Similarly central cities of both large and small SMSAs with mail nonreturn rates of 35 percent or higher had gross omission rates more than three times the average, while those cities with mail nonreturn rates below 10 percent had below-average rates.

Mail nonreturn rate appears to be a good indicator of gross omissions. Of course, the mail nonreturn rate is a symptom and not a cause of various problems pertaining to an area that result in higher-than-average rates of omissions (including not only the unwillingness of persons to be counted but also problems related to census procedures such as difficulty in delivering mail to individual households in some multiunit structures). Nevertheless, the mail nonreturn rate appears to provide valuable information to locate geographic areas in which coverage is particularly difficult. Further research on the characteristics of areas with high mail nonreturn rates that could assist development of effective coverage improvement techniques is hampered by the small sample sizes in the PEP for these areas. Moreover, at present, information on socioeconomic characteristics of the nonmatched PEP cases--for example, income and occupation--that might be useful to examine along with demographic and geographic characteristics is not in a ready form for analysis at the Census Bureau. (Fellegi, 1980a, provides estimates by a broad range of characteristics for persons missed in the 1976 census in Canada, as estimated by the reverse record check methodology.)

As already noted, the whole story regarding coverage problems in the census does not emerge solely by looking at gross omissions. In every census, some persons and housing units are counted more than once or are otherwise erroneously included (for example, via "curbstoning" or counting as an occupied unit one that was actually vacant on Census Day). The phenomenon of overenumeration may have more to do with census procedures, for example, quality control of the address list, than with the propensities of persons to be counted; nevertheless, it is necessary to examine gross overnumerations as well as omissions to obtain a complete picture.

With regard to gross overenumerations, the PEP results indicate the following patterns:

(1) Population groups with relatively high gross omission rates also tended to have relatively high rates of gross overenumerations. However, the dispersion in gross overenumeration rates was less than the dispersion in gross omission rates.

(2) By ethnicity categories, blacks, most Hispanics, and members of other nonwhite races had gross overenumeration rates moderately above the average. By household relationship, persons not related to the household head and relatives other than parent, child, or spouse had moderately high gross overenumeration rates relative to the average.

(3) Gross overenumeration rates also varied by type of enumeration procedure. Within mailout-mailback areas, enumerations obtained through follow-up for nonresponse exhibited a rate of gross overenumerations more than twice the average rate, while enumerations resulting from mail returns exhibited a below-average rate. Enumerations obtained in conventional areas also had a below-average rate of gross overenumerations.

The IRS-Census Match

A methodological study conducted after the 1980 census, the IRS-Census Match, provides, as a by-product, information indicative of differential rates of gross omissions from the census. (The Internal Revenue Service provided a sample of tax returns to the Census Bureau for the analysis but had no access to the census data for these returns.) This study, which matched a sample of about 11,000 filers of 1979 tax returns to 1980 census records, found the following patterns of gross omission rates (see Appendix 5.1 for further details):

(1) Categorizing tax filers by sex and ethnicity, black men had a gross omission rate more than twice the average for the study, while white women had a below-average rate.

(2) Categorizing tax filers by marital status (proxied by joint versus single return) and income level, blacks filing single returns at all income levels and most Hispanics filing single returns had gross omission rates more than twice the average, as did blacks filing joint returns with low incomes (less than $8,000) and most Hispanics filing joint returns. In contrast, blacks filing joint returns and whites filing single returns with higher incomes ($15,000 or more) and most whites filing joint returns had below-average gross omission rates.

Experience From Previous Censuses

Coverage evaluation programs for previous censuses provide additional information about groups in the population that are more apt to be undercounted compared with other groups. It is important to look at data available from previous censuses both for clues as to the correlates of the undercount and also to determine if there are any patterns over time. That is, are some population groups apparently getting easier to count and others harder to count? Any time patterns that can be discerned have implications for choice of coverage improvement methods in the next census. Unfortunately, only the post-enumeration survey program for the 1950 census provides separate gross overcount as well as undercount figures, and the great differences in enumeration methods make it hard to compare the 1950 with the 1980 results.

Demographic Analysis

Previous censuses show similar patterns, though higher levels, of net undercount for broad population groups as in 1980, using the method of demographic analysis. In every census since detailed coverage analysis began in 1950, blacks were more poorly counted than others and men more poorly counted than women (see Table 5.1).

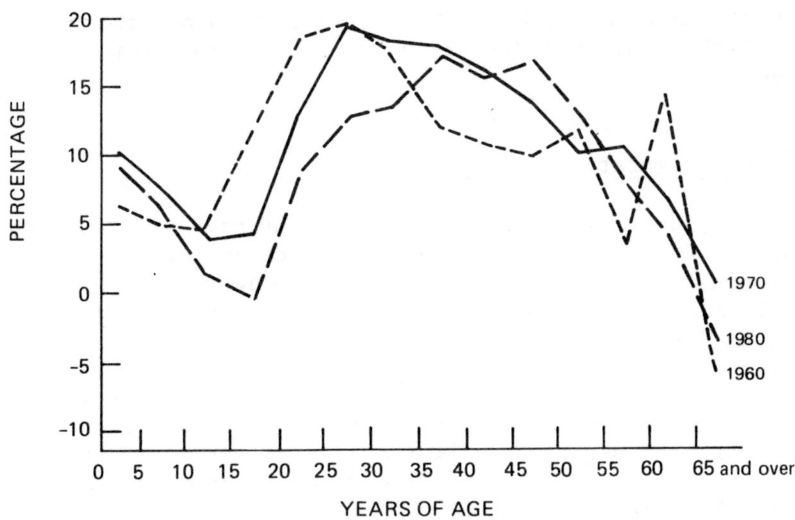

FIGURE 5.2 Percentage net undercount rates by age for black men: 1960-1980 censuses (determined from demographic analysis).

Looking at patterns of undercount for more finely stratified age, race, and sex groups reveals some intriguing differences over time. Black men of working age were the most heavily undercounted group in 1980. This has also been true in previous censuses, but the data show a shift in the age groups most affected (see Figure 5.2). In 1960, black men ages 15-39 were most heavily undercounted; in 1970, the age group experiencing the greatest undercount among black men had shifted to the range from 20 to 49; in 1980, black men with the greatest undercount rates were in the age range from 25 to 54.

This pattern does not clearly support a conclusion that undercount among black males is age-specific nor a conclusion that high rates of undercount are specific to a particular cohort of the population. Nevertheless, the data suggest that a group of black men who were ages 15-34 in 1960 is still proving particularly hard to count as the cohort grows older. The data also suggest that in every census young black men age 20 and over are much harder to count than black male teenagers. The phenomenon of black children under age 10 of both sexes being relatively hard to count appears to be a new pattern evident in 1970 and 1980 but not 1960 (based on data not shown for black female children as well as the data shown for males).

Post-enumeration Surveys

Post-enumeration surveys conducted in previous censuses provide data on relative rates of undercoverage for various population groups. Appendix 5.1 reviews the findings of these surveys in detail. Highlights of the survey results include:

(1) With respect to household relationship, the 1950 and 1960 survey results corroborate the finding from the 1980 PEP that persons not belonging to the nuclear family are harder to count than household heads, spouses, and their children.

(2) Survey data from 1950 suggest that fewer years of schooling are associated with a higher-than-average gross omission rate.

(3) Findings with regard to labor force status, occupation, and income are mixed. The 1960 survey found relationships of low income and unemployment to higher rates of gross omissions, but, in the case of income, the relationship appeared stronger for whites compared with blacks. Both the 1960 and 1950 survey results estimated high gross omission rates for persons employed as agricultural laborers, while farmers and farm managers had below-average gross omission rates.

Resident Observer Studies

The techniques of resident observation employed in ethnographic studies were used on one occasion to investigate factors affecting the coverage of household surveys. The findings from this study support and extend the findings about hard-to-count groups in the census based on traditional methods of coverage evaluation. Appendix 5.1 provides a full description.

Housing Coverage Studies

Rates of omission of housing units do not necessarily translate into comparable rates of missed persons;

nevertheless, studies of completeness of coverage of housing units conducted in every census since 1950 are another source of information on relative rates of gross omissions in the population. Persons can be missed in the census because the entire household is overlooked or because one or more persons in an otherwise enumerated household are missed. In 1950, the post-enumeration survey indicated that three-quarters of all missed persons were in whole households that were missed, while only one-quarter were in enumerated households (Bureau of the Census, 1960:Table C). By 1970, this distribution had changed: only half of missed persons were in missed households and the other half were in otherwise enumerated households. Among blacks, nearly three-quarters of those missed were in enumerated households (Siegel, 1975). With improvements in compilation and review of the address list used for the census, the remaining problem of coverage has, to a great extent, shifted from a problem of locating structures to one of finding everyone who is associated with a particular household. Appendix 5.1 reviews findings from the 1980 census and previous censuses on characteristics of missed housing units.

COVERAGE IMPROVEMENT PROGRAMS: PAST EXPERIENCE

In past censuses, the Census Bureau has implemented programs designed to improve coverage. Those programs have included general advertising and publicity to increase awareness of the census and encourage response, programs directed toward improving the quality of staff and operational procedures, and, finally, special programs targeted specifically to known problem areas. This section reviews the special coverage improvement programs implemented in 1970 and 1980 to address specific problem areas.

Coverage Improvement in 1970

The Census Bureau adopted specific coverage improvement procedures for the 1970 census predicated on three assumptions:

(1) The need for even greater accuracy in the population count than achieved in the past because of the use

of the data for legislative redistricting under "one man, one vote" court requirements and the growing use of the data for fund allocations.

(2) The perception that it was becoming increasingly difficult to obtain a complete count in the absence of additional coverage efforts.

(3) The belief that new methods would be required to effect any coverage improvement. As a history of the coverage improvement efforts in 1970 notes (Bureau of the Census, 1974b:1):

> The 1950 and 1960 programs were predicated on the assumption that undercounts were due largely to the enumerator's failure to follow instructions. Hence, stress was placed on simplified procedures, training, and quality control. Analysis of the results of the 1960 evaluation program . . . indicated that the reasons were more complex. In particular, a substantial part of the undercount appeared to be due either to deliberate attempts by some segments of the population to be omitted from the census or to the fact that they did not fit into any households by the conventional rules of residence. Even where the undercount was due to complete households being missed, the causes were frequently such that additional enumerator training, exhortation to the enumerators, and similar approaches appeared potentially capable of only marginal gains.

Programs to encourage public cooperation with the census, particularly among hard-to-count groups, were important components of the Census Bureau's strategy to obtain complete coverage in 1970. These programs included public information efforts and community education programs, assistance centers set up in 20 cities that the public could call or visit for help in filling out census forms, and providing instruction sheets and questionnaires in Spanish and Chinese where needed. Special efforts to improve enumerator performance in the 20 largest cities were also adopted.

The Census Bureau also implemented specific coverage improvement programs designed to add housing units and persons to the count, most of which were also used in the 1980 census. These programs are identified in Table 5.2, which indicates the number of housing units and persons added by each program, total costs, and costs per housing unit and person added (all costs are in 1980 dollars). The table categorizes the programs as: (1) programs carried out prior to Census Day with the primary purpose of correcting the address list, both in terms of entire structures and units within structures, (2) programs carried out during the data collection phase and designed to locate missed units within structures or to verify the occupancy status of listed units, and (3) programs carried out during data collection and designed to add missed persons. Note that the cost estimates provided are only approximate, as are the estimates of numbers of housing units and persons added to the count.

In brief, the 1970 coverage improvement programs included:

1.1 Advance Post Office Check (APOC). The APOC involved a check of the address list carried out from February through October 1969 by the U.S. Postal Service in areas for which the Census Bureau purchased commercial mailing lists. These areas included about three-quarters of the mailout-mailback population or 45 percent of the total population.

1.2 Precanvass. The Precanvass was an additional check that Census Bureau enumerators made several weeks before Census Day of the address list in selected enumeration districts of 17 large metropolitan areas expected to prove difficult to count. The enumerators concentrated on identifying multiple units within structures.

1.3 Casing and Time of Delivery Checks. These checks involved review of the address lists by the Postal Service just prior to Census Day both in mailout areas for which the Census Bureau purchased lists and in prelist areas for which Census Bureau enumerators developed the mailing list.

2.1 National Vacancy Check. In the National Vacancy Check, the Census Bureau carried out a sample survey of about 13,500 housing units originally classified as vacant to determine their occupancy status. On the basis of the findings, imputation procedures were used to reclassify 8.5 percent of all vacant units as occupied and to impute persons to these units.

2.2 Post-Enumeration Post Office Check. The PEPOC was administered in conventionally enumerated areas of 16 Southern states. The Postal Service checked the address lists developed by enumerators for completeness and Census Bureau staff followed up a sample of missed addresses in

TABLE 5.2 Additions and Costs of 1970 Census Coverage Improvement Programs

Program	Housing Units Added		Persons Added		Cost (1980 dollars)		
	Number ('000s)	Percentage of Total	Number ('000s)	Percentage of Total	Total ('000s)	Per Added HU	Per Added Person
Programs to improve address list prior to data collection							
Advance Post Office Check (APOC)[a]	1,200	1.7	3,600	1.8	8,250	6.88	2.29
Precanvass	108	0.2	234	0.1	743	6.88	3.18[b]
Casing and Time of Delivery Checks[a]	1,800	2.6	5,400	2.7	N.A.	N.A.	N.A.
Subtotal	3,108	4.5	9,234	4.5	8,993	6.88[c]	2.35[c]
Programs to improve housing unit count during data collection							
National Vacancy Check	—[d]	—[d]	1,069	0.5	225	—	0.21
Post-Enumeration Post Office Check (PEPOC)	174	0.3	484	0.2	1,538	8.84	3.18[b]
Report of Living Quarters Check	126	0.2	380	0.2	1,207	9.58	3.18[b]
Subtotal	300	0.4	1,933	1.0	2,970	9.15[e]	1.54

Programs to improve person count during data collection							
Missed Persons Campaign	—	—	—	—	N.A.	N.A.	N.A.
Movers Check	—	—	15	—	635	—	42.33
Supplemental Forms Operation	40	0.1	122	0.1	388	9.70	3.18[b]
Subtotal	40	0.1	137	0.1	1,023	9.70[f]	7.48
TOTAL	3,448	5.0	11,304	5.6	12,986	7.36[g]	2.20[h]

NOTE: Total 1970 housing unit and population counts, used as bases of percentages, were 68,672,000 and 203,302,000, respectively. Many programs were conducted in only some areas of the country. Hence, when evaluating the cost-effectiveness of such programs in adding to the count of persons or housing units, care should be taken to use the appropriate denominator, as noted in the text.

[a] Bureau of the Census (1976:3-39, 3-42, 4-21 to 4-24). Housing unit additions are approximate estimates; person additions are housing unit additions times 3 persons per unit. The figure for housing units added through APOC represents net additions (4.4 million additions minus 3.2 million deletions). The APOC also corrected about 1.8 million addresses within structures.

[b] Costs for the Precanvass, PEPOC, Report of Living Quarters Check, and Supplemental Forms Operation were estimated by the Bureau of the Census (1974b) at about $1 to $2 per person, and hence were calculated as $1.50 times 2.118, or $3.18, for this table.

[c] Per housing unit cost calculated as $8,993/1,308; per person cost calculated as $8,993/3,834; i.e., denominator includes only housing unit or person additions for programs for which total costs are available.

[d] The National Vacancy Check resulted in 250,000 housing units or 0.4% of the total being reclassified from vacant to occupied (Bureau of the Census, 1973c:15).

[e] Per housing unit cost calculated as $2,745 (cost of PEPOC and Report of Living Quarters Check) /300.

[f] Per housing unit cost calculated as $388/40.

[g] Numerator = $12,126 ($8,933 + $2,745 + $388); denominator = 1,648 (1,308 + 300 + 40).

[h] Numerator = $12,986; denominator = 5,904 (3,834 + 1,933 + 137).

SOURCE: Number of housing unit and person additions are from Bureau of the Census (1974b:Table A), except where otherwise noted; costs are approximate estimates from Bureau of the Census (1974b:18), except where otherwise noted. All costs are expressed in 1980 dollars (1970 cost estimates times 2.118).

the field. On the basis of this effort, housing units and persons were added to the census records via imputation.

2.3 Report of Living Quarters Check. This check involved comparing respondents' answers to Question A about number of living quarters at their address with the number recorded on the census address list. For structures listed as having fewer than 10 units, for which the respondent indicated a greater number of units than noted in the census list, enumerators made a field verification of the number of units.

3.1 Missed Persons Campaign. In this operation the Census Bureau left cards with community and other local organizations to distribute to persons in casual settings, such as carry-outs, barbershops, etc. The cards, which asked for minimal demographic information, were to be returned to the Census Bureau to match to the census records.

3.2 Movers Check. In the same metropolitan areas in which the Precanvass was conducted, the Census Bureau attempted to follow up persons reporting a change of address to the Postal Service during the census enumeration period.

3.3 Supplemental Forms Operation. The Census Bureau mounted special "Were you counted?" campaigns and enumerated persons who came forward on special forms. Residents traveling overseas were also enumerated with supplemental forms. In most cases, these forms were processed for an area and persons added only when the total number of supplemental forms represented 1 percent or more of the enumeration district population.

The programs in category 1 added about 4.5 percent to the housing unit and person count and were reasonably cost-effective (recognizing that cost-effectiveness of coverage evaluation programs is difficult to measure, particularly in the absence of information regarding the proportions of housing units and persons correctly added to the count, that is, not overcounted). The APOC added 1.7 percent to the overall housing unit count--3.8 percent in the commercial mailing list areas in which the program was conducted--in addition to correcting many addresses. The Casing and Time of Delivery Checks added 2.6 percent overall and fully 4.4 percent in the mailout areas in which these checks were performed. The Precanvass added only 0.2 percent to the total housing unit count, but the program was implemented in selected areas of only 17 metropolises. In these selected areas, the Precanvass added 2.3 percent to the housing unit count.

The 1970 programs carried out during the data collection phase and aimed at checking the count of housing units and their occupancy status (category 2) proved cost-effective as well, although these programs added a much smaller percentage to the population count than the address check programs. The National Vacancy Check added 0.5 percent to the population count and reclassified 0.4 percent of total housing units from vacant to occupied. The program cost very little per added person, because it was carried out on a small sample (about 0.2 percent) of units originally classified as vacant. Of course, in determining the cost-effectiveness of a coverage improvement program based on a sample survey, one must look not only at the cost per added person but at the reliability of the data obtained. A program with a smaller sampling fraction will cost less on a per person added basis compared with a more extensive program, but may also produce less reliable data.

Evaluation of the 1970 National Vacancy Check indicated that data quality was high, even with the error introduced by sampling (Waksberg, 1970, 1971). The program was implemented in a conservative manner in several respects. First, units in the sample of 13,500 were reclassified from vacant to occupied only if the enumerator determined that the same family had continuously occupied the house during the census enumeration period. On this basis, 11.4 percent of the sample units were reclassified. In the imputation procedure applied to the complete set of census records, instead of 11.4 percent, a total of 8.5 percent of vacant units (to attempt to account for the smaller average household size of misclassified units in the sample compared with correctly classified units) were changed to occupied and persons imputed to these units. It turned out that this procedure imputed somewhat fewer persons than expected because the imputed household size for the reclassified units on average was yet smaller than the average household size targeted for the imputation. The best estimate is that no more than another 0.1 percent should have been added to the population count (Bureau of the Census, 1974b:12-13).

The Post-Enumeration Post Office Check added 0.3 percent to the housing unit count overall and 0.2 percent to the population count. The program added 1.3 percent in the conventionally enumerated areas of the South in which it was carried out. The recheck of units in which the respondent reported more living quarters than there were addresses for the structure on the mailing list added at a minimum about 0.2 percent to the population count overall. The Census Bureau was only able to estimate the effects of this program for questionnaires returned by mail. For the latter universe, the added persons shown in Table 5.2 represent about 0.3 percent of the total. The Census Bureau estimated that the Report of Living Quarters Check was erroneously omitted in one of three cases; if the check had been made for all applicable addresses, at least 0.3 percent would have been added to the total population count (Bureau of the Census, 1974b:4).

The programs directed toward finding missed persons (category 3) were least effective in terms of additions to the count. The Supplemental Forms Operation added less than 0.1 percent to the total population count, although, as previously noted, these forms were generally processed only where they represented 1 percent or more of the initially enumerated population. The Movers Check added a negligible number of persons overall and 0.6 percent to the population of the areas in which it was performed (the same 17 large metropolitan areas in which the Precanvass was implemented). The Census Bureau estimated that the Movers Check would have added another 0.6 percent to the population of these 17 areas if the program had been carried out completely according to specifications (Bureau of the Census, 1974b:8).

As noted in a previous section, the 1970 census missed proportionately more persons in otherwise enumerated households than in missed households compared with the 1950 experience. This result is probably due at least in part to the relative effort and success achieved by the programs aimed toward housing unit coverage (the first and second categories in Table 5.2) versus the programs aimed at identifying missed persons. Another point to emphasize regarding the 1970 coverage improvement strategy is that many programs were carried out on a selective basis in areas in which it was felt they would be particularly effective or for which the effort was believed to be justified in terms of cost. Two programs, the National Vacancy Check and the PEPOC, were carried out on a sample basis and the results used to impute persons to the census. Finally, there was some effort evident in the 1970 program, specifically in the National Vacancy Check, to guard against overcounting as well as undercounting.

Coverage Improvement in 1980

The 1980 coverage improvement strategy exhibited three differences from 1970:

(1) The resources put into coverage improvement in 1980 exceeded the resources spent in 1970 (expressed in 1980 dollars) by several orders of magnitude, reflecting the belief that every effort was necessary to obtain accurate coverage to satisfy needs for fund allocation, redistricting, equal employment opportunity actions, and other important public policy uses of census data. Programs aimed at increasing public cooperation, particularly among hard-to-count groups, such as special publicity efforts, assistance centers, and foreign-language questionnaires, were greatly expanded, as were the number and extent of programs designed specifically to add housing units and persons to the count.

(2) The Census Bureau made a deliberate decision to conduct most specific coverage improvement programs on a nationwide basis and to avoid the use of sampling and imputation. However, some programs were implemented selectively in areas specifically designated for the purpose.

(3) Several new programs were adopted to tackle the problem of within-household undercoverage, although most programs, as in 1970, were directed toward improvement of the address list either before or after Census Day.

Table 5.3 provides statistics from Census Bureau evaluations (see Thompson, 1984; updated in Bureau of the Census, 1985c) regarding coverage improvement efforts in 1980 for programs implemented prior to Census Day directed at improving the address list and programs implemented during data collection. Again, estimates of cost and added housing units and persons are approximate. Overall, the 1980 census coverage improvement effort, including all the programs listed in Table 5.3, accounted for almost 9 percent of the total costs of the census and added about 8.4 percent to the total population count. In 1970, the coverage improvement programs listed in Table 5.2 accounted for about 3 percent of the total census costs and added about 5.6 percent to the total population. As in 1970, the cost-effectiveness of specific 1980 census coverage improvement programs varied greatly.

The 1980 census address list improvement programs carried out prior to Census Day (Table 5.3, Panel A)

TABLE 5.3 Additions and Costs of 1980 Census Coverage Improvement Programs

Program	Housing Units Added		Persons Added		Cost (1980 dollars)		
	Number ('000s)	Percentage of Total	Number ('000s)	Percentage of Total	Total ('000s)	Per Added HU	Per Added Person
Panel A: Programs to improve address list prior to data collection							
Advance Post Office Check (APOC)	2,000[a]	2.3	5,120	2.3	6,970	3.49	1.36
Precanvass	2,360[b]	2.7	6,030	2.7	11,800	5.00	1.96
Casing and Time of Delivery Checks	2,060	2.3	5,280	2.3	9,290	4.51	1.76
Subtotal	6,420	7.3	16,430	7.3	28,060	4.37	1.71
Panel B: Programs to improve housing unit count during data collection							
Local Review	53[c]	0.1	76[c]	—	4,310	44.74[e]	31.20[e]
Post-Enumeration Post Office Check (PEPOC)	50	0.1	130	0.1	990	19.80	7.62
Prelist Recanvass	120	0.1	220	0.1	10,290	85.75	46.77
Vacant/Delete Check	409[d]	0.5	1,720	0.8	36,320	36.41[f]	21.12
Subtotal	632	0.7	2,146	0.9	51,910	45.16[g]	23.29[h]

Panel C: Programs to improve person count during data collection							
Casual Count	—	—	13	—	250	—	19.23
Coverage Questions and Dependent Roster Check[i]	93	0.1	240	0.1	7,500	80.65	31.25
Nonhousehold Sources Program	—	—	130	0.1	9,820	—	75.54
Were You Counted	17	—	71	—	270	15.88	3.80
Subtotal	110	0.1	454	0.2	17,840	70.64[j]	39.30
TOTAL	7,162	8.1	19,030	8.4	97,810	8.99[k]	5.04[l]

NOTE: Total 1980 housing unit and population counts, used as base of percentages, were 88,207,000 and 226,546,000, respectively. Many programs were conducted only in some areas of the country. Hence when evaluating the cost-effectiveness of such programs in adding to the count of persons or housing units, care should be taken to use the appropriate denominator, as noted in the text.

[a] Also corrected 2.9 million addresses.
[b] Also transferred 570,000 units from one geographic area to another.
[c] Also transferred 48,000 housing units and 56,000 persons from one geographic area to another.
[d] Also reclassified 590,000 units from vacant to occupied, in addition to the 409,000 units reclassified from "delete" to housing unit additions. Also deleted 507,000 vacant units from the housing inventory.
[e] Per housing unit and per person cost calculated as 55% of total costs (share attributable to additions as opposed to transfers) = $2,371/53 and 76, respectively.
[f] Per housing unit cost calculated as 41% of total costs (share attributable to additions as opposed to reclassification) = $14,891/409.
[g] Numerator = $28,542 ($2,371 + $990 + $10,290 + $14,891).
[h] Numerator = $49,971 ($2,371 + $990 + $10,290 + $36,320).
[i] Housing unit and person additions and costs based on evaluation of report of living quarters question (H4) edit only.
[j] Numerator = $7,770 (costs of Coverage Questions and Dependent Roster Check plus Were You Counted).
[k] Numerator = $64,372 ($28,060 + $28,542 + $7,770).
[l] Numerator = $95,871 ($28,060 + $49,971 + $17,840).

SOURCE: Calculated from Bureau of the Census (1985c:2-3).

proved extremely cost-effective. The Advance Post Office Check performed by U.S. Postal Service staff in summer 1979 and the Precanvass carried out by Census Bureau staff in early 1980 each added well over 2 percent to the U.S. total housing unit count. Both of these programs were limited to the tape address register (TAR) areas (that is, city delivery areas for which the Census Bureau had developed computerized geographic coding files and purchased commercial mailing lists), and, in those areas, they added between 4 and 5 percent each to the housing unit count for a cost of about $4 per added housing unit. Comparable figures for the 1970 programs are 3.8 percent of housing units added by APOC in the TAR areas and 2.3 percent of units added by the Precanvass in 17 metropolitan areas, for a cost of about $7 (in 1980 dollars) per added unit. The 1980 Casing and Time of Delivery checks--implemented by Postal Service staff just prior to Census Day in the entire mail census area (including 95 percent of the population in TAR plus prelist areas)--also added over 2 percent to the U.S. total housing unit count for about the same cost as the other two programs. In 1970, these checks added over 4 percent of the housing units in the mailout areas.

The programs carried out during data collection that were primarily directed at checking the address list or at determining whether units were correctly classified as occupied or vacant (Table 5.3, Panel B) proved much more expensive than the pre-Census Day programs. These programs included:

- Local Review. The Census Bureau provided preliminary housing unit and also population counts to local officials after completion of the first stage of follow-up. Officials reviewed the counts and indicated problem areas for checking.
- Post-Enumeration Post Office Check. In contrast with 1970, PEPOC was carried out in all conventionally enumerated areas of the country on a 100 percent basis as part of the second stage of follow-up.
- Prelist Recanvass. In Prelist areas, the address list was rechecked during the second stage of follow-up. In some areas, only selected enumeration districts were recanvassed.
- Vacant/Delete Check. In contrast with 1970, the 1980 Vacant/Delete Check was implemented on a 100 percent basis during the second stage of follow-up.

Each of 8.4 million housing units originally classified as vacant or as "delete" because they were not residential were rechecked in the field.

These four programs added about 1 percent to the total population count for an average cost of $23 per person added. Over 80 percent of this improvement was due to the Vacant/Delete Check. The Prelist Recanvass had the highest unit costs, and there is evidence that it experienced severe operational problems that diminished its effectiveness. The Local Review program also had high unit costs and added less than 0.1 percent to the population count. Local Review was very unevenly implemented across the country; many areas did not participate. The effectiveness of the PEPOC in terms of adding persons is understated in Table 5.3 because it was carried out in conventional areas representing only 5 percent of the total U.S. population. In these areas, PEPOC added 1.2 percent to the population count, about the same as the performance in 1970, although the cost to add a person in 1980 was almost two and a half times the 1970 cost, reflecting the difference between a 100 percent and a sample operation. The Vacant/Delete Check, as discussed further below, probably introduced a measure of overcounting as well as reducing the undercount. The 1980 program added 0.8 percent to the population count compared with 0.5 percent for the 1970 effort. The cost to add a person from the 1980 Vacant/Delete Check was fully 100 times the 1970 cost, reflecting the great increase in the number of units that were rechecked in the field.

There are data on the characteristics of persons added to the census in 1980 from some of these programs. Evidence suggests that the Prelist Recanvass replicated the race distribution in the general population and hence did not help reduce differential undercount (Thompson, 1984:12). This further lowers the panel's assessment of its relative cost-effectiveness. The Vacant/Delete Check, by contrast, made a measurable impact on differential coverage rates. Based on available data, it appears that this program may have reduced the black versus white differential undercoverage by 0.5 percentage points (estimated from Thompson, 1984:23).

The programs carried out to improve the person count during data collection (see Table 5.3, Panel C) proved least cost-effective. These programs included:

• Casual Count. This operation was similar to the 1970 Missed Persons Campaign, except that, instead of relying on community organizations, the Census Bureau sent special enumerators about 6 weeks after Census Day to places frequented by transients who might otherwise be missed. The operation was limited to centralized (city) district offices.

• Coverage Questions and Dependent Roster Check. This program was directed both toward adding housing units and persons within households and also toward reducing erroneous inclusions. Responses to questions on number of units in the building and the roster of household members were edited and followed up as appropriate.

• Nonhousehold Sources Program. This operation--an innovation in 1980--involved matching several administrative lists to census records for selected census tracts in urban district offices. The lists used were driver's license records, immigration records, and public assistance records in New York City. About 6.8 million persons were checked against census records.

• Were You Counted. This program was similar to the 1970 Supplemental Forms Operation.

The above four programs added only 0.2 percent to the total 1980 population count for a cost of over $39 per added person. The component of the Coverage Questions Check that involved rechecking buildings in which the respondent reported more living quarters than there were addresses on the mailing list appeared less effective in adding persons and more costly than the comparable Report of Living Quarters Check in 1970. (The Census Bureau was not able to evaluate the effectiveness or cost of the other coverage questions in 1980.) The Casual Count and Were You Counted programs had negligible impact in both the 1970 and 1980 censuses. The one major innovation for 1980, the Nonhousehold Sources Program, which had appeared promising in pretests, added only 130,000 persons (less than 0.1 percent of the total population and less than 2 percent of the total number of administrative list entries checked against census records), for a cost of over $75 per person added. If the Nonhousehold Sources Program had been more effective in terms of persons added, the program could have had a pronounced effect on differential coverage rates. Among the small group of persons identified through the Nonhousehold Sources list matching operation, about one-third each were white, black, and Hispanic, compared with the breakdown in the general population of over 80 percent white, 12 percent black, and 6 percent Hispanic (Thompson, 1984:18-19).

In addition to programs designed to add persons during the data collection stage, the 1980 census effort included a program called Whole Household Usual Home Elsewhere, which was designed to increase the accuracy of the count by area. In this effort, about 1 million persons were transferred from one enumeration district to another in accordance with the Census Bureau's rules of usual place of residence. For example, persons residing in a vacation home on Census Day had their data transferred to the location of their usual home. Other programs, such as Local Review and the Precanvass, also produced transfers as well as net additions.

Evaluation of Coverage Improvement Experience in 1980

Looking at the 1980 coverage improvement programs, it appears evident that programs carried out prior to Census Day to check the address list were important in improving the count and low in cost in terms of dollars per housing unit added to the list. Moreover, because these programs were implemented before the enumeration, any additions that were in fact duplications could be corrected subsequently.

The costs per person added by the programs administered during data collection were quite high. The Nonhousehold Sources Program stands out in this regard, as does the Prelist Recanvass. The Vacant/Delete Check, although not the most costly on a per person added basis, was the most expensive program in total costs--but it significantly reduced the differential undercount, which is of key importance.

There is evidence that the Vacant/Delete Check contributed to overcount as well as importantly reducing undercount (see Bureau of the Census, 1985c:Ch.8). The 1980 program (in contrast to the 1970 National Vacancy Check) was designed not only to verify the status of units originally classified as vacant or delete but also to identify and enumerate persons who were missed in the census because they were moving from an old to a new residence. Enumerators were instructed to ask residents of units originally classified as vacant whether they had moved in since Census Day, and, if so, whether they had been counted at their previous residence. Movers who stated that they had not been counted were enumerated at the new address. However, people were often enumerated without being aware of the fact (for example, because some other household member filled out the form), and, hence, movers located in the Vacant/Delete Check were at risk of being counted twice.

Other 1980 census coverage improvement programs, such as Whole Household Usual Home Elsewhere, also probably contributed to overcount. The fact that all the coverage improvement programs were implemented clerically, with no use made of automation, undoubtedly served to increase cost and reduce effectiveness. This was particularly true for programs that were carried out in the final stages of follow-up, when there was great pressure on the district offices to close out their operations.

Overall, the three predata collection coverage improvement programs, together with the Vacant/Delete Check, accounted for over 95 percent of persons added but only 66 percent of the coverage improvement budget--casting doubt on the cost-effectiveness of the other approaches. These comparisons would be even more favorable to these specific programs if the Vacant/Delete Check had been carried out on a sample basis, as in 1970.

CENSUS BUREAU PLANS FOR TESTING COVERAGE IMPROVEMENT PROGRAMS FOR 1990

The Census Bureau's testing program for the 1990 census began in spring 1984 with tests in several urban and rural localities of improved methods of address list compilation--a key element in achieving completeness of coverage (Bureau of the Census, 1984b). Included in plans for 1986 pretests are many tests related to coverage improvement (see Johnson, 1984; updated in Bureau of the Census, 1985b). Almost all the programs implemented in 1980 are scheduled for further testing in 1986, along with some new programs. Current plans call for testing improved techniques and procedures for the following programs that were used in 1980:

- Advance Post Office Check. As a high priority pretest objective, the Census Bureau proposes to test the use of mailout-mailback procedures in rural areas that were conventionally enumerated in 1980. One procedure to be tested would be to have Census Bureau staff prelist the area, followed by an APOC, with the Postal Service delivering the questionnaires. There is a proposal in urban areas to test enhancing the APOC by adding identification of problem addresses (e.g., addresses where there is a mail drop for an entire building).

- Precanvass. The Census Bureau proposes testing an enhancement of the Precanvass that includes correcting addresses within all multiunit structures, even where the count in the structure from the Precanvass agrees with the count on the address register, and also to extend both the APOC and the Precanvass operations to prelist as well as tape address register areas.
- Casing and Time of Delivery Checks and Local Review. Various improvements to these operations are proposed for testing.
- Vacant/Delete Check. The Census Bureau proposes to test ways of improving the effectiveness of this program, not including, however, consideration of conducting the program on a sample basis.
- Casual Count. Tests of automating the process of searching for persons identified in the Casual Count operation and of adding them to the census are proposed.
- Coverage Questions and Dependent Roster Check. The Census Bureau proposes to examine the combination of questions used in 1980 to check within household coverage to determine if rewording, new instructions, or other changes will increase their effectiveness, and also to test adding questions about multiple residences that could help minimize overcounting. The Census Bureau also proposes to test improvements in the Whole Household Usual Home Elsewhere program.
- Nonhousehold Sources Program. Various possible improvements are proposed for testing in this program, such as the use of new sources of administrative lists and the use of automated matching and searching techniques.

The only programs used in 1980 that are not proposed for testing in 1986 are the Prelist Recanvass and the Post-Enumeration Post Office Check. (Conventional area enumeration methods, which include PEPOC, will not be tested in the 1986 round of pretests and may not be used at all in 1990.) A new program being considered for testing is the use of an update list/leave procedure in prelist areas, in which Census Bureau enumerators instead of the Postal Service would deliver questionnaires and at the same time update the address list. Update list/leave is also proposed for testing (although perhaps not until

1987) in multiunit structures in urban areas that pose special problems for mail delivery.

The Census Bureau has outlined an ambitious testing program related to coverage improvement. The panel stated its belief in Chapter 3 that the Census Bureau must choose among the ideas proposed for testing. In the following sections, we offer recommendations regarding priorities for testing and research in the area of improving the count. The discussion first addresses needed research on hard-to-count groups and on problems of overcount.

NEEDED RESEARCH ON UNDERCOUNT AND OVERCOUNT

The panel supports further work at the Census Bureau to analyze the characteristics of population groups and areas more subject to census undercount and also those more likely to be overcounted. The panel also supports further analysis, to the extent available data permit, of the effectiveness of coverage improvement programs in reducing differential undercount. This research can contribute importantly to the planning of special coverage improvement efforts for the next census and also to the planning of evaluation programs to determine the completeness of coverage that was achieved. At the present time, the undercount research staff at the Census Bureau is continuing investigation of gross undercount and overcount with the data from the Post-Enumeration Program, including analyzing enumeration districts that contain nonmatched cases (that is, gross omission cases in the Current Population Survey) on characteristics such as percentage not speaking English and percentage low income.

> Recommendation 5.1. We recommend that the Census Bureau assign a high priority to the completion of studies of undercount and overcount in the 1980 census.

Research on the characteristics of hard-to-count groups and of groups and areas prone to overcount will be more useful for planning coverage improvement and evaluation programs for the next census to the extent that the research is completed expeditiously. To be designing pretests for 1990 without having completed research on undercount and overcount diminishes the value of the research results and can result in less well-designed tests.

Recommendation 5.2. We recommend that the Census Bureau set up a timetable and assign staff to permit completion of the analysis of 1990 coverage evaluation results in time to be used in planning the first pretest of the 2000 census.

ISSUES IN COVERAGE IMPROVEMENT: QUESTIONNAIRE CONTENT

Next the panel discusses priorities for research and testing of coverage improvement programs, beginning with consideration of items on the questionnaire that relate to coverage. These items include the questions on race and Hispanic origin as well as questions designed specifically to help coverage, such as number of living quarters or addresses in the respondent's building. The population counts for race and Hispanic groups are affected by the accuracy of reporting race and ethnicity as well as by coverage errors, and it is important to understand what responses to these questions mean if appropriate estimates of coverage rates are to be developed (for example, from demographic analysis).

Race and Hispanic Origin Questions

Information about race and ethnicity, including particularly Hispanic origin, is required for the implementation of a number of federal and state laws pertaining to political representation, civil rights, and assistance to disadvantaged groups. Even if it were not for these specific legal requirements, such information would be needed as a basis for understanding the political and economic status of various racial and ethnic groups. The legal uses of racial and ethnic categories reflect basic political and economic concerns of U.S. society today. These concerns are evident in the importance attached to completeness of coverage in the census for race and ethnic groups. Differential rates of net undercoverage--for example, the net undercount rate of greater than 5 percent estimated for blacks in 1980 compared with a rate probably considerably less than 1.5 percent for all others--have excited more attention than the undercount rate for the entire population.

Information about race has been collected in each census since 1790. A specific separate question on Hispanic origin was introduced for the first time in 1970, when it was asked on a sample basis. In 1980, a question on Hispanic origin was included on the short form.

For 1990, issues related to the panel's work include:

(1) Whether question design can be improved to yield more accurate and/or more useful information, including whether the design should explicitly strive for comparability with other sources of race and ethnicity information, such as vital statistics.

(2) Whether, for considerations of coverage improvement, minimizing respondent burden, or other reasons, part of the race and ethnicity information could more appropriately be collected on a sample basis.

Race and Ethnicity Questions in Earlier Censuses

Changing information needs and societal attitudes about race and ethnicity have been reflected in changes in the design, content, and enumerator instructions for the race and ethnicity question(s) from one census to the next. The frequent changes severely limit data comparability across succeeding censuses.

In 1920, persons of mixed white and Negro blood were classified as Mulatto. Anyone who was not classified as White, Black, Mulatto, Chinese, Japanese, or Indian was classified as "Other." In 1930, the Mulatto designation was dropped. Enumerators were instructed to list persons with any Negro blood, no matter how small the percentage, as Negro. Persons of Mexican birth or parentage were to be listed as "Mexican" unless definitely Negro, Indian, Chinese, or Japanese. In 1940, Mexicans were listed as white unless definitely Indian or some other race.

There were apparently no further major definitional changes in 1950 or 1960. In 1960, racial designations, and, in 1970, ethnic designations, were placed on a self-identification basis, although, where data were collected by an enumerator, the enumerator was allowed to fill in blanks by observation when possible. In 1980, however, enumerators were no longer allowed to enter race by observation. In every modern census, missing responses have been filled in via editing and imputation routines.

The Directive to Standardize Federal Race and Ethnicity Information

Increased legal and program uses of racial and ethnic designations in the 1960s and 1970s produced a proliferation of race and ethnic data collections by various agencies, using a variety of concepts and definitions. To improve data comparability, the Office of Management and Budget's (OMB) Statistical Policy Division in 1977 established standard categories to be used by all federal agencies collecting data on race. The prescribed racial categories are: white, black, American Indian or Alaskan Native, and Asian or Pacific Islander. The ethnicity categories are: Hispanic origin, not of Hispanic origin. Alternatively, Statistical Policy Directive 15 allows agencies to use a combined race and ethnicity categorization: white (not Hispanic), black (not Hispanic), Hispanic, American Indian or Alaskan Native, Asian or Pacific Islander.

The 1980 Census

The race question on the 1980 census was designed with the aim of obtaining accurate information that could be aggregated into the OMB prescribed groupings with minimum need for hand tabulation. Since there was evidence that many respondents might be unaware that their racial background was one that the federal government includes in the "Asian and Pacific Islander" group, nine separate race or ethnic groups for aggregation into this category were listed. Also listed were white, black, Indian (Amer.), Eskimo, Aleut, and "other," for a total of 15 categories (see Figure 5.3 for question format).

A question on Spanish/Hispanic origin appeared separately (and with two other questions intervening) on the 1980 census. It requested information for four separate Spanish/Hispanic categories (see Figure 5.3).

Thus two of a total of seven population questions on the 1980 census short form were about race or ethnicity. Together these two questions took up about 30 percent of the space on the population part of the short form.

Almost 6 million individuals identifying themselves as Hispanic on the Hispanic origin question (about 40 percent of total Hispanics) marked "other" on the race question. In contrast to 1970, when similar responses were classified as "white" during tabulation, these responses were

Here are the QUESTIONS ↓	These are the columns for ANSWERS → *Please fill one column for each person listed in Question 1.*	**PERSON in column 1** Last name / First name / Middle initial

2. How is this person related to the person in column 1? *Fill one circle.* *If "Other relative" of person in column 1, give exact relationship, such as mother-in-law, niece, grandson, etc.*	*START in this column with the household member (or one of the members) in whose name the home is owned or rented. If there is no such person, start in this column with any adult household member.*

4. Is this person — *Fill one circle.*	○ White ○ Black or Negro ○ Japanese ○ Chinese ○ Filipino ○ Korean ○ Vietnamese ○ Indian (Amer.) *Print tribe* → ○ Asian Indian ○ Hawaiian ○ Guamanian ○ Samoan ○ Eskimo ○ Aleut ○ Other — *Specify*

7. Is this person of Spanish/Hispanic origin or descent? *Fill one circle.*	○ No (not Spanish/Hispanic) ○ Yes, Mexican, Mexican-Amer., Chicano ○ Yes, Puerto Rican ○ Yes, Cuban ○ Yes, other Spanish/Hispanic

FIGURE 5.3 Race and Hispanic origin questions on the 1980 census short form.

kept in the "other" category in 1980. This change reflected a joint OMB-Census Bureau decision that the great majority of the Hispanics who responded in this way understood the race question and did not consider themselves white. Some data users are critical of this decision, which they argue impairs the comparability of the 1980 data with the data from the 1940 through 1970 censuses. 1980 data have been tabulated and published in such a way as to permit users to reclassify this group if they wish, however. Even with such reclassification, data are not fully comparable from one census to the next, due to a variety of other changes in question design, enumerator instructions, and editing rules.

Considerations for 1990

Collection of information on race and ethnicity in a large, diverse country such as the United States is inherently difficult. With the introduction of the concept of self-identification, the racial and ethnic categories moved away from their former precise, or pseudo-precise, anthropological definitions and toward definitions stemming from commonly perceived cultural categories. This shift was appropriate. Certainly, questions requiring information about percentages of Negro and Indian blood (used, at least in theory, through 1950) would be generally regarded as offensive today.

The quest for accurate self-identification by respondents and the feasibility of computer tabulation produced, in 1980, a "race" question that was in fact a mix of racial, ethnic, and geographic categories. This was not inappropriate, but it does raise the question of whether the questions on race and Hispanic origin could be combined.

A related question is the possible need for information on additional ethnic or geographic categories in 1990. Since 1980 there has been substantial entry into the United States of refugee populations from Cambodia, Haiti, El Salvador, and elsewhere. These groups remain tiny relative to the total size of the U.S. population, but it may be that, as groups of particular policy concern, detailed information on their geographic location will be sought. This situation suggests the desirability, in the interest of keeping the short-form question of manageable length, of moving some of the detail on Asian and Pacific Islander categories to the long-form sample. Arguing against this is the probable difficulty of obtaining accurate short-form responses without listing all the detailed categories.

There is no clear evidence that inclusion of detailed race and Hispanic origin questions on the short form in 1980 was a barrier to a complete count. The group that logically might find these questions most irritating and irrelevant is the white, non-Hispanic majority of the population. Undercoverage among this group is believed to have been minimal. Other population groups seemed, in general, willing to supply race and ethnic information and, in many cases, insistent on doing so.

Design of the race and ethnicity question(s) is complicated by the limitations and ambiguities of common English-language usage. It is difficult to find brief,

Is this person: of Spanish/Hispanic Origin:	Not Spanish/Hispanic	Yes, Spanish/Hispanic (includes Puerto Rican, Cuban, Mexican, Chicano and other Hispanic)
White	0	0
Black	0	0
Japanese, Chinese, or Korean	0	0
Vietnamese, Cambodian, Laotian, or Tai	0	0
Filipino	0	0
Asian Indian	0	0
Hawaiian, Guamanian, or Samoan	0	0
Eskimo or Aleut	0	0
Indian (U.S. Tribes: print tribe ________)	0	0
Indian (Mexican, South, or Central Amer.)	0	0
Other (Specify ______________________)	0	0

FIGURE 5.4 Race and Hispanic origin information that may be required in 1990.

unambiguous, readily understood phraseology for distinguishing Indians (from India) from Indians (native U.S. tribes). The 1980 phraseology "Indian (Amer.)" is ambiguous. Does it apply only to tribes native to the United States or does it encompass all Indians of North and South America? Presumably, the former was intended, but should those of Mexican, South, and Central American origin not also have the opportunity to conveniently identify their origin--and would this not be useful information?

The matrix of information that may need to be collected on the short form is illustrated in Figure 5.4, but this illustration is not intended as format or phraseology for use in an actual census question.

> Recommendation 5.3. We recommend that the Census Bureau test a variety of question designs for the race and ethnicity information to be collected in the 1990 census, including some that combine the collection of information on Hispanic origin with the other race and ethnicity information.

Developing Race and Ethnicity Questions

The Census Bureau does not have many opportunities to test important questionnaire changes, such as changes in the race and Hispanic origin questions prior to a census.

Moreover, it is expensive to mount full-scale questionnaire wording tests, as was done prior to 1970 and 1980 and is planned for 1990 in a national content test currently scheduled for 1986.

The focus group technique has been successfully employed to design survey questions. This approach, originally developed in market research, involves in-depth discussions with small, usually homogeneous groups (Higginbotham and Cox, 1979; Slavson, 1979). Focus groups offer the advantage of being able to probe for underlying meanings and hidden associations evoked by different question wording that may affect responses in unforeseen ways. This feature may be particularly useful for the testing of questions on race and ethnicity. While focus group findings cannot be directly generalized, focus groups can help narrow the range of question alternatives that warrant testing with larger--and more costly--samples selected scientifically.

As a case in point, prior to the 1980 census the Census Bureau conducted numerous tests of different wording of the question on Hispanic origin. The various pretests and dress rehearsals tried out variations of this question, as did the 1976 National Content Test, which had a sample size of 28,000 housing units. A number of serious response problems were encountered. For example, in almost every case in which a question had a category with the term "American," such as "Central or South American" or "Central or South Amer. (Spanish)," there was evidence that some non-Hispanic Americans checked these responses (Fernandez and McKenney, 1980). Holding a number of focus group sessions at an early stage in the questionnaire content planning would probably have provided timely evidence, for a relatively low cost, of this behavior and other response problems. In a similar situation, the Social Security Administration successfully used focus group interviews to identify problems and ambiguities with the race and ethnicity items on a proposed revised application form and designed operational tests of using alternative versions based on the focus group findings (Scherr, 1980; Scherr and Nelson, 1980).

Focus groups cannot and should not replace other methods of questionnaire development, including sample surveys with alternative questionnaires and controlled laboratory or classroom experiments. (The Census Bureau conducted a number of classroom experiments prior to the 1980 census that provided useful findings regarding placement of instructions, the position of particular items on the questionnaire, requiring respondents to make machine-readable entries for date of birth, and the use of graphics; see Rothwell, 1983.) However, we believe that the use of focus groups for questionnaire development of sensitive and ambiguous items such as race and ethnicity would be very useful. We initially recommended the focus group technique in our interim report (National Research Council, 1984), and we note that the Census Bureau used focus groups in the 1985 pretest in Tampa to elicit reactions to the questionnaire format.

> Recommendation 5.4. We recommend that the Census Bureau, in addition to other methods that it has traditionally employed, use the technique of focus group discussions as one means to develop questions on particularly sensitive items such as race and ethnicity.

Comparability Considerations

Although changes in question wording and categories for the race and ethnicity items may be necessary to improve the information, it is vitally important to strive for historical comparability of race and ethnicity data from one census to the next to the extent possible. Historical comparability is important to permit reliable analysis of changes in the status of various groups. Cross-temporal comparability is also important for evaluation of completeness of coverage, for example, using demographic analysis or reverse record check methodologies.

> Recommendation 5.5. We recommend that, in 1990, as it did in 1980, the Census Bureau collect, tabulate, and release data on race and ethnicity in such a way that the data can be reaggregated as necessary to obtain maximum feasible comparability with 1980 and 1970.

Comparability of race and ethnicity data from the census with race and ethnicity information collected in vital statistics records is also important for at least two reasons. First, vital statistics on births and deaths are large components of the total population estimates by race that are compared with the census counts to estimate net undercoverage using the technique of demographic analysis. Second, vital rates, such as birth, death, marriage, and divorce rates, which have vital statistics data in the numerator and census counts in the denominator, are important social indicators that are commonly analyzed by race. For both of these purposes, it is desirable that the data on race from both vital statistics and the census be as comparable as possible.

There will probably always be differences between the concepts of race and ethnicity as collected in vital statistics and in the census, if only because the methods of data collection vary: self-enumeration in the census versus identification by others in vital statistics (parents or medical staff for newborns and relatives or medical staff for decedents). Nevertheless, discrepancies due to differences in categories and editing rules could be minimized.

Currently, definitions of race and ethnicity differ in vital statistics from those used in the decennial census in several important ways. First, vital statistics records include Mexicans, Cubans, and Puerto Ricans in the white race category. Second, not all states determine Hispanic origin, although the 22 states that do are estimated to account for 90 percent of Hispanic births. Third, there are some differences in editing rules when race is mixed or unclear. For example, in vital statistics birth records, newborns of mixed parentage are assigned the race of the father, unless the father is white or the mother is Hawaiian, in which case the child is classified according to the mother's race (see National Center for Health Statistics, 1982a, 1982b). In the 1980 census, by contrast, persons of mixed parentage who could not specify a single category were coded according to the race of the mother (in 1970, the rule was to use the race of the father--see Bureau of the Census, 1983c.)

At present, the National Center for Health Statistics is reevaluating the standard certificates for vital events. Specifically, the center is requesting comments on whether the birth and death certificates should include a question on ethnic origin or descent separate from the race item and whether the question should ask simply for Hispanic origin or ask for origin in every case, such as Italian, English, Cuban, etc.[1]

---

[1]Personal communication from John E. Patterson to Miron L. Straf, October 26, 1984.

Recommendation 5.6. We recommend that the Census Bureau, the National Center for Health Statistics, and other relevant federal agencies work closely together to design questions and response editing rules on race and ethnicity that minimize conceptual differences between census and vital statistics records to the extent feasible. The Office of Management and Budget should act as necessary to facilitate such coordination.

Coverage Questions

The 1970 and 1980 censuses included several questions on the short form designed to aid in achieving a complete and accurate count. In 1970, Question H-A asked, "How many living quarters, occupied and vacant, are at this address?" with categories provided from 1 to 10 or more. Answers to this question were checked against the address list for structures with under 10 units to identify missed households. In 1980, the same question was asked as Question H-4 and edited as in 1970. In addition, the 1980 questionnaire included as Question 1 on the first page a space to list the name of each person living there on Tuesday, April 1, 1980, or who was visiting and had no other home (see Figure 5.5). An edit was performed to check that the number of names listed in this household roster agreed with the number appearing on the inside of the questionnaire; field follow-up took place if there were more names on the roster than inside. Finally, the 1980 questionnaire included 3 questions (H-1, H-2, H-3) that probed for persons whom the respondent either failed to list in Question 1 or improperly included (see Figure 5.5).

As discussed above, evaluation indicated that the H-4 edit in 1980 was less successful in adding housing units and persons than the comparable edit in 1970. Neither effort added more than a fraction of 1 percent to the population count. Review of questionnaires in 1980 that failed the H-4 edit indicated that the census office staff had a difficult time in conducting the edit and also that some respondents may not have correctly interpreted the question (Thompson, 1984:15).

The Census Bureau was unable to evaluate the effectiveness of the household roster (Question 1) edit, because of the absence of appropriate records, but looking at Figure 5.5 suggests that respondents may well

Question 1

List in Question 1

- Family members living here, including babies still in the hospital.
- Relatives living here.
- Lodgers or boarders living here.
- Other persons living here.
- College students who stay here while attending college, even if their parents live elsewhere.
- Persons who usually live here but are temporarily away (including children in boarding school below the college level).
- Persons with a home elsewhere but who stay here most of the week while working.

Do Not List in Question 1

- Any person away from here in the Armed Forces.
- Any college student who stays somewhere else while attending college.
- Any person who usually stays somewhere else most of the week while working there.
- Any person away from here in an institution such as a home for the aged or mental hospital.
- Any person staying or visiting here who has a usual home elsewhere.

1. **What is the name of each person who was living here on Tuesday, April 1, 1980, or who was staying or visiting here and had no other home?**

Note

If everyone here is staying only temporarily and has a usual home elsewhere, please mark this box ☐.

Then please:
- answer the questions on pages 2 through 5 only, and
- enter the address of your usual home on page 20.

→ *NOW PLEASE ANSWER QUESTIONS H1—H12 FOR YOUR HOUSEHOLD*

If you listed more than 7 persons in Question 1, please see note on page 20.

H1. Did you leave anyone out of Question 1 because you were not sure if the person should be listed — *for example, a new baby still in the hospital, a lodger who also has another home, or a person who stays here once in a while and has no other home?*

- O Yes — *On page 20 give name(s) and reason left out.*
- O No

H2. Did you list anyone in Question 1 who is away from home now — *for example, on a vacation or in a hospital?*

- O Yes — *On page 20 give name(s) and reason person is away.*
- O No

H3. Is anyone visiting here who is not already listed?

- O Yes — *On page 20 give name of each visitor for whom there is no one at the home address to report the person to a census taker.*
- O No

H4. How many living quarters, occupied and vacant, are at this address?

- O One
- O 2 apartments or living quarters
- O 3 apartments or living quarters
- O 4 apartments or living quarters
- O 5 apartments or living quarters
- O 6 apartments or living quarters
- O 7 apartments or living quarters
- O 8 apartments or living quarters
- O 9 apartments or living quarters
- O 10 or more apartments or living quarters
- O This is a mobile home or trailer

FIGURE 5.5 Coverage questions in the 1980 census.

have had problems with the instructions indicating which persons to list in Question 1 and which to omit. Similarly, the instructions do not seem at all clear for households that on Census Day were at a vacation residence but had a usual residence elsewhere.

The panel believes it is important that the questions and instructions regarding composition of the household be clearly communicated to respondents and that responses to such questions be given special attention by the field offices. This extra care is needed to minimize the possibilities for incorrect enumeration, whether it be undercount, overcount, or misallocation of persons and/or housing units among geographic areas.

Americans have always been highly mobile--one-sixth of the population changes residence every year, and some of those persons are in the process of moving at the time of the census (Hansen, 1984:Table A). Movers complicate both completion of an accurate count and evaluation of the count. Households with second (vacation) homes also complicate accurate enumeration. The 1970 census found that about 5 percent of households had a second home (Bureau of the Census, 1982c:751), and the percentage is growing. Finally, recent trends in living arrangements, retirement, and the workplace have resulted in populations with two or more "usual" residences that present special problems for accurate census-taking. Some examples include:

- Retired persons who have two "usual" homes, one for the winter months in a warm climate and the other for the summer months in a cool climate;
- Children of divorced families in which the parents have joint custody and the children spend a substantial part of the year, month, or week with each parent; and
- Two-career couples with jobs and residences in two different locations.

It is debatable how each of these kinds of persons should be counted. Leaving aside the matter of assignment to a specific household and geographic area, populations such as these appear more than usually at risk of undercount as well as overcount.

The Census Bureau is proposing as part of its 1986 pretest program to consider alternative coverage and household roster questions and to test adding questions about multiple residences that could help minimize miscounting. The Census Bureau also plans to test improvements in the program that attempts to assign households found at their second (vacation) home to their regular residence (the Whole Household Usual Home Elsewhere program).

A range of questionnaire design techniques, including focus groups, would appear useful to employ for these questions to determine wording and formats that are clear to the respondent and also easy for census office staff to process. Research on trends in mobility, second homes, and multiple residences should also assist in decennial census planning. Identifying geographic areas particularly affected by these phenomena might suggest special efforts targeted to particular populations in these areas. It is particularly important in this regard to assess future trends. If, as appears probable, a growing part of the population is likely to have two or more usual places of residence, own a second home, or to be moving between an old and a new residence during the census enumeration, then planning for a complete and accurate count should give high priority to dealing with these groups.

> Recommendation 5.7. We recommend that the Census Bureau give high priority in its planning for 1990 to research and testing of questions and enumeration procedures that address problems of accurately counting persons in the process of moving, households with second (vacation) homes, and persons with more than one usual place of residence.

A Specific Suggestion for a Coverage Improvement Question

In the 1977 pretest in Oakland, California, the Census Bureau tested the concept of "network" or "multiplicity" response rules for coverage evaluation (Sirken et al., 1978). Such rules include asking parents to provide names and addresses of children and vice versa. Published results suggested that the address information furnished was not of sufficient quality to warrant further investigation of this method as part of a coverage evaluation program that included matching samples of persons to census records.

However, the panel believes that the concept of generating lists of individuals in an area from the census operation itself to use as a procedure to improve coverage is worth investigating, at least for hard-to-enumerate areas, and comparing with other procedures in terms of costs and effectiveness. The procedure would be to ask respondents in the census for lists of specific types of relatives not living in the household. Information needed for nonresident relatives to facilitate locating them and determining if they had been included in the census would include address and also basic demographic characteristics, such as age and sex. The panel believes that relatives may be at least as good a source of up-to-date address information to use for a matching operation for coverage improvement as other lists that are commonly suggested, such as driver's licenses or welfare records.

The Oakland results suggested that address information supplied by parents was somewhat more accurate than information supplied by most other categories of relatives. Moreover, parents would probably be the most reliable source of information on a critical match item: birth date. Hence, asking parents to provide basic demographic information and addresses for children not living in the household could improve coverage, particularly of hard-to-count groups such as young adult black and Hispanic males and young black and Hispanic children in central cities.

<ins>Recommendation 5.8</ins>. We recommend, as one procedure to consider for improving coverage of hard-to-count groups, that the Census Bureau pretest a question asking parents for names and addresses of children who are not part of the household. This question should be included in the 1986 pretests.

Specifically, we propose that a question similar to the following be added to the census form:

Does anyone living in this household have a son or daughter living somewhere else? Yes ____ No ____
If yes, please list sons and daughters below.

Name ____
(Last First Middle)

Sex _____ Age___ Birth Date __________________
(Month - Day - Year)

Address ____

The object is to improve coverage in hard-to-count areas, particularly of young children, and hence it would not be cost-effective or even feasible to follow up all children reported as not living in the household. Instead, the goal would be to examine census returns from areas identified as hard to enumerate and to follow up those children reported by their parents as living in the same area. The question suggested above is phrased to ask parents for the addresses of all children not living in the household, so that there is no opportunity for misinterpretation of which children should be listed, but the follow-up could be restricted to children in target age-race-sex groups.

The answers to this question would provide a list of individuals that can be matched against the census. Presumably the list could be constructed and follow-ups (perhaps on a sample basis) of nonmatches done during the census operation. Operational questions for a test include the accuracy of birth date and address obtained from parents, the method of identifying addresses that are from hard-to-enumerate areas and should be followed up, the method of locating addresses, the use of different procedures in urban and rural areas, and the method of sharing information in cities with multiple offices. The effects on response rates of asking this question also need to be examined.

The panel recognizes that there are problems in adding a question to the census short form, particularly a question that requires a lot of space and that may be viewed as invasive of privacy. Indeed, given its intended follow-up on a sample basis, the question should perhaps be included on the long form only.

Research and testing of the suggested multiplicity coverage question and of other such questions, including ones on multiple residences, should be closely coordinated. The wording and format of all such questions must be carefully considered to ensure that the entire package is communicated clearly. If there is concern over the increased respondent burden, particularly for recipients of the long form, the Census Bureau should consider deleting other questions. Chapter 6 suggests some long-form housing questions that could be deleted and collected instead from other sources. The Census Bureau should also consider the possibility of different questionnaire formats in different areas. For example, it might be possible to include the multiplicity coverage question only on questionnaires for enumeration districts with certain expected characteristics, such as a high poverty rate and, conversely, to include questions on multiple residences only on questionnaires administered in other kinds of areas.

Because the multiplicity question appears promising for coverage improvement and also relates to other coverage questions that the Census Bureau is proposing to test in 1986, it is important that the multiplicity question be tested in 1986 as well. The panel, in fact, recommended in its interim report (National Research Council, 1984) that the multiplicity question be tested in the first 1990 census pretest, that is, in 1985. The Census Bureau has proposed delaying a test until 1987. For the reasons outlined above, the panel believes that high priority should be given to testing coverage questions in 1986 and that these tests should include a multiplicity question.

ISSUES IN COVERAGE IMPROVEMENT: SPECIAL ENUMERATION PROCEDURES

The panel does not propose to comment in detail on each of the various coverage improvement procedures used in 1970 and 1980 and proposed for testing in 1986. We believe we can be most useful to the Census Bureau by recommending general strategies for deciding the priorities to assign in its 1990 census research and testing program. The Census Bureau staff exercised some selection in the process of drawing up the proposed package of 1986 pretests of coverage improvement programs, but the package still seems much too ambitious for the likely available staff and budget resources and for the time available to design, execute, and evaluate the results from this and subsequent pretests prior to 1990. Pretest results that cannot be assimilated in time to affect the next pretest or the dress rehearsals represent largely wasted effort.

The panel believes that the goal of a complete enumeration is very important and, as discussed more fully in Chapter 7, that adjustment procedures should not be viewed as an alternative to obtaining as complete a count as possible throuth cost-effective means. The panel also believes that special coverage improvement programs can make important contributions to improving the count. However, the panel does not subscribe to the view that every coverage improvement idea that is suggested should be pursued or that programs used in past censuses should automatically be included in the plans for the next census. The panel believes that evaluation results for coverage improvement procedures used in prior censuses should be carefully reviewed and that further research and testing should be conducted only for programs that meet certain criteria of cost-effectiveness, particularly in reducing differential undercounts. Similarly, proposed ideas for new kinds of procedures should be assessed against several criteria to determine the extent to which they appear promising and feasible.

With regard to assigning priorities for research and testing of coverage improvement programs with which the Census Bureau has prior experience, the panel recommends the following strategy:

> Recommendation 5.9. We recommend that the Census Bureau review coverage improvement programs used in past censuses and proceed with research and testing directed toward use in 1990 of those programs that: (1) exhibited a high yield in terms of numbers of missed persons correctly added to the count and/or contributed significantly to reducing differential undercoverage, (2) exhibited low-to-moderate costs per person correctly added, and (3) did not add many persons incorrectly. Programs that do not satisfy these criteria should be dropped from consideration unless: (1) the program exhibited low total dollar costs and had demonstrable public relations or goodwill value in previous censuses or (2) there is some particular reason to believe a revised program will yield greatly improved results.

The above recommendation does not quantify terms such as "high yield" or "low cost." Obviously, the previous performance of specific coverage improvement programs should be carefully and appropriately measured and a decision whether to include a program in the 1990 pretest plans carefully arrived at. For example, the proportion of housing unit or person additions to the count should be measured using the appropriate denominator. In the case of a program administered in specified areas, the denominator should be the total count only for those areas. Admittedly, the available evaluation data are subject to margins of error that may be wide for some programs. Nonetheless, it seems possible to assign priorities through a hard look at the information in hand.

Based on the data in Tables 5.2 and 5.3, it appears that the various address checking programs carried out in advance of Census Day easily qualify for further consideration both in terms of proportion of additions to the count and in terms of cost per addition. Some other programs, such as the Were You Counted program, yielded very little but were quite inexpensive and appear to have goodwill value in conducting the census. Still other programs are more problematical. Although the coverage questions and roster checks were low yield and costly to administer in 1980, it appears essential, as discussed above, that research be carried out to develop optimal formats and processing procedures for these questions to minimize problems of undercount, overcount, and misallocation among geographic areas. The Vacant/Delete Check met a minimum standard of 0.5 percent additions to the count, but it was costly in 1980. A high priority for further research on this program would involve investigation of ways to reduce costs, for example, by returning to the use of sampling, as in 1970 (see further discussion in Chapter 6, where the panel recommends that the Census Bureau conduct research on the use of sampling for the Vacant/Delete Check and possibly other coverage improvement programs). The Nonhousehold Sources Program appears to fail on tests both of additions to the count (even when the denominator is the number of addresses that were selected for matching) and cost. It is possible that the use of automation could improve the cost-effectiveness of this program as might selection of other kinds of lists, but, given that choices must be made, it appears that the program should be given low priority.

For ideas with which the Census Bureau has little or no experience, the panel suggests that questions such as the following be asked:

(1) To what extent is the proposed coverage improvement program directed toward known problem areas? For example, the Census Bureau is considering tests of a number of means of handling multiunit structures for which mail delivery is often problematical, including an update list/leave procedure that was tried experimentally in a few district offices in 1980. As another example, the proposed multiplicity coverage question is directed toward hard-to-count groups, specifically young minority children.

(2) To what extent does any available evidence suggest that the proposed procedure might prove effective? For

example, although the update list/leave procedure in 1980 resulted in significantly higher initial mail return rates in the experimental offices compared with the controls (81 versus 71 percent--see Mikkelson and McKelvey, 1983), no significant differences in coverage have been determined (see Bailey and Ferrari, 1984; Mikkelson, 1984).

(3) Do rough paper-and-pencil estimates of cost and yield suggest that the proposed program is likely to be cost-effective?

(4) Can the program be implemented in targeted areas as a means of improving cost-effectiveness, or can cost savings be effected through judicious use of sampling?

For coverage improvement procedures that the Census Bureau decides to retain in its research and testing program, the panel believes it is important to further categorize them into programs that need early field testing versus those that can be researched with other, less expensive, and less staff-intensive methods. For example, it may not be necessary to include the Casual Count program in any early full-scale pretest. Other procedures, such as trying out various address checks in prelist and conventional areas, probably need early testing, particularly to work on integrating these operations with the various automation efforts that are being given high testing priority. A strategy that does not attempt costly field tests of every program should help make the Census Bureau's budget and staff resources stretch farther and help reduce the problem of a proliferation of tests producing results that cannot be assimilated in time for 1990. Finally, one cost-effective means of gaining useful information for improving coverage programs would be to conduct focus groups that include members of hard-to-count populations. Such groups could consider reasons for failure to be counted and consider as well the likely impact of particular programs.

<u>Recommendation 5.10</u>. We recommend that the Census Bureau conduct full-scale pretests in 1986 only of those coverage improvement programs that require such testing. Furthermore, we recommend that the Census Bureau use focus groups that include members of hard-to-count populations as one means to explore coverage improvement techniques and to narrow the range of options to be field-tested.

APPENDIX 5.1

GROSS OMISSIONS AND GROSS OVERENUMERATIONS IN THE CENSUS

This appendix presents results of coverage evaluation programs that identify groups in the population that appear to have been less well counted--through omission and/or erroneous enumeration--in the 1980 and previous decennial censuses. Most of the results represent estimates of gross omissions from the census. Results of the demographic analysis method of coverage evaluation are discussed in the text but not in this appendix, because demographic analysis provides estimates of net undercoverage but not of the gross omission or gross overenumeration components. Results of studies of the completeness of census coverage of housing units are also briefly reviewed.

GROSS OMISSIONS OF PEOPLE

Findings From 1980 Census Coverage Evaluation Programs

The Post-Enumeration Program

The PEP program developed estimates of gross omissions in the 1980 census through matching interview records from the April and August Current Population Surveys (the P sample) to census records in the same small geographic areas (enumeration districts). The PEP design resulted in gross omission rates that represent overestimates because, among other reasons, the rates include persons who were enumerated in the census but at a location so far removed from their address in the CPS that it was outside the area of search for a match in the census records. The PEP program also encountered many problems in implementation. To date, there are 12 separate sets of estimates of undercount developed from PEP based on different treatment of problems such as nonresponse to the CPS (see Chapter 4 for a description and evaluation of PEP). Hence, the discussion that follows seeks to determine the order of magnitude of differences in gross omission rates among population subgroups, but it cannot provide precise estimates. The tables shown in this section express findings from the PEP in terms of ratios of the gross omission rate for a population group to the average rate experienced for the total population. Population groups are placed into one of five categories of relative gross omission rates:

(1) Very High: greater than or equal to 3 times the average rate;
(2) High: greater than or equal to 2 times and less than 3 times the average rate;
(3) Moderately High: greater than or equal to 1.25 times and less than 2 times the average rate;
(4) Average: greater than .75 times and less than 1.25 times the average rate;
(5) Below Average: less than or equal to .75 times the average rate.

Several tables show relative gross omission rates from the PEP for population groups categorized by household relationship, race and Hispanic origin (ethnicity), type of place, and by ethnicity and type of place crossed with rates of nonreturn of the mail questionnaires in the district offices. The data represent the results of preliminary exploratory analysis conducted by the Census Bureau of the PEP 3-8 series. This series was based on matching the April CPS to the census and estimated an average gross omission rate for the total population in 1980 of 5.4 percent.

The 3-8 series happened to be the first series to be put into a computerized form suitable for this kind of analysis at the Census Bureau. Further work is necessary to confirm that the 3-8 findings are reliable and representative of the results shown by other series of estimates. More limited tabulations of several other PEP series of estimates were recently prepared by the Census Bureau, and they generally confirm the picture shown by the 3-8 series regarding the population groups that were relatively harder to count in 1980 (see discussion at the end of this section).

Findings from the PEP 3-8 series. The preliminary findings from the 3-8 series with regard to which population groups proved relatively harder to count are not surprising, but the dispersion among the five categories of relative gross omission rates is not always as great as one might expect. On the dimension of household relationship, members of the nuclear family--head, spouse, and son or daughter--were relatively easy to find compared with other household members (see Table 5.4). Persons not related to the household head and relatives other

TABLE 5.4 Household Relationship by Relative Gross Omission Rate for a Sample of Persons, Post-Enumeration Program-Census Match (1980, PEP Series 3-8)

Relative Gross Omission Rate[a]	Household Relationship
Very high	—
High	Nonrelative
	Other relative
	Brother or sister
Moderately high	Mother or father
Average	Head
	Son or daughter
Below average	Spouse

NOTE: Average gross omission rate for the 1980 PEP was 5.4%.

[a]Categories of relative gross omission rates are as follows:
(1) Very high: greater than or equal to 3 times the average rate.
(2) High: greater than or equal to 2 times and less than 3 times the average rate.
(3) Moderately high: greater than or equal to 1.25 and less than 2 times the average rate.
(4) Average: greater than .75 and less than 1.25 times the average rate.
(5) Below average: less than or equal to .75 times the average rate.

SOURCE: Hogan (1983b:3).

than parents had high rates of gross omissions compared with the average for the total population. On the dimension of ethnicity (see Table 5.5), blacks were among the hardest-to-find groups, with a high relative gross omission rate. Persons classified as Hispanic had a moderately high rate overall but showed dispersion when further categorized by place of origin. Puerto Ricans and "other" Hispanics had high relative gross omission rates; the rate for Mexicans was moderately high; while the rate for Cubans was within the average category. Finally, American Indians and Asian-Americans had moderately high gross omission rates, while the rates for non-Hispanic whites and other races were average.

Distributions are not given for other demographic variables such as age and sex. Males and females both had average rates of gross omissions, as did most age groups. (The PEP findings of very little difference in coverage rates between men and women contrast with the results of demographic analysis, which showed worse coverage for men, particularly among blacks.) From unpublished PEP 3-8 series tabulations, young adults ages 15-24 had a moderately high relative rate of gross omissions, while persons age 45 and older had below-average rates. The PEP does not provide separate estimates of coverage of undocumented aliens, although the PEP sample probably included some representation of this group.

TABLE 5.5 Ethnicity and Mail Nonreturn Rate By Relative Gross Omission Rate for a Sample of Persons, Post-Enumeration Program-Census Match (1980, PEP Series 3-8)

Relative Gross Omission Rate Category[a]	Ethnicity (detailed categorization)		Mail Nonreturn Rate (mail areas only)[b] and Ethnicity[c]	
Very high	—		30% or higher:	Black
				Hispanic
High	Black (non-Hispanic)		30% or higher:	Total
	Hispanic:	Puerto Rican	15-29%:	Black
		Other		
Moderately high	Hispanic:	Total	30% or higher:	White
		Mexican	15-29%:	Hispanic
	American Indian		Less than 15%:	Black
	Asian			
Average	Hispanic:	Cuban	15-29%:	Total
	White (non-Hispanic)			White
	Other race (non-Hispanic)		Less than 15%:	Hispanic
Below average	—		Less than 15%:	Total
				White

NOTE: The average gross omission rate for the 1980 PEP was 5.4%.

[a] Categories of relative gross omission rates are as follows:
(1) Very high: greater than or equal to 3 times the average rate.
(2) High: greater than or equal to 2 times and less than 3 times the average rate.
(3) Moderately high: greater than or equal to 1.25 and less than 2 times the average rate.
(4) Average: greater than .75 and less than 1.25 times the average rate.
(5) Below average: less than or equal to .75 times the average rate.

[b] The mail nonreturn rate is the percentage of occupied households that did not mail their questionnaires to census offices.

[c] The three ethnicity categories shown are exhaustive: black non-Hispanic, Hispanic of all races, and white and other race non-Hispanic.

SOURCE: Hogan (1983b:2; 1983a:attached graphs).

Among the variables displayed, the dimension of type of place (see Table 5.6) shows the least dispersion. Central cities of large standard metropolitan statistical areas (SMSAs with 3 million or more population) had a moderately high relative gross omission rate, while all other place types had average rates. Note that areas enumerated using conventional techniques rather than a mailout-mailback approach had a below-average relative gross omission rate.

Distributions are not given for urban versus rural areas or region of the country (Northeast, Midwest, South, West), as all of these categories had average gross omission rates. This is not to say, however, that more in-depth analysis would not reveal interactions between region or urban versus rural and other variables.

TABLE 5.6 Type of Place and Mail Nonreturn Rate by Relative Gross Omission Rate for a Sample of Persons, Post-Enumeration Program-Census Match (1980, PEP Series 3-8)

Relative Gross Omission Rate Category[a]	Type of Place	Mail Nonreturn Rate (mail areas only)[d] and Type of Place	
Very high	—	35% or higher:	Central city, large SMSA
			Central city, small SMSA
High	—	30% or higher:	Other, SMSA
			Outside SMSA
		25-34%:	Central city, large SMSA
Moderately high	Central city, large SMSA[b]	25-34%:	Central city, small SMSA
		10-24%:	Central city, large SMSA
Average	Central city, small SMSA[c]	15-29%:	Other, SMSA
	Other, SMSA		Outside SMSA
	Outside SMSA	5-24%:	Central city, small SMSA
	All mailout-mailback areas		
Below average	Conventional areas	0-14%:	Other, SMSA
			Outside SMSA
		0-9%:	Central city, large SMSA
		0-4%:	Central city, small SMSA

NOTE: The average gross omission rate for the 1980 PEP was 5.4%.

[a] Categories of relative gross omission rates are as follows:
(1) Very high: greater than or equal to 3 times the average rate.
(2) High: greater than or equal to 2 times and less than 3 times the average rate.
(3) Moderately high: greater than or equal to 1.25 and less than 2 times the average rate.
(4) Average: greater than .75 and less than 1.25 times the average rate.
(5) Below average: less than or equal to .75 times the average rate.

[b] Large standard metropolitan statistical area (SMSA) is defined as an area with over 3 million population.

[c] Small SMSA is defined as an area with 3 million or less population.

[d] The mail nonreturn rate is the percentage of occupied households that did not return their questionnaires to census offices.

SOURCE: Hogan (1983b:4; 1983c; and unpublished worksheets).

When either ethnicity or type of place is crossed with the mail nonreturn rate for the district office (that is, 100 percent minus the percentage rate at which questionnaires were mailed back from households), the dispersion in relative rates of gross omissions increases dramatically. While blacks on average had a high relative gross omission rate, those blacks in district offices with mail nonreturn rates of 30 percent or more had a very high relative gross omission rate (3 or more times the average rate), and, conversely those blacks in district offices with mail nonreturn rates of less than 15 percent had only a moderately high relative gross omission rate. A similar spread is evident for Hispanics and for non-

Hispanic whites (see Table 5.5). The dispersion for type of place categories is even more extreme when the factor of mail nonreturn rates is introduced. Central cities of large SMSAs, which on average exhibited a moderately high relative rate of omissions, had a very high rate in those areas in which the district office mail nonreturn rate was 35 percent or greater and, conversely, a below-average rate in those areas of the central city in which the mail nonreturn rate was under 10 percent (see Table 5.6).

Findings from Other PEP Series. Unpublished tabulations of gross omission rates from two other PEP series, the 5-8 series based on matching August CPS records to the census, and the 14-20 series based like the 3-8 series on matching April CPS records to the census but with a different treatment of incomplete cases, generally support the findings reported above from the 3-8 series. The 5-8 series estimated an overall rate of gross omissions of 5.25 percent and the 14-20 series a rate of 3.45 percent compared with the 5.4 percent rate estimated by the 3-8 series. In relative terms, all three series found that blacks had a high relative gross omission rate, Hispanics a moderately high rate, men and women average rates, young adults ages 15-24 a moderately high rate, persons age 45 and older below-average rates, and other age groups average rates. In each case, the determination of the gross omission rate category for a population group was made relative to the average rate for the particular series. Data from the match of August CPS records to the census also generally support the 3-8 series of findings regarding the relationship of high mail nonreturn rates to high relative rates of omissions (Hogan, 1983a).

The IRS-Census Match

A methodological study conducted after the 1980 census, the IRS-Census Match, although not designed as a coverage evaluation study, provides some evidence on differential rates of gross omissions from the census. The purpose of the IRS-Census Match was to examine tracing and matching problems with pre-enumeration surveys and reverse record checks. The study attempted to match a sample of about 11,000 filers of 1979 tax returns to 1980 census records. Black and Hispanic filers were oversampled (Childers and Hogan, 1984a).

The average gross nonmatch rate for the total sample was 12.6 percent. There are many reasons for the high rate, including the facts that addresses supplied by taxpayers on IRS forms were not always the same as the residence address and that the matching study was carried out several years after the census and not intended to produce coverage estimates. Nonetheless, some insights can perhaps be gained when the IRS sample is categorized along several dimensions and gross omission rates for subgroups are compared with the average for the entire sample.

In the IRS-Census Match study, blacks and Hispanics exhibited moderately high relative gross omission rates (category 3), while the rate for non-Hispanic whites fell into the average category (category 4). Adding the dimension of sex increases the dispersion, with black males having a high relative gross omission rate (category 2) and white females a below-average rate (category 5). These findings are consistent with those from the PEP and demographic analysis.

The IRS-Census Match provides data on gross omission rates for two important dimensions: marital status (proxied by type of return--single or joint) and income (adjusted gross income reported to the IRS). These two dimensions help identify hard-to-count groups (see Table 5.7). Persons filing single returns had moderately high gross omission rates, while persons filing joint returns had below-average rates. Cross-tabulating type of return with ethnicity gives the result that, while black single return filers had a high relative gross omission rate, black joint return filers fell into the average category. Similarly, white single return filers had a moderately high relative gross omission rate, while white joint return filers were below average. Type of return did not discriminate to any important extent among the Hispanic group.

Adding the dimension of income refines the picture of hard-to-count groups. Black single return filers had high relative gross omission rates regardless of income level; however, income discriminated among black joint return filers, with those reporting less than $8,000 income showing a high relative rate of gross omissions but those reporting $15,000 or more income a below-average rate. Among whites, those filing single returns with reported income under $15,000 and those filing joint returns with income under $8,000 fell into the category of moderately high relative gross omission rates, while

TABLE 5.7 Ethnicity, Type of Return, and Income by Relative Gross Omission Rate for a Sample of Income Tax Filers Ages 18 to 64, IRS-Census Match (1980)

Relative Gross Omission Rate Category[a]	Ethnicity and Type of Return[a]		Income in 1979, Type of Return, and Ethnicity[b]	
Very high	—		—	
High	Black:	Single return	Under $8,000, single return:	Black
	Hispanic:	Single return		Hispanic
			Under $8,000, joint return:	Black
				Hispanic
			$8,000-14,999, single return:	Black
			$8,000-14,999, joint return:	Hispanic
			$15,000 or more, single return:	Black
				Hispanic
Moderately high	Black:	Total filers	Under $8,000, single return:	White
	Hispanic:	Joint return	Under $8,000, joint return:	White
		Total filers	$8,000-14,999, single return:	Hispanic
	White:	Single return		White
			$8,000-14,999, joint return:	Black
Average	Black:	Joint return	$15,000 or more, joint return	Hispanic
	White:	Total filers		
Below average	White:	Joint return	$8,000-14,999, joint return:	White
			$15,000 or more, single return:	White
			$15,000 or more, joint return:	Black
				White

NOTE: The average gross omission rate for the 1980 IRS-Census Match was 12.6%.

[a] Categories of relative gross omission rates are as follows:
(1) Very high: greater than or equal to 3 times the average rate.
(2) High: greater than or equal to 2 times and less than 3 times the average rate.
(3) Moderately high: greater than or equal to 1.25 and less than 2 times the average rate.
(4) Average: greater than .75 and less than 1.25 times the average rate.
(5) Below average: less than or equal to .75 times the average rate.

[b] The three ethnicity categories shown are exhaustive: black non-Hispanic, Hispanic of all races, and white and other race non-Hispanic.

SOURCE: Childers and Hogan (1984a:Tables 1 and 2).

the remainder fell into the below-average category. For Hispanics filing joint returns, the cutting point between high relative gross omission rates and average rates was an income level of $15,000; however, income level did not discriminate among Hispanics filing single returns to any great degree.

Findings From Previous Census Coverage Evaluation Programs

Coverage evaluation programs for previous censuses provide additional information about groups in the population

TABLE 5.8 Household Relationship by Relative Gross Omission Rate for a Sample of Persons, CPS-Census Match (1960)

Relative Gross Omission Rate Category[a]	Household Relationship
Very high	Brother- or sister-in-law
	Group quarters resident
High	Son- or daughter-in-law
	Other relative
	Nonrelative
	Grandson or granddaughter
Moderately high	Relationship not reported
	Mother or father
	Mother- or father-in-law
	Brother or sister
Average	Son or daughter
	Head
Below average	Wife

NOTE: The average gross omission rate for the 1960 CPS-Census Match was 6.5%.

[a]Categories of relative gross omission rates are as follows:

(1) Very high: greater than or equal to 3 times the average rate.
(2) High: greater than or equal to 2 times and less than 3 times the average rate.
(3) Moderately high: greater than or equal to 1.25 and less than 2 times the average rate.
(4) Average: greater than .75 and less than 1.25 times the average rate.
(5) Below average: less than or equal to .75 times the average rate.

SOURCE: Bureau of the Census (1964a:Table 19).

that are more apt to be undercounted compared with other groups. This appendix reviews the findings of post-enumeration surveys and resident observation but does not discuss demographic analysis. The chapter text reviews the estimates of net undercoverage provided by demographic analysis for the 1950, 1960, and 1970 censuses.

Post-enumeration Surveys

Post-enumeration surveys conducted in previous censuses provide data on relative rates of undercoverage for various population groups. Tables 5.8 through 5.11 show relative gross omission rates for the population categorized along several dimensions from the results of the match of the April 1960 Current Population Survey to 1960 census records and of the match of the Post-Enumeration Survey conducted in summer 1950 to 1950 census records. (The dimensions shown were chosen to try to present estimates based on large enough sample sizes for reliability.) The relative gross omission rate experienced for

TABLE 5.9 Employment Status by Sex and Income by Race by Relative Gross Omission Rate for a Sample of Persons, CPS-Census Match (1960)

Relative Gross Omission Rate Category[a]	Sex and Employment Status (persons 14 years and over)[b]		Race and Income in 1959 (males 14 years and over with income)[c]	
Very high	—		—	
High	Female:	Unemployed	Nonwhite:	Income under $7,500
	Male:	Agricultural (Ag.) wage worker		Total male 14 years and over with income
Moderately high	Male:	Not in labor force	Nonwhite:	Income $7,500 or more
		Unemployed	White:	Income under $5,000
Average	Female:	Total	White:	Income $5,000-9,999
		Nonag. wage worker		Total male 14 years and over with income
		Nonag. self-employed		
		Not in labor force		
	Male:	Total		
		Nonag. wage worker		
Below average	Male:	Ag. self-employed	White:	Income $10,000 or more
		Nonag. self-employed		

NOTE: The average gross omission rate for the 1960 CPS-Census Match was 6.5%.

[a]Categories of relative gross omission rates are as follows:
(1) Very high: greater than or equal to 3 times the average rate.
(2) High: greater than or equal to 2 times and less than 3 times the average rate.
(3) Moderately high: greater than or equal to 1.25 and less than 2 times the average rate.
(4) Average: greater than .75 and less than 1.25 times the average rate.
(5) Below average: less than or equal to .75 times the average rate.

[b]Groups not shown because of small sample size are male agricultural and nonagricultural unpaid worker; female agricultural wage worker, self-employed, and unpaid worker; and female nonagricultural unpaid worker.

[c]All income amounts are in 1979 dollars (1959 figures times 2.5).

SOURCE: Bureau of the Census (1964a:Tables 28 and 43).

the entire population was 6.5 percent in the 1960 CPS-Census Match and 2.2 percent in the 1950 Post-Enumeration Survey. (The lower rate for 1950 attests to the deficiencies of a "pure" post-enumeration survey in which enumerators are sent out to recanvass an area.)

On the dimension of household relationship, both 1960 and 1950 data support the findings from the 1980 PEP, namely that persons not belonging to the nuclear family were harder to find than household heads, spouses, and their children. Nonrelatives including residents of group quarters were particularly difficult to count (see Tables 5.8 and 5.10).

Looking at relative gross omission rates by extent of education, data from 1950 indicate that persons with education not reported exhibited a very high relative gross omission rate, while persons with 6 or fewer years

TABLE 5.10 Household Relationship and Education Level by Relative Gross Omission Rate for a Sample of Persons, Post-Enumeration Survey-Census Match (1950)

Relative Gross Omission Rate Category[a]	Household Relationship	Education Level (persons 25 years and over)
Very high	Nonrelative	Education not reported
High	—	—
Moderately high	Other relative	6 or fewer years of school completed
Average	Head	More than 6 years of school completed
	Wife	
	Son or daughter	
Below average	—	—

NOTE: The average gross omission rate for the 1950 Post-Enumeration Survey-Census Match was 2.2%.

[a] Categories of relative gross omission rates are as follows:
(1) Very high: greater than or equal to 3 times the average rate.
(2) High: greater than or equal to 2 times and less than 3 times the average rate.
(3) Moderately high: greater than or equal to 1.25 and less than 2 times the average rate.
(4) Average: greater than .75 and less than 1.25 times the average rate.
(5) Below average: less than or equal to .75 times the average rate.

SOURCE: Bureau of the Census (1960:Tables E and 4).

of schooling exhibited a moderately high rate. The gross omission rate for persons with more than 6 years of schooling fell into the average category (see Table 5.10). Comparable data are not available from 1960.

Both the 1960 and 1950 census coverage evaluation programs furnish data on differential rates of undercount among the population classified by labor force status, occupation, and income levels (see Tables 5.9 and 5.11). In 1960, unemployed women had a high relative gross omission rate, and men who were unemployed or not in the labor force had moderately high rates. Looking at employed persons, male agricultural paid laborers had a high relative gross omission rate, while the rate was below average for self-employed men both in farming and other lines of business.

On the dimension of income, looking only at males, there is a clearer picture for whites compared with nonwhites in 1960. In the case of white males, those with low income had a moderately high relative rate of gross omissions, while those with high income had a below-average rate. In contrast, income did not discriminate to any important extent among nonwhite males.

TABLE 5.11 Occupation by Sex and Income by Relative Gross Omission Rate for a Sample of Persons, Post-Enumeration Survey-Census Match (1950)

Relative Gross Omission Rate Category[a]	Sex and Occupation (persons 14 years and over)[b]		Income in 1949 (males 14 years and over)[c]
Very high	Female:	Farm laborer and unpaid worker	—
	Male:	Farm laborer	
High	Female:	Private household worker	Income not reported
	Male:	Nonfarm laborer	
Moderately high	Female:	All other occupations[d]	Income under $3,000
	Male:	Farm unpaid worker	
		Not employed	
Average	Female:	Not employed	Income $3,000-10,499
	Male:	All other occupations[e]	Total male 14 and over
Below average	Female:	Sales worker	Income $10,500 and over
	Male:	Farmer and farm manager	

NOTE: The average gross omission rate for the 1950 Post-Enumeration Survey-Census Match was 2.2%.

[a] Categories of relative gross omission rates are as follows:
(1) Very high: greater than or equal to 3 times the average rate.
(2) High: greater than or equal to 2 times and less than 3 times the average rate.
(3) Moderately high: greater than or equal to 1.25 and less than 2 times the average rate.
(4) Average: greater than .75 and less than 1.25 times the average rate.
(5) Below average: less than or equal to .75 times the average rate.

[b] Excludes male private household worker, female farmer, and female nonfarm laborer categories because of small sample size.

[c] All income amounts are in 1979 dollars (1949 figures times 3).

[d] Includes professional and technical, nonfarm manager, clerical, crafts, operative, and service worker categories.

[e] Includes categories listed in note *d* plus sales worker category.

SOURCE: Bureau of the Census (1960:Tables 6A, 6B, and 9B).

The 1950 data, which do not include race breakdowns, support the general patterns evident in 1960 on occupation and income. Persons with very high relative rates of gross omissions include farm laborers of both sexes and female unpaid farm workers. In contrast, male farmers and also female sales workers had below-average rates (female farmers were excluded because of very small sample size). Male nonagricultural laborers and female private household workers fell into the next category of high relative gross omission rates. On the dimension of income, low income is associated with a moderately high relative rate of gross omissions, while high income is associated with a below-average rate. Note that persons with various characteristics, such as income, not reported in the 1950 study tended to have very high or high relative gross omission rates, indicating that these persons represented a generally hard-to-count group.

Finally, tables are not shown by type of area or region of the country, as these dimensions did not discriminate significantly in either 1960 or 1950 on relative rates of gross omissions. In 1960 the population of urban areas, rural nonfarm, and rural farm areas all exhibited average relative gross omission rates (Bureau of the Census, 1964a:Table 8). In 1950 persons living in urban areas had an average rate of gross omissions, persons classified as rural nonfarm had a moderately high relative rate, and persons classified as rural farm had a below-average rate. By region of the country in 1950, the Northeast, North Central, and West regions had average rates, while only the South had a moderately high relative rate of gross omissions. Within the South, rural nonfarm areas were hardest to count, with a high relative rate of gross omissions (Bureau of the Census, 1960:Table F).

Comparable data were not published for 1970, but unpublished data from a match of the April Current Population Survey to the census records indicate the following patterns. (These findings should be viewed as suggestive only, however, because of high variances associated with the estimates.) First, employed whites had a below-average gross omission rate, but employed blacks had a moderately high relative rate. Similarly, higher-income whites had a below-average gross omission rate, but this was not true for higher-income blacks. Unemployed and low-income persons of both races had average rates of gross omissions. Finally, rates of gross omissions were higher in rural than in other types of areas (Siegel, 1975:8-9).

Resident Observer Studies

The techniques of resident observation employed in ethnographic studies were used on one occasion to study factors affecting the coverage of household surveys. Charles A. Valentine and Betty Lou Valentine, who were trained anthropologists, conducted a resident ethnographic study of a predominantly black inner-city community in 1968-1970, partially under the sponsorship of the Center for Research in Measurement Methods of the Census Bureau (Valentine and Valentine, 1971). Interviewers for the Current Population Survey, the Health Interview Survey, and the Quarterly Housing Survey conducted interviews in the area at the time when the Valentines had been in residence for approximately one year. The interviewers were unaware that the Valentines were studying the area. The Valentines independently identified the residents of a number of households in the area and ultimately compared their independently derived data on household composition for a total of 25 dwelling units with the corresponding data as reported by the survey interviewers. About three-fourths of the households were black and one-fourth Hispanic. The families lived in substandard housing, some lacking basic facilities. All families were judged to have very low incomes relative to the cost of living for the area. The Valentines described the community as "a typical polyethnic inner-city slum."

For the 25 households, the surveys reported a total of 127 individuals, whereas the Valentines identified 153 individuals as being associated with the dwelling units. Therefore, the survey procedures produced a 17 percent undercount relative to the count obtained by the resident observers. The most striking result was that the ethnographic evidence suggested that 61 percent (17 of 28) of the males age 19 and older were not counted by the survey procedures. The Valentines described the missed men as regularly residing in the households. The men contributed to financial support, took part in domestic activities, and shared in child-rearing. In nine of the households, the men were legally married and living with their spouses. The remaining common-law unions were relatively permanent and most were intact two years after the study. The Valentine estimates provided a much more realistic sex ratio than did the interview results.

The Valentines described a number of reasons that led them to believe that one cannot expect traditional interview or self-enumeration procedures to identify individuals of the type missed in the study area. The Valentines felt that the respondents understood the questions. They concluded that the men were not reported because the identification of resident males in the households could be detrimental to the economic welfare of the household and that the respondents behaved in a consistent manner in failing to report these men.

GROSS OVERENUMERATIONS OF PEOPLE

Findings From the 1980 PEP Program

The whole story regarding coverage problems in the census does not emerge solely by looking at gross omissions. It is necessary to examine gross overenumerations as well as omissions to obtain a complete picture. The PEP developed estimates of gross overenumerations in the 1980 census through rechecking a sample of census records (the E sample) to identify problems such as duplicate records, persons enumerated who were not alive on Census Day, and so on. As is true for the PEP estimate of gross omissions, the estimate of gross overenumerations is overstated. Also, the rates cannot be subtracted to give an estimate of the net undercount, because they have different denominators (see Cowan and Fay, 1984, for further explanation).

Data from the PEP 3-8 series (which is the only series for which tabulations for population groups are currently available) indicate an overall gross overenumeration rate of 3.6 percent in 1980 versus an overall gross omission rate of 5.4 percent. It is the case that population groups with relatively high gross omission rates also tended to have relatively high relative rates of gross overenumerations. However, the dispersion in gross overenumeration rates is less than the dispersion in gross omission rates.

Table 5.12, as an illustration, shows relative rates of gross overenumeration for ethnicity and household relationship in 1980. Blacks and Hispanics on average had moderately high relative rates of gross overenumerations, as did members of other races. American Indians, Asians, white non-Hispanics, and some categories of Hispanics, in contrast, were in the average category. This pattern is similar to the pattern evidenced in Table 5.5 for relative gross omission rates, but the dispersion is less for gross overenumerations. Similar findings emerge for categories of household relationship: household members outside the nuclear family had higher rates of both gross overenumerations and gross omissions compared with nuclear family members but were not as badly overenumerated relative to the average as they were underenumerated (see Table 5.4).

The rate of gross overenumerations also varied by type of enumeration procedure. Enumerations obtained in mail areas by follow-up because the questionnaire was not

TABLE 5.12 Ethnicity and Household Relationship by Relative Gross Overenumeration Rate for a Sample of Persons, Post-Enumeration Program-Census Match (1980, PEP Series 3-8)

Relative Gross Overenumeration Rate Category	Ethnicity (detailed categorization)	Household Relationship
Very high	—	—
High	—	—
Moderately high	Black (non-Hispanic)	Nonrelative
	Hispanic: Total	Other relative
	Cuban	Brother or sister
	Puerto Rican	
	Other race (non-Hispanic)	
Average	American Indian	Head
	Asian	Spouse
	Hispanic: Mexican	Son or daughter
	Other	Mother or father
	White (non-Hispanic)	
Below average	—	—

NOTE: The average gross overenumeration rate for the 1980 PEP was 3.6%.

[a]Categories of relative gross overenumeration rates are as follows:
(1) Very high: greater than or equal to 3 times the average rate.
(2) High: greater than or equal to 2 times and less than 3 times the average rate.
(3) Moderately high: greater than or equal to 1.25 and less than 2 times the average rate.
(4) Average: greater than .75 and less than 1.25 times the average rate.
(5) Below average: less than or equal to .75 times the average rate.

SOURCE: Hogan (1983b:2-3).

mailed back showed a high relative rate of gross overenumerations, while enumerations resulting from mail returns or obtained in conventional areas had below average rates (Cowan and Fay, 1984:6). It is not clear how much of the gross overenumeration was due to actual double counting and other kinds of erroneous enumerations in the census as opposed to problems with unresolved cases in the E sample. These problems are known to have been worse for groups exhibiting above-average gross overenumeration rates.

Findings from Earlier Censuses

The 1970 census relied on demographic analysis as the primary method for estimating net undercoverage; the CPS-Census Match provided estimates of gross omissions of persons but not of gross overenumerations. The 1960 Post-Enumeration Survey determined gross overenumerations of persons and housing units as well as gross omissions, but only net undercoverage rates were reported, while the 1960 CPS-Census Match determined only gross omissions (see Chapter 4 for further discussion).

Only the 1950 Post-Enumeration Survey, of pre-1980 census coverage evaluation programs, reported the components of net population coverage error. As was true for the 1980 PEP, the 1950 gross overenumeration estimate of 0.9 percent is overstated, as is the gross omission estimate of 2.2 percent, because the estimates included persons counted in the wrong geographic location (see Bureau of the Census, 1960). Findings with regard to gross overenumerations in 1950 are less clear-cut than the findings for 1980. In general, most population groups fell into the same categories of relative gross overenumeration and gross omission rates. Some groups appeared to have been less often overenumerated than underenumerated relative to the average rates (as was the general pattern in 1980), while a few groups appeared to have been more often overenumerated than underenumerated. The very different enumeration procedures used in the 1950 and 1980 censuses make it difficult to compare overenumeration experiences.

HOUSING COVERAGE STUDIES

Another source of information on relative rates of gross omissions in the census is provided by studies of completeness of coverage of housing units conducted in every census since 1950. Of course, rates of omission of housing units do not necessarily translate into comparable rates of missed persons; nevertheless, data on the characteristics of missed units add to the picture of hard-to-count elements in the population. Housing coverage evaluation studies also provide information on gross overenumerations, although the estimates from the 1980 census evaluation are not comparable with estimates from previous censuses because of the use of different methods.

Looking at missed units, the 1950 census estimated an overall gross omission rate for occupied housing units of 3 percent; the estimated rate was 2.1 percent in 1960, 1.4 percent in 1970, and 1.5 percent in 1980.

Data from 1950 on gross omissions of occupied housing units show that rented units as a group exhibited a moderately high relative gross omission rate, while owned units had a below-average rate. Within the rental category, units for which rent was not reported and with very low monthly gross rent had very high relative gross omission rates; in contrast, moderate-to-expensive units fell into the average category. The smallest units (only one room) and also units with number of rooms not reported exhibited very high relative rates of gross omissions, while the largest units (five or more rooms) had a below-average rate. Finally, close to 30 percent of missed occupied units were in buildings that were otherwise enumerated, while 70 percent were in buildings that were missed entirely (Bureau of the Census, 1960:Tables I, 11, and 15).

By region of the country or type of place (urban versus rural or metro versus nonmetro), there were no important differences in relative rates of gross omissions for occupied housing units in 1950 (Bureau of the Census, 1960:Table K). This was also true for 1960, 1970, and 1980. In 1960, the South had a moderately high relative rate of gross omissions, as did areas outside SMSAs. In 1970, the South's rate of gross omissions fell into the average category, while nonmetropolitan areas remained in the moderately high category. However, without special coverage efforts in the South in 1970, specifically a post-enumeration post office check of the address list, the South would have had a moderately high relative rate of gross omissions (Bureau of the Census, 1973c:Tables F and G). In 1980, rural areas had a moderately high relative rate of gross omissions and the West region and areas enumerated with conventional methods had below-average rates (Bureau of the Census, 1985a:Table 2).

In 1960 about 40 percent and in 1970 about 30 percent of missed occupied units were in buildings that were otherwise enumerated, with the remainder in structures that were missed entirely. Table 5.13 shows the percentage distribution of missed units by the enumeration status of the structure for type of place in 1960 and 1970 (comparable data are not available for 1980). A clear shift is evident from 1960 to 1970 in the distributions by area type, presumably due to the introduction of new procedures for developing address lists for using mailout-mailback enumeration procedures in 1970. The shift is toward a higher percentage of missed units within otherwise enumerated structures in central city areas in 1970 compared with 1960 and lower percentages for other metropolitan areas and areas outside SMSAs. Data not shown indicate that in 1970 one-half of the units missed within structures were in structures

TABLE 5.13 Percentage of Gross Omissions by Enumeration Status of the Building and Type of Area, for Samples of Occupied Units, CPS-Census Match (1970 and 1960)

	1960 Percentage of Occupied Units Missed in Buildings		1970 Percentage of Occupied Units Missed in Buildings	
Type of Area	Enumerated	Missed	Enumerated	Missed
Total[a]	38.1	61.9	28.6	71.4
Inside SMSA[b]	47.4	52.6	46.2	53.8
Central city	54.5	45.5	66.7	33.3
Other	33.3	66.7	25.0	75.0
Outside SMSA[c]	27.6	72.4	10.0	90.0

[a] 1970 percentages are calculated from Table G, Part A, "After Processing," based on the 1970 CPS-Census Match and assuming that processing changes reduced the miss rate in missed buildings but not in enumerated buildings.

[b] 1970 percentages are calculated from Table F, Part B, based on the 1970 Coverage Evaluation in Mail Areas.

[c] 1970 percentages are calculated from Table F, Part A, "After Processing," based on the 1970 CPS-Census Match and assuming that processing changes reduced the miss rate in missed buildings but not in enumerated buildings.

SOURCE: Bureau of the Census (1973c:calculated from Tables F and G).

classified as single-unit addresses on the mailing list, with another one-third in structures classified as having two to four units. Three-fourths of occupied units missed in 1970 were in structures built before 1939 (Bureau of the Census, 1973c:17).

Data from a study of housing units in the E sample of the 1980 census Post-Enumeration Program that contained at least one duplicated person provide an estimate that 0.9 percent of units were duplicated. This estimate, although based on methodology that the Census Bureau believes to be superior to the methodology used in previous censuses, is an underestimate because it excludes various other kinds of housing unit overenumerations. Looking at relative duplication rates, the South had a moderately high rate of housing unit duplications in 1980, as did mail areas where the address list was developed by Census Bureau staff (prelist areas), rural areas, and nonmetropolitan areas. Conventionally enumerated areas and the Midwest had below-average housing unit duplication rates (Bureau of the Census, 1985a:Table 4). The 1980 study estimated (Bureau of the Census, 1985a:30) that in 88 percent of the duplicated units the entire household was duplicated, while in the remaining duplicated units only some household members were duplicated.

6
Taking the Census II: The Uses of Sampling and Administrative Records

The charge to the panel called for assessment of the uses of sampling and administrative records to improve the cost-effectiveness of the decennial census. Recent census methodology has incorporated both of these techniques into one or more aspects of census operations, but there may well be room to extend their use. This chapter evaluates a range of uses of sampling for obtaining the count and characteristics and also considers the joint use of administrative records and sampling to improve the quality of certain census items.

SAMPLING IN THE CENSUS

Sampling has been employed since the 1940 census to obtain additional useful data without the burden and expense of asking all questions of the entire population. Sampling has also been used as part of census operations for purposes of quality control and has been extensively used in postcensal programs of coverage and content evaluation. Recently, it has been suggested that sampling could prove cost-effective in helping to fulfill the basic purpose of the decennial census--obtaining the population count for the nation, states, and small areas.

The panel examined the merits of the following potential uses of sampling for the count: (1) taking a sample census, (2) conducting follow-up of a sample of households that do not return their questionnaires, and (3) implementing coverage improvement programs for hard-to-count areas and population groups on a sample basis. The panel also reviewed issues in sampling for content, including criteria for deciding when to include questions on the short form administered to 100 percent of the population and when to include questions on one or more long forms administered to a sample. The panel also considered the merits of a follow-on sample survey to obtain additional information. Finally, the panel reviewed the uses of sampling in conjunction with administrative records for verification and improvement of the quality of subject items collected in the census. Sampling is also discussed in Chapter 8 in the context of coverage evaluation methods. Because we believe that the use of sampling in an operational context for quality control is a well-understood application, we do not comment on these uses of sampling in the census, despite the great importance of careful control of all aspects of census procedures.

The panel reviewed two papers prepared by staff of the Census Bureau outlining proposed research on uses of sampling for the head count and content in 1990. The paper by Miskura et al., "Uses of Sampling for the Census Count" (1984), describes four applications of sampling for the decennial census and proposes research projects for each type of use: (1) obtaining the census count on a sample basis, (2) using sampling for follow-up of unit nonresponse in the census, (3) using sampling for coverage improvement operations, and (4) using sampling for verification and possible correction of specific subject items during the census.

A package of papers prepared in summer 1984, "Interim Census Manager Reports on 1986 Pretest Objectives" (Johnson, 1984), describes proposals for the round of 1990 census pretests to be conducted in spring 1986. Proposed tests that involved the use of sampling for the count or content included: (1) a split panel test of sampling for unit nonresponse follow-up, (2) simulating the use of sampling for one of the coverage improvement programs--the Vacant/Delete Check, and (3) testing a general-purpose follow-on survey of 1-2 percent of short-form recipients conducted a few months after completion of the census enumeration. However, the Census Bureau has dropped the first two projects listed from the current 1986 pretest plans (see Bureau of the Census, 1985b).

Any evaluation of the costs and benefits of a particular sampling procedure must endeavor to assess the gains or losses on several dimensions compared with an alternate procedure. The comparison procedure could be a complete enumeration or another variant of sampling, for example, the use of a larger or smaller sampling fraction or a different sample selection procedure. Criteria considered by the panel include:

(1) Accuracy of the information obtained. Errors in surveys traditionally are thought of as having two components: sampling and nonsampling. Sampling error is inherent in sample surveys and necessarily increases the random variation of observed values from true values, compared with a complete enumeration. Nonsampling error may arise from question wording, field techniques, or many other sources and can occur both in samples and in complete enumerations. It is possible that a well-designed and executed sampling operation can reduce nonsampling error compared with a complete enumeration because the staff may be better trained and procedures more uniformly applied. It is, of course, also possible for the sample survey design to introduce nonsampling error. Furthermore, certain components of nonsampling error appear as variances that decrease with increasing sample size.

(2) Cost. In the context of the decennial census, which cost over $1 billion in 1980, the cost impact of any proposed methodology is an important consideration. Sampling is usually expected to reduce costs compared with a complete count, and small samples are expected to cost less than large samples; however, this is not always the case. The use of sampling introduces costs associated with sample design, selection of the sample, quality control of the sampling operation, processing of the data to estimate universe totals, and assessment of the quality of the information obtained.

(3) Timing. The length of time required for an operation is important in the census context. Shortening the time between Census Day and completion of the enumeration has positive implications for cost savings, for earlier availability of the data, and for improved accuracy of the numbers. (For example, the shorter the field operation, the less opportunity there is to miscount movers.) Sampling may have the benefit of reducing the calendar time required to complete the census field work.

(4) Feasibility. The enormous scale of census operations places a high premium on the feasibility of proposed methodologies in the field. Sampling may have drawbacks on this dimension if it proves more difficult to implement a sample operation than to conduct a complete enumeration. Because the census is a massive undertaking conducted within a brief time span only once every 10 years, there are not the opportunities to refine sampling procedures and to train field staff afforded in a continuing sample survey.

(5) Respondent burden. Sampling reduces the aggregate time the public must spend filling out questionnaires as well as the survey costs. Since the decennial census is conducted only once every 10 years, the panel does not view reducing respondent burden as an important argument for increased use of sampling to obtain the basic census counts. However, burden reduction has historically been an important justification for obtaining responses for most content items from samples of households. It is possible that greater use of sampling for content, with the consequent further reduction in burden, could have the benefit of improving the quality of the response.

(6) Legislative and political considerations. Although the panel was explicitly instructed to set aside legal considerations in examining choice of methodology for the decennial census, such considerations cannot be totally ignored. At present, clear legislative authority exists for the Census Bureau to use sampling to obtain answers to any and all items on the form, but there is a question whether this authority would extend to the use of sampling in determining population head counts for purposes of congressional reapportionment.

The decision to adopt a particular application of sampling in the decennial census must rest on a careful assessment of the net gain or loss (compared with the alternatives) on each of the above dimensions. Because an assessment is unlikely to show net pluses on every dimension (or net minuses for that matter), it will be necessary to make trade-offs and to answer hard questions such as how much reduction in accuracy is tolerable to achieve a specified level of cost savings. Quantification of the relative importance of the dimensions is difficult. In considering proposed changes in methodology, the panel has attempted to make explicit the degree to which various factors are affected.

SAMPLING FOR THE COUNT

The panel reviewed several possible applications of sampling for the count, ranging from replacement of the census with a large sample survey to the use of sampling in the final stages of follow-up. The panel concluded, for a variety of reasons, that sampling appears more likely to be cost-effective at the end of the census process than in the earlier stages. The panel supports further research directed toward evaluating the merits of limited use of sampling as part of the census enumeration process.

Taking a Sample Census

Currently, decennial census methodology involves collecting the majority of population and housing characteristics from a sample of households, who receive the "long-form" census questionnaire. (Sample sizes for the long-form items in recent censuses have ranged from 3.3 to 50 percent and are typically 20 or 25 percent.) However, counts of persons and housing units and basic characteristics, such as age, race, sex, and marital status, are obtained from 100 percent of the population.

The concept of taking a sample census, i.e., taking a large sample survey instead of a full census to obtain the count of the population and related basic characteristics, has been suggested as a means to effect a reduction in costs while satisfying the primary information needs served by a full census (see, for reference, Bureau of the Census, 1982a; Kish, 1979). Kish has also suggested, as a variant on the basic concept of a sample census, taking "rolling samples," whereby a different fraction of households is enumerated each year (Kish, 1979; Congressional Research Service, 1984:175).

Miskura et al. (1984) propose several research projects intended to result in a possible design for a sample census. These include projects to develop appropriate sampling error estimates for alternative designs, to develop total error models (including sampling and nonsampling error) and to investigate the theoretical reduction in nonsampling error required to obtain overall accuracy at least equal to that of a complete count, and to develop cost models and estimate their parameters for a sample census. At present, however, the Census Bureau has no plans to proceed with extensive research on a sample census, a decision the panel supported in its interim report (National Research Council, 1984:Ch.2).

Problems Involved in a Sample Census

The panel believes that the concept of replacing the census with a large sample survey should be excluded from the Census Bureau's 1990 research and testing program for a number of reasons that relate principally to census purposes, costs, and coverage.

The decennial census is the only comprehensive source of data for very small geographic areas such as towns, census tracts, and city blocks (see the discussion in Chapter 2). There are important needs for data about small areas, including: redistricting of national, state, and local legislative districts, which requires block counts by race to meet court-mandated criteria for equal size and compactness of districts (Bureau of the Census, no date-b), and revenue sharing, which requires population and income data for 39,000 political jurisdictions that include many very small towns, villages, and special districts. Small-area census data are also used in public planning and by the private sector for many purposes. Moreover, the model-based estimation techniques that are used to produce small-area data postcensally for revenue sharing and other purposes are recalibrated periodically against the census.

To obtain small-area population counts and basic characteristics from a sample survey to satisfy the uses outlined above with an acceptable level of accuracy would require a large sampling rate, probably 50 percent or greater for small jurisdictions. Moreover, it would not be acceptable to design a clustered area sample that included the population of only some geographic areas, such as selected counties or cities, because small-area data are needed for every political jurisdiction in the country. Hence, it would not be possible to reduce the number of field offices and thereby effect significant savings in administrative overhead costs. Moreover, while the size of the interviewer staff could be reduced somewhat, a large sample survey would entail additional costs for drawing and controlling the sample. Finally, to select a large unclustered sample would probably require complete address listing. Given a large sampling rate, an unclustered design, and 100 percent address listing, the panel is doubtful that costs could be significantly reduced in comparison with a full census.

The panel has reviewed Census Bureau cost estimates prepared in the mid-1970s for conducting a mid-decade census on a sample basis compared with a complete enumeration. These estimates appear to bear out the contention that there would be only minor cost savings in sampling on the scale necessary for satisfaction of present demands for small-area data (see Appendix 6.1 for details).

Finally, there is the issue of completeness of coverage obtained by a large sample survey compared with the full census. There is a large body of evidence in both the

United States and other countries that the census obtains more complete population coverage than even the best-executed sample survey (Redfern, 1983; Yuskavage et al., 1977). Furthermore, the coverage deficiency of sample surveys relative to censuses affects differentially precisely those population groups that are least well counted by the census in the first place. In fact, even the samples taken in conjunction with the census generally produce lower population figures than the complete census (Waksberg et al., 1973). One possible reason for this finding is that the publicity surrounding a census elicits greater cooperation from the public than can be obtained in surveys. While, of course, the Census Bureau would mount a publicity campaign for a sample census, it would be difficult to include a question like "Were you counted?" when only a fraction of the population is supposed to respond. Similarly, the field operations of a census, including follow-up and special coverage improvement programs, are geared toward finding every housing unit and person and adding missed units to the address list developed in advance of the census. For a sample census, it is unlikely that the same effort would or could be put into adding units to the sampling frame, and less complete coverage may result.

The less complete coverage obtained by a sample census compared with current methodology would have adverse implications for many important uses of census data. Concerns about inequities resulting from differential undercoverage of important subgroups of the population are already very strong. Substituting a large sample survey for the census would deepen these concerns still further--and probably with every good reason, given, as we noted before, that sample surveys appear to undercount even more disproportionately precisely those population groups already disproportionately undercounted by the census. The decennial census is also used as the basis for the design of current surveys in both the public and private sectors and to benchmark current population estimates. Less complete coverage would adversely affect these uses of census information as well.

We believe that rolling samples would also suffer from the disadvantages just discussed for a large-scale decennial sample survey compared with a complete enumeration, namely less complete coverage and either significantly reduced reliability of small-area data or only modest cost savings. Rolling samples may offer some advantages, such as improved ability to recruit and retain high-quality field staff, but have the added disadvantage that data are not available for comparative analysis across areas and population groups at a point in time. As described in Chapter 2, many uses of census data, including redistricting, fund allocation, and public policy analysis, depend on cross-sectional measures.

> Recommendation 6.1. We recommend that the Census Bureau not pursue research or testing of a sample survey as a replacement for a complete enumeration in 1990.

The Use of Sampling for Follow-up

Another proposed use of sampling for the count is to sample in the follow-up stage of census operations as a means of reducing costs (Bureau of the Census, 1982a, 1983a; Ericksen and Kadane, 1985; General Accounting Office, 1982). A census carried out with the use of sampling for follow-up could, for example, at a specified date after Census Day, draw a sample of addresses from which a completed census form had not been returned and follow up only those addresses. The total number of housing units and persons represented by the cases that were followed up would then be estimated and added to the number that returned questionnaires in the mail. The Miskura et al. paper outlines research projects intended to provide a sound methodological basis for designing follow-up operations to be carried out for a sample of nonresponding units. These projects are similar to those proposed in connection with conducting the entire census on a sample basis, namely to develop sampling error estimates and total error models for alternative sampling designs. These research endeavors were expected to lead to a pretest of sampling for follow-up and such a pretest was included in the Census Bureau's initial plans for 1986 (Johnson, 1984). The test would have used a split panel design, whereby census field staff in half the enumeration districts would follow up every household not returning a questionnaire, but follow up only a sample of nonresponding households in the remaining districts. Unfortunately, given the realization that not all objectives could be tested with a limited number of sites, the Census Bureau decided that other objectives took higher priority and dropped the test of sampling for follow-up in 1986.

Problems Involved in Sampling for Follow-up

The panel believes that the use of sampling for follow-up has some of the same drawbacks as the use of sampling for the entire census. The Miskura et al. and Johnson documents properly observe that, for sampling in follow-up operations to be effective, increases in total error (sampling plus nonsampling errors) must be counter-balanced by comparable cost savings. Because a heavily clustered design could not be used, given that follow-up operations must be carried out in every geographic area, there would be little opportunity to effect sizable savings by eliminating entire segments of field operations. Moreover, there would be the added costs of drawing and controlling the sample. The possibilities of confusion caused by a large sampling operation concurrent with the census should not be underestimated. For example, mail returns will come in after the cutoff date for drawing the follow-up sample and would introduce practical field problems and problems of integrating the late returns with the sample. Careful attention would need to be given to the sample design and determination of sampling fractions, given the likelihood of large variations in initial mail response rates across geographic areas. For example, in 1980, Madison, Wisconsin, had a mail return rate of over 90 percent, while the rate for the central Brooklyn district office was about 55 percent (Ferrari and Bailey, 1983:59). Carrying out follow-up operations on a sample basis would also add problems for coverage improvement and coverage evaluation programs that involved matching individual records. Furthermore, because low mail return rates very often characterize areas with relatively high coverage errors, sampling at this stage would probably introduce the largest sampling error into those estimates that already suffer from the largest coverage errors.

Sampling in the Final Stages of Follow-up

In light of the fact that it is never possible to obtain a 100 percent follow-up, there may be reason to believe that sampling could prove cost-effective in the final stages of follow-up operations. It is well known that the cost to count an additional person rises sharply as one moves toward those people who are harder to locate. That is, the per case cost to enumerate people requiring multiple follow-ups or special coverage efforts is many times the per case cost for those persons who mail back their questionnaires (Keyfitz, 1979; National Research Council, 1978; see also Chapter 5).

The administrative and recordkeeping problems associated with the use of sampling are much smaller if sampling is used only at later stages of follow-up. For example, it is anticipated that a much smaller fraction of persons in the final follow-up pool would subsequently return their census forms by mail. Certainly the total number of individuals for whom records are required is smaller if sampling is restricted to the final stages of follow-up. Therefore, the selection of the sample and recordkeeping could be handled by a smaller number of higher-level Census Bureau employees.

There is also the possibility that the use of sampling in the later stages of follow-up could lead to a decrease in the nonsampling component of error that would exceed the error introduced by sampling, thus resulting in a decrease in total error. We can imagine a situation in some regional offices in which the personnel who are involved in final stage follow-up operations vary greatly in their abilities to elicit accurate information from the nonresponding units. Total error may be reduced if, rather than using the whole field force in follow-up, only those interviewers with superior skills are employed in a probability sample of the final follow-up cases. To the extent that field personnel have differential skill levels--and there is reason to believe that qualified and dedicated personnel are becoming increasingly difficult to hire and retain (Hill, 1984)--this approach might have payoffs.

Determining the Final Stages of Follow-up

In the 1980 census, the first stage of follow-up for nonresponding households called for enumerators to make as many as four attempts to locate the residents. If no one could be found but the housing unit appeared to be occupied, the enumerators were instructed to obtain basic information from other persons, such as neighbors, resident managers, and the like. Census Bureau field staff estimate that as many as 98 percent of households were enumerated by the end of this first stage. The second phase of follow-up included attempts to locate the remaining 1 or 2 percent of nonrespondents and implementation of special coverage improvement programs such as the Vacant/Delete Check and Nonhousehold Sources Program discussed in Chapter 5. This second stage also included follow-up of households whose questionnaires had an unacceptable rate of missing data.

To obtain appreciable cost savings from sampling in the last stages of follow-up, it may be necessary to restructure the first and second stages. One possible scenario could be to restrict the first stage to perhaps two attempts to locate nonrespondents. The second stage could then encompass follow-up on a sample basis of the remaining nonresponding households, which would represent a larger fraction of all households than the second phase of the 1980 operation. Clearly, more study is needed before recommendations could be formulated.

It would also be possible, as discussed further below, to carry out the checking of vacant units on a sample basis in a combined operation with the second stage follow-up of nonrespondents. (In fact, the checking of vacant units is a particular type of follow-up.) Appendix 6.2 presents an illustrative scenario and gives crude estimates of possible cost savings.

Restructuring the first and second stages of follow-up in this manner and using sampling for the second stage could have beneficial effects on the quality of the data. The 1980 census procedures did not include any special quality control measures for households enumerated in the first follow-up stage based on responses of other persons such as neighbors (called "last resort" cases). If, after a limited number of initial follow-up attempts, sampling were initiated with higher-level staff and more stringent quality-control measures, there is the possibility that better data could be obtained in the second stage for a larger proportion of households.

The Merits of Research on Sampling

On balance we doubt that sampling the entire pool of nonresponding households for follow-up will prove cost-effective, but we believe there may be important benefits from the use of sampling for households that do not respond after one or two follow-up attempts. We urge the Census Bureau to study the feasibility of sampling and to estimate components of total error in the 1987 cycle of pretests. We also advise that maximum use be made of information that can be extracted by simulating sampling with data from the 1985 and 1986 pretests. The analysis should attempt to identify stages of follow-up (first round, second round, etc.) and, for each stage, determine cost structures and patterns of response, comparing these across different sized geographic areas and areas with differing initial mail response rates. In addition, we suggest that the Census Bureau investigate methods of making the most effective use of field staffs with varying skills and determine if there are new techniques that can be applied to reduce the nonsampling components of total error.

Recommendation 6.2. We recommend that the Census Bureau include the testing of sampling in follow-up as part of the 1987 pretest program. We recommend that in its research the Census Bureau emphasize tests of sampling for the later stages of follow-up.

A great deal can be learned about the nonresponse phenomenon from an analysis of past records of the number of callbacks and the time required to obtain information from various housing units. We have urged that this analysis be applied to the 1985 and 1986 pretests, for which we believe that increased automation should make it possible to capture the follow-up history of individual households. Analysis of the 1980 census experience would also be very useful, but the necessary data were not recorded in sufficient detail.

Recommendation 6.3. We recommend that the Census Bureau keep machine-readable records on the follow-up history of individual households in the upcoming pretests and for a sample of areas in the 1990 census, so that information for detailed analysis of the cost and error structures of conducting census follow-up operations on a sample basis will be available.

Telephone Follow-up

We noted with interest the report on the telephone follow-up experiment conducted during the 1980 census (Ferrari and Bailey, 1983). A sample of units in the address lists of seven district offices that were not in multiunit structures and had not sent back questionnaires by mid-April was selected for telephone follow-up using telephone directories organized by address. (In one district office, a sample of units in multiunit structures was also drawn.) The nonresponding units not in the sample were followed up by enumerators according to standard census practice. Preliminary results indicated several advantages for the telephone technique, namely lower costs per completed interview compared with personal follow-up, lower item nonresponse rates for many items, and fewer duplicate questionnaires. Refusal rates were similar for both techniques. A disadvantage of telephone follow-up was that the directories lacked listings or had out-of-date listings for many addresses. The Census Bureau's 1990 census research program includes further tests of telephone follow-up in 1986 (Johnson, 1984; Bureau of the Census, 1985b).

The report of the 1980 experiment, in addition to documenting results, describes in some detail operational problems that were encountered in administering the experiment. For example, a higher than expected rate of return of mail questionnaires after the sample selection date reduced the actual sample size of the telephone follow-up samples. The regular field office staff and the experiment staff also had problems working smoothly together in some offices. These kinds of problems may affect not only telephone follow-up but also sampling for follow-up in general.

> Recommendation 6.4. We support the Census Bureau's plans for further testing of telephone follow-up procedures in 1986. We recommend that the Census Bureau review the implications for sample-based follow-up operations of the operational difficulties that were encountered in the 1980 telephone experiment.

Sampling for Coverage Improvement

Along with proposals to follow up a sample of nonrespondents, proposals have been put forward to conduct specific coverage improvement programs on a sample basis. It is suggested that using sampling for coverage improvement has the potential to reduce costs, speed the completion of the census, and reduce nonsampling error and total error. With regard to considerations of data quality, coverage improvement programs can result in erroneous enumerations (overcount) as well as adding missed households and persons to the census. If coverage improvement programs are carried out on a sample basis by higher-quality staff using careful procedures, it is possible that quality may be improved--although experience with post-enumeration coverage evaluation surveys would not appear to support this hypothesis. On the negative side there are problems of costs and delays in estimation raised by the use of sampling for coverage improvement programs.

In 1970 the Census Bureau carried out two coverage improvement programs, the National Vacancy Check and the Post-Enumeration Post Office Check, for samples of households. In 1980 there was a deliberate decision to implement all procedures on a 100 percent basis and minimize imputation of entire households. There is evidence that the 1970 National Vacancy Check, which involved revisiting a small sample of units originally classified as vacant and making a careful determination of their status as of Census Day, came close to measuring the actual net undercount of occupied housing units. The 1980 Vacant/Delete Check, while importantly reducing undercount, also contributed to overcount (see Chapter 5).

Miskura et al. propose to consider the benefits of sampling for coverage improvement and describe four research projects geared toward developing sample-based coverage improvement programs for 1990:

(1) Work on sample design issues, such as development of a sampling frame, choice of sample unit, and possible stratification;
(2) Investigation of selection and data collection methodologies;
(3) Research on estimation from the results of coverage improvement sampling operations; and
(4) Research directed at translating the findings from the estimation work into required additions to the census, for example, imputation procedures to add "persons" corresponding to the estimated undercount.

The Census Bureau's 1986 pretest plans initially included a proposal to simulate implementing the Vacant/Delete Check on a sample basis. Simulation was proposed because a sample of vacant units at one pretest site would be too small to support reliable analysis (see Johnson, 1984). Current plans do not include this research (Bureau of the Census, 1985b).

In Chapter 5, the panel recommended that the Census Bureau carefully evaluate previously tried and proposed coverage improvement procedures to select only the most promising for inclusion in the 1990 research and testing program and to drop the rest from further consideration. For the procedures that are retained in the test plans, the panel recommends that the Census Bureau consider whether sampling offers any advantages. In accord with prior recommendations in this chapter, the panel suggests that sampling will be advantageous only for those programs that are carried out in the later stages of follow-up and where there is the possibility to achieve substantial cost savings.

Reviewing the coverage improvement procedures discussed in Chapter 5, sampling is not recommended for any of the address checks carried out prior to Census Day. These programs are important for developing a complete list of housing units, which is an essential tool for obtaining complete population coverage. Among the coverage improvement procedures implemented after Census Day, the Vacant/Delete Check stands out as a procedure that: (1) proved effective in reducing undercount in both 1970 and 1980 and will undoubtedly be used in 1990 and (2) cost a large sum of money in 1980 (at least $36 million) and therefore offers the potential for cost savings.

The panel therefore supports research on the use of sampling for the Vacant/Delete Check, particularly as the experience in 1970 with conducting this operation on a sample basis suggests that a carefully controlled sample operation affords the opportunity to reduce erroneous enumerations (overcount) as well as add overlooked households and persons to the census count. The panel urges that such research be carried out as soon as feasible.

> Recommendation 6.5. We recommend that the Census Bureau consider the use of sampling for those coverage improvement programs that are implemented in the final stages of census operations and where there is potential for significant cost savings. We recommend that the Census Bureau simulate sampling in the Vacant/Delete Check program in an upcoming pretest.

SAMPLING FOR CONTENT

Every census since 1940 has obtained responses for some content items from samples rather than from 100 percent of the population. The use of sampling in 1940 was very limited, but by 1980 the majority of population and housing items were asked on a sample basis (see Bureau of the Census, 1978b). We briefly recapitulate the highlights of the use of sampling for content collection in recent censuses:

- The 1940 census obtained most items from everyone; a few items were asked of a 5 percent sample of the population.
- The 1950 census extended the use of sampling for content and featured a fairly complex sample design. About two-fifths of the questions were asked on a sample basis. Sample sizes for population items were 20 percent and 3.3 percent (one-sixth of the 20 percent sample). A matrix design was used for housing sample items--each one-fifth of households was asked one or two housing items in addition to the complete count questions.
- In 1960, about three-fourths of the population and two-thirds of the housing items were asked on a sample basis. Sample sizes were 25 percent for population items and 25, 20, and 5 percent for housing items. The 1960 census first introduced the concept of "short" and "long" forms. In the first stage of census enumeration, every household filled out the short form. At every fourth residence, the occupants were also asked to complete one of two versions of a long form, each version containing the 25 percent population and housing items but either the 20 percent or 5 percent housing questions.
- The use of sampling for content in 1970 was similar to that in 1960. There was a short form sent out to 80 percent of households and two different versions of the long form. Each version included the 100 percent population and housing items and a common set of items asked of 20 percent of households, but one version included as well a set of questions asked of 15 percent of households and the other a set asked of 5 percent of households.
- In 1980, there was only one long form, but different fractions of households received the long form depending on the population size of their place of residence. In places expected to exceed 2,500 population, one in every six households received the long form, while, in smaller places, one in every two households received the long form. The overall sampling rate was approximately 20 percent. The primary reason for changing from a uniform 20 percent sampling rate to rates of 50 percent for small places (about 5 percent of the population) and 16.7 percent for all other places was to

provide reliable per capita income data for use in general revenue sharing allocations for all places.

The current short-form/long-form arrangement is the result, historically, of trading off, for each possible item, the costs of putting it on the short form, on the long form, or not including it at all against the benefits of acquiring responses on the item from either a sample or a complete enumeration. The costs of including items in census questionnaires comprise increased respondent burden and hence unit and item nonresponse, increased time and resources required for processing of the information, and, perhaps above all, increased difficulty of census operations. The Census Bureau cannot hope to collect every item that users might want. Benefits depend on how the census information collected will be used.

The Census Bureau has a long-established process for evaluating proposals for content items to include on the questionnaire and for determining whether it is acceptable to ask them only on the long form or whether they must be included on the short form. Generally, the presumption is that items should be restricted to the long form, in order to reduce burden and processing costs, unless it can be demonstrated that the data are required for very small geographic areas such as city blocks or small places (see the discussion in Chapter 2).

Sampling Plans for Content in 1990

The Census Bureau is currently in the process of obtaining reactions from data users regarding proposed content for 1990. The Census Bureau has also completed a preliminary assessment of population data needs for the 1990 census by subject item and level of geographic area detail based on a survey of federal, state, and local agencies of mandated requirements for census information (Herriot, 1984).

Current plans for the 1990 census are to continue the use of two different sampling rates for the long form as in 1980. The Census Bureau (Johnson, 1984) is also considering conducting a follow-on sample survey that would collect additional items that are not on either the long form or the short form for about 1-2 million households (1-2 percent). The sample for the follow-on survey would be drawn from households receiving the census short form and would be fielded about two months after the completion of nonresponse follow-up in the census. Items being considered include noncash income, disability, and education. Follow-on surveys have been conducted in connection with previous censuses, but usually directed toward specific populations and not fielded until a year or more after the census. (In this regard, the Census Bureau is considering for 1990 a special follow-on survey of residents of mobile homes; see Bureau of the Census, 1985b.)

The proposed follow-on survey of a nationally representative sample of households enlarges the set of choices with regard to inclusion of items in the census. It adds the possibility of obtaining data for items not currently on the long form for which a lower sampling rate is acceptable. It also offers the possibility of moving some items currently on the long form to the follow-on questionnaire and thereby perhaps increasing unit and item response rates in the census. Finally, greater detail can be obtained for items on the follow-on survey, given the much reduced sample size, compared with what is feasible for the long form. However, the need for a follow-on survey should be carefully assessed, as should the appropriateness of including particular items. It should not be assumed that such a survey will provide the vehicle for obtaining all the detail that the census itself cannot accommodate.

The panel had available only sketchy information on the content and purpose of the proposed 1990 follow-on survey for which a pretest is planned in 1986. The panel is concerned that the Census Bureau has not applied the same stringent criteria for determining items to include in the follow-on survey as has been the practice with regard to the long form. For example, the panel is troubled by the proposal to ask questions on noncash income, given that respondents may react negatively and that alternative data sources currently exist for information on this topic, including the new Survey of Income and Program Participation and administrative records. The panel suggests that the Census Bureau articulate explicit criteria for an item's inclusion on the follow-on survey. From there, decisions to include items on the follow-on survey (if it is carried out) can be made using a process that is similar to the one for including items on the long form.

Recommendation 6.6. We recommend that the Census Bureau refine and make more explicit its criteria for inclusion of items in the proposed follow-on survey that is being considered for the 1990 census.

Possible Alternatives

In considering issues of sampling for content, the panel noted a few alternatives to the current short-form/ long-form breakdown with or without a follow-on survey:

(1) Modified status quo. The sampling rates for the long form could be something other than 16.7 percent and 50 percent based on size of place. There might be three or more strata with different sampling rates for each. Perhaps there would be only a change in the sampling rates in the current two strata. The panel is not aware of any consideration of such alternatives by the Census Bureau.

(2) Matrix sampling for the long form. There would be several long forms each containing some items in common and some different items. The sampling frame would be divided into several groups and each group would receive a different long form. This procedure, which was followed to some extent in the 1950, 1960, and 1970 censuses, would allow a greater total number of questions on the long form. The panel believes that the logistical problems of such an approach are formidable. Moreover, user experience with two sets of data products in the 1970 census--one set based on the 15 percent sample and the other on the 5 percent sample--suggests that it is preferable to have one set of data records that permit cross-classifications among all items.

(3) One-form census with follow-on survey. The short form might be lengthened to include items that were important for small areas, for example, income. The proposed follow-on survey could include the remaining long-form items. Data from 1980 census returns suggest that a longer short form might not reduce initial response rates appreciably. Overall, the mail return rate in 1980 for short forms was about 1.5 percentage points higher than the rate for long forms. In centralized district offices, which were responsible for central cities containing hard-to-count areas the difference was about 2.5 percentage points (Turner, 1984, 1985). However, the proportion of questionnaires requiring follow-up for item nonresponse was much higher for long forms than for short forms, based on data from an experiment in the 1980 census using alternative questionnaires (see Fansler et al., 1981; Mockovak, 1982a, 1982b, 1983).

The one-form census is such a substantial departure from the current practice that it is probably only of interest for decennial censuses in the year 2000 or later. Historically, of course, censuses used to consist of only one form. The two-form census came about in order to reduce costs and respondent burden, while retaining the capability of producing small-area detail and detailed tabulations for most items. A one-form census with a follow-on survey would be likely either to be more expensive than the current practice, if the census form should include a large proportion of questions currently on the long form (particularly income, occupation, and industry, which have the highest processing costs), or to result in a severe loss of small-area and subgroup detail, if the follow-on survey included all or most of the current long-form items.

The panel has not tried to put together a comprehensive list of alternatives to the current short-form/long-form arrangement in terms of content breakdown or sampling rates, nor has it extensively analyzed the several alternatives outlined above. The current content of both the long- and short-form questionnaires is the result of an elaborate process with widespread consultation among potential users, and the panel has no specific modifications to propose. However, particularly in view of the Census Bureau's consideration of a follow-on survey, the panel believes it would be worthwhile for the Census Bureau to explore alternatives such as those listed above. If one or more alternatives look desirable, consideration should be given to pretesting them.

THE USE OF ADMINISTRATIVE RECORDS AND SAMPLING FOR IMPROVED ACCURACY OF CONTENT

Information on the wide range of content items covered in the census typically comes from individual responses to questionnaires (although a small proportion of responses are obtained in other ways, such as through imputation). One of the methods the Census Bureau has frequently used to evaluate the quality of reporting in the decennial census is to reinterview a sample of census respondents after Census Day. Matches with other surveys such as the CPS and with administrative records have also been used for content evaluation. To date, virtually all content evaluations have been carried out on a postcensal basis

(Bureau of the Census, 1978b; Miskura and Thompson, 1983). The results have been used to improve questionnaire design in subsequent censuses as well as to inform users of census data about limitations in the statistics, but have not been used to alter responses to the census itself.

Miskura et al. (1984) discuss the possibility of making an integral part of the census enumeration the use of survey procedures to reinterview samples of households to verify their responses and perhaps adjust content items. They propose several research projects in this area. Most of their discussion, however, concerns reinterview operations, such as the Vacant/Delete Check, that are more properly characterized as coverage improvement programs designed to add occupied housing units and persons to the count rather than to change responses to content items.

Brown (1984) discusses several kinds of uses of administrative records for content collection and evaluation:

(1) Content evaluation. Administrative records are frequently used for this purpose. For example, an evaluation of reporting of utility expenditures in 1980 compared census responses with administrative records from utility companies.

(2) Content improvement. Brown discusses the possible use of administrative records as a source of values for imputation of missing data in the questionnaire.

(3) Content collection. Brown notes (p. 5) that "the use of administrative records as a source of some census data may reduce respondent burden and improve the quality . . . without incurring enumeration costs."

(4) Administrative records census (ARC). Brown reviews proposals to replace the census both for the count and for content with data developed from administrative records, as is currently done in some European countries.

The panel considered the use of administrative records for content collection and improvement but did not consider the issue of an administrative records census. (Chapters 5 and 8 review uses of administrative records for coverage improvement and coverage evaluation.) The panel has made clear its belief in the importance, for 1990, of maintaining the traditional concept of enumeration as the heart of census methodology. However, the panel believes that administrative records can make important contributions to the census, particularly in the area of improved accuracy of content.

The Importance of Improving Accuracy of Content

The concern over completeness of population coverage in the census can obscure equally valid concerns over the accuracy of the content. Analysis of the fund allocation formula for general revenue sharing, for example, has shown that the per capita income component of the formula is more important than the population component in determining the distribution of funds among jurisdictions (Robinson and Siegel, 1979; Siegel, 1975). Yet reports of income in the census, as in household surveys, are known to be subject to large errors (Bureau of the Census, 1970a, 1973a, 1975b). These facts suggest that some resources can be usefully directed to improving the accuracy of content.

Evaluation research has documented problems in the reporting of many other items in the census besides income. The panel believes that serious attention should be directed to research that might lead to improved accuracy of selected census content items. We believe a research program should include design of operations to verify responses as part of the census enumeration and, as a corollary, consider the issue of adjusting census reports based on the outcome of such verification operations. We also support research into the possibility of obtaining some data items by methods other than traditional census responses. The primary alternative source is administrative records. Obviously, not all items can or should be included in verification or alternative data collection operations. For the content improvement programs that appear worthwhile, sampling will often be necessary to make the process manageable in the field and to keep costs within reasonable bounds.

Because programs to adjust census reports based on verification or alternative data collection operations have rarely been a part of decennial census methodology, it would be prudent for the Census Bureau to set forth and follow a step-by-step research and testing program. Extensive research should be concentrated on a few key items.

> Recommendation 6.7. We recommend that the Census Bureau conduct research and testing in the area of

improved accuracy of responses to content items in the census. We recommend further that the content improvement procedures examined not be limited to reinterviews of samples of respondents, but include the use of administrative records.

Improving the Accuracy of Housing Items

In considering the issue of content improvement, the panel looked most closely at questions on structural characteristics of housing units, particularly the item on age of the structure or year when the structure was built. We recognize that there are many other content items, such as income, that should be reviewed to identify means of improving their quality. However, time constraints precluded examining other items besides housing structure characteristics. The housing items offer the important advantage that concerns over possible invasion of privacy from using administrative records as a data source seem very unlikely to arise in contrast to the use of administrative records to obtain, for example, income data.

Age of structure is an important component of one of the two fund allocation formulas for the Community Development Block Grant Program. The intent of this formula is to direct funds to older, declining cities in which the housing stock includes a disproportionate share built prior to 1940 (Gonzalez, 1980). Reporting of this item in the census has observable problems (Bureau of the Census, 1972, 1975a; Katzoff and Smith, 1983). The nonresponse rate is fairly high, as is the index of inconsistency (a measure of the difference between census reports and reports obtained in reinterviews for a sample of census respondents). It has been observed that, in some cities, the proportion of housing reported as being built before 1940 has been increasing rather than decreasing.

It is not surprising that this item should be poorly reported. People who rent their living quarters, particularly if they recently moved into the unit, would be unlikely to have accurate information regarding the age of the structure. Even homeowners may be uncertain about when their homes were built. It would seem that buildings housing several families, such as apartments or condominiums, will be those for which response errors are largest. For these structures, information on age is likely to be available from administrative sources such as assessment and tax records. A specific suggestion for the use of administrative records for a sample of structures to obtain better data from the census on age and related items is outlined in Appendix 6.3.

A second set of items on the 1980 census form that deserves comment is the set of questions on utility bills. The discussion by Tippett and Takei (1983) establishes that there is an upward bias on the order of 50 percent in the responses to these items. A bias of this order strongly calls into question the usefulness of retaining such questions on the census form. Alternative methods of collecting such data, in particular from the utilities, should be considered.

We understand that the Census Bureau is considering testing questionnaires that would ask owners or managers of apartment buildings the items on the structure, such as year built, number of units, condominium/cooperative status, heating equipment, fuels used, source of water, etc. This method is used in the censuses of several European countries at present (Redfern, 1983). We believe that it is worthwhile to explore this approach, but we do not feel it should replace research on the use of administrative records.

For some housing items it may be appropriate to consider obtaining data from administrative records and dropping the items from the census. For example, if the primary use for age of structure is as input to the community development block grant formula, and cross-tabulation of this item with other census items is of low priority for users, then a cost-effective approach would be to devote resources to gaining access to and improving administrative records for the date of construction and to eliminate this item from the census questionnaire.

There are problems in using administrative records to obtain housing structure items. Records are kept in different ways and vary in quality and accessibility in different jurisdictions. For example, records such as tax assessors' rolls are highly computerized in some jurisdictions, while maintained on paper in other areas. The number and types of characteristics recorded for each property also vary (see Bureau of the Census, 1984a). Nonetheless, investment in research and testing of the use of administrative records for housing structure items offers the potential to improve the accuracy of the data while reducing respondent burden in the census (or, alternatively, permitting other useful items to be put on the questionnaire). Similarly, research into the feasibility of obtaining utility expenses from utility company records would appear very worthwhile.

Recommendation 6.8. We recommend that the Census Bureau investigate the cost and feasibility of alternative ways of obtaining data on housing structure items. Possibilities include: (1) obtaining housing structure information on a sample basis from administrative records and using this information to verify and possibly to adjust responses in the census; (2) obtaining structure information solely from administrative records and dropping these items from the census; and (3) asking structure questions of a knowledgeable respondent such as the owner or resident manager. We recommend that any trial use of a "knowledgeable" respondent procedure include a check of the data obtained from such respondents against data from administrative records.

APPENDIX 6.1

COST ESTIMATES FOR A SAMPLE CENSUS

At various times during the 1970s, the Census Bureau prepared cost estimates for conducting a mid-decade census. These estimates covered several different scenarios, including a large sample survey. The estimates were very rough and a mid-decade census has never been conducted, so that there is no experience with which to validate the numbers. Nonetheless, the estimates give a range for the proportionate cost of a large survey compared with complete enumeration.

Figure 6.1 shows several lines plotting costs against sampling rates developed from the Census Bureau estimates for a mid-decade census. These lines indicate that a 50 percent sample survey (the x's on the chart) would cost about 70 to 80 percent of the cost of a complete census and that a 75 percent sample survey (the y's on the chart) would cost about 85 to 90 percent as much.

The coefficient of variation for an estimate of the number of blacks for places of different sizes based on sampling rates of 50 percent and 75 percent would be approximately as shown in Table 6.1. For each size place, it is assumed that the black population is about 12 percent of the total. The table also assumes that the sampling rate used would not vary by size of place.

TABLE 6.1 Coefficient of Variation for Estimates of the Black Population by Size of Place and Size of Sample

	Coefficient of Variation for Estimate of Black Population (%)	
Place Size	50% Sample	75% Sample
10,000	5	3
5,000	7-8	5
2,500	10	7
1,000	15	10

NOTE: The black population is assumed to represent about 12% of the total for each area. The calculation of the coefficient of variation includes a factor of 2 for the design effect resulting from sampling entire households rather than conducting a simple random sample of persons.

SOURCE: Calculated from Herriot (1984:Table 1).

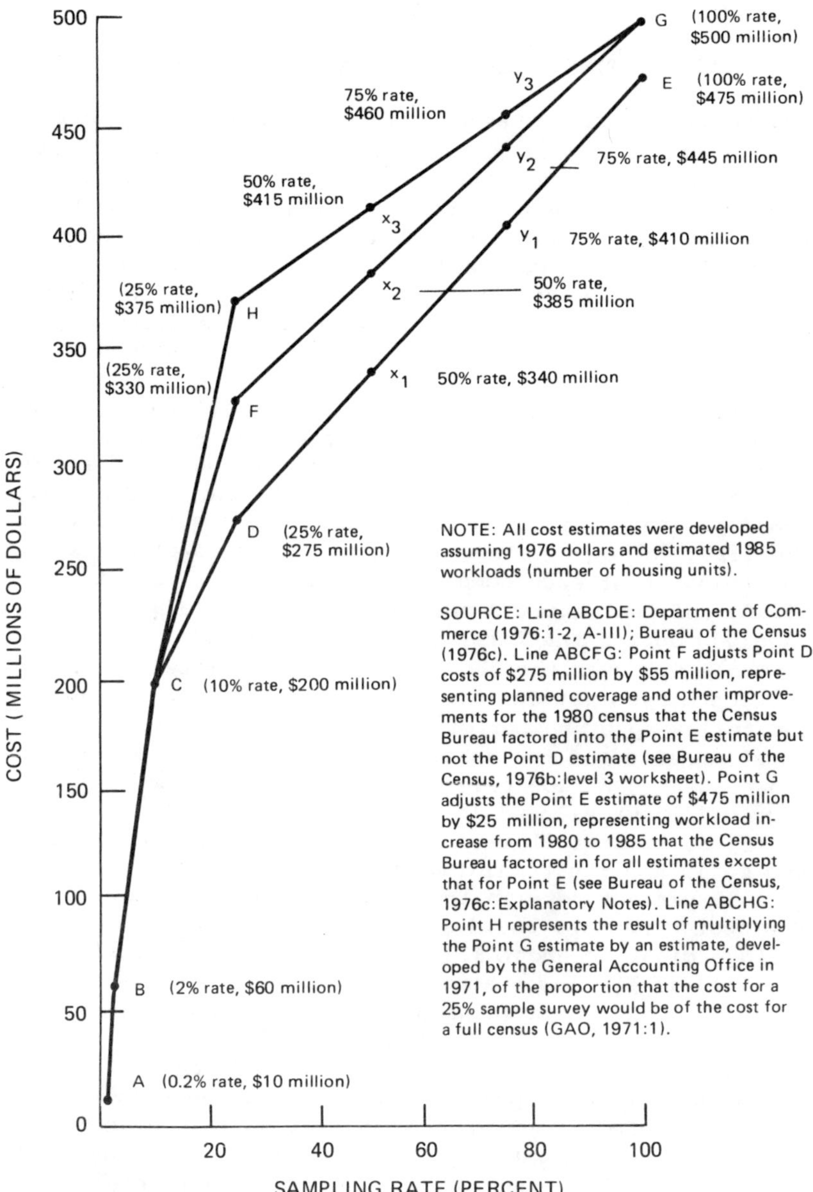

FIGURE 6.1 Census costs estimated for varying sampling rates.

APPENDIX 6.2

ILLUSTRATIVE FOLLOW-UP SCENARIO USING SAMPLING

Census Bureau staff have estimated that unit nonresponse follow-up for the 20 percent of households that did not mail back their questionnaires in 1980 cost about $145 million.[1] Follow-up was conducted in two stages in 1980. During the first stage, enumerators were instructed to make up to four callbacks to try to complete an interview. Households for which no information was obtained during this stage, even from neighbors or landlords as a last resort, were followed up as part of the second-stage operation.

Data are available for a few district offices in 1980 on the number of callbacks required for enumerators to obtain an interview from a nonresponding household and on the costs of completion. These data (Ferrari and Bailey, 1983) indicate that about 1.5 calls were required during the first follow-up stage for enumerators to complete an interview, that each completed interview cost about $3.90, and that about 3 percent of cases were not resolved during the first follow-up operation.

Table 6.2 uses the above, admittedly limited, data to develop a hypothetical distribution of households requiring follow-up by number of calls to obtain a filled-in questionnaire and the associated costs. The scenario shown assumes a two-stage follow-up operation with up to four callbacks allowed in the first stage.

If the first follow-up operation were restricted to two calls and the remaining nonrespondents were sampled at a 25 percent rate in the second stage of follow-up, the cost structure would appear as in Table 6.3. Net savings might be about $35 million ($146 minus $111 million) if the lower bound estimate of the costs of a 25 percent sample compared with a complete effort is used (from Figure 6.1). If the higher bound estimate is used, so that each call costs $12 in the second stage of follow-up with a 25 percent sample, then the total costs shown in Table 6.3 would be $126 million ($66 plus $60), and net savings might be about $20 million from the use of sampling ($146 minus $126). If the Vacant/Delete

[1]Personal communication from Peter Bounpane to the Panel on Decennial Census Methodology, March 9, 1984.

TABLE 6.2 Hypothetical Distribution of Follow-up Callbacks and Costs, Scenario 1: Up to Four Callbacks Permitted in First Stage of Follow-up

	Housing Units		Callbacks to Complete	Number of Callbacks	Cost ($) ($4/call)
	Number	Percentage			
First follow-up	8.5	9.7	1	8.5	34
	4	4.5	2	8	32
	2	2.3	3	6	24
	1	1.1	4	4	16
Subtotal	15.5	17.6		26.5	106
Second follow-up	2	2.3	5	10	40
Total	17.5	19.9		36.5	146

NOTE: Number of housing units, number of callbacks, and cost are in millions; 17.5 million housing units is about 20% of the total count of 88 million housing units in 1980.

SOURCE: See discussion in Appendix 6.2.

Check were also conducted on a 25 percent sample basis, savings for this program might be in the range of: $36 million x (100-58) = $15 million, to $36 million x (100-75) = $9 million. In total, the savings from conducting both nonresponse follow-up and the Vacant/

TABLE 6.3 Hypothetical Distribution of Follow-up Callbacks and Costs, Scenario 2: Two Callbacks Permitted in First Stage of Follow-up, Remaining Cases Sampled at 25% in Second Stage of Follow-up

	Housing Units	Callbacks to Complete	Number of Callbacks	Cost[a] ($)
First follow-up	8.50	1	8.5	34.0
	4.00	2	8.0	32.0
Subtotal	12.50		16.5	66.0
Second follow-up	.50	3	1.5	13.5
	.25	4	1.0	9.0
	.50	5	2.5	22.5
Subtotal	1.25		5.0	45.0
Total	13.75		21.5	111.0

NOTE: Number of housing units, number of callbacks, and cost are in millions.

[a] Costed at $4 per call in the first follow-up stage and $9 per call in the second follow-up stage, assuming that a 25% sample costs about 58% of a complete effort (see Appendix 6.1—note that 58% is the lower bound estimate; 75% is the upper bound estimate).

Delete Check with the use of sampling might be in the range of $30 to $50 million, or about 3 to 5 percent of the total cost of the 1980 census. This scenario makes no allowance for additional expenditure on each call that might be made to achieve higher quality through sampling.

The selection of a 25 percent sampling rate is purely for illustration. The impact of this rate and others on the quality of the population estimates for small areas would need to be assessed. We note that the overall rate of contact for the total population of an area using a 25 percent second-stage follow-up sample implemented after two calls in the first stage would be about 95 percent for an area with "average" unit nonresponse of 20 percent, while the rate of contact would be under 90 percent for an area with a 50 percent nonresponse rate.

APPENDIX 6.3

IMPROVING DATA ON HOUSING STRUCTURE ITEMS: A SUGGESTED METHOD

The panel offers the following scheme as a suggestion for obtaining more reliable data on age of structure and related housing items. The basic concept is to develop a sample of structures from the address lists compiled for the census and to obtain data from local administrative records about the characteristics of the structures in the sample. It may prove most feasible to carry out this scheme in urban areas in which census address listings and identifiers carried on local administrative records can most readily be matched.

Prior to the census, a reasonably complete list of housing unit addresses is constructed. Units that have the same basic address (such as Apt. A and Apt. B at the same street number) can initially be considered to be part of the same structure. Hence, it is possible to draw a sample of basic addresses that is a good proxy for a sample of structures.

The precise design and size of the sample would depend on the nature of the costs, among other considerations. We outline one possible procedure. Assume that the sample of basic addresses or structures is drawn with the probability of selection proportional to the estimated number of units in the structure. For concreteness, assume that single-unit buildings are sampled at a rate of 1 in 10, duplexes are sampled at a rate of 2 in 10, and so forth, up to structures with 10 or more housing units that are sampled with certainty. Administrative records data for age of structure and other items would then be obtained for the structures in the sample.

The sample of basic addresses or structures can be linked to the sample of housing units in the census as follows. Assume that one-fifth of the households are to receive the census long form, which asks for age of structure and related housing items. Given that the sample of basic addresses is specified at the time of the mailing of the census forms, all of the long-form households could be selected from those addresses. Specifically, one scheme would be to send long forms to: all single housing unit structures that are in the sample of basic addresses, two households in all other selected structures with less than 10 units, and one-fifth of the households in all structures with 10 or more units.

Recalling the sampling rates for different sized structures, this will achieve a one-fifth long-form sample for structures with more than one unit. To achieve a one-fifth long-form sample of single-unit buildings, it will also be necessary to send long forms to single-unit structures not in the sample of basic addresses. This sampling scheme has the drawback of increasing sampling variance for the long form due to the clustered design. However, it has the great advantage that all of the long-form sample for people living in structures with two or more housing units is included in the sample of basic addresses. Hence, data collected from administrative records for these structures are available to verify or to use in place of responses to the census.

Two options are available with respect to the question on age of structure in the census. It could be asked on the census form or it could be omitted. Assume that the question is retained on the census form. The simplest processing method would be to use the value obtained from administrative records for all individuals residing in the structures that are in the sample of basic addresses and to retain the answers of individuals not in the sampled structures. It would also be possible to use regression-type procedures to modify responses of individuals in structures that are not in the sample based on the information obtained for the sampled structures.

Now assume the question is not included on the census form. The values obtained from administrative records could simply be appended to the census data records for persons in structures that are in the sample of basic addresses. For persons not in sampled structures, it would be possible to assign values obtained from sampled structures located in the same area. This should be a very effective procedure in areas in which large groups of units, such as apartment complexes or suburban housing developments, were constructed at the same point in time.

7
Adjustment of Population Counts

THE NEED FOR ADJUSTMENT

"Since the first census in 1790 there have been problems in finding and accurately counting every person living in the United States" (Hogan, 1984a:2). However, two things are new in recent decades. First, the Census Bureau has developed and published quantitative measures of coverage error, measures that show that net undercoverage varies substantially by age, sex, race, and Hispanic origin. Second, the number and kind of uses to which census data are put have multiplied. Thus, concerns about the consequences of differential coverage error have increased as has pressure for the Census Bureau to reduce differential coverage error. Both improvements in the actual census count and subsequent statistical adjustment of that count have been urged. In 1980 the Census Bureau undertook a major effort to improve the actual count, especially for minority groups, but decided against subsequent statistical adjustment. However, many constituencies have urged adjustment and some have instituted litigation to require it.

The ultimate goal of the decennial census is that of accuracy of the final census numbers. The evaluation studies undertaken by the Census Bureau broadly identify inaccuracies and provide information that would be desirable to use. Therefore, the panel is led to recommend that adjustment procedures be developed with the objective of improving the accuracy of the census products.

Adjustment aims, by supplementing the census counts with other information, to produce more accurate population estimates than the raw counts. Adjustment may be carried on to characteristics data as well. The quality of the adjusted census depends, then, on the accuracy of the census counts and the other information used as well as on the adjustment procedure adopted.

An adjustment of census figures for a region with a low completion rate would produce numbers that, although closer to the true values than the unadjusted numbers as best one can tell, would still have a great deal of uncertainty attached to them. The panel thus attaches great importance to the goal of completeness of the census count and views possible subsequent adjustment of that count as a complement to--not a substitute for--continued efforts to improve census coverage. The traditional nature of the census as an operation in which "each person stands up and is counted" should be maintained. If public perception of the importance of being counted were to deteriorate, participation in what Kruskal rightly terms a national ceremony (Congressional Research Service, 1984:49) might decline, with serious consequences for the accuracy of the census numbers, adjusted or not.

The goal of accuracy is often unclearly specified and can have different meanings in different contexts. For government entitlement programs that use the census numbers by comparing them with a cutoff point, the degree of inaccuracy is critical only when a number is close enough to the cutoff point that a funding decision would be affected. For programs that use the relative change from census to census, the accuracy of the estimate of change is the goal. For programs that determine political representation or distribution of public monies through allocation procedures based on census information, the relative accuracy of the census in different geographic areas is crucial. As reviewed in Chapter 2, there is evidence that differential coverage errors importantly affect both political representation and fund allocation. The panel believes that adjustment procedures should focus on minimizing these errors. In recommending this aspect of accuracy as a primary goal, we recognize that statistical adjustments that help achieve it may reduce the accuracy of certain other census information, for example, measures of change from prior censuses. We also recognize the importance of other aspects of accuracy, in particular, errors in the counts themselves, for many research, planning, and program purposes of local and national users. Minimizing differential coverage errors should reduce rather than increase most of these, but a different focus might reduce them more. We invite further study and discussion of the implications of our focus on minimizing differential coverage errors.

In recent censuses, the production of what is referred to as the "actual census count" already involves, for a minority of the census households, a variety of statistical procedures: imputation for forms damaged in processing, imputations of persons in housing units believed to be occupied although no one was ever found at home, imputation of missing data in partially filled-in census forms, etc. (see Bailar, 1983c; also see Appendix 3.1). Although it would not be the first instance of the use of statistical modifications in the census, making further adjustments to the census of the kind we discuss in this chapter would importantly increase the use of statistical procedures in census-taking. The panel believes that it is not a question of taking a stand "for" or "against" adjustment, as adversarial circumstances press one to do. The decision-making process relative to adjustment requires a dispassionate rounded discussion recognizing the full range and complexity of the technical issues.

The adjustment question is in reality a series of interrelated questions: If an adjustment is to be made, what is to be adjusted--the count, or some or all of the other census information? By what procedure? At what level of geography? With what impact on the accuracy of a variety of census numbers? On what time schedule? For what uses of census data? So that the data set is internally consistent or not? In the remainder of this chapter, we summarize some of the technical information pertinent to these questions and present the recommendations to which we are led. Many technical questions remain to be answered if adjustment procedures are to be developed in time for their use in the 1990 census. On the whole, while much effort will be required, the panel is optimistic that substantial progress can be made, and many feel that this progress could well be sufficient to permit adjustment to become a feasible and desirable part of the 1990 census process.

One of the questions raised with respect to the issue of adjustment is the extent of adjustment of characteristics information. If an adjustment is implemented, the panel recommends that it be carried down to the microdata level. This would, practically speaking, be expressed as a reweighting of individual records and, hence, would represent a coverage-based adjustment of characteristics information as well as the counts. However, one could at the same time adjust characteristics information through models using information from content evaluation programs (see discussion in Chapter 6). Models for the misresponse of characteristics information, such as the underreporting of income, and models for the characteristics of uncounted people could be attempted. One possibility would be to develop models at an aggregate level and then carry the adjustment down to the micro level using methods discussed below. The development, testing, implementation, and evaluation of such models involve complicated, difficult issues that the panel has not had time to adequately discuss. For the purposes of this report, the panel has decided to concentrate on the adjustment of population counts, with the adjustment of characteristics that such a reweighting of individual records entails.

> Recommendation 7.1. Completeness of the count is an important goal, both for ensuring the accuracy of the census and for establishing the credibility of the census figures among all users. Adjustment should not be viewed as an alternative to obtaining as complete a count as possible through cost-effective means. Nevertheless, the ultimate goal is that of the accuracy of the published figures. Given the likelihood that the census will continue to produce different rates of undercoverage for various population groups, and given the equity problems caused thereby, we recommend that work proceed on the development of adjustment procedures and that adjustment be implemented if there is reasonable confidence that it will reduce differential coverage errors.

We note that there are several different methods of adjustment that have been suggested so far, and we anticipate that others will be proposed. It is possible that a variety of alternatives, including compromise possibilities, will be developed with evidence that each would be an improvement over the census count, but with no obvious basis for choosing among them. In our view, this situation should not by itself preclude the Census Bureau from making adjustments and picking one of the alternatives.

EVALUATING ADJUSTMENT: LOSS FUNCTIONS AND YARDSTICKS

One would like to evaluate the numbers produced by the census (either based on raw counts or based on adjustments to those counts) by comparing them with the true values of those numbers in the population if one had a completely accurate census. Since one cannot know those true values, one must use methods external to the actual census process to obtain an independent estimate of those values. (Some of the methods are described elsewhere in this report.) Each of the methods entails positing a model or assumptions about both the nature of the errors in the census (i.e., about the process by which individuals may be either not included or double-counted in the raw data) and about the nature of the method (and its underlying data) that produced the independent estimate of the census values.

Each of two considerations has a place in the evaluation of census numbers, the error in the number itself and the resulting loss to society due to erroneous treatment of political jurisdictions (or other uses of the census number). By error we mean the difference or the relative difference between the number produced by the census (either the raw or adjusted count) and the true value for that number in the population if we had a completely accurate census. By loss we mean a numeric measure of the impact of the error in the census number both for each political jurisdiction and for the United States as a whole. For this discussion we call these numeric measures "loss functions." As we are interested in net social gain, our prime consideration is the overall loss function for the country as a whole, and not the separate loss functions that may be adduced for each separate political jurisdiction. A jurisdiction's gain or loss of funds or political representation due to error is understood to be always a nonnegative loss from society's point of view. We are not taking the point of view of a single jurisdiction, which might be that any gain is a good thing, or of a social planner second-guessing the political process, which might be that some errors benefit society by counterbalancing deficiencies in laws and social policies, or even in other data, e.g., on income.

The determination of the appropriate loss function for the country as a whole is a difficult task. Moreover, it is impossible to determine a single loss function that is appropriate for evaluating every effect of an error in the census numbers: each use of the census numbers has a different effect resulting in different components of loss.

In the most general setting, loss functions should reflect the cost to society of data collection, data processing, and data dissemination as well as the costs of basing decisions on imperfect information. Decisions on data collection procedures themselves are influenced by costs difficult to evaluate. (For example, what is the cost to the respondent of one additional question on the census form?) Thus, loss functions influence census data collection procedures as well as estimation procedures and hence considerations of loss are involved in decision making for census procedures besides those involved with adjustment.

A discussion of loss functions should not be limited to issues related to the question of adjustment. The need to determine an appropriate loss function underlies most of the decisions that the Census Bureau makes. The determination of an appropriate loss function is typically accomplished, necessarily, without understanding the precise costs associated with various decisions. The panel feels that loss function considerations enter importantly into all aspects of census methodology and the panel's recommendations in other chapters have implicitly reflected such considerations. We are formally discussing loss functions in the context of adjustment because of the focus in the public debate on how to measure the consequences of introducing adjustment procedures into the census.

In what follows we first discuss loss functions from the point of view of the uses of the census numbers, after which we consider their relationship to adjustment procedures.

A User's View of Loss Functions and Adjustment

Concern about census coverage error arises less because of net national undercoverage than because of differential undercoverage by geographic location and demographic group. Differential undercoverage causes differences in political representation and distribution of public monies from the allocation that would result if a completely accurate census could be taken, differences that may work to thwart the intent of laws governing representation and fund distribution and that are often perceived as unfair. One of the principal reasons for adjustment of the counts of census data would be, by reducing differential coverage errors, to reduce the impact of these errors on political representation, fund distribution, and other public programs.

Because the data produced by the decennial census have many uses, the benefit of accuracy in the published numbers is difficult to measure. Indeed, the benefit may vary from use to use. Congressional apportionment, for example, requires only population totals by state, whereas the revenue sharing formula uses population and per capita income for each incorporated place. Whether adjustment of population totals by state--resulting in more accurate congressional apportionment--will also result in more accurate distribution of revenue sharing monies may depend on how the adjustment is distributed within the state and what, if any, adjustments are made to the per capita income estimates. How the different loss functions can or should be reconciled in order to preserve consistency between the uses of census data for different applications is an issue for which the panel has in the abstract little advice to offer.

Even for any single given use of census data, the benefit of adjustment may vary from place to place. Suppose, for example, that midwestern central cities were grouped into a domain and the census results for each city adjusted by the same formula. Since the precise undercounts and characteristics used in the adjustment for each city will differ among the cities, after adjustment some cities will be closer to the "true" count than others. Adjustment might improve accuracy in these cities as a group, but not in all cities equally, nor in every city. Nor would they benefit equally, and some might be adversely affected (lose federal funds or representation).

It must be accepted that no adjustment procedure can be expected to simultaneously reduce the error of all census information for every location in the United States. Rather, adjustment should be undertaken when there is reasonable certainty that appreciable reduction in the general differential coverage error will be achieved. A relatively trivial reduction would not be worthwhile, since adjustment will surely cost time and resources to implement, and doubt about whether the adjustment did or did not reduce differential coverage error would impair public confidence in census figures. Furthermore, knowledge of a subsequent adjustment might reduce public cooperation, thus lowering the completeness of the census count.

For an effective adjustment procedure to be widely accepted, given that not all localities will benefit, it is important that there be as widespread understanding and agreement as possible within the professional community of statisticians that a general reduction in differential coverage error is sufficiently desirable to accept adverse impacts on some individual localities. More important but difficult to obtain is this understanding throughout all levels of government (see Keyfitz, 1979).

In other words, localities need to recognize two important points regarding adjustment. First, the standard of comparison should not be the raw census count. That is, an adjustment that lowers the population count for an area may have reduced the error in the estimate for that area as much as an adjustment that raises the count for another area. Second, although adjustment may increase error for some localities, the country as a whole has benefited if adjustment has reduced overall differential error. One further point: although each locality will know whether its count was higher or lower after adjustment, we can reasonably require of an adjustment procedure that each locality's error is more likely to be reduced than increased, and that no locality will have good reason to believe otherwise, even post facto.

The panel believes that it is substantially more important to reduce the general error per person than the general error per place. Hence, the panel does not recommend the use of loss functions for measuring the total error that weight each political jurisdiction equally, e.g., that determine the proportion of the 39,000 revenue sharing jurisdictions that gained or lost through adjustment, regardless of the number of people in each jurisdiction. Rather, the panel believes that the contribution to total loss attributable to an area should reflect the size of its population.

> Recommendation 7.2. In measuring the total loss associated with an adjustment procedure, we recommend that the contribution to this loss attributable to a geographic region should reflect its population size. Thus, we recommend against loss functions based solely on the number of political entities losing or gaining through adjustment.

The next section discusses the properties of several kinds of loss functions and considers specifically how they take into account population size.

Loss Functions and Adjustment

The classical yardstick used by sample survey researchers to assess the accuracy of a single number, chosen principally for its convenient mathematical properties, is the square of the deviation between the number and its true value. Whatever loss function we use to assess the accuracy of a single number, we still must determine a rule for amalgamating the losses associated with each number into an overall loss function for the entire set of numbers produced. The usual tack taken is to sum the individual loss functions.

Using this rule for squared error applied to population gives disproportionate weight to large localities. Consider the following example. Suppose there are two areas, one with true population of 10,000 and estimated population of 11,000, and the other with true population of 5,000 and estimated population of 5,500. The loss for the first area is $(11{,}000-10{,}000)^2 = 1{,}000{,}000$, the loss for the second area is $(5{,}500 - 5{,}000)^2 = 250{,}000$, and the total loss is 1,250,000. The larger area with twice the population of the smaller area and the same percentage error counts for four times as much in the overall loss function.

Using this rule for squared error applied to relative or percentage error (that is, the square of the percentage deviation between the number and its true value, or squared relative error), also a very intuitive idea, gives disproportionate weight per person to small localities. To continue with our example, the squared relative error for the larger area is $((11{,}000-10{,}000) / 10{,}000)^2 \times 100 = 1$ percent; for the smaller area is $((5{,}500-5{,}000) / 5{,}000)^2 \times 100 = 1$ percent; and the total loss is 2 percent. In this case, the larger area counts for no more than the smaller area in the overall loss function.

The following argument gives an in-between notion that may be about right, although we make no absolutist claim for either the argument or the resulting loss functions. Tukey (1983) and Fellegi (1980b) have suggested as an appropriate alternative loss function that of "relative squared error," that is, squared error divided by the true value. In our example, the respective losses for the two areas would be $(11{,}000-10{,}000)^2 / 10{,}000 = 100$ and $(5{,}500-5{,}000)^2 / 5{,}000 = 50$, with the total loss equal to 150. In this case, the larger area with twice the population of the smaller area and the same percentage error also counts for twice as much in the overall loss function.

Tukey argues for the use of relative squared error on the grounds of its invariance properties. That is, relative squared error has the property that the contribution of the error for one area to the overall loss function is proportional to its size, assuming that the percentage error for all subareas is the same.

Another loss function that has this invariance property and is more tractable computationally (see Kadane, 1984) is squared error divided by the estimated value. Using the same example, the respective area losses would be $(11{,}000-10{,}000)^2 / 11{,}000 = 91$ and $(5{,}500-5{,}000)^2 / 5{,}500 = 45.5$, with the total loss equal to 136.5. Again, the area with twice the population size contributed twice as much to the overall loss function. Both of these loss functions, squared error divided by the true value and by the estimated value, are commonly used in the analysis of contingency tables.[1]

The foregoing discussion pertains to the construction of a loss function associated with census-produced numbers wherein it is the absolute accuracy of each number that is to be assessed. Concern with minimizing a differential coverage error indicates the need for a loss function that reflects not the error in each number _eo ipso_ but rather that error in relation to the errors in the other numbers within a set of census-produced numbers. For example, we do not so much want to gauge the accuracy of population counts for each county in a state as to gauge whether the inaccuracies are relatively evenly distributed across the counties. The loss functions needing consideration here really measure not the accuracy of the numbers but the "differential inaccuracy" of the numbers. If, for example, each number is 95 percent of its true

---

[1]Note that squared relative error (relative to either the true or estimated value) is different from relative squared error and does not have the same invariance property. All are weighted versions of one another. Thus relative squared error and squared relative error (relative to the true value) are simple squared error weighted by the reciprocal of the true value and the reciprocal squared, respectively; relative squared error is squared relative error weighted by the true value; and so on.

value, we would like a "differential inaccuracy" loss function to indicate this by having a value of zero.

Tukey (1983) calls such a loss function a "measure of misproportionality" and suggests that one can use for each number the squared difference between the relative error of that number and the relative error of the number of the aggregate of which that number is part. Relative error is defined as the error divided by the true number or, equivalently, as the ratio of the census-produced number to the unknown true number minus 1. If the aggregate is a state total and each component number is a county total, then this measure would be the squared difference between the relative error of the county number and that of the state number or, equivalently, between the ratio of the census to the true number for the county and the ratio for the state. Suppose, for example, that our two areas of population size 10,000 and 5,000, each of which had a relative error of 10 percent, were part of a larger area of population 50,000 that had a relative error of 8 percent. Then the measure of misproportionality for each of the two component areas would be $(.10 - .08)^2 = .0004$. If the area of 50,000 population instead had a 10 percent relative error, then the loss function for each of the components would be zero.

To aggregate this loss function across counties, say, Tukey suggests a weighted sum of the component (i.e., county) loss functions, wherein the weights are the true values of each of the components of the sum. In our example, the loss for the area of 10,000 population would count twice as heavily as the loss for the smaller area in the overall loss function.

Research on Loss Functions and Adjustment

One characteristic of the loss functions given above is that they are general in nature and not specific to census data uses, except in distinguishing absolute and differential inaccuracy. Some consideration has been given to use-specific loss functions, in particular in the work by Kadane (1984) on congressional seat allocation and the work by Spencer (1980b) on allocations of revenue sharing dollars to states. Kadane demonstrates the close relationship between loss functions proposed by Tukey (1983) and the loss function underlying the method currently used in seat allocation. (See Appendix 7.1 for a brief overview of loss functions and apportionment.)

In modeling the revenue-sharing loss function, Spencer suggests that the components are not merely the units receiving revenue sharing dollars but also the (one) source of funding. For each component he postulates as loss function a constant multiple of the magnitude of the overallocation (if one exists) or a possibly different constant multiple of the underallocation (if any). The overall loss function is an unweighted sum of component loss functions.

The Kadane paper exhibits a loss function for allocating congressional seats among states whose minimization results in the allocation procedure actually used in Congress. In the case of revenue sharing and other major uses of census data, the task of ascertaining an appropriate loss function is more complex. The loss function studied by Spencer was merely a convenient construct, a springboard from which he could proceed to investigate the central issue, the implications of data inaccuracy for revenue sharing.

Research on the effect of the choice of loss function on the effectiveness of adjustment procedures has been limited. Spencer (1980a) provides some evidence that the degree of improvement resulting from adjustment is not very sensitive to choice of loss function. Schirm and Preston (1984) studied the effect of a very simple synthetic adjustment (see the discussion of synthetic estimation in a subsequent section), using only two demographic groups, on population proportions across geographic areas using a number of different loss functions:

(1) The ratio of the sum of absolute errors in the proportions before adjustment to the sum of absolute errors in the proportions after adjustment.

(2) The ratio of the sum of squares of errors in the proportions before adjustment to the sum of squares of errors in the proportions after adjustment.

(3) The fraction of total national population that resides in states whose proportions after adjustment are closer to their true proportion than are their proportions before adjustment.

They found, in a limited simulation study, that the decision to adjust is sensitive to selection of the loss function in that the first two loss functions offer consistent recommendations about whether or not to adjust in only about 60 percent of the simulated cases.

Seeking the source of the 40 percent inconsistency can bring us closer to an understanding of the impact of choice of loss function on the adjustment problem. We note first that Schirm and Preston were comparing a particular kind of adjustment procedure with no adjustment. That particular procedure may have been a substantial overadjustment on average in the situations they considered, enough so to be worse than no adjustment in many cases. A milder adjustment might be better in most cases, by either loss function, as far as one can tell.

Second, Schirm and Preston also developed a number of theoretical insights on the effect of a synthetic adjustment, the most important of which was the observation that a synthetic adjustment will probably overcorrect the proportions in states in which the more heavily undercounted group is an unusually large fraction of the population and undercorrect the proportions in states in which it is an unusually small fraction of the population. This implies, of course, that simple synthetic adjustment is inappropriate if one can estimate or guess which states have these properties, or obtain information relevant or related to them. In their simulation study Schirm and Preston found that nearly two out of every three applications of adjustment procedures will bring the majority of the proportions nearer to the truth, and that on average 54 percent of the population proportions will be closer to the true values. Nonetheless, there is a small, but substantial, probability that a possibly large majority of the population proportions is taken further from the true values by adjustment.

In Schirm and Preston's paper, the choice of loss function does have a strong impact on the choice of adjustment procedure. But when the choice of adjustment procedure depends importantly on the choice of loss function, such dependence suggests that the particular adjustment procedures (or underlying models) under consideration have weaknesses that can be moderated or overcome, perhaps through a combined or compromise procedure. For example, one might average the procedures, or identify the regions for which each procedure is effective and then use the adjustment procedure that is most effective for that region. One might envision an iterative process, with one stage consisting of identification of the improved or compromise procedure and a second stage consisting of the determination of the regions in which the procedure may be improved yet further.

<u>Recommendation 7.3</u>. We believe that, in general, the results of an adjustment are likely to be affected more by the quality of coverage evaluation data and the models and methodology used than by the choice of loss functions. Given a family of loss functions with relatively similar objectives, it should be possible, and desirable, to determine an adjustment procedure that has good performance for most or all of them. We recommend that the Census Bureau investigate the construction of adjustment procedures that are robust to a reasonable range of loss functions.

Modifying Extreme Adjustments

There is a concern that the use of imperfect models could result in adjustments for some small areas that were so different from the census counts as to create a presumption of overadjustment. This could not occur with an ideal procedure and is very unlikely to occur for large areas and demographic groups. However, the models underlying the methods used for carrying down coverage evaluation information to small areas are rough and make little provision for a small area's special characteristics. Even if a model is effective by any reasonable definition of the term, it is possible that some very small areas will be adjusted to totals that differ substantially from the census counts. So when the adjustment is essentially finished, a reasonable procedure might involve checking the final adjusted estimates against the original raw counts. One diagnostic check would be to examine all cases in which the adjusted count differed from the census by more than a specified percentage. These might be labeled extreme adjustments. The notion of protection against an extreme adjustment has been discussed in the literature and at the Census Bureau. We mention three procedures that could offer protection against these extreme adjustments.

It has been suggested by Tukey (1985) that one not decrease any area's count as a result of adjustment. This suggestion is based on the belief that most areas are undercounted, in which case, at least area-by-area, a no-decrease policy is an improvement. Presumably fewer areas will be critical of an adjustment as long as they are not reduced in population as a result. It appears unlikely that such a constraint will cause undue damage to the primary goal of improving the differential undercount; however, it does not represent protection against extreme upward adjustments.

Hogan (1984c) has raised the possibility of using rough confidence intervals as a buffer against a poor adjustment. These confidence intervals could presumably be developed along the lines discussed below in the section on variance estimation. In his memorandum, Hogan adduces a procedure (one of a family of procedures) that does not adjust as long as the confidence interval includes the original census value. However, if the census counts are outside the confidence interval surrounding the adjusted counts, the adjustment is reduced to the conservative edge of the confidence interval. As an example, should the adjustment be 7 percent plus or minus 3 percent, the area would be increased by 4 percent. This method would help protect against extreme invalid adjustments.

Finally, a policy of refusing to adjust any area up or down by more than so many percentage points could be established. This would share some of the properties of the component protection technique of Efron and Morris (1972), which was used by Fay and Herriot (1979) in their hierarchical Bayes adjustment of postcensal per capita income estimates (see Appendix 7.2 on hierarchical Bayesian techniques).

These procedures would be needed either because the model for adjustment was imperfect or because the loss function was not appropriate. Since practical considerations inevitably enter into the choice of both model and loss function, such heuristic compromises are a consequence of our currently limited modeling and computational capability. All three methods for protection against extreme adjustments reviewed above are untested in the case of adjusting population counts, have quite different rationales and effects, and are in need of extensive research before they can be recommended for use.

Error Estimation

Our concern to this point has been with the magnitude of the error in the raw census data, i.e., the absolute or relative difference between the number produced by the census and the true value for that number in the population if one had a complete census. When one superimposes adjustment procedures on the raw counting process to produce census estimates, an additional consideration enters the picture, namely the statistical properties of the estimation procedure. We are not merely concerned with the error in the estimated census number, but also with the range of variation of that error that is associated with the estimation procedure adopted.

It is convenient to focus our concerns and discussion in terms of two statistical properties of the estimation procedure, its bias and its standard deviation. The determination of these properties presupposes the existence of a model of the process generating the original errors in the census data and, furthermore, knowledge of errors in whatever coverage evaluation information is used. Thus, the bias and variance of, say, synthetic estimation will be quite different depending on whether the unreported data are distributed over subpopulations and regions with probability proportional to size or with probabilities associated in some other specific way with subpopulation or region.

For every underlying model of the census and coverage evaluation error process, estimates of over- and undercoverage and any adjusted census data derived from such estimates will have a range of variation associated with them. A program to estimate the distribution of errors arising from the evaluation and adjustment procedures is needed. Although error can probably be measured only imperfectly, information about the distribution of error is important both for users of the data and for the Census Bureau itself, in the same way that sampling variances for sample surveys are useful even though they omit information on response biases, imperfections in the sampling frame, etc.

The possible errors of local area estimates, after adjustment, obviously enter into the analysis needed for most decisions discussed in this chapter, e.g., models to be used, loss functions, etc. Though we do not discuss error distributions and their impact for each such analysis, some comments on the types of error that affect the adjusted data and the kind of information that is relevant for analysts appear to be useful. We shall use terminology generally applied in sample survey reports, since most users of census data are familiar with those concepts.

The most commonly used models for errors in sample surveys are really about variability of estimates, and start off by decomposing estimation of errors into terms relating to their bias and to their variance. Even in relatively simple sample surveys these concepts cannot always be defined without some ambiguity, and this certainly applies to the complex statistical procedures being considered for use in adjusting the census. However, the decomposition seems useful as a way of thinking about one of the components of errors of the estimates, that due to sampling variability.

Bias can be thought of initially as the national overall error in the census derived from the coverage evaluation program estimate. Components of bias can also be considered, such as breakdowns by race and ethnicity. As in most survey situations, point estimates of bias terms will probably not be available (otherwise they could be used to modify the estimates). However, it may be possible to indicate likely bounds on the biases.

The first element in the variance component consists of the sampling variances of the post-enumeration survey (or allied evaluation efforts). Given usual sampling methods, these variances can be estimated. Distributing the estimated undercoverage among local areas involves another set of errors. The estimation error introduced into the estimate for a particular local area by the method used to carry down the coverage error can be considered as having components of both bias and variance. It is probably useful to think of these components as part of the total mean square error rather than decomposing into the traditional "bias" and "variance" terms. If the data used to provide the "improved" population count are from a post-enumeration survey or some other national sample, it should be possible to calculate between-area mean square errors and estimate parameters of the distribution of errors. An approach similar to the one used for evaluating corrections from the 1970 vacancy check may be feasible (see Waksberg, 1970, 1971). We recognize that the adjustments to be used may be more complex than the fairly simple synthetic adjustment used in 1970, but an adaptation of the general error estimation approach might possibly be applicable. Such calculations would be interesting and useful in assessing the impact of the adjustment procedures on local area estimates.

We suggest that the Census Bureau explore methods of implementing estimates of error distribution. It may be possible to carry out simulations with results from the 1980 Post-Enumeration Program. This would be useful, not only as part of a dress rehearsal for 1990 techniques, but also to provide important information for use in loss functions and other factors needed for decision making.

There is, however, another important component of error in the census, namely model error, that is not at all considered by the usual sample survey decomposition of errors, because traditional survey methods are model free. The standard sampling variability and bias calculations presume an underlying model of random sampling in the data collection process. Variations in this model, the model of nonresponse and multiple response to the census, will produce an additional error component. To provide no estimate of it because one knows little about how to calculate this component, and to publish merely the sampling variability error components (even if appropriately footnoted) may lead the unwary reader to believe that the published number represents the entire magnitude of the error. We therefore suggest that the Census Bureau investigate methods for providing estimates of this error component as well, for inclusion along with the census figures and the sampling variability error determinations.

There is an alternative way to view the choice of adjustment and the concepts of error and bias. In this alternative view, one does not first produce an "adjustment procedure" and then analyze its error. Rather, one starts with a probability distribution of the true population given the census counts and other information. If a decision is necessary (i.e., to estimate the undercount geographically), a loss function is chosen (see above), and the optimal decision minimizes expected loss (Savage, 1954). Thus, the adjustment procedure is implied by: (a) what the distribution on the true population is and (b) the consequence of various sizes of mistakes one might make, (i.e., the loss function). One implementation of this alternative view for estimated undercount is given by Ericksen and Kadane (1983, 1985) and Kadane (1984).

> <u>Recommendation 7.4</u>. We recommend that the Census Bureau explore methods for providing estimates of errors associated with estimates of census over- and undercoverage, with a view to publishing such error estimates along with coverage evaluation results and any adjusted census data that may be issued.

CONSIDERATIONS OF INTERNAL CONSISTENCY

Adjustment of census data could create problems of internal consistency of macro- and microdata from the census. Below we define what we mean by consistency in this context and offer our recommendation for dealing with this problem.

Suppose a set of parameters (unknown population quantities to be estimated) satisfies a mathematical relation. Let each parameter be separately estimated, perhaps even optimally with respect to some specified loss functions. Then it does not generally follow that the estimates satisfy the same mathematical relation as the corresponding parameters. For purposes of this discussion we call the set of estimates internally consistent, or for short, consistent, if they satisfy the same relation as the corresponding parameters. This use of the word "consistent" is quite different from the usual usage in statistics, namely, that, as the sample size increases to infinity, the estimator converges in probability to the corresponding population parameter.

The panel believes that there is a valid distinction to be made between the use of statistics designed specifically for a certain purpose and those designed to be used by many people to serve a wide variety of purposes. In the former case the only criterion that should be operative is that the statistics are "best" for the prescribed purpose; they may not be consistent with one another, and there is no requirement of consistency with other statistics or data sets. Typical cases of the latter situation are outputs from the general purpose survey vehicles of government statistical agencies. Given the exceptional range of output and its widespread use, internal consistency is an important quality for general purpose statistics.

The issue of internal consistency is important in relation to the possibility of adjusting census counts on the basis of combining coverage evaluation survey results with modeling. Should adjustment be used, two basic alternatives would arise: a set of adjusted population estimates could coexist with the unadjusted counts implicit in the census microdata set; or the microdata set could be adjusted.

In the former case substantial public confusion is likely to arise. It is difficult to explain, for example, that the population of a county is not necessarily the sum of the populations of its component school districts; or to explain that the population shares might only add up to 97 percent. Similarly, if the microdata set is unadjusted but some higher-level aggregates are adjusted for the estimated undercount, then _any_ substantive tabulation of characteristics at, say, the county level will necessarily have sums for groups or areas at the higher level of aggregation different from the published adjusted population of the county. Given the availability of adjusted counts for higher levels of aggregation, the panel believes that many users will perform their own adjustment of lower-level data, but presumably less effectively than the Census Bureau, at greater total cost, and with the result that different sets of numbers would be in use.

The panel recognizes that current census methodology produces tabulations that are not consistent in every respect. Specifically, the data products prepared from the long-form records are not always consistent with corresponding tabulations in data products produced from the short-form records. The Census Bureau uses iterative proportional fitting to promote consistency of the short-form and long-form data (see Appendix 3.2 and further discussion in this chapter), but inconsistencies remain. However, each data product from the census is internally consistent, for example, the marginals of a tabulation of income by race and sex contained in summary tape file 3, based on the long-form records, agree with the marginals from the same product of a tabulation of occupation or ancestry by race and sex, and totals for smaller geographic areas agree with those for larger areas. It is consistency in this respect that the panel supports.

Consequently, under the assumption that adjusted population estimates for _some_ geographic aggregations will be produced, the panel favors the alternative of carrying the adjustment down to the level of the microdata. Two basic approaches are available to accomplish this, imputation and weighting. Imputation consists of "creating" the required number and kinds of people in each area and assigning to them a full range of census characteristics, including the detailed set of geographic codes. Weighting attaches to each micro record a weight calculated in such a manner that the sum of the weights of records coded to an area for which an adjusted count is available is equal to that count. Some methods for carrying adjustment down to the level of microdata are given below in the section on procedures for adjustment.

Weighting and imputation are closely related and each presents some nontrivial problems. Problems arise because the census consists of at least three distinct but closely related microdata files: persons, families, and households. Therefore, together with the total number of persons, the numbers of families and households also have to be adjusted. Previous evaluation studies show that the total number of persons missed has significant proportions of both: (a) persons missed in partially enumerated households and/or families (these cases do not affect the number of families or households but do affect family and household characteristics) and (b) persons missed in completely missed households or families (these, of course, affect the number of such units). Moreover, the proportion of persons missed either in partially enumerated households, or in completely missed households, is known to vary from rural to large urban areas and is likely to vary by race, age, and other characteristics. If adjustment is to be carried out, then it is desirable to estimate the most important of these proportions so as not to cause possibly serious damage to such basic statistics as average family size.

The discussion of methods for carrying down an adjustment later in this chapter notes other problems posed by the various methods in addition to the problem of properly representing both person and family characteristics. Careful evaluation of these methods is essential to the implementation of an appropriate adjustment procedure.

The discussion above relates to the range of outputs provided by what is publicly and officially referred to as "the census." For special circumscribed purposes it may well be possible and desirable to compute special estimates not consistent with "the census." Finally, the panel's brief for consistency is not meant to preclude release of unadjusted census numbers for research purposes. For example, records on the public use microdata sample files could be flagged in such a way that researchers could analyze unadjusted data. As discussed in the next section, it may also be necessary to release unadjusted census figures prior to the availability of final adjusted numbers.

> Recommendation 7.5. The panel believes that it is important to strive for internal consistency of published census figures. Should adjustment appear feasible and effective, methods exist for distributing adjusted totals for aggregated groups down to subgroup values. We recommend that one of these methods be used to achieve internal consistency of census figures.

CONSIDERATIONS OF TIMING

As currently specified by law, the Census Bureau is required to meet two deadlines for specific data products from the decennial census: a deadline for the submission of state population counts within 9 months after Census Day for purposes of reapportionment of the House of Representatives, and a deadline for submission of small-area population counts within 12 months after Census Day for purposes of redistricting (see Chapter 2).

The panel assumes that the above deadlines are likely to be in effect for the 1990 decennial census. It is also reasonable to suppose that there will be pressures in censuses after 1990 for the release of information to meet deadlines at least this prompt. It is certainly conceivable (and considered to be likely by some members of the panel) that it will not be possible to prepare adjusted data in time to satisfy the above time constraints, especially the December 31st deadline for reapportionment. Another possibility is that relatively crudely adjusted state totals could be prepared by December 31st, with more carefully adjusted and more detailed data available later.

Given this contingency, the Census Bureau could first release the unadjusted census figures, to be followed by the adjusted figures when they become available. The first products might be identified as preliminary (or interim), and the later products labeled as final (or revised). Then users, public and private, could decide whether it was worthwhile for their purposes to wait for the adjusted figures. Included in this scenario is the possibility of the preliminary figures being used only for the purpose of reapportionment. This assumes that either the adjustment would be ready in time for redistricting, or that the redistricting deadline could be postponed enough to accommodate adjustment. In this special case, the inconsistency brought about by the existence of two sets of books would be limited to the counts by states. There is another possibility, that the Census Bureau might be asked to release only adjusted figures and users would wait until they were available. Then, of course, the deadlines given above would possibly have to be extended.

Each of the above scenarios is troublesome. The release of two sets of books would raise the specter of states, litigants, researchers, and others arguing over which set was the "proper" one to consult. It is easy to imagine the furor caused by states that would lose seats in the House of Representatives on the basis of the change from unadjusted to adjusted figures. It is also easy to imagine an equal employment opportunity case resting on the determination of whether the relevant percentage of minorities living in an area was the adjusted or unadjusted statistic. This possibility could be avoided if adjusted data could be released in time for redistricting, thereby releasing only one set of books with microdata. The other scenario, i.e,. the postponement of reapportionment and redistricting until possibly late 1991 (which corresponds to the date of completion of an initial version of the 1980 coverage evaluation program), extends the period during which political representation is based on population counts a decade or more out of date. Even if the postponement is politically acceptable, the misproportional representation implied by delay needs to be weighed against that implied by use for apportionment (and possibly redistricting) of figures somewhat less accurate than a careful adjustment might produce.

The existence of revised estimates is common today in the statistical system of the U.S. government. Statistics of the gross national product, energy production, consumer prices, and others all experience revisions and alterations, some on a regular basis, others as needed. Users accept the price of revisions and inconsistency (two sets of books) as the necessary cost of accuracy. Continued reliance for a decade on less accurate census data because adjustments to increase accuracy could not be completed by a specific date would, under that scenario, deny the country the potential benefits of more accurate data for uses other than apportionment.

The burden of choice among the above scenarios, which is essentially political, should not be left to the Census Bureau alone. Assuming that adjustment turns out to be feasible and desirable, but that adjusted data cannot meet legislated deadlines, it would be important to have a firm expression from Congress as to which scenario is preferable.

> Recommendation 7.6. Census data used for reapportionment and redistricting are required by law to be produced no later than specific dates. It is possible that adjustment of the 1990 census will prove feasible and effective in all respects, except for the ability to meet the required deadlines. This should not necessarily preclude subsequent issuance of adjusted

data for other uses. In this situation, we recommend that the Census Bureau seek determination by Congress of whether it desires that adjusted data be used and will therefore extend the deadlines, or wishes to adhere to current deadlines and will therefore stipulate the use of unadjusted (or partially adjusted) data for reapportionment and redistricting.

PROCEDURES FOR ADJUSTMENT

Inputs to Adjustment Procedures

Adjustment of the census must be based on one or more sources of information on the number of persons likely to have been missed, either nationally or in a given geographic region. Efforts to obtain good estimates of census over- and undercoverage have now been under way for four decades, and several methods exist for estimating coverage error (see Chapter 4). Up to now, these estimates of coverage error by race, sex, and age were made available to the public in the form of published reports, but they were not used to adjust the census results.

Among the reasons for not making such adjustments have been limitations on the quality of the information used to estimate coverage error and delayed availability of such information, as well as concerns about the public acceptability of adjusted data and about their legality for certain uses. Of these considerations, this panel has been concerned primarily with the technical possibilities for obtaining improved coverage estimates and adjustment techniques and using them in a timely manner. If the technical capability for adjusting the census in such a way as to increase its accuracy exists, we believe public acceptance of adjusted data will follow. (We note that there have been numerous questions raised about the quality of unadjusted data in 1980, evidenced in part by the litigation on this issue, and it is unclear that adjustment would appreciably increase the public concern.) Our detailed recommendations for improved evaluation of census coverage are given in Chapter 8. Here we briefly summarize the basic approaches to coverage evaluation that are available.

Until 1980, the Census Bureau felt that the best source of information about the completeness of the census counts was the demographic method first developed by Coale (1955). This method is designed to provide estimates of differential coverage by demographic groups. However, reasonably accurate estimates by geographic region within the country, using this methodology, have so far not been possible. A further limitation, which proved quite serious with respect to the 1980 census, is the failure of these estimates, as traditionally constructed, to include any estimate of the number of undocumented aliens. Several million undocumented aliens are believed to have been resident in the United States in 1980 and a substantial, but unknown, fraction of them to have been counted in the census. Thus, the census count included a large group of people (not readily identifiable in the census data) excluded from the demographic estimate. This definitional difference was of sufficient practical importance by 1980 to severely limit the usefulness of demographic analysis for coverage evaluation or for adjustment. Estimates of the number of undocumented aliens counted in the 1980 census by age, race, and sex have now been constructed and used to develop demographic estimates of the coverage of the legally resident population (see Passel and Robinson, 1984; Warren and Passel, 1983). However, only very rough estimates exist for the total population of undocumented aliens, and, hence, demographic analysis can at this time provide only very rough estimates of the coverage of the total population. In addition, the lack of subnational detail remains a serious limitation on the use of estimates from demographic analysis in any adjustment procedure, especially for reducing differential geographic coverage errors.

A program similar to the 1980 Post-Enumeration Program (PEP) provides an alternative approach to estimating coverage errors in the 1990 census. In Chapter 8, we identify four major areas of PEP methodology in need of improvement, some with more, others with less, concrete suggestions on how to proceed. Progress with respect to most of these problem areas is needed for PEP to provide usable estimates for adjustment--either to substantially reduce the errors in PEP or at least to obtain a substantially better understanding of the combined impact of the errors on the resulting estimates.

Other possible approaches to estimating coverage error, not used for coverage evaluation in the United States except in a testing mode, include the reverse record check, which has been used in Canada (see Fellegi 1976), systematic observation in a sample of areas, and the matching of census results against a sample drawn from the union of several lists of persons. We discuss some of these alternatives and give our recommendations for further research in Chapter 8.

Below we discuss possible technical approaches to the use of information generated from coverage evaluation programs for purposes of adjusting the decennial census data. Since the estimates derived directly from the coverage evaluation programs are necessarily restricted to a limited number of large areas, and since it is desirable for many purposes that the adjustment apply to small areas, adjustment procedures naturally separate into two components: (1) the manner in which the original estimates are derived for the limited number of large areas and (2) the manner in which the estimates are carried down from these larger areas to smaller areas. The objective of consistency argued for above results in the need for adjustment down to the level of the person or household, i.e., for some type of reweighting or imputation. Therefore, our discussion of methods for carrying the adjustment down to small areas focuses on carrying down to the level of the person or the household.

Methods for Starting Out

Combining Estimates from Different Programs

It appears that for 1990 the Census Bureau plans to concentrate on two techniques of coverage evaluation: demographic analysis and some version of a pre- or post-enumeration survey. In future censuses, additional techniques may become central to the coverage evaluation program. Indeed, the panel recommends in Chapter 8 that the Census Bureau, as part of its 1990 research program, work on developing other techniques of coverage evaluation, specifically, reverse record checks and systematic observation. Given the substantial indeterminacies involved, not surprisingly, different evaluation programs yield differing estimates of census errors. This is true even for variants of the same procedure. The Census Bureau has produced a range of coverage error estimates from the 1980 PEP based on alternate assumptions (e.g., about the nonresponse in PEP) and did not reach a conclusion as to which estimate was best. Thus, there arises the problem of combining information from various coverage evaluation programs.

One method of combining the information from the different evaluation programs is to use some methods to "benchmark" others. This approach is used when the totals from one method are considered to be much more reliable than the totals from another, even though the internal proportions of the latter are useful. For example, it is quite likely that the estimate of the black national undercount for various age-sex groups derived from demographic analysis will be quite accurate in 1990, since it will be relatively unaffected by the treatment of undocumented aliens.

A more general approach, encompassing benchmarking, is to consider combining the estimates from the various programs in some way. There has been very little work to date on the problem of determining reasonable weights to use in averaging the information from, say, demographic analysis and the PEP, or from various PEP estimates based on different assumptions to deal with nonresponse and record matching problems. More research needs to be conducted to identify models that might be useful in trading off the strengths and weaknesses of the various census coverage measuring instruments so as to form a superior estimate.

Modifying Estimates From Within One Program

Tukey (1985) has suggested that an effective way of tabulating the information from the PEP or a reverse record check with a view to subsequent adjustment is through cross-classification by homogeneous domains. That is, instead of directly producing estimates for political entities such as states, which have heterogeneous populations and therefore on average do not differ very greatly in coverage error, estimates can be produced for combinations of areas that are homogeneous on variables believed to be related to the undercount. For example, one domain might comprise central cities in northeastern industrial states and another nonmetropolitan areas in the Southwest. A benefit from the use of these domains is that the homogeneity within strata should result in lower variances within strata.

Given estimates at the level of homogeneous domains, it may still be possible to improve on these estimates. One can think of the PEP information as being composed of a systematic component and a random component. If the systematic component can be effectively modeled, the model can be used to modify the raw PEP estimates of undercoverage.

Regression is one technique for distilling the systematic component from the observed coverage estimates of the PEP. Variables are examined for their ability to explain the differences in PEP from domain to domain. If these variables (or close surrogates) can be identified, and how they affect the PEP estimates determined, then a model relating the PEP estimates to these variables will help reduce some of the random fluctuation present in the PEP estimates. The choice of these variables involves considerations such as the strength of the relationship to the observed PEP undercount estimates and the quality and availability of the data. Ericksen and Kadane (see Ericksen, 1984) have proposed an adjustment model that uses as variables for each area: percentage minority (black and nonblack Hispanics), percentage conventional census (i.e., the method used largely in rural areas, where enumerators called in person to collect census forms), and the crime rate. The testing of other variables for their explanatory power and robustness, already started, should continue so that these types of models are better understood, and the pool of useful variables is better developed.

In considering regression, another benefit from the use of domains is obtained. The values of the covariates for domains that enter into the estimation of regression coefficients should have wider ranges than they would have if one were using states because the domains should be less alike than the states. This increased range of values is known to reduce the variance of the estimated regression coefficients.

The hierarchical Bayesian method (see Appendix 7.2), advanced by Ericksen and Kadane (1985) in the adjustment context, is one technique for assessing the degree to which the systematic part of the PEP has been distilled and for assigning weights to the regression estimate and the estimate derived directly from the PEP program. Roughly, the observed sampling variances of the PEP estimates are compared with the estimated variances due to the regression. Estimates are combined with weights inversely related to their variances--those estimates with less variance getting more weight. As is true of all models, the hierarchical Bayesian method depends on a number of assumptions, which should be analyzed to the extent feasible to determine the degree to which they obtain. Freedman and Navidi (in press) question the validity of the assumptions underlying the application cited above and observe some lack of robustness with respect to departures from these assumptions as well as the choice of variables. Their work emphasizes the need to validate the assumptions underlying any models made use of in adjustment.

Tukey (1985) has proposed a similar adjustment technique that uses the regression estimates alone, uncombined with the observed PEP estimates. The relative merits of regression uncombined with the direct PEP estimates, the observed PEP estimates uncombined with regression estimates, or the combinations possible through the use of hierarchical Bayesian techniques as well as other models need to be researched.

Methods for Carrying Down

Assuming that usable adjusted estimates have been created for domains or states, it still remains to carry the adjustment down to lower levels of geographic and demographic aggregation. At least four methods have been advanced for this purpose: (1) synthetic estimation, (2) iterative proportional fitting, (3) imputation, and (4) regression. We discuss these techniques in turn below.

Synthetic Estimation

The synthetic method, in the context of adjustment, is defined as an estimation process that apportions an overcount or undercount for an area to subareas on the basis of the population sizes of the subareas (see Hill, 1980). This is usually done by maintaining the larger areas' under- or overcount percentages for demographic groups in the subareas. For example, suppose that there were two demographic groups, I and II, and we were calculating a synthetic estimate of the undercount for a small area A_1 within the larger area A. Also suppose, for the larger area, the census and a coverage evaluation program each estimated the population counts illustrated in Table 7.1. The synthetic method would now assume a 5 percent overcount of group I individuals and a 25 percent undercount of group II individuals in every subarea of area A. Thus, the synthetic estimate for area A_1 as shown in the table would be $20\text{x}(95/100) + 9(40/30) = 31$.

TABLE 7.1 Simple Example of Synthetic Estimation

	Demographic Group I	Demographic Group II	Total
Area A			
Census count	100	30	130
Coverage evaluation program estimate	95	40	135
Area A_I			
Census count	20	9	29
Synthetic estimate	19	12	31

NOTE: This procedure can be carried out for any number of subareas.

Adjustment via synthetic estimation involves reweighting each individual belonging to a domain and demographic group by the ratio of the count determined by a coverage evaluation program and that determined by the census. Since this procedure reweights individual records, it results in a consistent data set. To arrive at the resulting estimate for any subnational area, the weights for the individuals residing within the area are totaled. (Appendix 7.3 contains a discussion of a problem encountered through the accumulation of synthetic estimates.)

Iterative Proportional Fitting

Iterative proportional fitting is a generalization of synthetic estimation to multiway fitting. Consider first a two-way matrix or table, for which new totals are set for both rows and columns. A synthetic estimate can be computed for each row so that the row totals of the adjusted table agree with the new row totals. Next the columns of the adjusted table can also be adjusted via synthetic estimation, after which one returns to readjust the rows, then the columns, etc., with the entire process iteratively continued. Convergence will occur in most practical situations. This procedure generalizes to any multiway contingency table. The resulting estimated table entries will be completely consistent with the new totals for marginals of the multiway table.

Iterative proportional fitting is currently used by the Census Bureau to force certain tables produced from the sampled long-form records to be essentially consistent with the corresponding short-form data produced on a 100 percent basis[2] (see Appendix 3.2). It is a potential adjustment procedure for using external totals to adjust the census counts as well. As an example, one could use totals for demographic groups (provided by an improved demographic method) and PEP totals for domains (provided by an improved PEP method) with iterative proportional fitting so that the adjusted counts agreed with the more reliable totals. (This assumes that the overall totals of the national PEP and demographic estimates have been made to agree, perhaps after a combination or reconciliation of some kind.)

When the classification variables are related to the undercount, and reliable estimates of the marginal totals are available, iterative proportional fitting can be expected to result in improvements in the estimated counts (see Oh and Scheuren, 1978). However, when the estimates of the marginal totals are not reliable, or the classification variables are not related to the undercount, iterative proportional fitting can have a detrimental impact on the resulting estimated counts. Research needs to be carried out to determine what the problems are with the use of this technique in the adjustment setting.

Imputation

Imputation (in a manner somewhat similar to that used by the Census Bureau for unit nonresponse adjustment) has also been proposed as a method for carrying down an adjustment to lower levels of aggregation. This procedure is very closely related to synthetic estimation. Suppose that one determined from PEP or another coverage evaluation program that certain percentages of persons belonging to various demographic groups living in a particular domain were missed in the census. Then, instead of reweighting the records for the individuals belonging to each of these demographic groups, as one would in a syn-

---

[2]Consistency extends only to row and column totals of tables that are used directly in the iterative proportional fitting algorithm. For tables of data at either different levels of aggregation or cross-tabulated with variables not involved in the iterative proportional fitting, the algorithm will often result in less inconsistency, but not necessarily complete consistency.

thetic adjustment, the number undercounted could be added by duplicating at random the records of people already counted in the census in that domain and demographic group.

Regression

Another potential method for carrying down adjustment to lower levels of aggregation is regression. The use of regression methodology to carry adjustments to lower geographic levels consists of estimating the coefficients of the covariates in a regression model at one level of aggregation as already described, and then estimating the undercount for each subarea by using the same model, with covariate information for that particular subarea.

The panel believes that synthetic or iterative proportional fitting methods of carrying down are superior to simple regression because the regression model used in this way is fitted to a more aggregated set of data than the set to which it will be applied. Moreover, since the covariate information for smaller areas will have more extreme values than would have been used in fitting the model, there is the potential for extreme adjustments.[3]

However, the above comments do not rule out a regression approach that is modified by some type of limitation of the adjustment, constraining it to lie not too far away from the original census count (see the previous discussion of this topic). For example, one can use regression to construct weights for individual respondents such that weighted sums match designated population totals for a number of auxiliary variables. In this way regression can be used to derive a consistent data set. The generalized regression estimator of the total can be written as a weighted sum of the area subtotals, wherein the weights are functions of the auxiliary variables and are so constrained that the weighted sum of each of the auxiliary variables equals the known total of the auxiliary variable

[3] It may be confusing to some that we recommend synthetic estimation but not regression, when regression is merely a generalization of the synthetic method. The synthetic method is a special type of regression in that it has only one covariate, the census count, which is presumed to be well-behaved for even fairly small areas.

used in the construction of the weights. In the census adjustment context, the totals of each of the auxiliary variables might be the adjusted estimates of the total number of individuals in age-race-sex categories at a reasonably high level of aggregation, such as state.

Huang (1978) and Huang and Fuller (1978) have discussed the application of the regression technique to survey sampling for both discrete and continuous auxiliary variables. A computer program that implements the regression weight method is available (Huang, 1983).

Finally, it should be kept in mind in considering the use of any of the above methods of carrying down adjustments to the microdata level that there are unresolved problems of allocating "additional persons" resulting from an adjustment to partially counted households and/or families. These problems, not fully researched, need further investigation.

CENSUS BUREAU PLANS FOR RESEARCH AND TESTING ON ADJUSTMENT

The purpose of the last two sections is to describe the research and testing plans of the Census Bureau with respect to adjustment and present the panel's reactions to these plans and recommendations for priority research areas. Two documents--"Pretest of Adjustment Operations" (Bureau of the Census, 1984c) and "Requisite Planning and Research Relating to a Decision on Census Adjustment for 1990" (Wolter, 1984)--describe the Census Bureau's adjustment research and testing program, the former document relating solely to the 1986 pretest, and the latter document giving an overview of the research up until the 1990 census. Much of what is discussed in these two papers relates to coverage evaluation and is covered in Chapter 8. Here we concentrate solely on the aspects related to adjustment. The line separating these topics is not easily drawn, and the reader is referred to Chapter 8 for further discussion.

The paper on "Pretest of Adjustment Operations" outlines a plan for the adjustment of data collected in a census pretest. The idea is to carry out an adjustment and study its timing, costs, and quality. The quality of the adjustment cannot be directly measured, but the Census Bureau intends to examine various indirect indicators of quality, such as: (1) consistency of independent estimates, (2) estimates of components of variance of the estimated undercoverage, and (3) size of nonresponse.

There is also the hope that this pretest can identify any unanticipated operational problems with carrying out an adjustment. The product of this pretest will be adjusted tabulations and mock-up publications.

In order to carry out an adjustment, there will have to be a pretest of a coverage evaluation program. This same paper mentions two pretests, one of a post-enumeration survey akin to the 1980 census PEP program, and the other a pre-enumeration survey, whose purpose is to determine the time savings achieved by taking the independent sample survey before the census, balanced against the possible effects on data quality introduced by sensitization of the population (see Chapter 8 for a discussion of this point). The paper stresses the importance of conducting both types of surveys in the same pretest site so that they can be compared on equal terms.

Wolter (1984) describes the current attitude and approach of the Census Bureau toward planning and research with respect to making a decision on adjustment. The needs identified in this position paper are to: (a) measure coverage errors in the decennial census, (b) measure errors for small areas, (c) set standards to judge adjusted data against unadjusted data, (d) supply the input to these standards, and (e) develop the operational techniques and methods to implement an adjustment should it be decided to do so on the basis of (d).

Wolter outlines five major steps as necessary to address the above needs: (1) summarize the 1980 coverage evaluation studies, (2) determine criteria that can be used to assess when adjusted counts are better than unadjusted counts, (3) develop techniques for measuring the undercoverage, (4) decide on an adjustment methodology should the decision be made to adjust, and (5) make the final decision on adjustment. Of these five steps, steps two, four, and five concern plans on adjustment, and we discuss their details below. Steps one and three are covered in Chapter 8.

Step two deals with determining what criteria or loss functions to use in comparing adjusted data with unadjusted data. While there are few details given with respect to testing and research, the basic approach taken by the Census Bureau will be to: (1) examine the previous literature, including that of Fellegi (1980b), Tukey (1983), and Spencer (1980a, 1980b), some of which were discussed above; (2) examine appropriate loss functions specific to special uses of the census data, e.g., examine the revenue sharing formula; and, finally (3) look at the losses incurred by an inaccurate adjustment compared with losses when there is no adjustment. This third substep will be accomplished by: (a) assuming one post-enumeration survey estimate yields "true" counts and then examining the costs of using one of the other estimates based on alternative imputation techniques; (b) assuming regression yields "true" counts and then evaluating the loss incurred by using synthetic estimation; and (c) developing a decision theory analysis to balance probable gain from adjustment with the cost of the adjustment program. This program is related to the discussion on loss functions above, and recommendation 7.3 and the accompanying text are relevant as a comment on these plans.

Step four is concerned with the choice of methodology to use in carrying out an adjustment. The factors underlying this decision are measures of bias and variance for various components of the adjustment methodology for each of the proposed methodologies. For example, the sampling variances and biases given by the post-enumeration survey and the potential biases through the use of a synthetic adjustment might be included in making such a choice.

Finally, there is the decision on the degree of an adjustment. The three components making up the degree of an adjustment are the timing, the geography, and the characteristics detail. The first issue is whether evaluation data will be ready for adjustment in time for reapportionment, redistricting, or later. The second issue relates to which level the adjustment will be carried down to, e.g., states, major cities, counties, census tracts, enumeration districts, or city blocks. Finally, the third issue relates to whether any of the content data will be adjusted, or merely the counts.

Wolter introduces the concept of what is labeled a "complete census adjustment," or an adjustment that is in time for reapportionment, carried down to the individual household level, and carried out for all characteristics collected on the census questionnaire. Wolter states that a complete census adjustment is the Census Bureau's preferred outcome. He also notes that the Census Bureau would plan to make the unadjusted data available for interested researchers. The panel earlier in this chapter expressed its preference for carrying down an adjustment to the microdata level in order to promote consistency. With regard to timing, the panel indicated that it does not want to ignore the benefits of an adjustment if one can be developed effectively except for the fact that it may not be ready by December 31, 1990. The panel comments further on Wolter's paper in Chapter 8.

PRIORITIES FOR RESEARCH AND TESTING ON ADJUSTMENT

The panel recognizes that there are many issues and aspects of adjustment that need and would benefit from additional research. The panel believes that an intensive research program is called for in the area of adjustment and believes that researchers both within the Census Bureau and in the academic community can make significant contributions to furthering the development of feasible and effective adjustment methods. It is in the Census Bureau's interest to encourage related studies by academic researchers as well as to pursue a vigorous research program of its own in the area of adjustment. As mentioned earlier in the report, one of the major constraints on the Census Bureau's abilities to carry out research is the resulting increased demand on its technical staff. The opportunity to augment this staff through the use of academics and other researchers should therefore be investigated, not only for issues in adjustment, but also to perform research on many of the other research issues suggested throughout this report.

> Recommendation 7.7. The panel recognizes that considerable work is still necessary and likely to lead to improved procedures for adjusting census data. We therefore support the Census Bureau's stated plans to pursue, internally, research and development of adjustment procedures, and we also recommend that the Census Bureau vigorously promote and support related statistical research in the academic community.

The panel concurs in the need for the Census Bureau to carry out an adjustment, as an exercise, in its pretest plans for 1986, including the preparation of adjusted tabulations. Only in this way will the Census Bureau learn how to develop an operational capability to adjust. The identification of any unknown logistical problems with adjustment needs to be made as soon as possible. Thus, the panel is strongly in support of the plan to carry out a pretest of adjustment-related operations in 1986, even though one cannot completely determine the effectiveness of an adjustment in 1990 through any pretesting or research done in 1986.

<u>Recommendation 7.8</u>. The panel supports the Census Bureau in its plans for a 1986 pretest of adjustment operations, including the production of mock tabulations of adjusted census data. We recommend analysis of the resulting adjusted and unadjusted data sets, to help identify the strengths and weaknesses of the particular methods tried.

With respect to the theoretical investigation of an adjustment methodology, the panel has identified research it would like to see pursued that is not specifically mentioned in either of the above papers. The appropriateness of an adjustment procedure can certainly be measured to some extent by investigating the agreement between estimates based on different models, the errors involved in the adjustment process, and nonresponse. Two examples of this were mentioned in our interim report (National Research Council, 1984:39,40):

> We suggest starting with the national age-race-sex undercount estimates derived from demographic analysis for 1980 and deriving from them, through synthetic and related means, state-level estimates. . . . Comparison of the synthetic estimates with the "direct" PEP-derived undercount estimates for states should then be made to see whether the results shed light on the feasibility of using synthetic estimates based on national demographic estimates of the undercount to produce state and substate undercount estimates.
>
> The United States should be divided into two (or three) blockings of about 20-60 relatively homogeneous and not necessarily contiguous domains. . . . Then, using the first blocking, a regression model should be estimated, using from three to six covariates, which fits the PEP undercount estimates derived for the domains. The same should also be carried out for the second blocking (and perhaps the third), attempting to use a different set of covariates. Estimates for substate regions would make use of synthetic techniques based on the regression estimates for the homogeneous domains. Then the undercount estimates for the two (or three) models should be compared in a variety of ways. It would be interesting to see whether the substate regression estimates

summed to the state-level PEP estimates. The effect of these estimates on redistricting or reapportionment could also be examined.

Since publication of our interim report, the Census Bureau undercount research staff has been actively pursuing research along these lines.

There are other aspects of adjustment methods that can also be researched. One important component of any statistical estimation process is the assumptions that underlie it. Thus, the degree to which the assumptions hold for all the competing procedures should be investigated. This work has already begun through the efforts of Freedman and Navidi (in press). The robustness of the various procedures to assumptions should be examined as well.

The methods proposed for carrying down the adjustment to lower levels of geographic aggregation should also be investigated. In some respects this is even more important than similar investigations for higher levels of geographic aggregation, since the methods used to carry the information down are necessarily rough, being less specific to the population of the area being estimated. These methods are used as much for convenience as for validity. The validity of the models underlying the methods used to carry information down should also be investigated on the basis of considerations of variance, nonresponse, and plausibility of and sensitivity to the underlying assumptions.

Finally, the panel believes that the impact of adjusted data on a variety of users should be examined. This area is mentioned in the Wolter paper, but the panel believes that it should be explicitly given priority. An investigation would include the problems posed by the possible existence of two sets of books, the difficulties brought about by the need to allocate additional counts to households and families, and the effect on estimation for families, should these additional counts not have imputed family relationships.

Recommendation 7.9. We recommend that research on adjustment include: (1) investigations of the assumptions underlying the procedures, (2) an attempt to empirically evaluate the more important of the assumptions as well as the sensitivity of methods to violation of assumptions, (3) study of methods used for carrying down estimates to lower levels of aggregation, and (4) a study of the impact of adjustment on uses of census data.

APPENDIX 7.1

A QUICK LOOK AT LOSS FUNCTIONS AND APPORTIONMENT

The method currently used to apportion the House of Representatives derives from Hill (1911). Let a_i be the number of seats allocated to state i, and p_i be the known population of state i. Suppose h seats are to be allocated. The algorithm used proceeds as follows:

(1) Set $a_i = 1$ for $i = 1, \ldots, 50$
(2) Suppose h' seats have been allocated, i.e., $\Sigma\ a_i = h'$. Choose a state j for which $p_j/\text{sqrt}(a_j(a_{j+1}))$ is a maximum. Increase a_j by one, and h' by one.
(3) If h' < h, then return to step (2). Otherwise stop.

It has been shown (Huntington, 1921) that this method is equivalent to the minimization of

$$L = \Sigma\ p_i^2 / a_i, \qquad (7.1)$$

given that each a_i is at least one. To see this, roughly, consider that the choice at some stage of the process has been to give the last representative to state A by minimizing criterion (7.1). We now show that this choice also satisfies the Hill algorithm. Assume that state A has parameters p_A and a_A, and state B has parameters p_B and a_B, respectively, for their population and number of representatives. Since (7.1) has been minimized, we must have that:

$$p_A^2 / (a_A) + p_B^2 / (a_B) < p_A^2 / (a_A-1) + p_B^2 / (a_B+1)$$

for any choice of B

or, equivalently,

$$p_A^2 / (a_A) - p_A^2 / (a_A-1) < p_B^2 / (a_B+1) - p_B^2 / (a_B) \text{ or}$$

$$p_A / \text{sqrt}[(a_A)(a_A-1)] > p_B / \text{sqrt}[(a_B)(a_B+1)],$$

Note: Much of the discussion is taken from Balinski and Young (1980) and Kadane (1984).

and therefore the choice of A to minimize criterion (7.1) also maximized the Hill criterion.

The function L, the Huntington criterion, does not have the form of a loss function in a strict sense. But it is equivalent to an index of misproportionality, as defined above in Chapter 7. For purposes of reapportionment, the loss due to any state could well be a function of how relatively under- or overrepresented the people of that state are, probably a function of $(p_i/a_i - p_+/h)^2$, where p_+ is the total population of the United States.

Amalgamating these losses by forming the weighted sum $\Sigma\, a_i\, (p_i/a_i - p_+/h)^2$ is reasonable. This can be seen by the following argument. If state A has k times the number of representatives as state B, and if states A and B are equally underrepresented by some apportionment of the House of Representatives, then the number of seats needing change for state A will be k times the number of seats for state B. Rewriting the sum $\Sigma\, a_i\, (p_i/a_i - p_+/h)^2$ as the sum of three terms by taking the square of the indicated expression, it is easy to see that this loss function can be rewritten, as $\Sigma\, p_i^2/a_i - \Sigma\, p_+^2/h$. Since the second term is a constant, minimizing this index of misproportionality is equivalent to minimizing the Huntington criterion.

APPENDIX 7.2

AN INTRODUCTION TO HIERARCHICAL BAYESIAN TECHNIQUES

An important problem in statistics is how to effectively weight information obtained about certain quantities from more than one source, with each source's means and variances estimable but unknown. This problem arises in the decennial census in more than one context. For example, how to combine information from the raw data collected in the decennial census and information from the coverage evaluation programs is the fundamental statistical problem faced in the determination of a method for adjustment. In addition, the combination of postcensal estimates based on sampled long-form responses for small areas with information from more highly aggregated areas that enclose the smaller areas, investigated by Fay and Herriot (1979), is again a problem of combining information from more than one source.

Hierarchical Bayesian methods (Lindley and Smith, 1972) provide a technique for weighting information from different sources. There is a strong similarity between the empirical Bayesian model and the components of variance model (see, e.g., Kackar and Harville, 1984; Henderson, 1975). In this section we describe the basic approach used.

As an example, assume that we have a process that generates n values m_i, so that each m_i is normally distributed with mean m, and variance t^2 (denoted $m_i \sim N(m,t^2)$). Then, assume that the n random variables X_i are independently $\sim N(m_i,s^2)$, with m, s^2, and t^2 known. Unconditionally, $X_i \sim N(m,t^2+s^2)$. The problem is to estimate the value of m_i after observing X_i. Bayesian methods direct one to determine the posterior distribution of m_i given X_i, which can be calculated given the prior distribution for m_i, and the distribution of X_i given m_i. The Bayesian estimate of m_i, under squared-error loss, is then the mean of this distribution, $(t^2X_i+s^2m)/(t^2+s^2)$. It is a weighted combination of X_i and m, with weights $t^2/(t^2+s^2)$ and $s^2/(t^2+s^2)$. Thus the two sources of information for the value of m_i are weighted in an appropriate fashion to arrive at a reasonable estimate. However, the estimator required m, s^2, and t^2 to be known.

One form of empirical Bayesian methodology (see Efron and Morris, 1973; Harville, 1976) generalizes this basic approach by treating m, s^2, and t^2 as unknown parameters to be estimated from the data, rather than known a priori.

The term hierarchical derives from the realization that the modeling need not stop at a distribution for the mean and the estimation of the parameters for this distribution. It is, for example, possible, instead of estimating m and t^2 from the data, to place a prior on them. Furthermore, if the data have a hierarchical structure such that independent realizations of m and t^2 are available, they can be used to estimate the parameters of that distribution. Moreover, more complicated linear structures than components of variance, such as multiple regression with "random" coefficients, can be handled. This can go on indefinitely, as long as estimates for the various parameters can be achieved in some way. This nesting of models allows incomplete knowledge about quantities that affect the quantity to be estimated to be incorporated into the estimation process.

In the case of adjustment, one possible hierarchical model might be developed based on the following reasoning. For major central cities and states and remainders of states with these cities in them, or for homogeneous regions, it is reasonable to consider modeling the ratio of the census counts to the true counts, i.e., percentages of undercount. One could assume that the ratios of the Post-Enumeration Program counts to the census counts, denoted p_i, or some appropriate transformation of the p_i, were distributed approximately as $N(m_i, v_i)$. The next step might be to hypothesize a model for the means m_i. One possibility for this model could be a regression model such as that suggested in Fay and Herriot. Then, $m_i \sim N(X_i B, A)$, where A is unknown. The regression model for percentage undercount could include as explanatory variables such variables as mail return rate, percentage undercount in the previous census, percentage minority, crime rate, percentage conventional enumeration, socioeconomic status, and so on (see Ericksen, 1984). Here, $X_i B$ is assuming the role of the mean of the "true" undercount. The variance of the parent distribution, v_i, can be derived from the Post-Enumeration Program specifications, such as the sampling rate. However, this alone is not sufficient, since there are other components to the variance of the Post-Enumeration Program besides sampling variance, e.g., variance due to nonresponse. As a third stage, one could estimate B using classical least squares, or hypothesize a model for it as well. The only remaining difficulty is that of estimating A.

If we had hypothesized the v_i to be constant, over i, it would be relatively easy to estimate the common value by computing the sum of squared deviations of p_i about X_iB, and making some adjustments. This is what is suggested in the work by James and Stein (1961), and later in the work by Efron and Morris (1973). However, the variance heterogeneity forces one into a more sophisticated methodology. One relatively easy but unsatisfying way around this difficulty is to assume that A, the variance of the prior distribution, is not constant over i, but instead, is equal to Av_i. Carter and Rolph (1974) propose a method of moments estimator for the case with constant variance, A, for the prior distribution, which is a more satisfying assumption.

APPENDIX 7.3

AGGREGATION OF SYNTHETIC ESTIMATES: A COUNTERINTUITIVE EXAMPLE

While synthetic estimation is suggested for adjustment because of its arithmetic and computational simplicity, synthetic estimation is not necessarily an improvement over the census counts. Let us assume the situation depicted in Table 7.2.

An examination of the table shows that the estimates of area totals using synthetic estimation are further from the truth than the unadjusted census estimates for areas I and III, and no better for area II. That is, the synthetic values 108 and 92 are not equal to the true counts of 100, which is the case for the unadjusted census counts. This is indicative of the fact that the near-optimality of synthetic estimation, discussed by Tukey (1983) for subgroups, is not necessarily preserved when synthetic subgroup estimates are accumulated to synthetic geographic area estimates.

TABLE 7.2 An Example: Problems in Aggregating Synthetic Estimates

	Subgroup 1			Subgroup 2			Total		
Area	Census	Synthetic	True	Census	Synthetic	True	Census	Synthetic	True
I	10	9	5	90	99	95	100	108	100
II	50	45	45	50	55	55	100	100	100
III	90	81	85	10	11	15	100	92	100
Total	150	135	135	150	165	165	300	300	300

8
Measuring the Completeness of the 1990 Census

RECAPITULATION OF MAJOR ISSUES IN COVERAGE EVALUATION

Chapter 4 described the methods used to evaluate the population counts in past censuses and appraised the quality of the various evaluation procedures. There is no need to repeat the detailed information of Chapter 4 in discussing the methods planned for 1990, but it is useful to summarize the main features of the evaluation methods. We shall also repeat key comments on this subject from the panel's interim report (National Research Council, 1984).

The methods used by the Census Bureau, or suggested by others for use in evaluating coverage of decennial censuses, can be grouped into four types:

(1) Pre- or post-enumeration surveys, such as the 1980 Post-Enumeration Program (PEP);
(2) Reverse record checks;
(3) Matching with administrative records, including multiple and composite list techniques; and
(4) Demographic analyses.

We later suggest a fifth method for coverage evaluation, which we call systematic observation. Systematic observation is a close relative of ethnographic studies, or resident observation.

Starting with the 1950 census, the Census Bureau's evaluation of coverage concentrated on the first and fourth methods above. A reverse record check study was carried out in 1960 but its quality was judged too poor for it to be used. (By contrast, this procedure has been judged successful in Canada and considerable reliance has been placed on it.) Administrative list matching has been used for special studies relating to coverage evaluation, but not for the production of overall estimates of net undercount.

There are known weaknesses to each of these methods, at least in the way they have been carried out in the past. Through 1970, the Census Bureau's judgment was that demographic analysis provided the best estimates of undercoverage, and these estimates were generally used in discussions of the undercount. Subsequent events, particularly the large level of presumed undocumented immigration, caused the Census Bureau to anticipate that this would no longer be true in 1980 and to rely on the PEP for coverage evaluation of the 1980 census.

Demographic analysis relies on estimates of populations independent of the current census, using such information as annual figures on births and deaths, immigration and emigration, and past census data. In earlier uses of the method, it was recognized that the net immigration statistics were somewhat shaky, but it was felt that a moderate error in this component could be tolerated without an important effect on the total estimate. However, by 1980, the uncertainty regarding the number of undocumented aliens in the United States changed perceptions of the accuracy of the independent population figures. New importance was attached to questions about the general quality of data on immigration and emigration. For the 1980 census, demographic analysis initially showed a net overcoverage of the white population, a result that the Census Bureau staff and most other analysts considered unlikely. The PEP and other survey-related procedures have the advantage over demographic analysis of providing subnational data, although cost constraints severely limit the number of areas for which separate estimates can be produced. (It is probably unrealistic to assume that reliable estimates will be available for more than at most 100 subareas of the United States.)

The most recent Census Bureau statements indicate that the Census Bureau intends for PEP-type surveys to be the basic evaluation tool in 1990. Demographic analysis will be continued, primarily for use in checking the reasonableness of the survey results for aggregate sex-age-race groups. The panel considers the Census Bureau to be acting prematurely in making a decision at this time for the evaluation method for 1990, particularly in light of the improvements that may be possible in other methods of coverage evaluation, as well as in the PEP. These possibilities are discussed in a later section of this chapter. We first repeat several assessments of evaluation methods from the panel's interim report:

1. Each of the various methods currently used in the United States and other countries to measure the completeness of census coverage is subject to serious limitations, including biases, in measuring the coverage of various population groups.
2. There is at present no reason to expect a breakthrough in the methodology of coverage evaluation before 1990. However, some significant improvements are possible, expected, and important.
3. There is, at this time, very little information on the quality of subnational estimates of coverage derived from any of the currently used evaluation programs.

These assessments are not meant to discourage evaluation efforts, but to encourage the Census Bureau to continue to explore methods of reducing the levels of uncertainty. One other general point about evaluation should be made. Information about the quality of the national census count is important in its own right. However, its value would be considerably increased if it could be used to modify population counts in subnational geographic areas. In Chapter 7 we have identified research whose successful completion might make it possible to use evaluation results for subnational adjustments. For such modifications to be of greatest use, the evaluation results should be known soon after the census is completed. While the accuracy of the evaluation methodology and ability to provide subnational estimates should be given the first priority, the ability to produce data quickly should also be an important criterion in choosing the evaluation methodology for 1990.

APPRAISAL OF CENSUS BUREAU PRETEST PLANS FOR COVERAGE EVALUATION

We begin by describing the current coverage evaluation research and testing program of the Census Bureau and the panel's views toward these programs as expressed and updated from its interim report. Then follows a description and assessment of a recent Census Bureau position paper, by Kirk Wolter, on plans for coverage evaluation and adjustment in the 1990 decennial census.

Current Program for Testing and Research of Coverage Evaluation

1985 Pretest of Post-Enumeration Survey Methodology

The Census Bureau experienced a number of problems in conducting the 1980 Post-Enumeration Program, and it planned a pretest in 1985 on post-enumeration survey (PES) methodology (Hogan, 1984a:Appendix A) to try to explore ways of overcoming some or all of these difficulties. The pretest involves selecting a sample of 200 blocks in Tampa, Florida, one of the two 1985 pretest sites. The blocks will be completely relisted and matched to the pretest census records. The matching will be a two-way computer match between the sample and the census listings, which will enable the Census Bureau to estimate the overcount as well as the undercount. Nonmatches will be followed up using many different sources, e.g., telephone directories, the post office, local welfare rolls, etc.

Problem areas that the Census Bureau identified for research are:

(1) Computer matching;
(2) Balancing the undercount with the overcount;
(3) Evaluating the overcount;
(4) Nonresponse research;
(5) Alternate questionnaire design;
(6) Rules on whether the current or the listed resident should be enumerated;[1]
(7) The use of the Post-Enumeration Program to benchmark other evaluation methods of interest;
(8) Homogeneous domains and their effect on block sampling; and
(9) Limited follow-up.

Originally the Census Bureau hoped to obtain information in the 1985 pretest about each of the problem areas listed above. Because many of them cannot be tested independently, the panel was concerned that the pretest might be unable to produce meaningful results for specific areas.

---

[1]Rules on whether the current or the listed resident should be enumerated in the PES refer to the problem of movers and whether new residents or the residents listed as present on Census Day are counted.

There was some indication that the Census Bureau had not identified methods and criteria for the evaluation of some of the components of this test. Furthermore, the likely sample size was too small to identify the differences in alternative methods of estimating the net undercount, because, in total, the undercount would probably be substantially less than 5 percent. Therefore, in our interim report, we recommended narrowing the scope of the 1985 pretest. The panel believed that priorities for the post-enumeration survey pretest should be based on an error profile of the Post-Enumeration Program in 1980, and the most promising improvements investigated. As a result of the panel's recommendations, the Census Bureau decided to focus its Pretest of Post-Enumeration Survey Methodology on the areas of computer matching and nonresponse.

Research Study on Hard-to-Count Groups

In this pretest, which runs simultaneously with the Tampa post-enumeration survey, a sample from various administrative lists of males ages 18-40 and children under age 10 who live on 1985 PES blocks will be drawn in order to examine an administrative records matching approach to coverage evaluation of hard-to-count groups. The people found on these various lists will be matched to the 1985 pretest census and post-enumeration survey lists to see if they were included in either (no composite list will be created). People who do not match to either will be followed-up for verification of address and other information. However, no tracing to determine the status of cases not living in the sample block at the time of the census will be done. The major objective is to determine if administrative records matching is feasible as a technique for improving coverage of the post-enumeration survey. The feasibility of this approach will be measured by the number of individuals located who were missed by the census and the PES, the political sensitivity raised by this operation, and the accessibility of the various list sources. The following administrative lists were initially under consideration:

(1) The 1983 Internal Revenue Service Individual Master File;
(2) Unemployment records;
(3) Immigration and Naturalization Service files;

(4) Job Training Partnership Act files;
(5) Draft registration files;
(6) Driver's license files; and
(7) Other lists, e.g., police blotters or records of local hospital admissions.

Since this pretest will not form a composite list, there will be no testing of this important component of administrative list-based coverage evaluation programs. Many of the lists proposed for use (e.g., police blotters and unemployment records) have been tried previously with poor results (see Bureau of the Census, 1976a:2-8) and also pose problems of duplicates. In addition, the possible nonrepresentativeness of a composite list formed from these administrative lists will have to be accommodated if dual or triple-system estimation with either the census list, or the census and post-enumeration survey lists, is contemplated. For these reasons, the panel recommended in the interim report against proceeding with this pretest until these difficulties were resolved. However, the panel is in favor of continued non-field-test research of this methodology. For example, the panel believes that research is needed for assessing the relative advantages of various alternative approaches to estimation of coverage of the total population using several administrative lists (see the discussion in Appendix 4.1).

As a result of the panel's interim report recommendations, the Census Bureau focused its attention on a more limited number of administrative lists. Otherwise, the hard-to-count study is proceeding as described above.

The Forward Trace Study

The Census Bureau designed the Forward Trace Study (Hogan, 1984a:Appendix C) to test various methods for tracing people from their 1980 census address to their current address. The purpose is to determine which tracing method would be most effective for use in a reverse record check.

The success of the reverse record check in Canada has suggested the use of a similar procedure in the United States. A major difference between the United States and Canada in the application of this technique is the 10-year time span between censuses in the United States, compared with 5 years in Canada. This time difference increases the difficulty in tracing people from the previous census to their present residence. The Forward Trace Study principally addresses this time effect.

The Forward Trace Study began in October 1981 when a sample was selected from the 1980 census supplemented by a sample of missed persons derived from the 1980 PEP. A third sample of immigrants was added later. Unfortunately, problems arose in obtaining the fourth sample of intercensal births, due to the sensitivity of records for out-of-wedlock births and adoptions. The approximate sample sizes for the four subsamples are:

(1) 1980 census	11,900	
(2) People missed	4,000	
(3) Immigrants	2,700	
(4) Births	2,700	(proposed)

Three different tracing methods are being investigated: (1) periodic tracing with periodic personal contact, (2) periodic tracing with initial personal contact, and (3) tracing only at the end of the period. The three different tracing procedures will be compared for cost and completeness, especially for hard-to-enumerate groups. One concern is that the people for whom the first tracing method is used may become sensitized to the census, and therefore may be enumerated with greater or lesser frequency than the general population. The extent of this sensitization would have to be well estimated in order to reliably estimate the degree of underenumeration from such a system.

The panel feels that the Forward Trace Study is likely to yield useful information as to the feasibility of using a reverse record check to evaluate the completeness of coverage of the 1990 decennial census, and therefore should be completed.

Description and Critique of the Wolter Paper

In October 1984, Kirk Wolter of the Census Bureau presented a position paper that represented both a change and a narrowing of focus for the research and testing of methods of coverage evaluation and adjustment for the 1990 census. Adjustment-related issues are discussed in Chapter 7. Here we discuss the issues related to coverage evaluation. In his paper, Wolter offered the possibility of major modifications to the Post-Enumeration Program used in 1980. In addition, he outlined the basis for the decision on whether to release adjusted data, at what time adjusted data might be released, and to what level of geographic detail adjusted data might be presented. We summarize this paper and the panel's reaction to it.

i. Wolter suggested that the Census Bureau might use an independent survey, rather than the Current Population Survey (CPS), which was used in 1980, as the survey of the population of the United States for the Post-Enumeration Program in 1990.

There are many advantages to the use of an independent survey. Restrictions come with the use of the Current Population Survey, including the sampling design, the timing of the survey, the type of interviewing and follow-up used, the questions asked, etc. A survey dedicated to coverage evaluation will give the Census Bureau the opportunity to consider many possibilities, including: (1) the use of administrative records in frame development, (2) the use of a compact area sample design, and (3) the use of more intensive interviewing and follow-up techniques to reduce nonresponse. However, these freedoms bring with them certain disadvantages. The methodology underlying the Current Population Survey is well-tested. The interviewers are skilled at their jobs (it is suggested below that an independent survey use, wherever possible, Current Population Survey interviewers), and the frame development is well-understood. Moreover, the Current Population Survey, already budgeted, would avoid the possibly substantial costs entailed in developing and running a new sample survey of the United States.

ii. The paper suggests that this independent sample be made up of compact area clusters, unlike the sampling design of the Current Population Survey.

The advantages of a sample of compact area clusters (such as entire city blocks) grow primarily from the ability to concentrate the enumeration and matching efforts on these small, geographically compact areas. Thus, two-way matching between the sample survey and the census records can be contemplated. The inability to perform a two-way match was one of the major problems of the 1980 PEP program. In addition, small-area estimates of net undercount could be used in model development and validation with compact area clusters. An added possibility is the use of national and local administrative records in the same regions, also for purposes of model development and validation.

There are also disadvantages to this proposal. The measurement of undercoverage may not be an ideal application for a highly clustered sample design. If undercoverage is extremely homogeneous within clusters, the effective sample size achieved by clustering could be well below that of the 1980 Post-Enumeration Program, even though the same number of individuals were sampled.

On balance the panel favors proposals (i) and (ii) of Wolter's paper, i.e., the use of an independent survey, which samples compact area clusters, for use in the 1990 Post-Enumeration Program, particularly if subsequent testing shows the intracluster correlations to have only a moderate impact on the effective sample size.

iii. Wolter strongly puts forward the post-enumeration survey as the key element of the 1990 coverage evaluation program, to the exclusion of methods such as administrative records, reverse record checks, and systematic observation.

Wolter presents many arguments for the discontinuance of research on a coverage evaluation program based on a reverse record check. The reasons given are: (1) the Census Bureau has little experience in running reverse record checks; (2) the program in 1990 would have to be experimental, since it would be the first time this method was used on this scale; (3) there have been problems maintaining current addresses for the sample created; (4) unexpected difficulties have arisen in acquiring birth records from the states because of the sensitive nature of these records; (5) the Forward Trace Study is as yet incomplete; and (6) all indications are that a reverse record check would be more expensive than a post-enumeration survey.

Throughout this report, one of the major themes has been the need for the Census Bureau, in its research and testing programs, to focus on priority areas, to the exclusion of less promising ideas. There are advantages to the narrowing of efforts, and coverage evaluation is certainly an area in which some narrowing is needed. Only in this way can the Census Bureau develop the expertise and assurance needed to implement successful coverage evaluation techniques. However, in this instance, the panel feels that the focusing is premature. The panel is of the opinion that the available information comparing the various approaches to coverage evaluation is inconclusive as to the relative merits of these approaches. More information needs to be gathered before strong directions can be recommended. The panel has recommended a substantial amount of winnowing down elsewhere in the decennial census research and testing program to accommodate a liberal approach to research and testing here.

The objections Wolter presents to further investigation of the use of reverse record checks are not compelling. An experimental reverse record check was a part of the 1960 coverage evaluation program in the United States, and Canada's experience cannot be disregarded. Furthermore, experimental programs can and should be used during the 1990 census so as to be ready for the census in the year 2000. Also, the serious problems associated with reverse record checks do not seem to be any more serious than those posed by the use of a post-enumeration survey.

As mentioned above, the post-enumeration survey has special problems with respect to certain populations. Reverse record checks, administrative list methods, and systematic observation are real possibilities for measuring undercount for these groups. The panel feels that the exclusive reliance on a post-enumeration survey methodology for coverage evaluation in 1990 is, at this time, premature.

> Recommendation 8.1. We recommend that the Census Bureau conduct research and tests of alternative coverage evaluation methodologies in addition to the post-enumeration survey, specifically reverse record checks and systematic observation.

iv. Wolter emphasizes the necessity for the development of a fast and accurate matching algorithm whether or not the 1990 PES is to be used for adjustment or coverage evaluation.

Record matching forms an essential part of most of the existing workable coverage evaluation methodologies at this point in time, including a PES or a reverse record check. The panel is in full agreement with the spirit of the above statement emphasizing the importance of the development of matching capabilities. Much of the research ongoing at the Census Bureau to expedite the matching process is devoted to the development of algorithms for computer matching. The panel applauds these efforts.

Wolter's paper bases a great deal of the adjustment decision on the successful development of a fast matching algorithm. To quote Wolter (1984:6, emphasis in original):

> A major assumption underlying both the research program and the decisions set forth here is that _fast_ and _accurate_ matching techniques will be developed. . . . It is already clear to us that there is no fall-back position if we fail to develop an accurate matching methodology. In this circumstance, the Census Bureau will not have the means of adjusting the 1990 census so as to improve those census data in any sense.

The strength of this statement necessitates some quantification of what a fast and accurate matching algorithm actually is capable of doing. Once this quantification has been made, if it then appears likely that fast and accurate matching will not be possible for 1990, we encourage the Census Bureau to investigate and develop possible fallback procedures that could then be considered for use.

> _Recommendation 8.2_. We agree that matching algorithms are very important to the success of several adjustment methods. We recommend that the Census Bureau investigate the development of a fallback position in case adequate matching is not available in 1990.

v. Finally, as a first step in the process toward a decision on adjustment, Wolter calls for summarization of current evaluation studies from the 1980 decennial census.

The Census Bureau has completed a number of studies based on the 1980 census that, when summarized, promise to provide useful information pertaining to coverage evaluation and possible adjustment of future censuses. There are a number of other studies as yet uncompleted or unreported that would also yield important information on strategies for coverage evaluation. For example, the Census/CPS/IRS

Match Study provides a three-way match that could be used to form estimates for certain subgroups of the population. Estimates using this three-way match might have smaller variance and possibly smaller bias than estimates using the two-way match performed in the PEP. Other studies, e.g., the Demographic Analysis of National PEP Estimates, Local Area Estimation Research, and the Exploratory Analysis of PEP Data (Hogan, 1984a), have direct implications for the feasibility of adjustment procedures.

The panel supports Wolter in urging that the above summarization be prepared and that the Census Bureau allocate sufficient staff resources to this task. However, the panel is also concerned that important studies from the 1980 evaluation program may not be completed or fully documented. The results have potential implications with respect to the effective design of other field tests currently being planned. The panel has an overall concern that the history of tests completed by the Census Bureau has not always been available to help in the design and consideration of new tests.

> Recommendation 8.3. We recommend that the Census Bureau complete and report analyses of 1980-based tests related to coverage evaluation, especially the Census/CPS/IRS Match Study.

THE 1990 DEMOGRAPHIC ANALYSIS PROGRAM: POSSIBLE IMPROVEMENTS

Demographic analysis requires data from sources, independent of the current census, to estimate the number of persons in a given age-race-sex category. The corresponding number recorded in the census can be evaluated by comparison with the demographic approximation. The simplest form of such analysis is illustrated by the construction of the estimated number of white females ages 20-24 in 1990 from:

(1) The number of white female births from April 1, 1966, to April 1, 1970;
(2) The number of white female immigrants from April 1, 1966, to April 1, 1990, whose age on arrival would place them into the target age group as of April 1, 1990;
(3) The number of deaths prior to April 1, 1990, occurring in the United States to all white female

residents born in the time period April 1, 1966, to April 1, 1970; and

(4) The number of white female emigrants born during the target period. The group includes both persons born in the United States and those who migrated there.

The number of births is determined from birth registration data adjusted for the estimated proportion of underregistration; the number of deaths is the registered number; and the number of legal immigrants is derived from Immigration and Naturalization Service statistics. The number of emigrants is unknown and is estimated from a variety of fragmentary information, mostly from immigration data of other countries and cohort analysis of consecutive censuses.

This basic form of calculation is applicable only to persons born in 1935 or later, because well-founded estimates of completeness of registration of births begin in 1935. Other forms of analysis have been used for cohorts born before 1935. For persons over age 65, Medicare files provide reliable data on the size of that population. For persons between 45 and 64 for the 1980 census, and between 55 and 64 for the 1990 census, more complex procedures attempt to estimate the true size of a cohort at each census date by pooling information about the number of persons recorded in the cohort in several censuses, making allowance for the estimated differential overall completeness of different censuses, for broadly similar but systematically evolving patterns of age-misreporting, and for differential undercounts by age.

As indicated in Chapter 4, the main weaknesses of demographic analysis are the following:

(1) No subnational estimates of undercount are available (and it is the geographically differential undercounting that leads to possible inequities in apportionment and fund allocation);
(2) No estimate of the undercount for Hispanics can be constructed because Hispanic groups, until very recently, have not been identified in birth and death registrations and are not identified in immigration records;
(3) It is necessary to use relatively crude and largely unverifiable methodology in estimating emigration;

(4) There are no sufficiently accurate estimates available on the number of illegal immigrants; and

(5) There are no available estimates for the reliability of the various component estimates.

Points (1) and (2) above, unlike (3) and (4), limit the available detail provided by demographic analysis but do not affect the reliability of the resulting estimates. Notwithstanding (3), (4), and (5), the method is generally thought to have provided better national estimates of undercounts by age, sex, and a limited breakdown of race for the censuses of 1950, 1960, and 1970 than did the post-enumeration surveys.

Demographic analysis was found less useful in evaluating the completeness of the coverage of the 1980 census. This is attributed primarily to the large number of unrecorded immigrants who are thought to have entered the United States during the 1970s (see Appendix 8.1). Another problem with the application of demographic analysis to the 1980 census is that the methodology of treating race, particularly Hispanics, was changed. This change created difficult problems of consistency with other data sources, includ- ing earlier censuses. The unknown number of emigrants continued to be a problem in 1980. Nevertheless, demographic analysis remained useful for those groups less affected by these shortcomings, particularly blacks. For blacks it is believed that demographic analysis provided a reasonable measure of undercount by age; however, it failed for whites and failed to provide estimates for Hispanics. Thus, it no longer provided reasonable measures of the <u>differential</u> undercount by race.

A useful modification of the procedure seems to be to apply demographic analysis separately to persons born in the United States and to the foreign born, provided the reliability of reporting of country of birth is high enough. One advantage is the potential availability of good national estimates by age and sex for the native white and native black populations, at least up to age 55 (i.e., for persons born in 1935 or later). The only estimates of international migration needed for this group are allowances for the movements of persons born in the United States. A portion of this movement could be inferred from immigration information from other countries. Estimates of emigration could also be derived, as a by-product, from a reverse record check, if one is carried out in conjunction with the 1990 census, or perhaps by a multiplicity-sampling approach incorporated in the Current Population Survey. If this modification is successful, the resulting demographic estimates could presumably be used to check the results of a reverse record check or a PES, or could be used as a benchmark for those methods as they relate to persons born in the United States.

The Census Bureau should investigate the value of the native American approach to modifying demographic analysis. Of course, an analysis of the quality of the information on reported place of birth would be required. The value of PES information on place of birth should also be investigated.

> Recommendation 8.4. We recommend that the Census Bureau conduct research into using demographic analysis to develop estimates of coverage for the native-born population. The research should consider whether these estimates could usefully be combined with other estimates of coverage.

THE REVERSE RECORD CHECK PROGRAM: CONSIDERATIONS FOR 1990

A reverse record check methodology has been used by Statistics Canada since 1961 in its assessment of the completeness of the coverage of its censuses. This procedure is described in Chapter 4, so we summarize only the basic methodology here.

A reverse record check is an evaluation program in which a sample of the population is drawn from a frame created prior to the census and traced forward to the time of the census. The proportion of the sample that is determined through tracing to be residing in the United States on Census Day provides an estimate of the total population. Usually, the sample is a combination of samples from the following four lists: (1) the previous census, (2) births in the intercensal period, (3) immigrants from the intercensal period, and (4) people missed in the previous census as determined from the previous coverage evaluation program. This technique has not been used extensively in the United States.

Compared to post-enumeration surveys of the kind conducted by the United States to evaluate its censuses, the reverse record check seems to offer several advantages:

(1) Unlike the "do it again, but better" method, it does not rely on the assumption that the post-enumeration survey might succeed very much better where the census failed. And unlike the "do it again, but independently" method, it does not have to rely on the unverifiable and unlikely assumption that the events of being missed by the census and by the post-enumeration survey are independent.
(2) The coverage error estimates do not depend in a major way on matching errors--a significant point of vulnerability of "do it again, but independently" methods of the type carried out after the 1980 census and planned for the 1990 census.
(3) The reliability of 1980 United States census coverage evaluation is significantly affected by nonresponse in the post-enumeration survey. There is no nonresponse in the reverse record check per se. There is an analogous category of tracing failed--but here again, the reverse record check has some advantages in that the tracing of a small number of residual cases can be (as it is in Canada) carried out over several months, as opposed to the tight time schedule of the field work of post-enumeration surveys.
(4) Imputation in the post-enumeration survey cannot be validated. By contrast, imputing for tracing failed cases can be partially assessed by reference to independent control totals. Indeed, the reverse record check provides an estimate of the number of persons who died since the previous census--a verifiable number. After matching with the census, the method also provides an estimate of the number of persons enumerated in the census--another verifiable number.
(5) The reverse record check provides a direct estimate of the number of emigrants since the last census, which can be used to overcome one of the significant data gaps of demographic estimation--both to evaluate the current census and as a benchmark for its intercensal population estimation.

One problem for the reverse record check method is the lack of records for undocumented aliens, so that they cannot be represented in the reverse record check sample. Another significant disadvantage of the reverse record check is the need for the tracing operation. However, with a 5-year gap between censuses, the 5 percent tracing failed rate achieved in Canada compares favorably with the over 8 percent imputation needed in the 1980 evaluation program used in the United States.

The panel believes the Census Bureau's experimental initiative called the "Forward Trace Study" may provide some information as to ways of overcoming the problem posed by the 10-year intervals between censuses in the United States. As discussed above, the Forward Trace Study is testing three modes of tracing a sample of individuals counted in the previous census, a sample of individuals missed in the previous census, and a sample of intercensal immigrants. The outcome of this study may help determine an effective method for tracing people in the United States. As indicated in Recommendation 8.1, the panel is concerned that a reverse record check be given more attention as a potential coverage evaluation methodology in 1990. Assuming that Recommendation 8.1 is persuasive and the decision is made to proceed in 1990 with a reverse record check in either a testing mode or as a primary coverage evaluation program, it is then necessary to know very soon which of the three versions of tracing will be used. If it happens that either of the methods for more intensive tracing in the Forward Trace Study wins out over tracing at the end of the period, the intensive tracing must begin by 1986 in order to benefit from the shortened period between contact. Therefore the samples need to be drawn by 1986.

> Recommendation 8.5. We recommend that the Census Bureau move quickly to complete the Forward Trace Study to determine the feasibility of using forward trace methods in a reverse record check program for 1990. If the methodology is effective, a national sample for this purpose needs to be initiated by 1986.

THE 1990 POST-ENUMERATION PROGRAM: POSSIBLE IMPROVEMENTS

Recent Census Bureau reports indicate that a type of post-enumeration survey will be the predominant component of the coverage evaluation effort in the 1990 decennial census, as it was in 1980. Assuming this and given the weaknesses of the 1980 version of this program outlined in Chapter 4, what possibilities are there for improvement in the Post-Enumeration Program for 1990?

There are two purposes for which a post-enumeration survey might be used. The first is to evaluate coverage, for example to identify subgroups of the population, by state and major city, that were disproportionately missed by the census. The second is to use the results for purposes of adjusting the population counts of states, major cities, and smaller geographic regions. These two purposes of coverage evaluation and adjustment overlap to a considerable degree. It is this second purpose, adjustment, on which we concentrate. We consider possible areas for improvement to the techniques of the 1980 Post-Enumeration Program; however, any improvements to the Post-Enumeration Program as a potential adjustment program are clearly improvements to it as a coverage evaluation program.

We organize this section as follows. First, we provide a description of the general procedure used in the 1980 Post-Enumeration Program. Then we identify the features of the Post-Enumeration Program in which worthwhile gains appear to be possible. For each feature identified, possible approaches for improvement are discussed.

The 1980 Post-Enumeration Program

As a coverage evaluation program, the 1980 Post-Enumeration Program was useful in identifying demographic subsets of the population, by state and major city, that were disproportionately missed by the census. For example, the 1980 Post-Enumeration Program indicated that, nationally, blacks and nonblack Hispanics were missed more frequently than whites. In addition, the PEP provided considerable information about erroneous enumerations, duplications, and incorrectly geocoded addresses, which indicated limitations of the decennial census methodology (see Wolter, 1983; Cowan and Bettin, 1982). Thus, the Census Bureau derived a substantial amount of information on the quality of the 1980 decennial census data set as well as information about which populations to direct its energies to for coverage improvement in 1990. In this sense, the 1980 Post-Enumeration Program can be seen as a continuation of, and improvement on, methods used for coverage evaluation in the 1950, 1960, and 1970 decennial censuses.

Chapter 4 contains a detailed description of the 1980 Post-Enumeration Program. However, for convenience, we repeat the overall strategy here. The basic idea was to recount <u>independently</u> a sample of households, and subsequently match individuals included in the two enumerations to determine those missed by the census but included in the recount. An estimation model, often referred to as capture-recapture, or dual-system estimation, was then applied to supplement the direct coverage estimates by adding an estimate of the number of individuals missed by the census. The Current Population Survey was the enumeration system used to perform this recount in 1980, and in this context was called the P sample. Although the sampling frame for the Current Population Survey is not independent of the decennial census, it undergoes sufficient changes over the intercensal period so that the listing of addresses used is fairly distinct from that of the decennial census (see Bureau of the Census, 1978a). This along with the independence of surveying operations in the Current Population Survey and the census helps promote the desired independence. The P sample included about 185,000 persons each for April and August 1980.

It was possible to search the census files for matches of individuals enumerated in the Current Population Survey. However, the search had to be restricted to a limited geographic area. Thus a person counted by the census within the "wrong" area (as per Current Population Survey definitions and operations) appeared at the conclusion of this match as if he or she were missed by the census. Due to the sampling design of the Current Population Survey, which did not make use of compact area clusters, it was essentially impossible to search the Current Population Survey files for individuals counted in the census. (This would then be a two-way match.) As a result, there was no mechanism in the P sample, by itself, for checking the validity of census enumerations. Invalid or erroneous census enumerations include not only improperly geocoded census addresses, but also curbstoning, individuals who should not have been included in the census, such as foreign visitors and people who were born after Census Day, duplicate enumerations, etc. The need to measure the frequency of these problems gave rise to a second sample, this time a sample of 100,000 individuals from the decennial census itself, called the E sample. The latter sample was used partly to "balance out" from the P sample the contribution of persons included in the census but at the wrong address and partly to estimate the number of persons erroneously included in the census--in order to derive, with dual-system estimation, net under- or overcount estimates. We note that there may be less need for the E sample in 1990 due to the possibility (mentioned above) of the use of a sample of geographically compact clusters for the PES, since in that case two-way matching may be feasible.

Improving the 1980 Post-Enumeration Program Methodology

We have identified four aspects of the 1980 Post-Enumeration Program that might benefit from special attention, although we do not necessarily have unambiguous recommendations to offer in every instance:

(1) Reduction in the level of survey nonresponse;
(2) Reduction in the percentage of unresolved matches;
(3) Improvement in methods to balance the local undercount with the overcount; and
(4) Estimation of the degree of independence between survey and census.

Reduction in the Level of Survey Nonresponse

Like any sample survey, the survey used for the Post-Enumeration Program will suffer from an imperfect sampling frame and interview refusals. As mentioned in Chapter 4, over 4 percent of the Current Population Survey interviews in April 1980 were refusals. Even when an interview is conducted, a lack of detailed information on address or to a lesser extent age, sex, and race for a record can create situations in which the status of a match with the census is unclear. The resulting problem of a large percentage of unresolved matches is addressed in the next section. Here we are concerned with people in the sample for the PEP, or who would have been in the sample had the sampling frame been complete, for whom no information was collected. This is a central issue, since there is a possibility that the same types of people who are missed in the census are either missing from the PEP sampling frame or refuse to cooperate with the PEP interviewer.

It would, obviously, be highly desirable to decrease the rate of refusal. In 1980, the Census Bureau used the April and August Current Population Survey samples as the P sample of PEP and utilized essentially the same Current Population Survey procedures as for other months. Therefore, one possibility for reducing refusal, assuming that the Current Population Survey is again used for the PEP, is to employ more intensive follow-up than is usually done, perhaps after the end of the regular survey week of the CPS. The possibility of making cooperation legally required should also be explored. This approach may introduce a discontinuity into the time series of employment and unemployment estimates, although this risk might be reduced by appropriate measures. An alternative, currently under consideration by the Census Bureau and discussed above in the critique of the paper by Kirk Wolter, is the use of a separate survey for coverage evaluation. Should a separate survey be used, it might still be highly desirable to employ experienced Current Population Survey interviewers during the non-CPS weeks.

Reduction in the Percentage of Unresolved Matches

In the 1980 Post-Enumeration Program, after completing a Current Population Survey interview, Census Bureau staff geocoded the address of each sample residence to determine the enumeration district in which that residence should have been placed in the 1980 decennial census. Then that (and only that) enumeration district was searched clerically for a name-address-race-sex-age combination that matched, according to defined criteria, a record from the Current Population Survey. Each Current Population Survey interview was categorized in one of three ways: matched with the census, not matched with the census, and match status unresolved. This last group is the most troublesome, at least if one assumes that errors involving the first two categories are well controlled. These cases can easily give rise to very significant matching errors, and hence errors in the estimated undercount.

When the April 1980 Current Population Survey was used, matching status could not be determined for approximately 8.5 percent of cases. This was due to a variety of causes, especially incomplete responses, response errors in either the census or the CPS, refusals to respond to the Current Population Survey, and ambiguities related to addresses (particularly in rural areas). Use of the August Current Population Survey resulted in over 10 percent of cases with unresolved matching status, larger than the April CPS presumably because of the problems introduced by mobility (see Wolter, 1983). In order to derive estimates of the number of persons missed, a match status had to be imputed to the unresolved cases. Over 30 percent of the April imputations resulted from an incomplete follow-up interview of CPS interviewees who were not initially matched with the census.[2] Depending on the method of imputation used (combined with some other factors), the Census Bureau generated 12 different sets of PEP estimates of the undercount for states and major cities. These estimates appeared sensitive to the method of imputation (and other factors) used (see the discussion in Chapter 4).

Improvements to the geographic system in 1990 may be helpful in reducing the number of unresolved matches. The Census Bureau's TIGER (Topologically Integrated Geographic Encoding Register) system, currently under development, could very well represent a substantial improvement over previous geographic systems, and could be in place by 1990. However, any resulting benefits from this new system would be dependent, to a large extent, on the quality of the responses that are to be coded. There are also efforts by the Census Bureau to avoid the necessity of geocoding, by treating the address as an alphanumeric response, which can then be used to block the census data set for matching in ways that do not require knowledge of the precise enumeration district of the individual.

Fractional matching is an idea that could be explored as an alternative method of imputing match status to cases for which the match status was unresolved. Assume that the likelihoods outlined in Appendix 4.2 from the Fellegi-Sunter mathematical model for matching are stored and available for the cases that are left unresolved, along with the several likely matches for these unresolved cases. It is conceivable that a function of these likelihoods could be developed empirically that would impute to each unmatched post-enumeration survey record (by computer algorithm and suitable personal follow-up) a fractional match status in such a manner that the sum of these fractions is equal to the unknown number of matched cases. Fractional matching is therefore merely a model relating match status to likelihoods from some model, e.g., the Fellegi-Sunter model. Assuming a computer matching success rate of 60-70 percent--perhaps an optimistic rate--this, without clerical assistance, would result in a massive imputation of match status. Given the substantial impact on undercoverage estimates of imputing match status to only about 8 percent of cases, such a major increase in the reliance on imputation

---

[2] From conversations with Robert Fay, III.

cannot be recommended on the basis of our current state of knowledge. However, there is the possibility of using fractional matching solely for those cases for which the match status is either very likely or very unlikely, leaving the remainder for clerical follow-up. Finally, its use to impute match status to the residual number after clerical follow-up of unresolved cases should be explored.

Another suggestion that has been made is for the Census Bureau to subsample the unresolved cases in order to concentrate efforts on them. There are two possible applications of this idea. The first is to sample from all cases unmatched by the computer algorithm. Not all members of the panel favor this idea. The use of sampling of all the matches left unresolved by the computer algorithm would result in estimates of undercoverage with substantially increased variances for important subpopulations and subnational regions. The second notion is to sample after a first-stage personal follow-up of unmatched cases has been attempted. The advantages of this approach parallel those discussed in Chapter 6 on sampling for follow-up. The full panel endorses this idea.

We point out that the use of especially intensive interviewing, discussed in the previous section, should improve the reporting of identifying information and hence might reduce the problem of individuals with unresolved match status. Finally, the use of computer matching might permit an extension of the area of search with the census file for each PES sample case, as well as the use of more matching variables and more advanced methodology. These improvements may well result in a significant reduction of the nonmatch rate.

Improvement in Methods to Balance Local Undercount With Overcount[3]

In the 1980 version of the Post-Enumeration Program, the E sample was used to estimate the genuine overcount of the census. It was also used to offset the Current Population Survey sample cases that could not be matched to the census _within_ the local area to which matching was

[3]The terms undercount and overcount are understood here to mean gross undercount and gross overcount.

restricted, often as a result of faulty determination of census geography, or indistinct addresses.

As described above in Chapter 4, the form of the dual-system estimate used in the 1980 Post-Enumeration Program for a particular demographic stratum was as follows (see Cowan and Fay, 1984):

$$N_T = N_P \ (NC - E - G - D - I) \ / \ M$$

where N_T is an estimate of the total population, N_P is the weighted sample total of the number of persons in the P sample, M is the weighted number of persons who are in both the census and the P sample, NC is the census count of persons, E is the weighted number of persons who were census erroneous enumerations from the E sample, G is the weighted number of persons in incorrectly geocoded housing units in the census from the E sample, D is the weighted number of duplicate counts in the census from the E sample, and I is the count from the census of field-related imputations.

The four subtracted quantities are therefore: (E) people who were counted in the census who should not have been, e.g., people born after Census Day, (G) people who were counted in the census but placed in the wrong area and therefore, given the blocking used in the clerical match, were incapable of being matched, (D) people who were counted in the census more than once in the same enumeration district, and (I) people who were imputed into the census, e.g., people for whom no questionnaire was returned or residences that were imputed to be occupied. An error for these four quantities substantially less than the magnitudes being measured is necessary for a reasonable estimate of those missed in the census, since the magnitudes of the quantities being added and subtracted is of the same order as that of the undercount. From Cowan and Fay (1984) we have the national percentage rates for the above four quantities:

Erroneous Enumerations	1.6
Geocoding Errors	1.0
Duplicates	0.8
Imputations	1.3

The question thus becomes, how can this balancing of the undercount and the overcount be reduced or eliminated from the Post-Enumeration Program estimation process?

The Census Bureau has recently advanced one possibility, discussed above, for avoiding the necessity of balancing (see Wolter, 1984). The idea is to use an independent survey in the Post-Enumeration Program in place of the Current Population Survey. The independent survey would sample geographically compact clusters and check for both over- and underenumeration in the same clusters using a two-way match. With a two-way match: (1) census duplicates are easier to find by checking post-enumeration survey records that match with more than one census record and (2) census erroneous enumerations and mis-geocoded records can be estimated from an examination of census records that do not match to any post-enumeration survey records. This avoids the need for intricate assumptions of balancing errors. In addition, local area estimates of net undercount could be exploited in model development (through the use of local area characteristics as auxiliary variables) as well as in model validation (by comparing for a subsample of small areas the direct and model-based estimates of undercount). As indicated above, the panel is in favor of this proposal.

Estimation of the Degree of Independence Between Survey and Census

A major and untested assumption of the 1980 Post-Enumeration Program is that, for each person, the events of being included in the census and the Current Population Survey are independent. However, there is evidence supporting the belief that many of the types of individuals missed in the census are also missed disproportionately by the Current Population Survey and, for that matter, by any type of household survey technique. For example, the CPS estimates of young males, particularly blacks, are consistently below the corresponding demographic estimates. The ethnographic study sponsored by the Census Bureau provided additional evidence of this phenomenon (see Valentine and Valentine, 1971). This lack of independence of inclusion in the evaluation survey and the census may be particularly likely for persons with tenuous or irregular household connections, for undocumented aliens, and for other groups who have reason to avoid visibility of any sort. For these people, the frequency of being missed by both the census and the survey may be substantially different than would be indicated if these events could be regarded as probabilistically independent. (Equivalently, the probability of inclusion in the census, given inclusion in the post-enumeration survey, may not equal the unconditional probability of inclusion in the census.) Thus k, the parameter mentioned in Chapter 4, may be substantially different from 1.

As mentioned in Chapter 4, the Census Bureau makes use of a stratified dual-system estimator, that is, the population is first stratified using certain demographic characteristics, then the dual-system estimator is applied separately within strata. This serves two purposes. First, the k's for each subtable formed with the stratification may all be closer to 1 than for the unstratified case. (However, the dependence is still likely to be substantial.)

Second, the stratification helps keep the probabilities of inclusion constant within strata. This is another assumption often used in the model underlying dual-system estimation. These two assumptions, independence of inclusion probabilities for the two lists, and the equality of the inclusion probabilities within one list (within strata), both need to be carefully studied. These assumptions are at least partially confounded. Thus, any study of the degree of validity or robustness of the independence assumption will be enhanced by simultaneously studying the degree of validity or robustness of the equality assumption. It is possible to examine the individuals missed by the census to see whether they differ with respect to various covariates not used in the determination of the strata. The extent of the differences would then be a test for equality of inclusion probabilities. However, if the individuals examined are only those caught by the post-enumeration survey, the results may be affected by any nonindependence between census and post-enumeration survey. Therefore, an important factor is the gathering of information for individuals missed by both the census and the post-enumeration survey.

A method that should be tested for its potential to count some of the individuals who typically escape the counting method used by censuses and surveys is the reverse record check. Systematic observation, discussed below, should also be tested for this purpose. Within the context of the Post-Enumeration Program itself, an approach that deals with certain aspects of this exceptionally difficult problem is triple system estimation (see Marks et al., 1977, and Appendix 4.1). In this approach, the independence assumption for two lists is often replaced by an assumption of conditional independence involving three lists. Validation of the assumption of conditional independence would be needed. Unfortunately, there is at present no "third" system with a reasonably complete coverage of the population of the United States. A union of suitably selected administrative records might be envisaged, but various problems, outlined in Chapter 4, make this possibility appear unlikely for the immediate future.

Ericksen and Kadane (1985) and Fellegi (1985) emphasize the sensitivity of dual-system estimation to the assumption of the independence of inclusion frequencies. Ericksen and Kadane (1985) propose a method that may be applicable to some special groups. They argue that, for blacks in the 1970 census, the probability of inclusion in the census, given inclusion in the post-enumeration survey, was not equal to the probability of inclusion in the census, as the assumption of independence would indicate, but was instead greater than twice the probability of inclusion in the census. The method used assumed that the demographic estimate of the national black undercount was correct for 1970. The general applicability of this approach is limited since the estimation of k would require knowledge of the total population--which is the end objective in wishing to estimate k in the first place. Furthermore, Fellegi (1985) argues that the numerical stability of their estimate is not good. Nevertheless, the panel supports the call of Ericksen and Kadane for further research to understand the degree of dependence that exists for various subpopulations and for various lists or surveys, i.e., how k depends on the list, in addition to the census, that is used and on the population studied.

Recommendation 8.6. We support the Census Bureau's research directed toward developing the 1990 Post-Enumeration Program and recommend that such research emphasize the following areas:

(a) Reduction of post-enumeration survey nonresponse;
(b) Reduction of unresolved matches between records for individuals listed in the post-enumeration survey and the decennial census;

(c) Validation of the assumptions and/or development of alternative methodologies with respect to netting-out of overcounts and undercounts with reference to the place of enumeration; and

(d) Investigation of alternatives to the assumption that the inclusion of individuals in the post-enumeration survey is unrelated to their inclusion in the decennial census and the estimation of the strength of this relation.

Some Remaining Considerations

Below we consider two remaining problem areas of the 1980 PEP program, timeliness and variance estimation, and discuss the current approach of the Census Bureau to their resolution. The panel has no recommendations to offer here other than endorsing the efforts of the Census Bureau.

Timeliness

One of the most important aspects of a potential adjustment program, resulting from the current deadlines for reapportionment and redistricting, is the timeliness of the program. In 1980, even preliminary estimates were not available from the Post-Enumeration Program until late in 1981. Apart from other considerations, this factor alone caused the results to be unusable for some purposes of adjustment. There is consequently a substantial interest in speeding up the Post-Enumeration Program process, without compromising its quality. In fact, one of the key elements now under investigation by the Census Bureau, and mentioned prominently in the position paper by Kirk Wolter, is testing of the operational feasibility of an adjustment by December 31, 1990. The possibility of meeting such a deadline would be enhanced by the use of a pre-enumeration survey and extended use of automation, both under consideration by the Census Bureau.

Use of a Pre-enumeration Survey. In order to boost the total sample size, the 1980 Post-Enumeration Program made use of the April and August Current Population Surveys, which served as more or less independent post-enumeration surveys. It has been suggested that earlier months of the Current Population Survey could be used, which would be ready for matching at the time of the decennial census. The January through March Current Population Surveys would be possibilities, with March having the additional advantage of containing a wealth of characteristics information that could be used for purposes of content evaluation and possibly modeling. Even if the Current Population Survey is not used in the 1990 PEP, the timing of the PEP will involve similar considerations.

The advantage of the use of a pre-enumeration survey is the possibility of having the survey files ready and waiting for the creation of the decennial census files. Even so, an appreciable fraction of the matching could not be done until personal follow-up was completed.

A possible disadvantage of a pre-enumeration survey is the potential sensitization of the population to the decennial census. As a result of the survey experience, the pre-enumeration survey interviewees would probably be more aware of the upcoming decennial census than the general population, and this may affect their actions regarding inclusion in the census. (It is not clear whether this is likely to lead to a greater or lesser desire to be enumerated.) However, sensitization is also possible with the use of a post-enumeration survey, since the taking of the census may affect cooperation with the survey. Sensitization could be reduced by the use of a survey that either precedes or succeeds the decennial census by a longer time period, say, one or two years. However, the panel has strong reservations about that idea. As the time period between survey and census lengthens, population mobility, deaths, etc., are likely to increase problems of accuracy.

The relative trade-off between a possible sensitization of the population versus the early preparation of pre-enumeration survey files to be matched to the census is at this time unknown. This is an area in which research is needed; it is a major part of the Census Bureau's 1986 pretest program for coverage evaluation methodologies.

Automation. There are currently a number of field tests planned by the Census Bureau to determine the most effective use of new automation technologies for information collection, transfer, storage, and retrieval (see Chapter 3). To date, these tests have concentrated on the roles of collection offices, processing offices, and logistics. Of key importance from the point of view of coverage evaluation are attempts to generate, very early on, machine-readable records of the basic identification of enumerated persons and households, adequate for computer matching.

In order to exploit the potential existence, at an early date, of both census and post-enumeration survey records in machine-readable form, effective computer matching algorithms have to be developed. In 1980, the matching was done clerically, a slow process that limited the search to one enumeration district for each CPS record. In trying to improve the timeliness of Post-Enumeration Program estimates, the Census Bureau (see Wolter, 1984) is placing a great deal of emphasis on its ability to develop software for automated matching.

The algorithm used by the Census Bureau (see Kelley, 1984a; Jaro, 1985) for computer matching was discussed in Chapter 4 on matching procedures. We are not recommending any modifications to that basic strategy. However, we do have one suggestion that the Census Bureau may wish to investigate further. The idea is to utilize computers to assist the clerical matching. A large proportion of cases unresolved by the computer matching algorithm take the form of records in one or the other of the two files having a multiplicity of possible matching cases in the other file, but with inadequate evidence to make a unique status assignment by computer. Such cases can be presented to clerks on display terminals in a split-screen fashion for visual inspection and decision. Some proportion of cases will still remain unresolved because the reported information is inadequate for match status determination. However, the efficiency and speed of dealing with clerically resolvable cases should be greatly enhanced. (A recent paper indicates that the Census Bureau is already planning something quite close to this; see Jaro, 1985).

Automation will have a much greater impact on matching operations at the Census Bureau than merely speeding up the processing. For example, it might allow the possibility of searching a wider geographic area for a matching record, and hence lessen reliance on the need for finely balancing local over- and undercounts.

Estimation of Variance Due to Matching

Should a 1990 version of the Post-Enumeration Program be used to adjust the population counts, it will be important to derive estimates of the error attributable to various causes, including matching. We concentrate here on the estimation of the variance of the matching process.

Matching can be considered to consist of three phases. An initial computer match, a subsequent clerical operation to resolve the more difficult cases, and imputation for cases whose match status could not otherwise be resolved. Given two files to be matched, the very nature of a computer algorithm is such that, conditional upon the files and the computer algorithm, there is no variance. Of course stochastic response errors in both the census and the post-enumeration survey will undoubtedly induce some matching variance. The estimation of this variance is technically feasible but would probably introduce serious operational difficulties when superimposed on the other rigorous requirements of a coverage evaluation program. The rough magnitude of this variance might, however, be estimated using some intercensal experiments.

For the component of the matching that is done clerically, a combination of designs involving interpenetration of a sample of matching clerks, together with some rematching, can readily be established. The design can be fully analogous to the estimation of interviewer and response variance (see Hansen et al., 1971; Fellegi, 1964).

SYSTEMATIC OBSERVER METHODOLOGY: CONSIDERATIONS FOR 1990

It is generally recognized that a serious undercount problem exists for some members of poor minority groups living in large central cities. There are also indications that in these areas the largest number of individuals are missed through incomplete reporting of household members rather than through failure to enumerate the households themselves. In particular, demographic studies using sex ratios seem to indicate that a disproportionate number of adult black males are missed by the census. Other studies suggest that it is unrealistic to expect improved traditional interview or self-enumeration procedures to increase substantially the coverage of such individuals. Finally, it is also for such individuals and for such areas that the Census Bureau has experienced the greatest difficulties in using matching to estimate undercount. These general perceptions, in conjunction with the resident observer study of Charles and Betty

Valentine described in Chapter 5, provide the motivation for this section, which outlines a research program aimed at finding out who is missed and at developing a procedure to estimate the number of individuals missed.

In 1972, the Census Bureau asked the Advisory Committee on Problems of Census Enumeration of the National Research Council to assess the Valentine study. The committee reviewed the study and suggested that the Census Bureau continue to support such studies. The Census Bureau contacted additional anthropologists and undertook to support graduate student participant observer studies. For a number of reasons, including personnel problems, none of the studies was completely successful. All of them took the form of Census Bureau support for graduate students in a graduate program at a university.

We believe in the potential of a trained individual, through normal, day-to-day encounters, to become aware of people in his or her neighborhood who would be difficult to enumerate through typical census procedures. There is a major difference between an effort of this kind and the anthropological studies such as the Valentine study. In the Valentine study, a considerable amount of personal information, such as sources of income and personal relationships, was obtained (and kept confidential, of course). In the type of study proposed in this section, the only information obtained would be name, age, race, sex, and address. This difference in degree of invasiveness might prevent the occurrence of the problems experienced in resident observer studies conducted since the Valentine study. The proposed study makes use of a type of enumeration similar to that used in Casual Count, described in Chapter 5. The different objectives of the proposed study require the use of a term different from the anthropological one of resident observers. We have adopted the term systematic observers.

Research activity on systematic observation can be coordinated with pretests being conducted for the 1990 census, but such research is not restricted to pretest activities. Consistent with the two terms resident observation and systematic observation, we envision two possible types of studies. In resident observation, similar to the Valentine study, anthropologists work in an area on an essentially full-time basis for a considerable period of time. In such studies, highly trained professionals attempt to identify the reasons for noncompliance and misreporting as well as to quantify the magnitude of the problem. The identification of the reason for noncompliance, especially with respect to different population subgroups, is vital for understanding how coverage improvement and coverage evaluation might be improved to help minimize the problem of differential undercoverage. Observers of this type could be placed in a number of different types of localities. Brooks (1974) suggested that research could profitably be conducted in the following types of study areas:

(1) A Mexican-American community in the Southwest;
(2) A transplanted Appalachian community in the urban north central region;
(3) An urban black community in the north central region;
(4) A northeastern Puerto Rican community;
(5) A northeastern black urban community;
(6) A Navajo reservation;
(7) A black southern rural community;
(8) A white ethnic community; and
(9) A white or mixed southern urban area.

Resident observer studies might provide information leading to the development of alternative data collection procedures.

The second type of activity, called systematic observation, would employ less highly trained professionals. The observers would live in the area and become familiar enough with the residents to make reliable reports on the number of persons in each of a small number of households at a particular date, as well as their name, age, sex, and race. It is conjectured that this activity would require only a fraction of an employee's time. By initiating several systematic observer studies at the earliest possible time, the following questions can be investigated:

(1) How difficult is it to recruit, train, and position systematic observers?
(2) How long must systematic observers reside in an area before they can provide reliable data on residents?
(3) How large an area (number of households) can a systematic observer be expected to provide reliable data for?
(4) What procedures can be used to validate the quality of the data provided by the systematic observers?

(5) Are different procedures required in different types of areas?
(6) Can problems of perceived invasion of privacy be overcome?

Recommendation 8.7. We recommend that the Census Bureau initiate a research program on systematic observation with a view toward the use of this method for a sample of areas at the time of the 1990 census.

Naturally, the results of a research program are unknown at the present time. However, to make clear the nature of our objectives, we outline a possible scenario for the use of systematic observers. The first step in the process would be the delineation of the area of study. This would include, but would not necessarily be limited to, the low-income areas of large central cities. The Census Bureau would draw an area sample of segments, each containing, say, 20 housing units. The Census Bureau would then recruit a full-time Census Bureau employee to live in or near each sample segment for a period of, say, one year beginning at least nine months prior to Census Day for the 1990 census. The individuals recruited would be employees of the Census Bureau, and as such would be sworn to uphold the confidentiality of the information collected, and would be subject to fines and imprisonment for any betrayal of that responsibility. In those areas in which the Census Bureau had offices, the individuals could spend part of their time as office employees of the Census Bureau. A condition of their employment would be that they live in the study area and that they become knowledgeable about the nature and composition of households in the area assigned to them. Living within the area, they would identify themselves as employees of the Census Bureau and would explain that part of their job is to become familiar with the community. As full-time employees of the Census Bureau, they would be instructed in procedures for data collection and in the techniques of systematic observation. At some point in the census procedure, presumably a few weeks before Census Day, the systematic observers would prepare a listing of households in their designated area, and indicate the household composition.

The need for the systematic observers to identify themselves as employees of the Census Bureau raises an important question as to whether the local area will be sensitized to the decennial census when it is taken, that is, whether the individuals residing in the area will be counted more or less well than the population in general. The proposed studies should attempt to measure the extent of any such sensitization.

The systematic observers could be used in other aspects of the census operation. For example, they might be used as enumerators or supervisors in the general area, but at some distance from the area segment for which they had primary responsibility. The area segment for which the systematic enumerator reported household composition would be enumerated in the census by a different census enumerator operating under an independent supervisor.

The data collected in the regular census enumeration could be matched against the data collected by the systematic observer. Because the original study area segments were randomly chosen, it would be possible to construct an estimator of the net number missed by race, age, and sex. It would also be possible to make estimates of household composition for the population. Some details of the sampling calculations underlying this statement are contained in Appendix 8.2.

It must be stressed that the ethical and public relations dimensions of such an operation are the most problematic and must be considered with great care, since there is the possibility of these type of studies being perceived as an invasion of privacy. The authors of the Valentine report, of ethnographic and anthropological studies such as Tally's Corner (Liebow, 1967), and of internal memos of the Census Bureau conclude that the ethical problems are not insurmountable. Moreover, the resident observer studies indicate that a person whose avowed interest is the study of the community will be tolerated by that community. Some of these issues were addressed in an October 1974 memo by Harold Nisselson, Chairman of the 1980 Census Coverage Committee. The basic feeling of the coverage committee was that such studies, while sensitive, can be defended as being responsible scientific studies. They can be designed in a manner such that little or no disruption of the activities of the members of the community need occur, and such that information has a minimal chance of being disclosed. As mentioned above in Chapter 5, the possibility of using focus groups should be considered here, both to assess the ethical and public relations dimensions of systematic observation, as well as to help understand ways in which these studies may be made more effective.

Systematic observer studies are expensive, but the total cost of including in the census a broad sample of the type described might be comparable to many of the activities used in the 1980 census to increase coverage. The cost of a large systematic observer study is also on the same order of magnitude as the post-enumeration studies being considered as a part of a census evaluation and adjustment program. Some rough cost considerations are also contained in Appendix 8.2.

APPENDIX 8.1

THE POPULATION OF ILLEGAL ALIENS: METHODS AND ESTIMATES

Over the past 10 years or so, concern with the number of illegal migrants, and particularly with those coming from Mexico, has been accompanied by a plethora of estimates of their numbers. In most cases the interest is in estimating the stock of illegal migrants at some point in time. There are a few examples, however, of attempts to estimate yearly flows. A sufficiently long series of estimates of the latter, in combination with appropriate information on survival patterns (determined by mortality and return migration), yield an estimate of the stock of migrants. The estimates for illegal aliens residing in the United States have ranged from as little as 600,000 during the mid-1970s (Robinson, 1980) to a high of about 8.2 million around 1975 (Lesko and Associates et al., 1975). In a recent study, Warren and Passel (1983) provided a lower bound for the estimates of illegal migrants by estimating all those who were counted during the 1980 census. Their final figure of about 2.0 million is reasonably close to other estimates of total illegal migrants residing in the United States during the 1970s. Thus, Lancaster and Scheuren (1978) obtained a figure for the age range 18-44 in 1973 of about 4.0 million as the midpoint of a subjective confidence interval with 1.4 and 5.72 million as extremes. Bean et al. (1983) calculated that the correct figure for Mexicans in 1980 should be not less than 1.5 million and no more than 3.8 million (though the lower bound depends heavily on numerous assumptions), whereas Korns (1979) calculated an estimate of about 2.0 million.

Table 8.1 classifies the available estimates according to a combination of characteristics. The first one is the quantity being estimated, stocks or flows. Estimates of stocks that are derived from original estimates of flows are classified as being part of the latter's set. The second characteristic is the type of information source used. We distinguish three autonomous sources--special surveys of migrants (or of migrants' families), apprehension data, and departure and arrival records--that can be used in combination with conventional sources such as censuses, surveys, and vital statistics of the country of origin of the migrants or of the United States or both.

TABLE 8.1 Types and Magnitudes of Estimates of Illegal Migrants

Source of Information	Estimate of: Stocks	Estimate of: Flows[a]
Special surveys	Direct: (1) Mexican National Survey on Emigration; (2) CENIET, 1981. Range of estimates: For 1978-1979, Mexican population illegally residing in the United States is 0.4-1.2 million.	
Data on apprehensions of illegal entries	Indirect: Lesko and Associates use of Immigration and Naturalization Service (INS) apprehension statistics for Mexican illegal aliens (1975). Range of estimates: For 1975, not less than 5.2 million Mexican illegal aliens residing in the United States.	Indirect: Lesko and Associates use of INS apprehension statistics for Mexican illegal aliens (1975). Range of estimates: Not more than 3 million in the period 1970-1975. Indirect: Morris and May (1980) used INS data on apprehension of Mexican illegal migrants. Range of estimates: For 1978, 1.1-1.7 million of Mexican illegal migrants (net).
Records of arrivals and departures[a]		Direct: INS study matching arrival and departure documents (1976). Range of estimates: For period 1974-1976, a maximum of 0.74 million illegal overstayers. Direct: Vining estimated a flow with data on arrivals and departures from international airports. Range of estimates: From 1974 to 1977, net illegal entries fall within the range 0.18-0.38 million annually.

Combination of U.S. census and other surveys (CPS) administrative records	Residual: Lancaster and Scheuren (1978) three-way match of CPS, IRS, and SSA records.	
	Range of estimates: 2.9-5.7 million for 1973.	
	Residual: Warren (1981) comparison of estimates from CPS and INS counts.	
	Range of estimates: For 1979, a point estimate of 1 million illegal residents.	
Combination of U.S. census and other surveys and vital statistics	Residual: Robinson (1980) estimates based on mortality rates specific by age, sex, race, and state.	Residual: Heer (1979) estimated net illegal flow from Mexico using the 1970 and 1975 CPS and vital statistics.
	Range of estimates: For 1970-1975, 0.6-4.7 million.	Range of estimates: 0.1-1.2 million in the period 1970-1975.
Combination of Mexican census and vital statistics	Residual: Bean et al. (1983) analysis of 1980 sex ratios for Mexican population.	Residual: Goldberg's analysis of the 1970 census and intercensal births, deaths, and legal migrants.
	Range of estimates: For 1980, the estimated range of illegal Mexican residents is 1.5-3.8 million.	Range of estimates: Point estimate of 1.6 million.

[a] Estimated flows can and frequently have been converted into estimates of stocks by assuming an initial population of migrants and patterns and levels of survivorship.

SOURCE: Palloni (1985).

Finally, the third characteristic is the type of method used. Partially dependent on the data sources, the methods of estimation can be classified as being direct, indirect, and residual. A direct method is one that permits the calculation of migrants based on a direct count of the population of interest. For example, an estimate obtained by surveying households in Mexican localities and probing into the number of relatives residing in the United States is a direct estimate (CENIET, 1981). This differs from indirect estimates such as those obtained by applying an estimated ratio of successful to unsuccessful illegal entries for a fixed period of time. In this case, the desired quantity--flow of illegal entries--is obtained only after a secondary quantity is estimated or assumed.

An estimate obtained through a residual method involves the accurate estimation of two quantities, with the difference taken to be a measure of the number of illegal persons residing in the United States. For example, the application of expected death rates to a base population yields an expected number of deaths, which is then compared to the observed number. Differences between the two are then used to calculate the size of a population contributing to the death records but not to the exposure (Robinson, 1980). Analogous procedures have been used through the matching of different sources of information such as the United States census, the Current Population Survey, and a variety of administrative records (Lancaster and Scheuren, 1978). In all cases, the estimate obtained relies on the prior estimation of two quantities. Errors in these estimates are potentially large, since they depend on a difference between <u>two</u> separate estimates, both of which are subject to errors.

It is important to notice that some of the methods and estimates described above and in Table 8.1 are not necessarily tailored to the measurement of illegal migration but to the fine tuning of estimates of net migrants who are not counted in official statistics (missed by the census, for example), whereas others are only geared to the production of estimates of flows or stocks of illegal migrants. While the former subpopulation group possibly contributes to census undercount, the second escapes altogether from migration records and may affect the accuracy of methods to evaluate census coverage.

As methods of improved census coverage are refined, the magnitude of the net undercount may become, in absolute terms, quite insignificant. However, the differentials in undercount by geographic areas, ethnic groups, sex, and age may be more resistant to elimination. One of the factors that contributes to differential undercount is the differential composition of the resident population in terms of their legal status in combination with differential success in counting each of them. If the population that has entered illegally is more difficult to enumerate, the differential undercount could be reduced by applying improved procedures to harder-to-enumerate areas (groups) with high concentrations of illegal residents. If, however, harder-to-count groups are equally drawn from the legal and illegal resident population, a focus on areas (groups) with heavy concentrations of illegal migrants will not necessarily reduce the differential undercount. However, even in the latter case, some methods of census coverage evaluation (e.g., demographic methods and reverse record checks) are affected by errors that vary directly with concentration of illegal residents, since migration records and statistics do not include illegal migrants. This is one of the reasons for the importance of developing new data sources to obtain estimates of flows of illegal migrants entering during the intercensal period. In a recent report, Hill (1985) has explored the feasibility of a variety of indirect procedures to estimate illegal immigration from collected (but not regularly processed) data or from new data that could be collected in relatively simple and economic ways using an infrastructure already in existence. These methods are highly dependent on assumptions regarding the distribution of illegal migrants by duration of stay and the process through which they are removed from a "current" population of illegal migrants. However, since they require relatively simple information, they are worth pursuing. The same applies to other methods to estimate the changes in the size of the population of illegal migrants, methods that in one way or another have been used in other disciplines (window, tagging, and indicator relationships) to estimate hidden populations.

APPENDIX 8.2

ESTIMATES OF VARIANCE AND COST FOR A LARGE SYSTEMATIC OBSERVER STUDY

Some very crude estimates of variance and cost are developed in this appendix to demonstrate the order of magnitude of costs that might be involved in a large systematic observer study. Because it would be desirable to concentrate systematic observers in problem areas such as central cities, we have based estimates of variability and costs on areas that have higher miss rates than are observed in the general population.

The Valentines reported a 17 percent undercount for the inner city neighborhood they observed, but a 5 percent figure for the 20-30 percent of the population that is most difficult to enumerate represents a figure that will give a conservative estimate of the accuracy per unit cost. If we assume that a systematic observer is responsible for an area containing about 40 people, that 50 percent of the time 4 people are not counted as part of the census and that 50 percent of the time no people are missed, the coefficient of variation for the miss rate for the population of sampling units would be 100 percent. Based on these assumptions, a study containing 400 resident observers would yield a coefficient of variation for the sample mean miss rate of about 5 percent.

If the cost per systematic observer were $12,000, the direct cost of the systematic observers for 400 sampling units would be approximately 4.8 million dollars. This cost is based on the assumption that systematic observers are paid approximately $24,000 per year, including fringe benefits (GS-7). The cost calculations assume that observation of a sample unit requires the equivalent of one-half person per year. If we assume that supervision and processing costs are equal to direct field costs, a study utilizing 400 systematic observers would cost on the order of $10 million.

References

Alvey, Wendy, and Scheuren, Frederick

1982 Background for an administrative records census. Pp. 137-146 in American Statistical Association 1982 Proceedings of the Social Statistics Section. Washington, D.C.: American Statistical Association.

American Statistical Association

1984 Report of the ASA technical panel on the census undercount. American Statistician 38(4):252-256.

Arellano, M.G., Petersen, G.R., Petitti, B.B., and Smith, R.E.

1984 The California Automated Mortality Linkage System [CAMLIST]. American Journal of Public Health 74(12):1324-1330.

Bailar, Barbara

1983a Error profiles: Uses and abuses. Pp. 117-130 in Tommy Wright, ed., Statistical Methods and the Improvement of Data Quality. New York: Academic Press.

1983b Counting versus estimation in a census--A difficult decision. Pp. 42-49 in American Statistical Association 1983 Proceedings of the Social Statistics Section. Washington, D.C.: American Statistical Association.

1983c Affadavit Presented to District Court, Southern District of New York, Mario Cuomo, et al., Plaintiff(s), Malcolm Baldridge, et al., Defendant(s), 80 Civ. 4550 (JES).

1984 Comment from the Census Bureau. American Statistician 38(4):257-260.

Bailey, Leroy, and Ferrari, Pamela
1984 1980 Census Update List/Leave (ULL) Household Roster Check - Preliminary Report. Preliminary Evaluation Results Memorandum No. 70. Bureau of the Census, Washington, D.C.

Balinski, M.L., and Young, H.P.
1982 Fair Representation: Meeting the Ideal of One Man, One Vote. New Haven: Yale University Press.

Bean, F.D., King, A.G., and Passel, J.S.
1983 The number of illegal migrants of Mexican origin in the United States: Sex ratio-based estimates for 1980. Demography 20(1):99-110.

Bishop, Y.M.M., Fienberg, S.E., and Holland, P.W.
1975 Discrete Multivariate Analysis: Theory and Practice. Cambridge, Mass.: MIT Press.

Bounpane, Peter
1983 Affidavit Presented to District Court, Southern District of New York, Mario Cuomo, et al., Plaintiff(s), Malcolm Baldrige, et al., Defendant(s), 80 Civ. 4550 (JES).

Brooks, C.A.
1974 Proposed Use of Participant-Observers in Studying the Problems of Census Undercoverage in Selected Areas. Unpublished memorandum. Bureau of the Census, Washington, D.C.

Brooks, C.A., and Bailar, B.A.
1978 An Error Profile: Employment as Measured by the Current Population Survey. Statistical Policy Working Paper No. 3. Washington, D.C.: U.S. Department of Commerce.

Brown, Rachel
1984 Research plan on the uses of administrative records for the 1990 census. Pp. 443-448 in American Statistical Association 1984 Proceedings of the Social Statistics Section. Washington, D.C.: American Statistical Association.

Bryce, Herrington J.
1980 The impact of the undercount on state and local government transfers. Pp. 112-124 in Proceedings of the 1980 Conference on Census Undercount. Bureau of the Census. Washington, D.C.: U.S. Department of Commerce.

Bureau of the Census
1944 U.S. Census of Population: 1940, Differential Fertility 1940 and 1910, Standardized Fertility

Rates and Reproduction Rates. Washington, D.C.: U.S. Department of Commerce.

1953 Infant Enumeration Study: 1950. Procedural Studies of the 1950 Censuses, No. 1. Washington, D.C.: U.S. Department of Commerce.

1955 The 1950 Censuses: How They Were Taken. Washington, D.C.: U.S. Department of Commerce.

1960 The Post-Enumeration Survey: 1950. Technical Paper No. 4. Washington, D.C.: U.S. Department of Commerce.

1964a Evaluation and Research Program of the U.S. Censuses of Population and Housing, 1960: Accuracy of Data on Population Characteristics as Measured by CPS-Census Match. Series ER 60, No. 5. Washington, D.C.: U.S. Department of Commerce.

1964b Evaluation and Research Program of the U.S. Censuses of Population and Housing, 1960: Record Check Studies of Population Coverage. Series ER 60, No. 2. Washington, D.C.: U.S. Department of Commerce.

1966 1960 Censuses of Population and Housing: Procedural History. Washington, D.C.: U.S. Department of Commerce.

1970a Evaluation and Research Program of the U.S. Censuses of Population and Housing, 1960: Record Check Study of Accuracy of Income Reporting. Series ER 60, No. 8. Washington, D.C.: U.S. Department of Commerce.

1970b 1970 Census User's Guide. Part 1. Washington, D.C.: U.S. Department of Commerce.

1971 Testing Census Coverage Through Drivers' Licenses. 1970 Census Preliminary Evaluation Results Memorandum Series No. 21. Washington, D.C.

1972 1970 Census of Housing. Vol. I, Chapter B, Detailed Characteristics. Part 1, United States Summary. Final Report HC(1)-A1. Washington, D.C.: U.S. Department of Commerce.

1973a 1970 Census of Population. Vol. I, Chapter C, General Social and Economic Characteristics. Part 1, United States Summary. Final Report PC(1)-C1. Washington, D.C.: U.S. Department of Commerce.

1973b Population and Housing Inquiries in U.S. Decennial Censuses, 1790-1970. Working Paper 39. Washington, D.C.: U.S. Department of Commerce.

1973c *1970 Census of Population and Housing Evaluation and Research Program: The Coverage of Housing in the 1970 Census.* PHC(E)-5. Washington, D.C.: U.S. Department of Commerce.

1973d *1970 Census of Population and Housing Evaluation and Research Program: The Medicare Record Check: An Evaluation of the Coverage of Persons 65 Years of Age and Over in the 1970 Census.* PHC(E)-7. Washington, D.C.: U.S. Department of Commerce.

1973e *1970 Census of Population and Housing Evaluation and Research Program: Test of Birth Registration Completeness 1964 to 1968.* PHC(E)-2. Washington, D.C.: U.S. Department of Commerce.

1974a *1970 Census of Population and Housing Evaluation and Research Program: Estimates of Coverage of Population by Sex, Race, and Age: Demographic Analysis.* PHC(E)-4. Washington, D.C.: U.S. Department of Commerce.

1974b *1970 Censuses of Population and Housing Evaluation and Research Program: Effect of Special Procedures to Improve Coverage in the 1970 Census.* PHC(E)-6. Washington, D.C.: U.S. Department of Commerce.

1975a *1970 Census of Population and Housing Evaluation and Research Program: Accuracy of Data for Selected Housing Characteristics as Measured by Reinterviews.* PHC(E)-10. Washington, D.C.: U.S. Department of Commerce.

1975b *1970 Census of Population and Housing Evaluation and Research Program: Accuracy of Data for Selected Population Characteristics as Measured by the 1970 CPS-Census Match.* PHC(E)-11. Washington, D.C.: U.S. Department of Commerce.

1976a *1970 Census of Population and Housing: Procedural History.* Final Report PHC(R)-1. Washington, D.C.: U.S. Department of Commerce.

1976b Cost Estimates for a 1985 Mid-Decade Census (Distributed by Fiscal Year). Unpublished tables (March 3, 1976).

1976c Cost Approximations for Alternative 1985 Population and Housing Census, Survey Purposes. Unpublished tables (March 4, 1976).

1978a *The Current Population Survey: Design and Methodology*. Technical Paper No. 40. Washington, D.C.: U.S. Department of Commerce.

1978b An Overview of Population and Housing Census Evaluation Programs Conducted at the Bureau of the Census. Background paper for the March 1978 meeting of the Census Advisory Committee of the American Statistical Association, Washington, D.C.

1982a *The Meaning of Enumeration*. 1990 Planning Conference Series No. 1. Washington, D.C.: U.S. Department of Commerce.

1982b *User's Guide - 1980 Census of Population and Housing*. Part A, *Text*. Washington, D.C.: U.S. Department of Commerce.

1982c *Statistical Abstract of the United States: 1982-83*. 103rd Edition. Washington, D.C.: U.S. Department of Commerce.

1982d Report of the United States Bureau of the Census in Response to the Order of the Court, Ordered August 6, 1982. Report submitted to the District Court, Southern District of New York, Mario Cuomo, et al., Plaintiff(s), Malcolm Baldrige, et al., Defendant(s), 80 Civ. 4550 (JES).

1983a Some Major Issues in Planning the 1990 Census. Background paper for Data Needs of America in Transition, Workshop on the 1990 Census, Congressional Research Service, Washington, D.C.

1983b Introduction and overview of the 1980 census. Chapter 1 in History of the 1980 Census of Population and Housing. Draft. Washington, D.C.

1983c *Census of Population and Housing 1980: Public Use Microdata Samples Technical Documentation*. Washington, D.C.: U.S. Department of Commerce.

1983d *1980 Census of Population*. Vol. 1, Chapter B, *General Population Characteristics*. Part 1, *U.S. Summary*. PC 80-1-B1. Washington, D.C.: U.S. Department of Commerce.

1983e Population and Housing Content Items. Chapter 13 in History of the 1980 Census of Population and Housing. Draft. Washington, D.C.

1983f *1980 Census of Population*. Vol. 1, Chapter C, *General Social and Economic Characteristics*. Part I, *U.S. Summary*. PC 80-1-C1. Washington, D.C.: U.S. Department of Commerce.

1984a 1982 Census of Governments. Vol. 2, Taxable Property Values and Assessment-Sales Price Ratios. Washington, D.C.: U.S. Department of Commerce.

1984b 1990 Census Planning. Background paper for the Census Advisory Committee on Population Statistics, Washington, D.C.

1984c Pretest of Adjustment Operations. Unpublished paper. Washington, D.C.

1985a The Coverage of Housing in the 1980 Census. Unpublished paper. Washington, D.C.

1985b General Description of Tasks and Where Testing Will Be Done. Draft (rev. April 2, 1985). Washington, D.C.

1985c Report on 1980 Census Coverage Improvement Program Evaluation. Draft. Washington, D.C.

no date(a) Coverage Evaluation and Coverage Improvement at the Census Bureau Since 1950. Unpublished paper. Washington, D.C.

no date(b) Redistricting and the Decennial Census. Unpublished paper. Washington, D.C.

Butz, William

1984 Data Confidentiality and Public Perceptions: The Case of the European Censuses. Paper presented to the Population Association of America, Minneapolis, Minnesota.

Carlucci, Carl P.

1980 The impact of an adjustment to the 1980 census on congressional and legislative reapportionment. Pp. 145-152 in Proceedings of the 1980 Conference on Census Undercount. Bureau of the Census. Washington, D.C.: U.S. Department of Commerce.

Carter, Grace M., and Rolph, John E.

1974 Empirical Bayes methods applied to estimating fire alarm possibilities. Journal of the American Statistical Association 69:880-885.

Cassel, Claes-Magnus, Sarndal, Carl-Erik, and Wretman, Jan H.

1983 Some uses of statistical models in connection with the nonresponse problem. Pp. 143-160 in William Madow and Ingram Olkin, eds., Incomplete Data in Sample Surveys. Vol. 3, Proceedings of the Symposium. Panel on Incomplete Data, Committee on National Statistics, National Research Council. New York: Academic Press.

CENIET

1981 Informe Final: Los Trabajadores Mexicanos en los Estados Unidos (Encuesta Nacional de Emigracion a la Frontera Norte del Pais y a los Estados Unidos--ENEFNEU--). Secretaria del Trabajo y Prevision Social. Centro Nacional de Informacion y Estadisticas del Trabajo. Mexico City.

Childers, Danny R., and Hogan, Howard R.

1983 Census experimental match studies. Pp. 173-176 in American Statistical Association 1983 Proceedings of the Survey Research Section. Washington, D.C.: American Statistical Association.

1984a The IRS/Census Direct Match Study - Final Report. SRD Research Report No. Census/SRD/RR-84/11. Bureau of the Census, Statistical Research Division. Washington, D.C.: U.S. Department of Commerce.

1984b Matching IRS records to census records: Some problems and results. Pp. 301-306 in American Statistical Association 1984 Proceedings of the Survey Research Section. Washington, D.C.: American Statistical Association.

Citro, Constance F.

1984 Imputation Rates for Selected Decennial Census Population and Housing Items. Unpublished paper. National Research Council, Panel on Decennial Census Methodology, Washington, D.C.

Coale, Ansley J.

1955 The population of the United States in 1950 classified by age, sex, and color - A revision of census figures. Journal of the American Statistical Association 50:16-54.

Coale, Ansley J., and Rives, Norfleet W., Jr.

1973 A statistical reconstruction of the black population of the United States, 1880-1970: Estimates of true numbers by age and sex, birth rates, and total fertility. Population Index 39(1):3-36.

Coale, Ansley J., and Zelnik, Melvin

1963 New Estimates of Fertility and Population in the United States: A Study of Annual White Births from 1855 to 1960 and of Completeness of Enumeration in the Censuses from 1880 to 1960. Princeton, N.J.: Princeton University Press.

Congressional Research Service

1984 Federal Statistics and National Needs. Prepared for the Subcommittee on Energy, Nuclear Proliferation, and Governmental Affairs. Washington, D.C.: U.S. Government Printing Office.

Conk, Margo, A.

1981 Accuracy, efficiency, and bias: The interpretation of women's work in the U.S. census of occupations, 1890-1940. Historical Methods 14(2):65-72.

1984 The 1980 census in historical perspective. In William Alonso and Paul Starr, eds., The Political Economy of National Statistics. New York: Basic Books.

Cormack, R.M.

1981 Loglinear models for capture-recapture experiments on open populations. Pp. 197-215 in R.W. Hiorns and D. Cooke, eds., The Mathematical Theory of the Dynamics of Biological Populations II. New York: Academic Press.

Cowan, Charles D.

1983 Affidavit Presented to District Court, Southern District of New York, Mario Cuomo, et al., Plaintiff(s), Malcolm Baldrige, et al., Defendants, 80 Civ. 4550 (JES).

Cowan, Charles D., and Bettin, Paul J.

1982 Estimates and Missing Data Problems in the Post Enumeration Program. Unpublished paper. Statistical Methods Division, Bureau of the Census, Washington, D.C.

Cowan, Charles D., and Fay, Robert E.

1984 Estimates of undercount in the 1980 census. Pp. 560-565 in American Statistical Association 1984 Proceedings of the Survey Research Methods Section. Washington, D.C.: American Statistical Association.

Deming, W.E., and Stephan, F.F.

1940 On a least squares adjustment of a sampled frequency table when the expected marginal totals are known. Annals of Mathematical Statistics 11:427-444.

Department of Commerce

1976 Mid-Decade Census. Unpublished memorandum (June 15, 1976). Washington, D.C.

Doyle, Brian
1980 Adjustment for census underenumeration: The Australian situation. Pp. 157-163 in Proceedings of the 1980 Conference on Census Undercount. Bureau of the Census. Washington, D.C.: U.S. Department of Commerce.

Efron, Bradley, and Morris, Carl
1972 Limiting the risk of Bayes and empirical Bayes estimators--part II: The empirical Bayes case. Journal of the American Statistical Association 67:130-139.
1973 Stein's estimation rule and its competitors--An empirical Bayes approach. Journal of the American Statistical Association 68:117-130.

Emery, Danuta, Campbell, Valencia, and Freedman, Stanley
1980 Distributing federal funds: The use of statistical data (preliminary report). Statistical Reporter December:73-90.

Ericksen, Eugene P.
1983 Affidavit Presented to District Court, Southern District of New York, Mario Cuomo, et al., Plaintiff(s), Malcolm Baldrige, et al., Defendants, 80 Civ. 4550 (JES).
1984 Surrebuttal Presented to District Court, Southern District of New York, Mario Cuomo, et al., Plaintiff(s), Malcolm Baldrige, et al., Defendants, 80 Civ. 4550 (JES).

Ericksen, Eugene P., and Kadane, Joseph, B.
1983 Using administrative lists to estimate census omissions: An example. Pp. 361-365 in American Statistical Association 1983 Proceedings of the Survey Research Methods Section. Washington, D.C.: American Statistical Association.
1985 Estimating the population in a census year: 1980 and beyond. Journal of the American Statistical Association 80: 98-131.

Fansler, Elaine, Rothwell, Donny, and Mockovak, William
1981 Analysis of Mail-Return Rates for the Alternative Questionnaires Experiment. Preliminary Evaluation Results Memorandum No. 16. Bureau of the Census, Washington, D.C.

Fay, Robert E., III, and Herriot, Roger
1979 Estimates of income for small places: An application of James-Stein procedures to census data. Journal of the American Statistical Association 74(366):Part I, 261-277.

Federal Committee on Statistical Methodology
1980 Report on Exact and Statistical Matching Techniques. Statistical Policy Working Paper 5. Washington, D.C.: U.S. Department of Commerce.

Fellegi, Ivan
1964 Response variance and its estimation. Journal of the American Statistical Association 59:1016-1041.
1980a Evaluation programme of the 1976 Census of Population and Housing - A sampling. The Statistician 29(4):275-312.
1980b Should the census count be adjusted for allocation purposes--equity considerations. Pp. 193-203 in Proceedings of the 1980 Conference on Census Undercount. Bureau of the Census. Washington, D.C.: U.S. Department of Commerce.
1984 Notes on Census Coverage Estimation Methodologies. Prepared for the March 1984 meeting of the Panel on Decennial Census Methodology, National Research Council.
1985 Discussion of "Estimating the population in a census year: 1980 and beyond." Journal of the American Statistical Association 80:98-131.

Fellegi, Ivan, and Holt, D.
1976 A systematic approach to automatic edit and imputation. Journal of the American Statistical Association 71:17-35.

Fellegi, Ivan, and Sunter, Alan
1969 A theory for record linkage. Journal of the American Statistical Association 64:1183-1210.

Fernandez, Edward, and McKenney, Nampeo
1980 Identification of the Hispanic population: A review of Census Bureau experiences. Pp. 358-363 in American Statistical Association 1980 Proceedings of the Survey Research Methods Section. Washington, D.C.: American Statistical Association.

Ferrari, Pamela W., and Bailey, Leroy
1983 The 1980 Census Telephone Follow-up Experiment - Preliminary Assessments and Implications. Unpublished paper. Bureau of the Census, Washington, D.C.

Fienberg, Stephen E.
1970 An iterative procedure for estimation in contingency tables. The Annals of Mathematical Statistics 41(3):907-917.

Freedman, David, and Navidi, W.C.
in press Regression models for adjusting the 1980 census. Statistical Science.

General Accounting Office
1971 Bureau of the Census Cost Estimates for Mid-Decade Census Proposals. Report to the Subcommittee on Census and Statistics, Committee on Post Office and Civil Service, House of Representatives. Washington, D.C.: U.S. Government Printing Office.
1982 A $4 Billion Census in 1990? Timely Decisions on Alternatives to 1980 Procedures Can Save Millions. Washington, D.C.: U.S. Government Printing Office.

Gilford, Leon
1983 Affidavit Presented to District Court, Southern District of New York, Mario Cuomo, et al., Plaintiff(s), Malcolm Baldrige, et al., Defendants, 80 Civ. 4550 (JES).

Goldberg, H.
1974 Estimates of Emigration from Mexico and Illegal Entry into the United States, 1960-1970, by the Residual Method. Unpublished graduate research paper. Center for Population Research, Georgetown University.

Gonzalez, Maria Elena
1980 Characteristics of formulas and data used in the allocation of federal funds. The American Statistician 34(4):200-211.

Gosselin, J.F.
1980 Reverse record check: Tracing people in Canada. Pp. 269-274 in American Statistical Association 1980 Proceedings of the Survey Research Methods Section. Washington, D.C.: American Statistical Association.

Gosselin, J.F., and Theroux, G.
1977 RRC - Methodology Report, Part I. Internal report, Statistics Canada, Ottawa.
1978a RRC - Results on Population and Household Undercoverage. Internal report, Statistics Canada, Ottawa.
1978b RRC - Supplementary Results on Population and Household Undercoverage. Internal report, Statistics Canada, Ottawa.
1979 RRC - Methodology Report, Part II. Internal report, Statistics Canada, Ottawa.

Grindley, W.C., et al.
1974 General Revenue Sharing Data Study. Vol. II, Current and Alternative Data Sources. Menlo Park, Calif.: Stanford Research Institute.

Hansen, Kristin
1984 Geographical Mobility: March 1982 to March 1983. Current Population Reports, Population Characteristics P-20, No. 393. Bureau of the Census. Washington, D.C.: U.S. Department of Commerce.

Hansen, M., Hurwitz, W., and Bershad, M.
1971 Measurement errors in censuses and surveys. Bulletin of the International Statistical Institute 38:359-374.

Harville, David A.
1976 Extension of the Gauss-Markov theorem to include the estimation of random effects. Annals of Statistics 4:384-395.

Henderson, Charles R.
1975 Best linear unbiased estimation and prediction under a selection model. Biometrics 31:423-447.

Herriot, Roger A.
1984 Final Report of 1990 Requirements Planning Committee. Unpublished paper. Bureau of the Census, Washington, D.C.

Herriot, Roger, A., and Speaker, Robert C.
1984 Residence rules for the 1990 decennial census. Pp. 449-451 in American Statistical Association 1984 Proceedings of the Social Statistics Section. Washington, D.C.: American Statistical Association.

Higginbotham, J.R., and Cox, K.K.
1979 Focus Group Interview: A Reader. Chicago: American Marketing Association.

Hill, J.
1911 Letter to William C. Huston, Chairman, House Committee on the Census, April 25, 1911. In U.S. Congress, House Apportionment of Representatives. H.R. 12. 62nd Congress, 1st Session.

Hill, Kenneth
1985 Indirect approaches to assessing stocks and flows of migrants. Pp. 205-224 in App. B of Daniel B. Levine, Kenneth Hill, and Robert Warren, eds., Immigration Statistics, A Story of Neglect. Panel on Immigration Statistics,

Committee on National Statistics, National Research Council. Washington, D.C.: National Academy Press.

Hill, Robert B.

1980 The synthetic method: Its feasibility for deriving the census undercount for states and local areas. Pp. 129-144 in Proceedings of the 1980 Conference on Census Undercount. Bureau of the Census. Washington, D.C.: U.S. Department of Commerce.

Hill, Robert B., and Steffes, Robert B.

1973 Estimating the 1970 Census Undercount for State and Local Areas. Unpublished paper. National Urban League Data Service, Washington, D.C.

Hill, William F.

1984 Data Collection in a Changing Environment. Paper presented at the October 1984 meeting of the Census Advisory Committee, Washington, D.C.

Hogan, Howard

1983a Preliminary Analysis of the Relation Between Census Mailback Rates and Gross Undercoverage. Unpublished paper. Bureau of the Census, Washington, D.C.

1983b Exploratory Analysis of PEP Data. Unpublished paper. Bureau of the Census, Washington, D.C.

1983c Exploratory Analysis of PEP Data - Addendum to Interim Report. Unpublished paper. Bureau of the Census, Washington, D.C.

1984a Research Plan on Adjustment for the 1990 Decennial Census. Unpublished paper. Bureau of the Census, Washington, D.C.

1984b Research plan on adjustment. Pp. 452-457 in American Statistical Association 1984 Proceedings of the Social Statistics Section. Washington, D.C.: American Statistical Association.

1984c Thoughts on a Rule for When to Adjust. Unpublished memorandum. Bureau of the Census, Washington, D.C.

Hogan, Howard, and Cowan, Charles

1980 Imputations, response errors, and matching in dual-system estimation. Pp. 263-268 in American Statistical Association 1980 Proceedings of the Survey Research Methods Section. Washington, D.C.: American Statistical Association.

Huang, E.T.

1978 Nonnegative Regression Estimation for Sample Survey Data. Unpublished Ph.D. thesis. Iowa State University, Ames, Iowa.

1983 Regression M-Weights Computer Programs. Unpublished manuscript. Statistical Research Division, Bureau of the Census, Washington, D.C.

Huang, E.T., and Fuller, W.A.

1978 Nonnegative regression estimation for sample survey data. Pp. 300-303 in _American Statistical Association 1978 Proceedings of the Social Statistics Section_. Washington, D.C.: American Statistical Association.

Huntington, E.V.

1921 The mathematical theory of the apportionment of representatives. _Proceedings of the National Academy of Sciences USA_ 7:123-127.

Ireland, C.T., and Kullback, S.

1968 Minimum discrimination information estimation. _Biometrics_ 24:707-713.

James, W., and Stein, C.

1961 Estimation with quadratic loss. Pp. 361-379 in _Proceedings of the Fourth Berkeley Symposium on Mathematical Statistics and Probability_. Berkeley: University of California Press.

Jaro, Matthew

1984a Record Linkage Research Plan. Unpublished paper. Bureau of the Census, Washington, D.C.

1984b Record linkage research and the calibration of record linkage algorithms. Pp. 599-601 in _American Statistical Association 1984 Proceedings of the Social Statistics Section_. Washington, D.C.: American Statistical Association.

1985 Current Record Linkage Research. Paper presented at the April 1985 meeting of the Census Advisory Committee, Washington, D.C.

Johnson, Bruce E.

1984 Interim Census Manager Reports on 1986 Pretest Objectives. Unpublished paper. Bureau of the Census, Washington, D.C.

Kackar, Raghu, and Harville, David A.

1984 Approximations for standard errors of estimators of fixed and random effects in mixed linear models. _Journal of the American Statistical Association_ 79:853-862.

Kadane, Joseph B.
1984 Allocating Congressional Seats Among the States When State Populations are Uncertain. Technical Report No. 309 (revised). Pittsburgh, Pa.: Department of Statistics, Carnegie-Mellon University.

Kadane, Joseph B., and Ericksen, Eugene
1984 Revised estimates of state and central city populations on Census Day, 1980. Pp. 208-210 in American Statistical Association 1984 Proceedings of the Social Statistics Section. Washington, D.C.: American Statistical Association.

Kadane, Joseph B., and Lehoczky, J.
1976 Random juror selection from multiple lists. Operations Research 24:207-219.

Katzoff, Ellen, and Smith, Robert
1983 Preliminary Results of the 1980 Content Reinterview Study. Preliminary Evaluation Results Memorandum No. 67. Bureau of the Census, Washington, D.C.

Kelley, R. Patrick
1984a Notes on the Theory and Practice of Exact Matching. Unpublished paper. Bureau of the Census, Washington, D.C.

1984b Blocking considerations for record linkage under conditions of uncertainty. Pp. 602-605 in American Statistical Association 1984 Proceedings of the Social Statistics Section. Washington, D.C.: American Statistical Association.

Keyfitz, Nathan
1979 Information and allocation: Two uses of the 1980 census. The American Statistician 33(2):45-50.

1980 Facing the fact of census incompleteness. Pp. 27-36 in Proceedings of the 1980 Conference on Census Undercount. Bureau of the Census. Washington, D.C.: U.S. Department of Commerce.

Kish, Leslie
1979 Samples and censuses. International Statistical Review 47(2):99-109.

Korns, Alexander
1979 Cyclical fluctuations in the difference between the payroll and household measures of employment. Survey of Current Business 59(5):14-44 and 55.

Lancaster, C., and Scheuren, F.J.
1978 Counting the uncountable illegals: Some initial statistical speculations employing capture-recapture techniques. Pp. 530-535 in 1977 Proceedings of the Social Statistics Section. Part 2. Washington, D.C.: American Statistical Association.

Lesko and Associates
1975 Final Report: Basic Data and Guidance Required to Implement a Major Illegal Alien Study During Fiscal Year 1976. Washington, D.C.: U.S. Department of Justice.

Levine, D.B., Hill, K., and Warren, R., eds.
1985 Immigration Statistics, A Story of Neglect. Panel on Immigration Statistics, Committee on National Statistics, National Research Council. Washington, D.C.: National Academy Press.

Liebow, E.
1967 Tally's Corner, A Study of Negro Streetcorner Men. Boston: Little, Brown and Co.

Lindley, D.V., and Smith, A.F.M.
1972 Bayes estimates for the linear model. Journal of the Royal Statistical Society. Series B 34:1-19.

Marks, Eli S., and Waksberg, Joseph
1966 Evaluation of coverage in the 1960 census of population through case-by-case checking. Pp. 62-70 in the American Statistical Association 1966 Proceedings of the Social Statistics Section. Washington, D.C.: American Statistical Association.

Marks, Eli S., Seltzer, William, and Krotki, Karol J.
1977 Population Growth Estimation: A Handbook of Vital Statistics Measurement. New York: The Population Council.

Marks, Jennifer
1980 Census Bureau data sources on immigration. Pp. 15-20 in American Statistical Association 1980 Proceedings of the Social Statistics Section. Washington, D.C.: American Statistical Association.

Matchett, Stanley D.
1984 Major Objectives and Priorities for 1986 Pretest. Unpublished paper. Bureau of the Census, Washington, D.C.

Maurice, Arthur J., and Nathan, Richard P.
1982 The census undercount: Effects on federal aid to cities. Urban Affairs Quarterly 17(3):251-284.

Mikkelson, Gordon
1984 Results of the Enumerator-Supplied Roster Portion of the Update List/Leave Procedures Evaluation. Preliminary Evaluation Results Memorandum No. 76. Bureau of the Census, Washington, D.C.

Mikkelson, Gordon, and MeKelvey, Karen
1983 Preliminary Results from Administrative Records for the Update List/Leave Experiment Program Procedures Evaluation. Preliminary Evaluation Results Memorandum No. 66. Bureau of the Census, Washington, D.C.

Miskura, Susan M., and Thompson, John H.
1983 1980 census findings and their implications for 1990 census planning. Pp. 353-360 in American Statistical Association 1983 Proceedings of the Social Statistics Section. Washington, D.C.: American Statistical Association.

Miskura, Susan M., Woltman, Henry, and Thompson, John
1984 Uses of sampling for the census count. Pp. 458-463 in American Statistical Association 1984 Proceedings of the Social Statistics Section. Washington, D.C.: American Statistical Association.

Mockovak, William
1982a Analysis of Item Nonresponse in the Alternative Questionnaires Experiment. Preliminary Evaluation Results Memorandum No. 19. Bureau of the Census, Washington, D.C.

1982b Analysis of the Effect of Questionnaire Length on Item Nonresponse. Preliminary Evaluation Results Memorandum No. 25. Bureau of the Census, Washington, D.C.

1983 Comparison of Data Obtained Using Alternative Questionnaires in the 1980 Census. Preliminary Evaluation Results Memorandum No. 56. Bureau of the Census, Washington, D.C.

National Center for Health Statistics
1982a Vital Statistics of the United States, 1978. Vol. II, Mortality. Part A, Section 6, Technical Appendix. Washington, D.C.: U.S. Department of Health and Human Services.

1982b *Vital Statistics of the United States. 1978*. Vol. 1, *Natality*. Section 4, *Technical Appendix*. Washington, D.C.: U.S. Department of Health and Human Services.

National Research Council

1972 *America's Uncounted People*. Advisory Committee on Problems of Census Enumeration. Washington, D.C.: National Academy of Sciences.

1978 *Counting the People in 1980: An Appraisal of Census Plans*. Panel on Decennial Census Plans, Committee on National Statistics, National Research Council. Washington, D.C.: National Academy of Sciences.

1984 *Planning the 1990 Census: Priorities for Research and Testing, Interim Report*. Panel on Decennial Census Methodology, Committee on National Statistics, National Research Council. Washington, D.C.: National Academy Press.

Nichols, Roy

1948 *The Disruption of American Democracy*. New York: Macmillan.

Nisselson, H.

1974 Request for Policy Guidance on Participant Observer Studies. Unpublished memorandum. Bureau of the Census, Washington, D.C.

Office of Management and Budget

1985 *Major Themes and Additional Budget Detail, FY 1983*. Washington, D.C.: U.S. Government Printing Office.

Oh, H. Lock, and Scheuren, Fritz

1978 Some unresolved application issues in raking ratio estimation. Pp. 723-728 in *American Statistical Association 1978 Proceedings of the Section on Survey Research Methods*. Washington, D.C.: American Statistical Association.

Palloni, Alberto

1985 The Population of Illegal Aliens: Data Sources, Methods, and Estimates. Unpublished paper. Center for Demography and Ecology, University of Wisconsin.

Passel, Jeffrey S.

1983 Affidavit Presented to District Court, Southern District of New York, Mario Cuomo, et al., Plaintiff(s), Malcolm Baldrige, et al., Defendants, 80 Civ. 4550 (JES).

Passel, Jeffrey S., and Robinson, J.G.
1984 Revised estimates of the coverage of the population in the 1980 census based on demographic analysis: A report on work in progress. Pp. 160-165 in American Statistical Association 1984 Proceedings of the Section on Social Statistics. Washington, D.C.: American Statistical Association.

Passel, Jeffrey S., Siegel, Jacob S., and Robinson, J. Gregory
1982 Coverage of the National Population in the 1980 Census, by Age, Sex, and Race: Preliminary Estimates by Demographic Analysis. Current Population Reports, Special Studies P-23, No. 115. Bureau of the Census. Washington, D.C.: U.S. Department of Commerce.

Passel, Jeffrey S., and Woodrow, Karen
1984 The judicial basis for enumeration of undocumented aliens in the 1980 census and implications for 1990. Pp. 464-469 in American Statistical Association 1984 Proceedings of the Social Statistics Section. Washington, D.C.: American Statistical Association.

Pollock, K.H., Hines, J.E., and Nichols, J.D.
1984 The use of auxiliary variables in capture-recapture and removal experiments. Biometrics 40(2):329-340.

Price, Daniel O.
1947 A check on underenumeration in the 1940 census. American Sociological Review 12(1):44-49.

Redfern, Philip
1983 A Study of the Future of the Census of Population--Alternative Approaches. Unpublished paper commissioned by the Statistical Office of the European Communities.

Riche, Martha Farnsworth
1984a 1984 demographic services directory. American Demographics 6(1):32-41.
1984b The state of the states' data centers. American Demographics 6(10):28-31, 36-37.

Robinson, J.G.
1980 Estimating the approximate size of the illegal alient population in the United States by the comparative trend analysis of age-specific death rates. Demography 17(2):159-176.

Robinson, J. Gregory, and Siegel, Jacob S.
1979 Illustrative assessment of the impact of census underenumeration and income underreporting on revenue sharing allocations at the local level. Pp. 646-656 in American Statistical Association 1979 Proceedings of the Social Statistics Section. Washington, D.C.: American Statistical Association.

Rothwell, Naomi D.
1983 New Ways of Learning How to Improve Self-Enumerative Questionnaires: A Demonstration Project. Unpublished paper. Bureau of the Census, Washington, D.C.

Rubin, D.B.
1978 Multiple imputations in sample surveys - A phenomenological Bayesian approach to nonresponse (with discussion and reply). Pp. 1-9 in Imputation and Editing of Faulty or Missing Survey Data. Washington, D.C.: U.S. Social Security Administration and Bureau of the Census.

Savage, I. Richard, and Windham, Bernard M.
1973 The Importance of Bias Removal in Official Use of United States Census Counts. Unpublished paper. Department of Statistics, Florida State University.

Savage, Leonard J.
1954 The Foundations of Statistics. New York: Wiley.

Scherr, Marvin G.
1980 The use of focus group interviews to improve the design of an administrative form: A case study at the Social Security Administration. Pp. 347-352 in American Statistical Association 1980 Proceedings of the Section on Survey Research Methods. Washington, D.C.: American Statistical Association.

Scherr, Marvin G., and Nelson, William J., Jr.
1980 Collection and analysis of data on race and ethnicity questions in social security number applications. Pp. 353-357 in American Statistical Association 1980 Proceedings of the Section on Survey Research Methods. Washington, D.C.: American Statistical Association.

Schirm, Allen L., and Preston, Samuel H.

1984 Census Undercount Adjustment and the Quality of Geographic Population Distributions. Technical Report. Philadelphia: Population Studies Center, University of Pennsylvania.

Sekar, C.C., and Deming, W.E.

1949 On a method of estimating birth and death rates and the extent of registration. Journal of the American Statistical Association 44:101-115.

Siegel, Jacob S.

1970 Coverage of population in the 1970 census: Preliminary findings and research plans. Pp. 64-69 in American Statistical Association 1970 Proceedings of the Social Statistics Section. Washington, D.C.: American Statistical Association.

1974 Estimates of the coverage of the population by sex, race, and age in the 1970 census. Demography 11(1)1-23.

1975 Coverage of Population in the 1970 Census and Some Implications for Public Programs. Current Population Reports, Special Studies P-23, No. 56. Bureau of the Census. Washington, D.C.: U.S. Department of Commerce.

Siegel, J.S., and Passel, J.S.

1979 Coverage of the Hispanic Population of the United States in the 1970 Census: A Methodological Analysis. Current Population Reports, Special Studies P-23, No. 82. Bureau of the Census. Washington, D.C.: U.S. Department of Commerce.

Siegel, Jacob S., Passel, Jeffrey S., Rives, Norfleet W., Jr., and Robinson, J. Gregory

1977 Developmental Estimates of the Coverage of the Population of States in the 1970 Census: Demographic Analysis. Current Population Reports, Special Studies P-23, No. 65. Bureau of the Census. Washington, D.C.: U.S. Department of Commerce.

Siegel, Jacob S., and Zelnik, Melvin

1966 An evaluation of coverage in the 1960 census of population by techniques of demographic analysis and by composite methods. Pp. 71-90 in American Statistical Association 1966 Proceedings of the Social Statistics Section. Washington, D.C.: American Statistical Association.

Sirken, Monroe, Graubard, Barry, and La Valley, Richard
1978 Evaluation of census population coverage by network surveys. Pp. 239-244 in American Statistical Association 1978 Proceedings of the Social Statistics Section. Washington, D.C.: American Statistical Association.

Slavson, J.R.
1979 Dynamics of Group Psychotherapy. New York: Jason Aronson, Inc.

Spencer, Bruce
1980a Benefit-Cost Analysis of Data Used to Allocate Funds. Lecture Notes in Statistics 3. New York: Springer-Verlag.

1980b Implications of equity and accuracy for undercount adjustment: A decision-theoretic approach. Pp. 204-216 in Proceedings of the 1980 Conference on Census Undercount. Bureau of the Census. Washington, D.C.: U.S. Department of Commerce.

Starsinic, Donald E.
1983 Evaluation of Population Estimation Procedures for States, 1980: An Interim Report. Current Population Reports, Population Estimates and Projections P-25, No. 933. Bureau of the Census. Washington, D.C.: U.S. Department of Commerce.

Strauss, Robert P., and Harkins, Peter B.
1974 The 1970 Census Undercount and Revenue Sharing: Effects on Allocations in New Jersey and Virginia. Unpublished paper. Joint Center for Political Studies, Washington, D.C.

Tippett, J., and Takei, R.
1983 Evaluation of Reporting of Utility Costs for Selected Cities. Preliminary Evaluation Results Memorandum No. 59. Bureau of the Census, Washington, D.C.

Thompson, John
1984 Preliminary Summary Results from the 1980 Census Coverage Improvement Program Evaluations. Preliminary Evaluation Results Memorandum No. 85. Bureau of the Census, Washington, D.C.

Tukey, John W.
1981 Discussion of Paper by Bailar and Keyfitz. Paper presented to the American Statistical Association, Detroit, Michigan.

1983 Affidavit Presented to District Court, Southern District of New York, Mario Cuomo, et al., Plaintiff(s), Malcolm Baldrige, et al., Defendants, 80 Civ. 4550 (JES).

1985 Discussion of "Estimating the population in a census year: 1980 and beyond." Journal of the American Statistical Association 80:98-131.

Turner, Frederick Jackson

1894 The Significance of the Frontier in American History. Proceedings of the 41st meeting of the State Historical Society. Madison, Wis.: State Historical Society.

Turner, Marshall L., Jr.

1984 1980 Census Mail Response Rates. 1990 Decennial Census Informational Memorandum No. 45. Bureau of the Census, Washington, D.C.

1985 1980 Census Mail Response Rates. 1990 Decennial Census Informational Memorandum No. 45, Revision 1. Bureau of the Census, Washington, D.C.

U.S. House of Representatives

1982 Impact of Budget Cuts on Federal Statistical Programs. Hearing before the Subcommittee on Census and Population of the Committee on Post Office and Civil Service. 97th Congress, 2nd Session (March 16, 1982), Serial No. 97-41. Washington, D.C.: U.S. Government Printing Office.

Valentine, Charles, and Valentine, Betty Lou

1971 Missing Men, A Comparative Methodological Study of Underenumeration and Related Problems. Unpublished paper. Bureau of the Census, Washington, D.C.

Waksberg, Joseph

1970 Analysis of Synthetic Estimates. Unpublished memorandum. Bureau of the Census, Washington, D.C.

1971 Mean Square Error of Revisions in Population Count from Vacancy Check. Unpublished memorandum. Bureau of the Census, Washington, D.C.

Waksberg, Joseph, Hanson, Robert, and Bounpane, Peter

1973 Estimation and Presentation of Sampling Errors for Sample Data from the 1970 Census. Paper presented at the 39th session of the International Statistical Institute, Vienna, Austria.

Warren, Robert, and Passel, Jeffrey S.
1983 Estimates of Illegal Aliens from Mexico Counted in the 1980 United States Census. Paper presented to the Population Association of America, Pittsburgh, Pa.

Warren, Robert, and Peck, Jennifer Marks
1980 Foreign-born emigration from the United States: 1960-1970. Demography 17(1):71-84.

Wolter, Kirk M.
1983 Affidavit Presented to District Court, Southern District of New York, Mario Cuomo, et al., Plaintiff(s), Malcolm Baldrige, et al., Defendants, 80 Civ. 4550 (JES).
1984 Requisite planning and research relating to a decision on census adjustment for 1990. Paper presented at the October 1984 meeting of the Census Advisory Committee, Washington, D.C.

Yuskavage, Robert, Hirschberg, David, and Scheuren, Frederick J.
1977 The impact on personal and family income of adjusting the Current Population Survey for undercoverage. Pp. 70-80 in American Statistical Association 1977 Proceedings of the Social Statistics Section. Washington, D.C.: American Statistical Association.

Biographical Sketches of Panel Members and Staff

JOHN W. PRATT (Chair) is a professor at the Harvard University Graduate School of Business. He received an A.B. from Princeton in 1952 and a Ph.D. in statistical theory and methods from Stanford in 1956. He is a former director of the Social Science Research Council and is a fellow of the American Statistical Association, the Econometric Society, and AAAS. He is interested particularly in statistical theory and methods and is a coauthor of *Social Experimentation: A Method for Planning and Evaluating Social Intervention*. He is a member of the Committee on National Statistics and chaired the Committee on National Statistics' study group on environmental monitoring.

PASTORA SAN JUAN CAFFERTY is a professor of social service administration at the University of Chicago. She received a B.A. from St. Bernard College in 1962 and an M.A. and a Ph.D. in American literary and cultural history in 1971 from George Washington University. Her research includes the effects of immigration on urban areas and use of census statistics.

CONSTANCE F. CITRO is an ASA/Census research fellow at the U.S. Bureau of the Census and served as study director for this study. She received a B.A. from the University of Rochester in 1963 and an M.A. and a Ph.D. in political science from Yale University in 1964 and 1969, respectively. She is a former vice president and deputy director of Mathematica Policy Research, Inc., and a former director of the Information Documentation Center of DUALabs. Her research has included many projects to add to the usefulness and accessibility of large, complex microdata files as well as analysis related to income measurement and demographic change.

MICHAEL L. COHEN is a research associate with the Committee on National Statistics. He received a B.S. from the University of Michigan in 1975 and an M.S. and a Ph.D. in statistics from Stanford University in 1977 and 1981, respectively. His interests lie in data analysis, regression, and sample design and estimation.

ANSLEY J. COALE is a professor of demography at Princeton University. He received a B.A. in 1939, an M.S. in 1941, and a Ph.D. in demography in 1947 from Princeton. He is a former chairman of the Committee on Population and Demography of the National Research Council. He is the coauthor of *New Estimates of Population and Births in the United States*, *Regional Model Life Tables and Stable Population*, and *The Growth and Structure of Human Populations*.

DONALD R. DESKINS, JR., is professor of urban geography and sociology and associate dean of the Horace H. Rackham School of Graduate Studies at the University of Michigan. He received a B.A. in 1960, an M.A. in 1963, and a Ph.D. in geography in 1970 from the University of Michigan. He serves as a contributing editor to *Urbanism Past and Present* and is a member of numerous professional societies. His most recent research is focused on the analysis of academic degree production in the United States and its public policy implications.

IVAN P. FELLEGI is the deputy chief statistician of Statistics Canada. He received a B.Sc. from the University of Budapest in 1956 and an M.Sc. in 1958 and a Ph.D. in survey methodology in 1961 from Carleton University. He is a former director of the Sampling and Survey Research Staff and a former director general of the Methodology and Systems Branch of Statistics Canada. He is current president of the International Association of Survey Statisticians and president-elect of the International Statistical Institute. He has published extensively in the areas of census and survey methodology and was a member of the Committe on National Statistics' panel on privacy and confidentiality as factors in survey response.

WAYNE A. FULLER is a distinguished professor in the Department of Statistics at Iowa State University. He received a B.S. in 1955, an M.S. in 1957, and a Ph.D. in statistical theory and methods in 1959 from Iowa State

University. He is a fellow of the American Statistical Association and the Institute of Mathematical Statistics and is the author of Introduction to Statistical Time Series. His fields of interest include times series, survey sampling, and econometrics. He is a member of the Committee on National Statistics and was a member of its panel on statistics for rural development.

JOSEPH B. KADANE is a professor of statistics and social sciences at Carnegie-Mellon University. He received a B.A. in 1962 from Harvard University and a Ph.D. in statistical theory and methods in 1966 from Stanford University. He is the editor of Robustness of Bayesian Analyses and is the applications and coordinating editor of the Journal of the American Statistical Association. He was a member of the American Statistical Association's technical panel on the census undercount and is interested particularly in statistical inference in the social sciences and computational complexity.

BENJAMIN F. KING is the director of survey methods at the Educational Testing Service in Princeton, New Jersey. He received an A.B. in 1958, an M.B.A. in 1960, and a Ph.D. in survey methodology in 1964 from the University of Chicago. He is a former professor of quantitative methods in the School of Business Administration and a former professor in the Department of Statistics at the University of Washington. His research interests include survey methods, logic, applications of statistics in business and economics, and policy research.

ALBERT MADANSKY is associate dean for Ph.D. studies and professor of business administration in the Graduate School of Business of the University of Chicago. He received a B.A. in 1952, an M.S. in 1955, and a Ph.D. in economics and statistics in 1958 from the University of Chicago. He has been a research mathematician at the RAND Corporation, senior vice president of a large advertising agency, president of a computer software and data processing firm, professor and chairman of computer sciences at City College of New York, and a fellow of the Center for Advanced Study in the Behavioral Sciences. He is the author of Foundations of Econometrics and has done research in multivariate statistical analysis.

ALBERTO PALLONI is an associate professor in the Department of Sociology and a research associate at the

Center for Demography and Ecology at the University of Wisconsin, Madison. He received a B.A. in 1971 from Catholic University of Chile and a Ph.D. in demography in 1977 from the University of Washington. He is a former associate professor in the Department of Sociology and research associate in the Population Research Center at the University of Texas. He has published in the fields of population studies and demography.

JOHN E. ROLPH is a senior statistican and associate head of the Economics Department of the Rand Corporation as well as a faculty member of the Rand/UCLA Health Policy Studies Center. He received an A.B. in 1962 and a Ph.D. in statistics in 1966 from the University of California, Berkeley. He has taught at the University of London, Columbia University, the Rand Graduate Institute, and the University of California, Los Angeles. He is the coauthor of Introduction to Data Analysis and Statistical Inference and, among other areas, is interested in empirical Bayes methods, sequential decision problems, actuarial methods, and jury representativeness.

COURTENAY M. SLATER is the president of CEC Associates, Washington, D.C. She received a B.A. from Oberlin College in 1955, and an M.A. and a Ph.D. in economics from American University in 1965 and 1968, respectively. She is a former staff economist with the Council of Economic Advisers and a former chief economist of the Department of Commerce. She is a member of the Committee on National Statistics and has been involved in the planning of decennial censuses.

JOSEPH WAKSBERG is the vice president and director of the statistical staff at Westat, Inc. He received a B.S. in mathematics from City College of New York in 1936. He is a former associate director for methodology and research at the U.S. Bureau of the Census. His fields of interest include survey methods, sampling theory, and sampling practice. He is the author of numerous publications in sample design for surveys and survey methodology.

Index

B

C

F

G

J

K

L

Q

R